D0203071

WITHDRAWN
UTSA LIBRARIES

Feminisms in Social Work Research

Social work as a profession and academic discipline has long centered on women and issues of concern to women, such as reproductive rights, labor rights, equal rights, violence, and poverty. In fact, the social work profession was started by and maintained in large part by women and has been home to several generations of feminists, starting with recognized first-wave feminists. This wide-ranging volume both maps the contemporary landscape of feminist social work research and offers a deep engagement with critical and third-wave feminisms in social work research.

Showcasing the breadth and depth of exemplary social work feminist research, the editors argue that social work's unique focus on praxis, daily proximities to privilege and oppression, concern with social change, and engagement with participatory forms of inquiry place social workers in a unique position both to learn from and to contribute to broader social science and humanities discourse associated with feminist research. The authors attend here to their specific claims of feminisms, articulate deep engagement with theory, address the problematic use of binaries, and engage with issues associated with methods that are consistently of interest to feminist researchers, such as power and authority, ethics, reflexivity, praxis, and difference.

Comprehensive and containing an international selection of contributions, *Feminisms in Social Work Research* is an important reference for all social work researchers with an interest in critical perspectives.

Stéphanie Wahab is an Associate Professor at Portland State University's School of Social Work, USA, and Honorary Research Associate Professor, Department of Sociology, Gender and Social Work, University of Otago, New Zealand.

Ben Anderson-Nathe is Associate Professor and Program Director of the Child and Family Studies program at Portland State University, USA.

Christina Gringeri is Professor in the College of Social Work at the University of Utah, USA.

Routledge Advances in Social Work

New titles

Analysing Social Work Communication
Discourse in Practice
Edited by Christopher Hall, Kirsi Juhila, Maureen Matarese
and Carolus van Nijnatten

Feminisms in Social Work Research
Promise and possibilities for justice-based knowledge
Edited by Stéphanie Wahab, Ben Anderson-Nathe
and Christina Gringeri

Forthcoming titles

Chronic Illness, Vulnerability and Social Work
Liz Walker and Elizabeth Price

Social Work in a Global Context
Issues and Challenges
Edited by George Palattiyil, Dina Sidhva and Mono Chakrabarti

Contemporary Feminisms in Social Work Practice
Edited by Nicole Moulding and Sarah Wendt

Domestic Violence Perpetrators
Evidence-Informed Responses
John Devaney, Anne Lazenbatt and Maurice Mahon

Feminisms in Social Work Research

Promise and possibilities for justice-based knowledge

Edited by Stéphanie Wahab, Ben Anderson-Nathe and Christina Gringeri

Routledge
Taylor & Francis Group

LONDON AND NEW YORK

First published 2015
by Routledge
2 Park Square, Milton Park, Abingdon, Oxon OX14 4RN

and by Routledge
711 Third Avenue, New York, NY 10017

Routledge is an imprint of the Taylor & Francis Group, an informa business

© 2015 Stéphanie Wahab, Ben Anderson-Nathe and Christina Gringeri

The right of the editors to be identified as the authors of the
editorial material, and of the authors for their individual chapters,
has been asserted in accordance with sections 77 and 78 of the
Copyright, Designs and Patents Act 1988.

All rights reserved. No part of this book may be reprinted
or reproduced or utilised in any form or by any electronic,
mechanical, or other means, now known or hereafter invented,
including photocopying and recording, or in any information
storage or retrieval system, without permission in writing from the
publishers.

Trademark notice: Product or corporate names may be trademarks
or registered trademarks, and are used only for identification and
explanation without intent to infringe.

British Library Cataloguing-in-Publication Data
A catalogue record for this book is available from the British
Library

Library of Congress Cataloging-in-Publication Data
Feminisms in social work research: promise and possibilities for
justice-based knowledge/edited by Stéphanie Wahab,
Ben Anderson-Nathe, and Christina Gringeri.
pages cm. — (Routledge advances in social work)
1. Social work with women. 2. Feminism. 3. Social
service—Research. I. Wahab, Stephanie. II. Anderson-Nathe,
Ben. III. Gringeri, Christina E.
HV1444.F457 2014
361.3072–dc23   2014003828

ISBN: 978-0-415-70711-4 (hbk)
ISBN: 978-1-315-88699-2 (ebk)

Typeset in Baskerville
by Swales & Willis Ltd, Exeter, Devon, UK

**Library
University of Texas
at San Antonio**

Contents

Contributors

Editors

Ben Anderson-Nathe holds masters degrees in social work and public policy, and a doctorate in community education and youth studies from the University of Minnesota. He has worked with youth in a variety of settings, including out-of-home care environments, community mental health, homeless and street youth centers, religious institutions, and lesbian, gay, bisexual, transgender, and queer (LGBTQ) services since the mid-1990s. Ben's research and teaching focus on youth worker development; young people and incarceration; gender, sexuality, and feminisms; social justice; and critical pedagogies and epistemologies. He is currently Associate Professor and Program Director of the Child and Family Studies program at Portland State University.

Christina Gringeri is Professor in the College of Social Work at the University of Utah. In 1990, she graduated from the University of Wisconsin-Madison with the MSW and Ph.D. in Social Welfare, and a graduate certificate in Women's Studies. Christina's long-term research interests have included women's economic activities, adult perceptions of childhood maltreatment, and the nexus of women's activism and spirituality. She teaches Qualitative Methods for Social Inquiry, as well as Social Policy and Macro Social Work Practice. She served 11 years on the Editorial Board of *Affilia: Journal of Women and Social Work*, and several years as director of Gender Studies.

Stéphanie Wahab is an Associate Professor at Portland State University's School of Social Work and Honorary Research Associate Professor, Department of Sociology, Gender and Social Work at the University of Otago, New Zealand. Her areas of specialization include intimate partner violence, commercial sex work, and anti-oppressive practice, as well as critical and constructivist inquiry. Her scholarly projects typically revolve around the intersections of gender, sexuality, race/ethnicity, privilege, oppression, and relationships. Dr. Wahab currently serves as an editorial board member of *Affilia: Journal of Women and Social Work*.

Contributing Authors

Rupaleem Bhuyan is an Associate Professor at the Factor-Inwentash Faculty of Social Work and Affiliate Faculty with the Women & Gender Studies Institute, University of Toronto. She campaigns for women's rights and immigrant rights in the United States and Canada through advocacy, community organization, and participatory action research.

Moshoula Capous-Desyllas is an Assistant Professor at California State University Northridge. Her interests include arts-based research methods, community organizing and advocacy, transglobal migration issues, commercial sex work, and intersecting oppressions. Moshoula's passion lies in highlighting the voices of marginalized communities through art as a form of activism and empowerment.

Lucy Costa is a Systemic Advocate with the Empowerment Council, an independent organization representing the client voice within the Centre for Addiction and Mental Health, Toronto. She is co-collaborator on Recovering our Stories Collective, a grassroots group critically examining the ethics and overuse of patients' personal narratives in the mental health sector.

Ann Curry-Stevens is on faculty with Portland State University's School of Social Work, where she heads the school's community practice concentration, and has been leading the research partnership with the Coalition of Communities of Color for the last six years. Her teaching centers on community practice, social justice, qualitative research, and building student capacity for undoing racism, poverty, and other forms of oppression.

Andrea Daley is an Associate Professor at the School of Social Work, York University, Toronto. Her research interests include access issues in healthcare policy and delivery for members of LGBTQ communities; examining gendered, sexualized, raced, and classed discourses on women's "mental illness"; and critical research methodologies.

Joseph Nicholas DeFilippis worked for 20 years as social justice activist before entering academia. In the 1990s, he volunteered as a welfare rights organizer and served as the Director of SAGE/Queens, an organization for LGBT senior citizens. In 2003, Joseph became the founding director of Queers for Economic Justice, an organization working with low-income and homeless LGBT people, and led the organization for six years.

Victoria Foster is currently Senior Lecturer in Social Sciences at Edge Hill University in Lancashire, UK. Originally trained in Fine Art, Victoria is particularly interested in innovative, collaborative research methods and how these can be employed in relation to consciousness raising and critiquing policy initiatives.

Flavia Genovese is a front-line social worker in Toronto, with experience addressing homelessness, domestic violence, economic vulnerability, and women's health. She currently coordinates a peer mentorship program for street-involved women in a community health center, focused on improving women's health through outreach and educational activities.

K. D. Hudson received her Ph.D. in Social Welfare from the University of Washington. Kimberly's research is grounded in feminist and critical race frameworks and draws upon a variety of interdisciplinary methods, including narrative inquiry and community-based research. Kimberly's primary areas of interest include identity-based communities (mixed-race and queer experiences); counterstories and digital storytelling; ideas of health and well-being; and social justice education.

Wendy Hulko is an Associate Professor in the School of Social Work and Human Service at Thompson Rivers University in Kamloops, B.C., Canada. She holds degrees in Sociology (Ph.D. – with Social Policy; B.A.Hons – with Spanish) and Social Work (MSW). Wendy's teaching and research interests include aging, queer studies, theory, diversity, and Cuba.

Martha Kuwee Kumsa is Oromo, born and raised in Ethiopia. A committed *siiqqee* feminist, she worked as a journalist and activist in the Oromo anticolonial national liberation struggle. She was a prisoner of conscience in Ethiopia and came to Canada as a refugee. She is now a Canadian citizen and teaches on the Faculty of Social Work, Wilfrid Laurier University.

Sandra M. Leotti is a doctoral student in Social Work and Social Research at Portland State University. Her practice experience includes community mental health, wilderness therapy, violence education and prevention, community case management for adults and children with disabilities and long-term illnesses, clinical practice with youth, and leadership development. Sandy's research interests include the criminalization of women, gender and disability, and feminist methodologies.

Rachel Mehl is a popular educator from Lawrence, Kansas. She learned Spanish while doing solidarity work with the Zapatista movement in Chiapas, Mexico and received her M.Ed. from the Ontario Institute for Studies in Education. She currently lives in Queens, New York, where she teaches English for Speakers of Other Languages and Civics at an immigrants' rights organization.

Gita Mehrotra is on faculty at the University of Utah. Her work focuses on promoting the well-being of women and LGBTQ people of color. Gita's interests include intimate violence in minoritized communities, intersectional experiences of queer people of color, social justice education, and feminist and critical theory/methodologies for social work.

Karen Morgaine is an Assistant Professor in Sociology at California State University Northridge. Her teaching focuses on social justice, community organizing, and lesbian, gay, bisexual, transgender, queer, questioning, intersex, pansexual (LGBTQQIP) communities. She uses qualitative research methodologies to examine power/privilege in social movements. Areas of interest include LGBTQQIP and radical/progressive social movements and framing of social problems.

Jennifer S. Muthanna obtained her BSW (Honours) from the University of Windsor in 2001 and her MSW (Advanced Clinical Practice) from Memorial University of Newfoundland in 2004. She currently is enrolled in the Ph.D., Social Work and Social Research program at Portland State University. Her areas of interest include postadoption issues and services, social work education, social justice, and feminist theories.

Bethany J. Osborne completed her Ph.D. in Adult Education and Community Development at the Ontario Institute for Studies in Education of the University of Toronto in 2013. She has worked with women in marginalized communities over the last two decades and has a keen interest in participatory action research.

Bob Pease is Professor of Critical Social Work at Deakin University in Geelong, Australia. He has been involved in profeminist politics with men for many years and has published extensively on masculinity politics and critical social work practice, including four books as single author and ten books as co-editor.

Margarita Pintin-Perez graduated from the MSW program at the University of Toronto in 2011. Her work experience includes community-based programming and clinical counseling for women and children who have experienced violence. Margarita is studying for her Ph.D. in Mexico on the topic of gender-based violence in the context of migration.

Lori E. Ross is a Research Scientist in the Social & Epidemiological Research Department, Centre for Addiction & Mental Health, Toronto, Canada. Her primary research focus is women's mental health, with a specific focus on the experiences of sexual and gender minority women and community-based participatory action research approaches.

Jen Self received her Ph.D. in Social Welfare and graduate certificate in Feminist Studies from the University of Washington (UW) in 2010. She is the founding Director of the UW Q Center and affiliate faculty at the UW School of Social Work. She is committed to critical queer, feminist, interpretive scholarship aimed to disrupt entrenched systems of sociopolitical power, with specific focus on social work praxis.

Fernanda Villanueva is the community outreach coordinator for the Migrant Mothers Project and remains inspired by the collective work that has been achieved. Fernanda received her MSW from the University of Toronto and has worked in the areas of women's mental health and health, in order to ensure women's stories remain heard.

Carole Zufferey is a lecturer at the School of Psychology, Social Work and Social Policy, University of South Australia. Her research focuses on housing, home, and homelessness, with attention to social work and social policy responses, including intimate partner violence. She is a Chief Investigator on several government- and university-funded research projects.

Acknowledgments

We would like to acknowledge Virgina Olesen for her thoughtful contributions to mapping the landscape of feminisms in qualitative inquiry. We also wish to thank Joan Orme, Emma Gross, and Susan Kemp for their contributions to feminist scholarship in social work. Thank you for pushing us individually and the field in general. Thank you for the gentle and sometimes not so gentle critiques and challenges. Thank you for mentoring generations of feminist scholars in social work. You've all paved the way for this book.

We dedicate this volume to present and future critical feminist scholars in social work.

1 Introduction

*Stéphanie Wahab, Ben Anderson-Nathe
and Christina Gringeri*

This book presents a collection of scholarship by social workers engaged in feminist social work research. Social work as a profession and academic discipline has long concerned itself with women and issues related to women and their social conditions (suffrage, reproductive rights, labor rights, equal rights, violence, poverty, etc.). In fact, the social work profession was started by and maintained in large part by women and has been home to several generations of feminists, starting with recognized first-wave feminists. Central to both feminisms and social work has been the attention to diversity, inherent worth and dignity of the individual, power (personal and political) and the various ways power, in all its dimensions (interpersonal, intrapersonal, social, political, economic, spiritual, etc.), informs individual and collective experiences. Perhaps the most salient of these similarities, however, is the centrality of social change within social work and feminisms, particularly social change focused on challenging systems and institutions that perpetuate power inequities, privilege, and oppression. While some have suggested that feminisms' influence on social work practice, teaching, and research has been "almost breathtaking" (Shaw, 1999, p. 114), others have commented that social work lacks an appreciation for and engagement with the complexities of feminisms, calling for a deeper engagement with feminist theories (Orme, 2003; Sands & Nuccio, 1992). This book addresses both impressions by showcasing exemplary feminist social work research and charting a course for social work scholars to engage with critical feminisms in their research.

Setting the Stage

Social work and feminisms have a lengthy and intertwined history of identifying social justice as a core goal; likewise, both arenas have based their work on broad and shifting definitions of the construct (Kemp & Brandwein, 2010). Social work has historically advocated for politically and economically marginalized populations and communities in the United States and abroad, focusing in its early years on children, women, and immigrant communities, and later expanding to include people of diverse backgrounds, low wage and/or poorly protected workers, refugees, lesbian, gay, bisexual, transgender, and queer (LGBTQ) persons, and others. Feminists in different historical periods have overlapped somewhat with social workers in advocating for equality and empowerment for women, and more recently expanding the work to include men and masculinities, transgender and gender queer people, and constructs of gender more broadly. Nevertheless, essentialized constructs, particularly associated with gender, have limited the scope and impact of social work efforts. This, coupled with the diverse priorities across feminisms and social work, has challenged social work, especially in higher education, to make obvious the ways in which feminist research and practice overlap.

There is growing international enthusiasm for competency-based education (Kovacs, Hutchison, Collins, & Linde, 2013), and social work curricula are now framed by standards and competencies. In the United States, both the Council on Social Work Education (CSWE) and the National Association of Social Workers (NASW) Code of Ethics claim social justice as a core professional value and purpose of social work. According to CSWE (2008), the "purpose of social work is actualized through its quest for social and economic justice, the prevention of conditions that limit human rights, the elimination of poverty, and the enhancement of the quality of life for all persons." The Educational Policy Statements (EPAS) issued and approved by CSWE in 2008 are intended to "support academic excellence by establishing thresholds for professional competence" (CSWE, 2008). The 2008 EPAS offer an operational definition of justice in 2.1.5: students are:

> required to recognize the global interconnections of oppression and be knowledgeable about theories of justice and strategies to promote human and civil rights. . . . Social workers ensure that these basic human rights are distributed equitably and without prejudice . . . and engage in practices that advance social and economic justice.

These goals dovetail well with the Global Standards for the Education and Training of the Social Work Profession (IASSW, 2004), which promote "inclusion of marginalized, socially excluded, dispossessed, vulnerable and at-risk groups of people; address and challenge barriers, inequalities and injustices that exist in society; formulate and implement policies and programs that enhance people's well-being, promote development and human rights." While these statements mention "theories of justice," that is left wide open to interpretation; they do not suggest how social work educators might accomplish justice in education, practice, and research. Reisch (2013) has argued that, while these organizations continue to highlight the importance of social justice, the actual practice of social work and the preparation and socialization of students for practice, research, and teaching have significantly diverged from the profession's stated mission (p. 716).

Given the influence of neo-liberalism on social work education (Reisch, 2013), the broad treatment of social justice in the education standards, and the lack of any mention of feminist approaches to justice, it is not surprising that many students do not understand the connections between feminisms and social work, especially as related to research. Many struggle to understand the connections between feminisms, anti-oppression, social justice, and broader human rights issues, and are challenged by how to conceptualize these concerns in social work research and practice. Orme (2003) argued that a key difficulty in this struggle is social work's resistance to theory, reinforced by the technical and instrumental focus of education standards mandating "competency-based" training. Social work students, practitioners, and many scholars underutilize theory in research and teaching. While ecological theory, systems theory, and the overall concept of person-in-environment represent the most influential theories in shaping social work practice and research, they also "include a linearity of bio-psycho-social and spiritual needs; the notion of fixed boundaries of various environmental systems; the presence of a universal, static hierarchy of human needs" (Jani & Reisch, 2011, cited in Reisch, 2013, p. 723).

Social work's resistance to theory and to feminisms have often gone hand in hand because both are perceived as activities of the elite (Orme, 2003); this resistance tends to produce feminist research in social work that is largely atheoretical (Gringeri, Wahab, & Anderson-Nathe, 2010; Wahab, Anderson-Nathe, & Gringeri, 2012). Social work's emphasis on developing curricula principally in response to community needs may help to explain the field's reluctance to critically engage with theory; we may have sacrificed theory for practicality. Consequently, although praxis is a central contribution of feminist social work research, it often unfolds only partially and in the absence of critical engagement with theory.

We contend that including feminisms in social work education will help students develop a clearer sense of justice that may be brought into research to help generate knowledge that advances social and economic justice, as well as for the purposes of theory development. One approach that supports students in reconnecting with feminisms in social work education and research is to focus on the operation of power and the causes of oppression, and to conceptualize how gender constructs support and critique power and oppression. This is well aligned with the EPAS regarding social justice, and offers a clear lens to students in applying theory and developing justice-based knowledge for critical practice. Orme (2003, pp. 141–142) has argued that a focus on power rather than group identity can contribute to critical practice and research in several ways: gendered structures of power can be oppressive for men as well as women, it allows social workers to engage in transformational work with people of all gender identities, it highlights the process and value of knowing as well as the power linked to knowledge, and it promotes understanding of the shifting and complex interconnections between theory, research, and practice. In this volume, we aim to recenter critical feminisms in social work research, teaching, and practice as a set of tools to foreground and develop social workers' commitment to social and economic justice, equality, and promotion of human and civil rights.

What Has Come Before

In addition to recentering critical feminisms in social work research, this book represents the outgrowth of our previous collaborative efforts, in which we analyzed and offered commentary on the state of feminist research within social work (Gringeri et al., 2010), the location and role of feminist social work research within the larger conversation of feminist research across the social sciences (Wahab et al., 2012), and opportunities for feminist social work researchers and teachers of research to more deliberately and critically engage third-wave, postcolonial, and other contemporary feminisms in our own teaching and research (Anderson-Nathe, Gringeri, & Wahab, 2013).

Our first paper (Gringeri et al., 2010) grew out of our interest in the state of contemporary feminist social work research, based on a suspicion that critical feminist approaches were sparse in social work research and that the field could improve on foregrounding the confluence between feminist principles and social work's cardinal values. In this project, we randomly sampled and analyzed 50 feminist research articles published in high-impact social work and social work-related journals between 2000 and 2010. Informed by Olesen's (2005) articulation of central features of feminist research, we developed a template to evaluate each research article for its inclusion of or attention to these features. As the iterative analysis unfolded, we finally reduced the template to four dominant questions: (1) what made the paper feminist? (2) how did it treat binary or dichotomous thinking? (3) how did it treat or incorporate theory? and (4) how did the article treat its discussion of methodology and methodological concerns of particular relevance to feminism?

Although a handful of the articles in our sample attended directly and critically to all four questions (we considered these exemplars of feminist social work research), the majority reflected overly simplistic claims to feminisms (Orme, 2003), reinforced rather than challenged essentialized and binary thinking, failed to critically integrate (or occasionally even state) theory into the project, and/or attended to only the most conventional of methodological considerations. We concluded from this review that feminist research in social work lagged significantly behind other social sciences in terms of incorporating critical perspectives. In this paper, we called our colleagues among feminist social work researchers to reconceptualize their work with greater attention to critical feminist principles of praxis, reflexivity, power, and deliberate critique of binary and dualistic thinking.

Our second paper (Wahab et al., 2012) expanded on this call, suggesting that in spite of our field's historic absence from broader feminist research conversations in the social sciences, social work has much to gain and much to offer these conversations. We articulated examples of feminist social work's engagement with second-wave feminist thought and the reluctance to take up more critical analyses of the categories and binaries accepted as givens by our profession. Presented in contrast to the epistemological and conceptual richness of third-wave, postcolonial, and other critical feminisms evident in the social sciences, we suggested that social work has much to gain by joining in more deliberate conversation and ideological exchange with these other fields.

We also discussed what social work can offer to the broader conversations among feminist social science researchers. Central to these contributions is social work's emphasis on praxis, offering practical application of feminist principles in action, and in the service of critical feminisms' larger aims of social justice, elimination of oppression, and resolution of power imbalances and abuses. We presented the exemplary feminist social work research identified in our earlier map of the landscape, highlighting articles that demonstrated concrete evidence of social work's contribution to feminisms through praxis. We concluded by inviting feminist social work researchers to join us and other feminist social science researchers in deliberate dialogues to challenge binaries and center critical perspectives on feminism, while also offering to our feminist social science colleagues the potential benefit of social work's emphasis on praxis.

Our final work in the initial project (Anderson-Nathe et al., 2013) presented as praxis our own reflections on feminist social work research, highlighting what we have learned and what meaning our learning holds for our work as teachers, researchers, and feminists within the social work tradition. This paper centered our belief, in agreement with others, that "as feminists we are committed to the dictum that *how* we study determines *what* we know" (Kaufman, 2007, p. 681). Through a series of case illustrations and questions to facilitate researchers' grounding their projects in critical feminist epistemologies and methodology, we offered concrete recommendations for our social work colleagues to seek greater alignment between the liberatory potential of critical feminisms and social work's cardinal values.

Building on the foundation we laid in the previous two publications, we examined three primary methodological and epistemological concerns central to exemplary feminist social work research: critical integration of theory; deliberate attention to reflexivity and researcher positionality; and researchers' willingness to critically grapple with, challenge, and destabilize binary or essentialized thought. In our treatment of each concern, we engaged in our own praxis of transparency and reflexivity by offering first-person accounts of how these concerns inform our work as feminist researchers and educators in social work. In modeling this praxis, we extended an invitation to other feminist social work researchers and teachers of social work research to join us in this project.

The contributors to this volume accepted the invitation. Many came to our attention through their exemplary work in feminist social work research, which we first encountered in our mapping of the social work landscape. Others are students and colleagues whose work in these areas has informed our own, and whose contributions reflect the engagement with feminisms and critical feminist analyses we hope this book will encourage for the field as a whole. In all cases, we provided the contributors with access to our collaborative writing on feminist social work research and invited them to locate themselves in conversation with that work and the tensions in the field, as articulated above.

Framing the Book

This book is organized in four main sections, each representing cardinal features of exemplary feminist research identified by Olesen (1994, 2000, 2005) and expanded in our previous publications (Anderson-Nathe et al., 2013; Gringeri et al., 2010; Wahab et al., 2012). These central features include claims of feminism and what constitutes feminist research, articulation and integration of theory in research, the treatment of binaries and dualistic or essentialized thinking, and critical engagement with methodology. They are grounded in the core mission of social work to engage in practice and action for social justice.

Historically, social work developed out of compelling engagement with social justice and praxis. In contrast to other professions such as counseling and psychology, praxis in social work uniquely emphasizes the interactive and reflexive relationships between research, theory, practice, and social action. It is a spiral in which social justice undergirds research, teaching, and practice, while contributing to new theories and refining old ones, as well as develops interventions for purposes of social change. Social work's professional Code of Ethics commits practitioners to ongoing praxis (NASW, 1996); by foregrounding praxis in feminist research and underscoring feminist contributions to social change, social work contributes information about context and process associated with the lived experiences of those who are often at the center of feminist social science research. Research based in participants' lived experiences, while acknowledging structural realities, can support social work feminist researchers to engage participants and clients around the issues important to them while engaging all of us as co-creators of knowledge, and partners in social change.

Our profession articulates an explicit value for and commitment to applying social justice principles for the purpose of social change, which also informs our research. Social workers are involved daily with many of the topics and problems central to feminist research, not only in terms of the problems and issues experienced by women, but in terms of how women, men, trans* people, children, families, and communities nationally and internationally experience the influences of gendered structures. Practice in the arenas of interpersonal violence, sex work, poverty, employment and discrimination, health and mental health, community organizing, and welfare policies and programs offer social workers ample opportunities to witness and participate in the ways in which gender, difference, and social identities shape human experiences, potential, conflicts, and resolutions. These experiences form a compelling foundation from which feminist social work researchers can strengthen and extend the social justice commitment of feminist research in the social sciences, as well as engage the tensions and trespasses (Rossiter, 2001) facilitated by research with anti-oppressive claims.

Praxis and a commitment to ethical and socially just knowledge creation (and knowledge production in the service of social justice) constitute the connective tissue of this volume. These principles unite the four categories of exemplary feminist social work research presented in this book; each contribution represents not only the authors' attention to one or more feature of critical feminist social work research but also those authors' praxis of research-in-action.

Even as the four central features of exemplary feminist social work research constitute the conceptual framework for this book, we felt challenged to organize the contributions to represent the breadth and depth of feminist social work research without "boxing in" each contribution to only one particular category. After all, truly exemplary feminist research in social work attends to all these features in one way or another (Gringeri et al., 2010). We have highlighted the more obvious streams addressed in each chapter, with an explicit reminder that many contributions address more than one stream.

Feminist Claims in Research

The first contributors in this book pay particular attention to feminist claims in research. Moving beyond Orme's (2003) "it's feminist because I say so" critique of feminist social work research, the contributors in this section address, head on, what makes their work feminist. These scholars engage feminist tenets and principles and feminist practice, articulate theory, and attend to issues of power, reflexivity, praxis, and social justice in their research. Although constructions of feminism in social work too often rely on the taken-for-granted and essentialized understandings of feminism as being "for women, by women, about women," exemplary scholarship attends directly to bringing social work into the critical feminist discourse evident in other disciplines.

Andrea Daley, Lucy Costa, and Lori E. Ross stake their feminist claims by explicitly centering multiple femininities informed by feminist, critical race, and post-colonial theories as a focus of analysis for understanding the interpretive nature of psychiatry in relation to gender, sexuality, race, and class within a particular time and place of one urban, Canadian psychiatric clinic.

Joseph Nicholas DeFilippis presents an open letter to feminist advocates entering academia. He presents an overview of some of the difficulties graduate students might encounter, as academic life is often at odds with feminist tenets. He draws on feminist community-based praxis to provide suggestions for navigating these tensions. Also informed by feminist practice, Bob Pease reflects on the implications of 20 years of writing, research, teaching, and activism in profeminist social work practice on men doing research on men's lives.

Theory in Research

As the profession of social work maintains an ambivalent relationship with theory, social work as an academic tradition remains limited in its engagement with theoretical positions and associated explanatory or illustrative offerings. Although its impacts on social work research are clear, the reasons for this reluctance to critically take up theory are somewhat more elusive. At least part of this explanation may rest in the field's historic development as a pragmatic and practice-centered profession, which was and remains one of social work's greatest strengths. Nevertheless, this history may also have contributed to the elevation of professional practice to the expense or neglect of theoretical, structural, or socially critical perspectives.

We have foregrounded praxis as one of the central contributions of feminist social work research (Wahab et al., 2012), and we appreciate that praxis is central to both social work and feminisms. But we also recognize that the field's elevation of practice *over* theory has compromised how social work research (even that claiming feminist orientations) engages in critical praxis, which we understand to highlight the inextricable and mutually reinforcing relationship between practice *and* theory. As a result, social work has tended to be more receptive to the liberal, radical, and postmodern streams (Freeman, 1990; Kemp & Brandwein, 2010; Nes & Iadicola, 1989) that have constituted second-wave feminism than contemporary, reflexive, and praxis-oriented feminist discourses characterized by cultural studies, post-feminisms, post-colonial, and other critical theories (Baines, 1997; Barnoff & Moffatt, 2007; Mehrotra, 2010; Orme, 2003; Sands & Nuccio, 1992).

This book addresses social work's reluctance to engage deeply with those critical feminisms that hold the potential to enrich and refocus the field's commitment to engaged praxis, both in social work practice and research. Specifically, in recent years, scholars examining the history and relationship between feminisms and social work in the United States have articulated key historical moments and ideological developments that have shaped both feminism and social work research and practice (Gray & Boddy, 2010; Kemp & Brandwein, 2010). Central to these ideological shifts has been an increase in critical feminisms and their potential to ultimately transform essentializing claims about oppression, master narratives and theories with claims to universalized experience or applicability, and the unexamined reliance upon and reinscription of binary and dualistic thought (Gray & Boddy, 2010; Gringeri et al., 2010; Kemp & Brandwein, 2010; Orme, 2003).

Although still emerging, some critical feminist social work researchers have taken up these ideologies. These chapters illustrate how critical feminist social work researchers have attended to theory in their projects as a central organizing principle to shape research decisions and activities, from question formulation and study design, to interpretation and presentation of findings, and ultimately to application or impacts for the field as a whole.

Wendy Hulko focuses on theory and its application to research methods. She argues that it is important for feminist researchers to embody praxis by enacting theoretical commitments, or at least by ensuring that theory and practice are in conversation with one another. Specifically, she focuses on the application of intersectionality theory across five separate research projects.

Using the example of social work responses to homelessness to theorize how masculinity and femininity are constructed and performed in social work, Carole Zufferey highlights how gender, power, and class are embodied and performed by men and women who work around issues of homelessness. Also informed by intersectionality, she discusses how social workers can engage reflexivity as a means of incorporating structural and individualist constructions of homelessness into practice.

K. D. Hudson discusses the theoretically pluralist feminist lens that informs her construction and use of borderlands as a conceptual tool. She includes: borderland epistemology, which considers the relationship between knowledge and colonization, and the emergence of hybrid knowledges (Mignolo, 2000); transnational feminism, providing insights to systems of dominance and resistance, with specific attention to interstitial power configurations, discontinuity, and flexibility (e.g., Mohanty, 2003; Swarr & Nagar, 2010); Chicana feminism, framing the body and sexuality as subversive tools (e.g., Anzaldúa, 1987; Hurtado, 2003); and post-colonial studies, positioned to shift voice, context, and power, and to explore "other" possibilities (e.g., Alexander, 2008).

Drawing on her ethnographic research with Sure Start in the United Kingdom, Victoria Foster draws on Gramsci's concept of hegemony to critically explore the ways in which poor working-class women have historically been viewed and theorized in their role as mothers. She discusses how theory informs the design of the study, relationships in research, and the process of dissemination of research findings.

Treatment of Binaries

The influence of postmodernism in social work has facilitated a rich and discursive exploration of binaries in social work teaching and research. Social work has historically relied on numerous binaries, including social worker/client, empowered/disempowered, victim/perpetrator, male/female, oppressed/privileged, just to name a few. Social change movements have often used these and other binary categories to construct unified positions in opposition to forms of oppression. The category *woman*, for instance, while challenged by some for its essentialism, has been central to the gains made by feminist movements (Mohanty, 1988). Wilchins (2004) argues, "a political category called Woman may sound like a good idea in theory, but it hides immense racial, economic, gender, and cultural differences within it" (p. 124). Dichotomous identity categories associated with gender, class, sexual orientation, ethnicity, race, ability, and age, while problematic, offer potential for solidarity and alliances by assuming a shared group experience.

However, binary categories leave little room for multiple and sometimes competing realities. They also fail to take into account how language and power produce our multiple subjectivities. Butler (1990) has suggested that the construct of gender around which the early feminist movement was built may "work to limit . . . the very cultural possibilities that feminism is supposed to open up" (pp. 200–201). Kumsa (2007) similarly troubles the self/other binary and argues that, "the biggest roadblock to ethical practice is the absolute sense of the binary relationship between Self and Other" (p. 102). She poignantly describes how this binary prohibits us from understanding how our "encounters" with people and our own sense of selves are constituted and mediated through webs of power dynamics, history, and discourse.

Influenced by feminists of color, lesbian feminists, and others who have argued for a critical understanding of intersectionality and the complexity of interlocking identities, powerful and useful merits can be realized when social work researchers actively critique binaries and dualistic thinking. As we have stated elsewhere (Wahab et al., 2012), research that actively destabilizes or challenges taken-for-granted constructions opens the possibility for that research to more fully engage with and report on the complex realities of people's lives.

Social workers' daily proximity with oppression and privilege (through systems, people's experiences, and our locations) positions us well to deconstruct taken-for-granted binary assumptions, including those not specifically associated with gender. While all authors in this book embrace and trouble binaries at different times, contributors in this section specifically complicate them in order to name and critique the assumptions and taken-for-granted constructs in research.

Ann Curry-Stevens troubles the subject/object binary in research by drawing on Butler (2009), applying this work to her own experience as a white researcher working with a coalition of communities of color around disparities research in the Northwestern United States. She argues for intersubjective research and its potential for reconfiguring power relationships across academic and community partners.

Martha Kuwee-Kumsa troubles the notion of social work as a helping profession and positions it within the discursive practices of the colonial nation-state. She reflects on a participatory action research project with an Oromo women's grassroots movement to reclaim and revive their ancient ancestral spirituality of their foremothers in the dire context of their own exile. In this chapter, she calls for a critical engagement of both the dualisms and the complexities of the in-between spaces of ontology/epistemology, ethics/politics, concepts/methods, and theory/practice in feminist social work research and practice.

Traditionally, feminist theories and values have been aligned with qualitative methods due to epistemological and ontological assumptions. Sandra M. Leotti and Jennifer S. Muthanna challenge these taken-for-granted assumptions by troubling the qualitative/quantitative binary in feminist research, and by exploring the progressive possibilities for utilizing quantitative methods in a way that supports feminist theories and values.

Engagement with Methodology

As feminists, we are committed to the dictum that *how* we study determines *what* we know. Therefore, it is critical that feminist methodology survive as a critical part of any curriculum if the feminist perspective is to have any academic base (Kaufman, 2007, p. 681).

We begin by affirming Kaufman's statement that a feminist methodology (read here as the theory and philosophy of knowledge and the research process) holds significant promise for feminist research in general and feminist social work research in particular. We understand feminism as "the search to render visible and to explain patterns of injustice in organizations, behavior, and normative values that systemically manifest themselves in *gender-differentiated ways*" (Ackerly & True, 2010, p. 464, italics in original).

While feminist scholars agree that there is no uniquely feminist research method, feminist beliefs and tenets can be brought to the research process (Burt & Code, 1995; Cook & Fonow, 2007; Cummerton, 1986; Fonow & Cook, 1991; Harding, 1991; Reinharz, 1992). While feminist researchers engage a wide range of methods informed by a range of ontologies and epistemologies, most research that calls itself feminist affirms a feminist belief that conventional science functions within a male-dominated paradigm (Harding, 1991, 1993; Hartsock, 1998; Reinharz, 1992) and presents a challenge to androcentric bias. Other shared features across feminist research, though fraught with tensions, include feminist researchers' attention to power, authority, ethics, reflexivity, praxis, and difference, and while these features surface across diverse feminist projects, they represent contested, dynamic, and often controversial spaces within feminist research (Olesen, 2005).

Here, we comment on our profession's reluctance to engage fully with critical feminist methodological developments. This is particularly true with regard to the field's potential to move beyond a conventional emphasis on "women's issues" toward incorporating a dynamic understanding of gender and sexualities (and other markers of identity) as intertwining systems and social structures affecting people's lives. Thus, more deliberately integrating critical feminist methodologies into social work curricula (particularly, though not exclusively, as regards social work research curricula) offers the possibility for social workers to develop more critical research agendas and perspectives on the research process and other social processes that affect clients and research participants.

The contributors in this section provide detailed methodological discussions associated with feminist research. Topics include issues associated with power, ethics, reflexivity, and various choices made around approaches to difference, the roles of participants and the possible dilemmas generated by those roles, as well as choices regarding representation and dissemination of findings.

Arts-based research has the potential to unsettle stereotypes, challenge dominant ideologies and hegemonic ways of representing knowledge, build bridges across differences, promote understanding, foster empathetic connections, and raise critical consciousness; all vital aspects of feminist research. Inspired by her artistic roots and passions, Moshoula Capous-Desyllas discusses her engagement with and understanding of power, voice, authority, ethics, representation, reflexivity, and praxis in her arts-based research (photovoice) with female commercial sex workers.

University-led research that employs "community-based" methods has become a reinvigorated form of knowledge production within social work. Increased resources from government sources have recruited social work academics to develop community partnerships while popularizing the use of community engagement methods (i.e., arts-based research, community advisory boards, knowledge dissemination) without providing adequate funding to community partners for their participation. Meanwhile, community organizing and activism have been criminalized by governments; community-based organizations that are government-funded risk losing core funding if they actively critique public policy or engage in activism against the state. Rupaleem Bhuyan, Flavia Genovese, Rachel Mehl, Bethany J. Osborne, Margarita Pintin-Perez, and Fernanda Villanueva illustrate their varied standpoints while engaging in participatory action research with the Migrant Mothers Project, a study that explores how women with precarious migratory status practice substantive citizenship for themselves and their children in Canada.

In her chapter presenting methodological reflections on a study of university LGBT centers, Jen Self articulates the contributions and potential of critical queer feminisms for social work research. Drawing on lessons learned from her own critical self-examination as a researcher engaged in critical queer and feminist scholarship, Self invites future researchers to consider the role of critical queer theories in interrogating and destabilizing normative features of the research process, including questions related to the role of the researcher, formulation of research questions, and process of analysis and representation of findings.

Karen Morgaine reflexively engages an exploration of the interplay between insider/outsider associated with her research experiences and agenda. Specifically, she unpacks how she has navigated identity politics and material issues of privilege and oppression in her own research. She concludes by asking: what does it mean to be a "good enough insider" in research?

From the position that feminist social work research is inherently and intentionally a political project, Gita Mehrotra argues that conducting feminist, qualitative research entails a form of affective labor where attention to emotional, personal, and sensory elements of the research process are consistent with the goals and assumptions of feminist research. She asks what it might mean for feminist social work scholars to: (1) better understand and acknowledge the emotional component of knowledge production; and (2) view emotional labor as an integral, salient, and legible part of the research work we do. Using her own research as an example, she shares the experience of managing intersectional social identities and power dynamics in the research process as a form of emotional labor.

While the "perfect storm" of globalization, rapid technological advances, and massive cultural and demographic transformations in the United States (Reisch, 2013) has facilitated tremendous challenges (and opportunities) for social work research and education during the past several decades, we find critical hope and possibilities in the words and voices present in this book. By highlighting the many faces of critical feminisms in social work research, we hope to support social workers to bridge the perceived divide between feminisms and social work research. Each contributor moves beyond "it's feminist because I say so" (Orme, 2003) by laying clear and explicit claims to feminisms, demonstrating multiple ways researchers can claim feminisms in research without relying on a "by and for women" research focus. These contributions help us more concretely understand the importance of theory to research and how theory can make research more just, more liberatory, and more attuned to power and ethics. Contributors also help us complicate and trouble accepted binaries associated with identity categories in addition to those frequently found in social work discourse and research (client/helper, insider/outsider, researcher/ study participant). Contributors in this book challenge us to expand our approaches to methods by raising ontological and epistemological questions. The numerous methods discussed in this book remind us that, while there is no uniquely feminist method for research, feminist principles, tenets and epistemologies can be brought into the inquiry process.

References

Ackerly, B. & True, J. (2010). Back to the future: Feminist theory, activism, and doing feminist research in an age of globalization. *Women's Studies International Forum, 33*, 464–472.

Alexander, K. B. (2008). Queer(y)ing the postcolonial through the West(ern). In N. K. Denzin, Y. Lincoln, & L. T. Smith (Eds.), *Handbook of critical and indigenous methodologies* (pp. 101–133). Thousand Oaks, CA: Sage.

Anderson-Nathe, B., Gringeri, C., & Wahab, S. (2013). Nurturing "critical hope" in teaching feminist social work research. *Journal of Social Work Education, 49,* 277–291.

Anzaldúa, G. (1987). *Borderlands: The new mestiza = La frontera.* San Francisco: Spinsters/Aunt Lute.

Baines, D. (1997). Feminist social work in the inner city: The challenges of race, class and gender. *Affilia, 12* (3), 297–317.

Barnoff, L. & Moffatt, K. (2007). Contradictory tensions in anti-oppression practice in feminist social services. *Affilia, 22* (1), 56–70.

Burt, S., & Code, L. (1995). *Changing methods.* Ontario, Canada: Broad View Press.

Butler, J. (1990). *Gender trouble: Feminism and the subversion of identity.* New York: Routledge.

Butler, J. (2009). *Frames of war: When is life grievable?* London/New York: Verso.

Cook, J. A. & Fonow, M. M. (2007). A passion for knowledge: The teaching of feminist methodology. In S. N. Hesse-Biber (Ed.), *Handbook of feminist research: Theory and praxis* (pp. 705–712). Thousand Oaks, CA: Sage.

Council on Social Work Education (CSWE). (2008). *Educational policy and accreditation standards.* Retrieved from www.cswe.org/File.aspx?id=13780.

Cummerton, J. M. (1986). A feminist perspective on research: What does it help us see? In N. Van Den Bergh & L. B. Cooper (Eds.), *Feminist visions for social work* (pp. 80–100). Silver Spring, MD: National Association of Social Workers.

Fonow, M. G. & Cook, J. A. (1991). *Beyond methodology: Feminist scholarship as lived research.* Bloomington: Indiana University Press.

Freeman, M. (1990). Beyond women's issues: Feminism and social work. *Affilia, 5,* 72–89.

General Assemblies of the International Association of Schools of Social Work (IASSW) and International Federation of Social Workers (IFSW). (2004). *Global standards for the education and training of the social work profession.* Adelaide, Australia.

Gray, M. & Boddy, J. (2010). Making sense of the waves: Wipeout or still riding high? *Affilia, 25* (4), 368–389.

Gringeri, C., Wahab, S., & Anderson-Nathe, B. (2010). What makes it feminist: Mapping the landscape of feminist social work research. *Affilia, 25,* 390–405.

Harding, S. (1991). *Whose science? Whose knowledge?* Ithaca, NY: Cornell University Press.

Harding, S. (1993). Rethinking standpoint epistemology: What is "strong objectivity"? In L. Alcoff & E. Potter (Eds.), *Feminist epistemologies* (pp. 49–82). New York: Routledge.

Hartsock, N. (1998). *The feminist standpoint revisited and other essays.* Boulder, CO: Westview Press.

Hurtado, A. (2003). Theory in the flesh: Toward an endarkened epistemology. *International Journal of Qualitative Studies in Education, 16* (2), 215–225.

Jani, J. S. & Reisch, M. (2011). Common human needs, uncommon solutions: Applying a critical framework to perspectives on human behavior. *Families in Society, 92,* 13–20.

Kaufman, D. R. (2007). From course to discourse: mainstreaming feminist methodology. In S. N. Hesse-Biber (Ed.), *Handbook of feminist research: Theory and praxis* (pp. 681–688). Thousand Oaks, CA: Sage.

Kemp, S. & Brandwein, R. (2010). Feminisms and social work in the United States: an intertwined history. *Affilia, 25* (4), 341–364.

Kovacs, P. J., Hutchison, E. D., Collins, K. S., & Linde, L. B. (2013). Norming or transforming: Feminist pedagogy and social work competencies. *Affilia, 28* (3), 229–239.

Kumsa, M. K. (2007). Encounters in social work practice. In D. Mandell (Ed.). *Revisiting the use of self: Questioning professional identities* (pp. 87–103). Toronto: Canadian Scholars Press.

Mehrotra, G. (2010). Toward a continuum of intersectionality theorizing for feminist social work scholarship. *Affilia, 25,* 417–430.

Mignolo, W. (2000). *Local histories/global designs: Coloniality, subaltern knowledges, and border thinking.* Princeton, NJ: Princeton University Press.

Mohanty, C. (1988). Under western eyes: Feminist scholarship and colonial discourses. *Feminist Review, 30,* 51–80.

Mohanty, C. T. (2003). *Feminism without borders: Decolonizing theory, practicing solidarity.* Durham, NC: Duke University Press.

NASW. (1996). *Code of ethics.* Washington, DC: NASW Press.

Nes, J. A. & Iadicola, P. (1989). Towards a definition of feminist social work: A comparison of liberal, radical, and socialist models. *Social Work, 34,* 12–21.

Olesen, V. (1994). Feminisms and models of qualitative research. In N.K. Denzin & Y.S. Lincoln (Eds.), *Handbook of qualitative research* (pp. 158–174). Thousand Oaks, CA: Sage.

Olesen, V. (2000). Feminisms and qualitative research at and into the millennium. In N.K. Denzin & Y.S. Lincoln (Eds.), *The handbook of qualitative research* (pp. 215–256). Thousand Oaks, CA: Sage.

Olesen, V. (2005). Early millennial feminist qualitative research: Challenges and contours. In N.K. Denzin & Y.S. Lincoln (Eds.), *The Sage handbook of qualitative research* (pp. 235–278). Thousand Oaks, CA: SAGE.

Orme, J. (2003). "It's feminist because I say so!' *Qualitative Social Work, 2* (2), 131–153.

Reinharz, S. (1992). *Feminist methods in social research.* New York: Oxford University Press.

Reisch, M. (2013). Social work education and the neo-liberal challenge: The U.S. response to increasing global inequality. *Social Work Education, 32* (6), 715–733.

Rossiter, A. (2001). Innocence lost and suspicion found: Do we educate for or against social work? *Critical Social Work, 2* (1), 1–5.

Sands, G. R. & Nuccio, K. (1992). Postmodern feminist theory and social work. *Social Work, 37* (6), 489–494.

Shaw, I. (1999). Seeing the trees for the wood: The politics of evaluation in practice. In B. Broad (Ed.). *The politics of social work research evaluation* (pp. 109–126). Birmingham: Venture Press.

Swarr, A. L. & Nagar, R. (2010). *Critical transnational feminist praxis.* Albany, NY: SUNY Press.

Wahab, S., Anderson-Nathe, B., & Gringeri, C. (2012). Joining the conversation: Social work contributions to feminist research. In S. Hesse-Biber (Ed.), *Handbook of feminist research: Theory and praxis* (2nd ed., pp. 455–474). Thousand Oaks, CA: Sage.

Wilchins, R. (2004). *Queer theory, gender theory.* Los Angeles: Alyson Books.

Section 1

Feminist Claims in Social Work Research

2 Doing Critical Feminist Research

A Collaboration

Andrea Daley, Lucy Costa and Lori E. Ross

Introduction

In this chapter, we examine our engagement with critical feminism in research within the context of an ongoing critical, collaborative, and interdisciplinary research project. We speak from our respective social identities and locations to explore feminist research issues including epistemology, collaborative methodology and representation, ethics, collaborative knowledge production, and communication with relevant audiences. Throughout the chapter we contextualize our reflections in current debates within both feminist and service user research literature as informed by the disability rights and consumer/survivor (C/S) movements.

Before engaging with the substantive objectives of this chapter, we want to address the interdisciplinary nature of our research given the book's focus on feminist social work research. In particular, in "writing ourselves into" (Presser, 2005) this examination of critical feminist research it seems important to note that, while the chapter is written for a text on feminist social work research, we do not characterize our research exclusively as such. That is, we have differing relationships—understandings of and experiences with—the social work profession. Moreover, in preparing for this chapter we asked questions about how feminist social work research might be demarcated from other critical research (i.e., critical disabilities, critical race theory) that centers the experiences of women. We queried the imperative to move beyond disciplinary confines in relation to research that identifies as its primary purposes the examination of social injustices in women's lives and social and structural transformation. This is a particularly critical query recognizing critiques that implicate social work in social injustices experienced by women, including its participation in colonial violence against Aboriginal/Indigenous communities (e.g., residential schools, the Sixties Scoop) (Cowie, 2010; Faith, 2008; Hart, 2003) and people with lived experiences of the psychiatric system (Poole, Jivraj, Arslanian, Bellows, Chiasson, Hakimy, Pasini, & Reid, 2012).

Having said this, while we do not characterize our work as exclusively social work research, the issues examined in this chapter are undoubtedly relevant to social work research that is informed by feminist and other critical epistemologies, methodologies, purposes, and goals. To this end, our exploration of how we engaged with principles of feminism in our research is guided by the following objectives:

1   To examine how feminist and other critical epistemologies contribute to our research.
2   To describe how we came to form a research collaboration *vis-à-vis* our respective relationships to the research topic.
3   To describe our critical feminist research practices in relation to the issues of ethics, representation, and collaborative knowledge production.
4   To outline challenges we experienced as critical feminist researchers related to the communication of research findings to C/S and institutional stakeholders.
5   To identify transformative outcomes of our research collaboration.

Background

The project on which this chapter is based identifies as its primary objective the examination of the interpretative nature of psychiatry in relation to the construction of women's distress and gender (femininities), sexuality, race, and class within the particular time and place of one urban, Canadian, clinical psychiatric setting (for a detailed account of the study purpose and methodology, see Daley, Costa, & Ross, 2012). The project included a retrospective review of 25 women's inpatient charts and five charts each from the following programs: women's, schizophrenia, mood disorders, geriatrics, and women and law. Our analysis indicated that mental health practitioners' use of language, the minimal inclusion of the sexualized, racialized, and classed structural contexts of women's lives (e.g., the impact of structural oppressions related to sexuality, race, and class), and the imperative to locate women's experiences in the mutually exclusive categories of "truth" or "untruth," as evidenced in chart documentation, function to construct narrow, medicalized representations of women's mental distress.

Methods

This chapter is written using the transcript of an audio-recorded discussion between us [Andrea (AD), Lucy (LC), and Lori (LR)], during which we explored the overarching question, "Why and how have we engaged feminisms in our research?" AD drafted an interview guide, which included a series of subquestions related to the overarching question. The interview guide was distributed to LC and LR for review, feedback, and revisions. The final iteration of the interview guide was agreed upon by each of us. Our discussion lasted approximately three hours, and the audio-recording was transcribed verbatim. The transcript was coded by AD using grounded theory methods (Charmaz, 2000, 2006) to identify themes, which were then verified by LC and LR. AD drafted the first iteration of the chapter, which was reviewed and revised by LC and LR towards its final iteration. Use of these data collection and analysis methods and the writing process for the purpose of this chapter is significant for two reasons. First, they allow for our unique perspectives, opinions, and ideas as informed by our respective subject positions to be more accurately represented through a collaborative process of knowledge production. Second, they reflect the method of collaborative knowledge production used in the project on which the chapter is based (to be discussed below), and thus convey a consistency in the principles of representation, collaboration, and egalitarianism between the "doing of" and "talking about" our research.

Themes

The analysis of the transcript identified key themes related to the overarching question, "Why and how have we engaged feminisms in our research?" including: (1) how our research is feminist; (2) forming a collaboration; (3) critical feminist research practices; and (4) transformative outcomes.

How Our Research Is Feminist

On the question of whether our research is feminist research, we agreed that throughout the research process we have explicitly and implicitly taken up feminist politics, principles, and methods. To this point, AD commented that:

> If we were talking to somebody and they asked us to explain the project even in not using the language of feminism or feminist, they would probably walk away having heard principles of feminism operating through our research.

More specifically, our research constitutes a process of "studying up" (Harding & Norberg, 2005) the psychiatric institution from a politicized stance to expose how policies and practices (re)shape unjust gender relations through chart documentation, and the implications of this practice of power for constructions of and responses to gendered distress. Our research is emancipatory in intent (McColl, Adair, Davey, & Kates, 2013; Moosa-Mitha, 2005) and is undergirded by the goals of transforming institutional practices that may have contributed to women's oppression and consciousness-raising within C/S communities (Fanow & Cook, 1991, 2005; Ramazanoglu & Holland, 2002; Reinharz, 1992; Sarantakos, 2005).

Notwithstanding our project's alignment with these characteristics of feminist research, identifying our research as exclusively feminist left us somewhat unsettled. Upon reflection, our discussion on the question of whether our research is feminist research became animated in tensions associated with competing/coexisting feminist epistemologies and critiques of White feminism. It is conceivable that the source of our "unsettledness" was a collective taking up of the tensions resulting from a convergence of feminist standpoint and feminist postmodernism epistemologies in our research (Harding, 1987). Our exclusive focus on an analysis of women's psychiatric charts to the exclusion of men's charts may suggest that we engaged with a feminist standpoint epistemology, whereby we recognized "woman" as a unified category, and as having experiences distinct from those of men. Alternatively, our taking up of the intersections between gender, sexuality, race, and class suggest a desire to disrupt the unified category of "woman" as informed by a feminist postmodern epistemology. In this regard, our analysis of women's psychiatric inpatient charts is guided by an understanding of the interconnected nature of gender, sexuality, race, and class and related structures of oppression (Cole, 2009; Collins, 2000; Davis, 2008; Hankivsky et al., 2010; King, 1990; Metzl, 2009; Phoenix & Pattynama, 2006). LR referred to anti-oppression and intersectional frameworks (Dominelli, 2002, 2003; Healy, 2005; Hill-Collins, 2000) to articulate that while gender is centered in our research:

> [It is not] extractable from thinking about women's experiences within the psychiatric system in relation to sexual orientation, gender identity, race, and class . . . we have always been looking at gender through those other lenses . . . so, labelling it a feminist project without acknowledging all of the other anti-oppression lenses that we've also used feels limited.

In other words, while our project does rely on the category of "woman," we also approach our analysis with an understanding of, and attempt to reveal, the multiple standpoints of diversely situated women by attending to intersections between gendered, sexualized, racialized, and classed oppressions. So, while the project centers gender (femininity) as a focus of analysis by identifying as its primary data source women's psychiatric inpatient charts, it presumes multiple femininities (genders) as they are produced by intersections between psychiatric disability, gender (femininity), sexuality, race, and class. AD stated:

> There seems to be something important about . . . using the category of woman in an essentializing way because there is the history of the psychiatric regulation of women's bodies and sexuality, so I think there's something important about not losing sight of that . . . but it's also recognizing that women's bodies are differently regulated because of how they're sexualized, racialized, and classed.

While exploring the feminist "nature" of our research, LC similarly took up a critique of feminism, stating that "theoretically feminism has a way to go towards understanding and taking up disability issues across the spectrum of intersectionality." Towards addressing this particular limitation of feminism she reflected on the importance of other critical theoretical frameworks central to our research, including disability studies, the C/S paradigm, and newly emerging mad studies (Menzies, LeFrançois, & Reaume, 2013), which foster different C/S voices, perspectives, and analyses. Similarly to feminism, these frameworks serve the purpose of our research by advocating for politicized and emancipatory disability research processes (Russo, 2012; Schneider, 2012); yet they also facilitate the centering of women as psychiatric subjects within the particular context of psychiatry and the psychiatric institution. In this regard, the alignment of our research to feminism *and* disability studies, the C/S paradigm, and mad studies is quite appropriate as there are "historically and currently explicit experiences where women have been pathologized and psychiatrized because of . . . PMS [premenstrual syndrome], hysteria, nymphomania, masochism" (LC).

Our taking up of intersectionality in the ways described above is allied with feminists of color and Black feminists who critique White feminism for its theorizing of a monolithic identity category of "woman" with little attention to interlocking systems of oppression across gender, sexuality, race, class, and disability (Combahee River Collective, 1977; Crenshaw, 1991; Hill-Collins, 2000; Mehrotra, 2010; Phoenix & Pattynama, 2006). However, our focus of analysis on "the many ways that gender interweaves with other factors in women's lives" (Moosa-Mitha, 2005, p. 55) rather than the many ways that "difference . . . is interwoven in the lives of women" (Moosa-Mitha, 2005, p. 55) suggests centering a gendered standpoint within a research process that seeks to deconstruct mainstream psychiatric narratives towards an uncovering of how knowledge about women's distress is linked to gendered relations of power.

Forming a Collaboration

The collaborative methodology that characterizes our research project draws upon feminist and other critical epistemologies that seek to foster egalitarian, democratic, emancipatory, empowering, and transformative effects and serve to challenge academic knowledge, expertise, and power (Beresford, 2002; Beresford & Wallcraft, 1997; Chamberlin, 1978; McColl et al., 2013; McLaughlin, 2010; Morrison, 2005; Oliver, 1992; Reaume, 2002; Shimrat, 1997; Wallcraft, Schrank, & Amering, 2009), and as such is fundamental to our understanding of this study as constituting feminist research. While the principle of collaboration has been operationalized through a broad group of action research methodologies, including social action research, feminist participatory action research, and community-based research, we are careful in using these particular research terms given how our project unfolded. The research project grew out of AD's social work practice experience in community mental health and, specifically, her experiences of the constraints of chart documentation and potential tensions associated with constructing women through dominant psychiatric discourses and documentation processes. AD conceptualized the problem of documentation as institutionalized violence/oppression whereby women become intelligible only through psychiatric discourse (Butler, 1999). Her interest in this area was informed by intersections between feminist critiques of the psychiatric regulation of women (Chesler, 1972; Jimenez, 1997; Showalter, 1985; Ussher, 1997, 2011), the legacy of the psychiatric pathologization of "homosexuality" (Drescher, 2010; King, 2003), her participation in lesbian, gay, bisexual, transgender, and queer (LGBTQ) activism in relation to barriers in access to good-quality health services, and training in critical social work theories and practice (Fook, 2012; Healy, 2005). In terms of the latter, exposure to feminist post-structuralism (Butler, 1999; Rossiter, 2001; Weedon, 1987) provided an important theoretical framework for this work.

As described above, the research did not begin with a self-identified problem of a group, a community, or an organization (Stringer, 1996). In recognition of historical and contemporary harms done through research "about" rather than "with" C/S communities, AD's first action was to ensure C/S community accountability of the work by seeking meaningful partnership with a C/S community organization. To this end, she sought out a partnership with the Empowerment Council (EC), a non-profit organization with the mandate of ensuring an independent voice for clients at a tertiary care mental health organization in Toronto (ON, Canada) (Empowerment Council, 2013). LC, systemic advocate for the EC, agreed to serve as a co-investigator on the project, upon agreement of the EC Board and establishing a Memorandum of Understanding between the Board and AD.

From the perspective of the EC, the research collaboration signaled "an important addition to the work that the Empowerment Council was already doing" in relation to "looking at prejudice, predetermination of clients' experiences by staff, and potentials beyond narratives of illness" (LC). The project was also seen as meeting the advocacy mandate of the EC by providing access to information about the institution and women's experiences within it that would otherwise be difficult or impossible for the EC to access. We anticipate that this type of research would not have been supported by the institution had it been initiated directly by the EC, rather than by academics in collaboration with the EC. Wallcraft et al. (2009), for example, state that:

> Collaborative research is, in most cases, the only way for survivor researchers to contribute to the production of knowledge. It is very difficult for user/survivor-controlled research to get funding and recognition so collaborative research often remains the only way for us to take part in research. (p. 62)

Conceivably, collaboration has supported the EC to strategically challenge and resist institutional (structural) power that might otherwise operate to create "barriers" to accessing medical records for advocacy purposes *vis-à-vis* research. This includes contributing to the analysis of the psychiatric charts "not from the perspective of medicine but from a consumer/survivor perspective" (LC). To this point, LC stated that the collaboration presented an opportunity for the EC, as a community-based advocacy service, to engage with academic discourse in order to leverage academic privilege and bring visibility to conversations and concerns that date back to the early years of C/S political mobilization. A historical account of these conversations and concerns within the C/S movement is evident in a mid-1980s issue of *Phoenix Rising*, a community-based publication produced by "present and former psychiatric inmates" that served as both a source of information about the injustices of the Canadian mental health system and a "rallying point" for people to make changes to it (On Our Own, 1980–1990). Importantly, the publication speaks to a history of community knowledge about the operations of sexism in the psychiatric system as well as within the context of C/S community mobilization, which informs and serves as a foundation for our research. In this regard, our collaboration is important for contextualizing our research within "its political and ideological relations" (Beresford, 2002, p. 100). That is, LC holds us accountable to recognizing that our research is possible because of, and is informed by, historical and contemporary grassroots C/S organizations that have worked tirelessly to challenge and resist oppressive psychiatric practices that impact women (Blackbridge, 1996; Funk, 1999; On Our Own, 1980–1990). LC's contributions of "community knowledge" and a "deep knowing" of the impacts of psychiatric institutional practices on women serve as a reminder and caution against past practices of academic researchers that have appropriated service user knowledge(s).

While collaboration in relation to the C/S community was integral to our project, we would be remiss not to explore our institutional collaboration as well. Institutional collaboration is important given that our project constitutes a "studying up"—that is, the studying of psychiatric institutional documentation practices rather than women's subjective experiences of being documented within a psychiatric institution. While the process of "studying up" holds potential emancipatory or consciousness-raising relevancy to C/S communities, our focus is also on social and structural transformation through changes to institutional practices. Our institutional collaboration with LR has not only been relevant to data collection (e.g., accessing our data source—women's psychiatric inpatient charts), but also to thinking about the communication and uptake of research-informed recommendations by the institution and related settings.

As indicated above, the origins of our research lie with AD, and in this way, the project may not reflect the full potential of the feminist research principles underlying a collaborative research methodology. Our collaboration is also limited in other ways. In particular, given our analytical framework of intersectionality (gender, sexuality, race, class, disability), we do not bring lived experiences of all relevant social identity categories to the research. Collectively, we hold identities as White, lesbian, bisexual, queer-identified women and members of C/S communities with lived experiences of being psychiatrized; have differing professional identities and relationships within the mental health system; have various experiences with social and economic marginalization; and have historical and contemporary relationships with immigrant/newcomer communities. As such, while our collaboration is not exhaustive, it does include key representatives of interested groups in relation to the area of inquiry (Minkler & Wallerstein, 2001). Importantly, however, none of us bring lived experiences as racialized women. While we do not intend to reduce the complexity of representation in research to placing researchers in essentialized and fit categories, we recognize the limitations to knowledge production in the absence of representation. In response, at the time of writing, we are expanding the research collaboration to include racialized community-based and academic researchers.

Critical Feminist Research Practices

While we appreciate a need to interrogate how our various subject positions influence research practices (Ramazanoglu & Holland, 2002), we also heed warnings about the inadvertent centering of (privileged) researchers through processes of reflexive positioning. Moreover, as Doucet and Mauthner (2006) state, "naming subject positionings does not address the question of how these subject positionings affect knowledge construction" (p. 42). As such, they urge feminist researchers to consider reflexive positionings beyond social identities to ask how institutional and pragmatic influences, among others, shape research practices (Doucet & Mauthner, 2006). In the remainder of the chapter we engage reflexive positioning to examine some of our research practices as they have been influenced by our various social identities and institutional and pragmatic influences. We rely on these examples of critical feminist research practices as an attempt to operationalize the principles of shared decision-making, egalitarian interactions, and multiple perspectives towards the development of a communal model of scholarship (Rhoades, 2000).

Ethics

At the beginning of our project, as with any research, we developed our ethics protocol. A central question that emerged in relation to data collection was consideration of how to access women's charts. More specifically, we needed to decide whether to work exclusively through the psychiatric institution or with women themselves to gain access to their psychiatric inpatient charts. Through a series of discussions we decided to work through the institution. This was a difficult decision to make in light of the feminist social justice and C/S principles and perspectives guiding our research.

Given our understanding of the potential implications for women who access the mental health system having agency around research conducted about their lives, it was essential that this decision was made jointly with representation and consultation with the EC.

Throughout this process we engaged a principled orientation to ethics (Preissle, 2007) that attended to benefits versus harms, privacy, and confidentiality. When exploring the potential benefits of the study, we considered its potential to redress the legacy of psychiatric regulating and pathologizing of women in general, and racialized, sexual minority, and poor women in particular (Dykeman, 1999). Central to our decision-making was our concern that seeking informed consent might, inadvertently, compromise women's right to privacy and confidentiality with regard to their medical histories. That is, despite taking measures to maintain privacy and confidentiality by, for example, sending letters to women's home addresses in non-descript envelopes and/or leaving telephone messages with minimal information, contacting women to obtain informed consent might have led to the inadvertent disclosure of their involvement with psychiatric services. We were concerned that this may pose a particular risk for those women who are economically and socially marginalized and who often reside in settings that afford little privacy (e.g., shelters, boarding homes). In addition, LC critically reflected on the need to weigh the potential harm of working through the psychiatric institution against those potentially encountered by women during their interactions with the psychiatric institution. In the end, we reached consensus that working through the institution posed no harms greater than those potentially encountered by women during their interactions with the institution.

It is important to note that this decision is not uncontested—likely there are readers of this chapter who will disagree with our ultimate decision around this—and we are called to account for this decision on an ongoing basis. LR provides the following explanation:

> If we are not able to produce social change as a result of the work than the risks to women of having their records reviewed by us without their explicit consent don't outweigh the benefits of the work.

It is also important to recognize that we do not equally share accountability for this decision. LC, in her role as a systemic advocate for, and identified member of, the C/S community, shoulders more accountability with regard to her participation in our research. In addition, she is more likely to come into professional and personal contact with women who see this as a personally relevant issue. This is consistent with writing about ethical issues in community-based research, which has highlighted the need to attend to the personal risks encountered by community-based researchers, who may risk damaging personal or supportive relationships through being held accountable by their communities for decisions of the research team

(Flicker, Roche, & Guta, 2010). This is a concern that we have not resolved, but one that we think requires more attention and discussion within the realm of critical feminist research.

Collaborative Knowledge Production

Our methods of data collection and analysis were shaped by the institutional requirement that only AD would have access to women's psychiatric inpatient charts. This required that she make decisions about which charts to include for review, and which documentation excerpts to extract from each chart for the purpose of analysis. This created the problem of having the "raw" data being interpreted through service provider and academic standpoints in the absence of a C/S perspective. We wanted to ensure that a C/S advocacy perspective was as deeply embedded as possible in our analysis, and thereby our conclusions. In order to work towards this, we used as our data source not only relevant documentation excerpts from the charts themselves, but also transcripts of the discussions the three of us had about the chart extracts. To be more specific, documentation excerpts from each chart were manually transferred into individualized, corresponding documents that served as a "text" for the purpose of analysis. Texts from each chart were read independently by each of us. We then came together to discuss our responses and insights to the chart extractions, and these discussions were recorded and transcribed verbatim. The verbatim transcripts, together with the chart extracts, were reviewed and coded to identify themes across investigators' insights, opinions, and interpretations (Daley et al., 2012).

In this way, LC's perspective as a systemic advocate and identified member of the C/S community was not simply applied to analysis done by service provider and academic members of the research team, but rather was embedded within the analysis process itself. LC noted the potential usefulness of this collaborative data analysis method to build upon strategies that are not merely about inclusion in research but that seek to transform research practices of power by "tackling diffuse epistemological frictions and identity politics, and engaging in theoretical discussions in an effort to respond to structural inequality." LR talked more specifically about the potential usefulness of the method for responding to requests from community members to have their knowledge and contributions to the research acknowledged, stating, "I feel like this is a way in which people can have their words attributed to them and to be part of the research process." The decentering of a singular self as "academic expert" was also imagined as possible through this method by LR, "I remember times [during data analysis] where I had emotional reactions to what we were reading [charting data] that were not exclusively about my positioning as an academic researcher but about me as a person."

Notwithstanding the promise of this method of participatory data analysis and knowledge production, we identified some potential limitations which deserve critical examination. First, we did not always speak the same "language" with respect to our analysis of the charts. At times, one or more of us would be discussing the chart extracts using language or frameworks that were unfamiliar to the other(s). For example, AD and LR, wearing our academic hats, would at times refer to theories that were not familiar or central in LC's everyday work. On the other hand, LR credits LC with contributing knowledge that further developed her understanding of "the C/S movement as a movement," and "pushing [me] in the direction of being more critical in the research process." Theoretical and experiential disjunctures are common problems of interdisciplinary collaborations (O'Cathain, Murphy, & Nicholl, 2008), and it is an ongoing challenge to think about how we can describe theoretical concepts in ways that resonate with all collaborators. This is a challenge we have not resolved, but one that is made easier by the time we have spent building trust in our collaborative relationship, in which we now feel comfortable seeking clarification around academic language, as well as the history, values, and politics of the C/S community.

Second, as underscored by LR, in any academic process there comes a point when people's ideas "get re-written into a language that's palatable"—quite often this is academic language. This raised a concern within the collaboration about the appropriation of community knowledge(s). In this regard, the value of our approach relied on the lead academic writer to appropriately attribute community contributors' ideas and insights, without co-opting them and reproducing them as academic knowledge. Our approach also considered the expected time commitment of community-based researchers who most likely negotiate multiple workload demands and responsibilities. LC stated that "writing cannot always be prioritized in ways that it may be for an academic researcher . . . that often systemic advocates are contending with the complexity of addressing pressing rights issues . . . putting out fires." So, while our participatory data analysis and knowledge production approach may constitute an innovative research practice towards the feminist research aim of egalitarian relationships, representation, and collaborative knowledge production, it does not resolve potential power imbalances in collaborative knowledge production.

Communicating With Relevant Audiences

By and large, a challenge we have experienced as researchers engaged with a critical feminist, social justice, and emancipatory paradigm is the communication of our findings to C/S and institutional audiences. We examine each of these areas below.

We take up communication about our research and, more specifically, our analysis to the C/S community as a foundational empowerment principle of collaborative research guided by feminist and critical C/S frameworks. As argued by Sweeney (2009), service user involvement in research is "committed to empowerment through research participation *and output*" [our emphasis] (p. 28). As such, collaboration:

> is related to the whole range of research processes and activities, from the origination of research focus and questions, control of research funding, data collection and analysis, *to dissemination and follow-up action* [our emphasis] (Beresford, 2002, p. 101).

This includes challenging traditional ways in which research "outputs" are conceptualized and delivered beyond publications in academic peer-reviewed journals. As such, we have presented our findings back to the Board of the EC, as well as held one community forum. While some EC Board members were able to readily engage with the research findings, other members described the findings as somewhat abstract and not especially relevant to their own experiences, or how they would be useful in their advocacy efforts. In particular, we have found it challenging to present the material in a way that is accessible and meaningful to community members and that facilitates community discussion. In preparation for the community forum we worked with a university-based knowledge mobilization unit to develop a "plain language" document of our findings. However, as described by AD, the final product "failed to capture the complexity and nuances of our analysis," and in turn "depoliticized a politicized project." This, we think, reflects the challenges in disseminating research that is quite political and theoretical in its approach within the context of constant neoliberal rhetoric around "predominant understandings of technical-rational [dissemination] models that are based on positivist understandings of social reality" (Barnes, Clouder, Pritchard, Hughes, & Purkis, 2003, p. 148).

We met with key institutional stakeholders interested in women's issues and/or charting practices at the institution where the research was conducted. The purpose of our meeting was to share some of our preliminary findings and discuss the potential implications for policy and practice. In this regard, LR noted that "it's really hard to make theoretical work action oriented and to translate into specific concrete action steps." However, this meeting was invigorating and helped us think about strategies to ensure the research is taken up within the institution, for example, through partnering with others involved in a "strategy" to better understand the barriers women may be facing to access services. LC expressed hope that social workers within the institution take up the research given her experience, as a systemic advocate, of witnessing social workers' professional institutional practices implicated in "barriers to making change . . . to doing progressive work and taking critically strong positions" in response to systemic injustices as they impact women. It may be that when we can share these specific concrete action steps with members of the EC Board, the relevance of the research will become clearer, and Board members may be better able to identify other ways in which the research can serve empowerment, advocacy, and social justice efforts.

Transformative Outcomes

Notwithstanding the challenges identified above, our project has been taken up by academics, community agencies, and women's health services. Our research publications are being used as course content in critical social work and critical disabilities courses, the research has been featured in a national (Canadian) women's health E-newsletter, and we have presented to a bioethics think tank. The use of our research in these ways constitutes potential opportunity for engaging in social change by building upon existing connections with community, institutional, and academic partners towards the goal of social and structural transformation.

In addition to these transformative outcomes, we note significant and impressive process-related outcomes of the research collaboration. LC explained:

> I think through working together I would say we've spun off into other projects. I feel like you [LR] and the Empowerment Council we work more closely now. And there's been like specific projects that we now communicate on more closely and the same with you [AD]. We can say that's connected to the work that we have been doing.

LR added that the idea that process can be as important as outcome is consistent with principles of feminist research, and that:

> The fact that part of this process was that we have developed stronger working relationships that have led to other projects, which are less theoretical and more practical . . . more action oriented is a valuable output of this project.

AD recognized the community-based connections as valuable outcomes of our collaboration; however, she also highlighted broadened connections with other social work academics doing similar work as an integral outcome. She noted that "there is something about the critical nature of our work that has been helpful in terms of building those connections," and that she hopes there is "trickle down in terms of how those academics take the work up [the analysis and associated social action] within their local communities." As an example, LR added that collaboration with the EC "has really deepened my willingness and ability to be an advocate through an academic role . . . by the fact that we've done this work I have a much deeper understanding of what the C/S movement is about."

Conclusion

In this chapter we explored the question of "Why and how have we engaged feminisms in our research?" Our exploration started with a description of our research as it seeks to redress the social and structural oppression of differently sexualized, raced, and classed women as they are produced through psychiatric discourse *vis-à-vis* chart documentation. We identified feminist epistemologies, including critiques of White feminism and critical disabilities and C/S frameworks as integral to our conceptualization of the research problem/question that centers women within the particular context of the psychiatric institution. We examined how the shared principles of egalitarianism, democratic decision-making, multiple perspectives, and reflexivity; and their consciousness-raising, emancipatory, and transformative goals informed the formation of our collaboration and research practices related to ethics, collaborative knowledge production, and communication with relevant audiences. We concluded by identifying transformative outcomes that build upon and enhance these critical research principles in ways that are specific to the overarching purpose of our research; this is to deconstruct institutionalized practices of power as they impact women within psychiatric settings.

Central to our discussion was whether our research is feminist research. In the ways described above, we would collectively answer "yes" to this question. However, we would also urge the reader to consider that the question defies a "yes/no" answer. We feel this is particularly true given historical and existing critiques of, and challenges to, feminism generally and feminist research specifically by feminists of color and Black feminists, as well as the disability rights and C/S movements—that is, given the ongoing evolution of feminisms and other critical theories. In this regard, we offer an uncertain and unsettled relationship with feminism in relation to critical research that takes up an intersectional approach to examine gender (femininities), sexuality, race, and class. Our discussion offers a challenge to social work researchers to adopt a stance of ongoing engagement with, and response to, the tensions of conducting critical, emancipatory research that is informed by intersecting theories and frameworks.

References

Barnes, V., Clouder, D.L., Pritchard, J., Hughes, C., & Purkis, J. (2003). Deconstructing dissemination: Dissemination as qualitative research. *Qualitative Research, 3* (2), 147–164.

Beresford, P. (2002). User involvement in research and evaluation: Liberation or regulation? *Social Policy & Society, 1* (2), 95–105.

Beresford, P. & Wallcraft, J. (1997). Psychiatric system survivors and emancipatory research: Issues, overlaps and differences. In C. Barnes and G. Mercer (Eds.), *Doing disability research* (pp. 66–87). Leeds, UK: The Disability Press.

Blackbridge, P. (1996). *Sunnybrook a True Story.* Vancouver, BC: Press Gang Publishers.

Butler, J. (1999). *Gender trouble: feminism and the subversion of identity* (10th Anniversary edition.) (pp. 3–44). New York: Routledge.

Chamberlin, J. (1978). *On our own: Patient controlled alternatives to the mental health system.* New York: McGraw-Hill.

Charmaz, K. (2000). Grounded theory: Objectivist and constructivist methods. In N.K. Denzin and Y.S. Lincoln (Eds.), *Handbook of qualitative research* (2nd ed.) (pp. 509–535). Thousand Oaks, CA: Sage.

Charmaz, K. (2006). *Constructing grounded theory: A practical guide through qualitative analysis.* Thousand Oaks, CA: Sage.

Chesler, P. (1972). *Woman and madness.* New York: Doubleday.

Cole, E.R. (2009). Intersectionality and research in psychology. *American Psychologist, 64* (3), 170–180.

Collins, P. (2000). *Black feminist thought: Knowledge, consciousness, and the politics of empowerment.* New York: Routledge.

Combahee River Collective. (1977). *Combahee River Collective Statement.* Retrieved on February 19, 2013 from: http://circuitous.org/scraps/combahee.html.

Cowie, A. (2010). Anti-oppressive social work practice in child welfare: Journeys of reconciliation. *Critical Social Work 11* (1), 46–51.

Crenshaw, K. (1991). Mapping the margins: Intersectionality, identity politics, and violence against women of color. *Stanford Law Review, 43,* 1241–1299.

Daley, A., Costa, L., & Ross, L. (2012). (W)righting women: Constructions of gender, sexuality & disorder through psychiatric documentation practices. *Culture, Health and Sexuality: An International Journal for Research, Intervention and Care, 14* (8), 955–969.

Davis, K. (2008). Intersectionality as buzzword: A sociology of science perspective on what makes a feminist theory successful. *Feminist Theory, 9* (1), 67–85.

Dominelli, L. (2002). *Feminist social work theory and practice.* London, UK: Palgrave Macmillan.

Dominelli, L. (2003). *Anti-oppressive social work: Theory and practice.* London, UK: Palgrave Macmillan.

Doucet, A. & Mauthner N.S. (2006). Feminist methodologies and epistemologies. In C.D. Bryant & D.L. Peck (Eds.), *Handbook of 21st century sociology* (pp. 36–42). Thousand Oaks, CA: Sage.

Drescher, J. (2010). Queer diagnoses: Parallels and contrasts in the history of homosexuality, gender variance, and the diagnostic and statistical manual. *Archives of Sexual Behavior, 39* (2), 427–460.

Dykeman, M.J. (1999). Addressing systemic issues in women's mental health: An inquest into the death of Cinderella Allalouf. *Journal of Women's Health and Law 1* (115), 15–30.

Empowerment Council. Retrieved on February 19, 2013 from: http://www.empowermentcouncil.ca/.

Faith, E. (2008). Indigenous social work education: A project for all of us. In M. Gray, J. Coates, & M. Yellow Bird (Eds.), *Indigenous social work around the worlds: Towards culturally relevant education and practice* (pp. 245–256). Hampshire, UK: Ashgate Publishing.

Fanow, M.M. & Cook, J. (1991). *Beyond methodology: Feminist scholarship as lived research.* Bloomington: Indiana University Press.

Fanow, M.M. & Cook, J. (2005). Feminist methodology: New applications in the academy and public policy. *Signs: Journal of Women in Culture and Society, 30* (4), 2211–2236.

Flicker, S., Roche, B., & Guta, A. (2010). *Peer Research in Action III: Ethical Issues.* Community Based Research Working Paper Series. The Wellesley Institute. Retrieved on February 15, 2013 from: http://www.wellesleyinstitute.com/wp-content/uploads/2011/02/Ethical_Issues_WEB.pdf.

Fook, J. (2012). *Social work: A critical approach to practice* (2nd ed.). London: Sage.

Funk, W. (1999). *What difference does it make?* Cranbrook, BC: Wildflower Publication.

Hankivsky, O., Reid, C., Cormier, R., Varcoe, C., Clark, N., Benoit, C., & Brotman, S. (2010). Exploring the promises of intersectionality for advancing women's health research. *International Journal for Equity in Health, 9* (5), 15.

Harding, S. (1987). Conclusions: epistemological questions. In S. Harding (Ed.), *Feminism and methodology* (pp. 181–190). Bloomington: Indiana University Press.

Harding, S. & Norberg, K. (2005). New feminist approaches to social science methodologies: An introduction. *Signs: Journal of Women in Culture and Society, 30* (4), 2009–2015.

Hart, M. (2003). Am I a modern-day missionary? Reflections of a Cree social worker. *Native Social Work Journal, 5,* 299–313.

Healy, K. (2005). *Social work theories in context: Creating frameworks for practice.* London, UK: Palgrave MacMillan.

Hill-Collins, P. (2000). *Black feminist thought: Knowledge consciousness, and the politics of empowerment* (10th anniversary ed.). New York, NY: Routledge.

Jimenez, M. (1997). Gender and psychiatry: psychiatric conceptions of mental disorders in women, 1960–1994. *Affilia, 12* (2), 154–175.

King, D. (1990). Multiple jeopardy, multiple consciousnesses: The context of a black feminist ideology. In M. Malson, E. Mudimbe-Boyi, J. O'Barr, & M. Wyer (Eds.), *Black women in America: Social science perspectives* (pp. 265–295). Chicago: University of Chicago Press.

King, M. (2003). Dropping the diagnosis of homosexuality: did it change the lot of gays and lesbians in Britain? *Australian and New Zealand Journal of Psychiatry, 37* (6), 684–688.

McColl, M.A., Adair, B., Davey, S., & Kates, N. (2013). The learning collaborative: An approach to emancipatory research in disability studies. *Canadian Journal of Disability Studies, 2* (1), 71–93.

McLaughlin, H. (2010). Keeping service user involvement in research honest. *British Journal of Social Work, 40,* 1591–1608.

Mehrotra, G. (2010). Toward a continuum of intersectionality theorizing for feminist social work scholarship. *Affilia, 25* (4), 417–430.

Menzies, R., LeFrançois, B., & Reaume, G. (2013). Introducing mad studies. In B. LeFrançois, R. Menzies, & G. Reaume (Eds.), *Mad matters: A critical reader in Canadian mad studies* (pp. 1–22). Toronto: Canadian Scholars' Press.

Metzl, J.M. (2009). *The protest psychosis: How schizophrenia became a black disease.* Boston: Beacon Press.

Minkler, M. & Wallerstein, N. (2001). Introduction to community based participatory research. In M. Minkler & N. Wallerstein (Eds.), *Community based participatory research for health* (pp. 3–26). San Francisco: Jossey Bass.

Moosa-Mitha, M. (2005). Situating anti-oppressive theories within critical and difference-centered perspectives. In L. Brown & S. Strega (Eds.), *Research as resistance: Critical, Indigenous, & anti-oppressive approaches* (pp. 38–72). Toronto: Canadian Scholars' Press.

Morrison, L.J. (2005). *Talking back to psychiatry: The psychiatric consumer/survivor/expatient movement.* New York: Routledge.

O'Cathain, A., Murphy, E., & Nicholl, J.P. (2008). Dysfunctional, multidisciplinary or interdisciplinary? Team working in mixed methods research. *Qualitative Health Research 2008, 18* (11), 1574–1585.

Oliver, M. (1992). Changing the social relations of research production. *Disability, Handicap & Society, 7,* 101–115.

On Our Own. (1980–1990). *Phoenix rising: The voice of the psychiatrized.* Toronto, ON.

Phoenix, A. & Pattynama, P. (2006). Intersectionality. *European Journal of Women's Studies, 13* (3), 187–192.

Poole, J.M., Jivraj, T., Arslanian, A., Bellows, K., Chiasson, S., Hakimy, H., Pasini, J., & Reid, J. (2012). Sanism, "mental health", and social work/education: A review and call to action. *Intersectionalities: A Global Journal of Social Work Analysis, Research, Polity, and Practice, 1,* 20–36.

Preissle, J. (2007). Feminist research ethics. In S.N. Hesse-Biber (Ed.), *The handbook of feminist research: Theory and praxis* (pp. 515–532). Thousand Oaks, CA: Sage.

Presser, L. (2005). Negotiating power and narrative in research: Implications for feminist methodology. *Signs: Journal of Women in Culture and Society, 30* (4), 2067–2090.

Ramazanoglu, C. & Holland, J. (2002). *Feminist methodology: Challenges and choices.* London: Sage.

Reaume, G. (2002). Lunatic to patient to person: Nomenclature in psychiatric history and the influence of patients' activism in North America. *International Journal of Law and Psychiatry, 25* (4), 405–426.

Reinharz, S. (1992). *Feminist methods in social research.* Oxford: Oxford University Press.

Rhoades, K.A. (2000). Collaboration and collaborative research. In L. Code (Ed.), *Encyclopedia of feminist theories* (p. 96). New York: Routledge.

Russo, J. (2012). Survivor-controlled research: A new foundation for thinking about psychiatry and mental health. *Forum Qualitative Sozialforschung / Forum: Qualitative Social Research, 13* (1), Article 8. Retrieved from: http://nbn-resolving.de/urn:nbn:de:0114-fqs120187.

Sarantakos, S. (2005). *Social research* (3rd ed.). New York: Palgrave Macmillan.

Schneider, B. (2012). Participatory action research, mental health service user research, and the hearing (our) voices projects. *International Journal of Qualitative Methods, 11* (2), 152–165.

Shimrat, I. (1997). *Call me crazy: Stories from the mad movement.* Vancouver: Press Gang Publishers.

Showalter, E. (1985). *The female malady.* New York: Pantheon.

Stringer, E.T. (1996). *Action research: A handbook for practitioners.* Thousand Oaks, CA: Sage.

Sweeney, A. (2009). So what is survivor research? In A. Sweeney, P. Beresford, A. Faulkner, M. Nettle., & D. Rose (Eds.), *This is survivor research* (pp. 22–37). Ross-on-Wye, UK: PCCS Books.

Ussher, J.M. (1997). Framing the sexual "Other": the regulation of lesbian and gay sexuality. In J. Ussher (Ed.), *Body talk: The material and discursive regulation of sexuality, madness and reproduction* (pp. 131–158). New York: Routledge.

Ussher, J.M. (2011). *The madness of women: Myth and experience.* London: Routledge.

Wallcraft J., Schrank, B., & Amering, M. (2009). *Handbook of service user involvement in mental health research.* Oxford: Wiley Blackwell.

Weedon, C. (1987). *Feminist practice & poststructuralist theory.* Cambridge, MA: Blackwell Publishers.

3 A Letter to Activists Entering Academia

Joseph Nicholas DeFilippis

Dear Activists

Hello, fellow traveler. I presume that if you are reading a text on feminist social work research, there is a good chance you were engaged in activism before becoming a researcher. I make this assumption because feminist social workers often do community-based work, engaging in advocacy, organizing, and social justice work. Additionally, since this is a research book, I also presume you are now located in academia. As someone who traveled a similar path from activism to the academy, I hope some of what I experienced might prepare you for what lies ahead. I am writing you the letter I wish someone had written to me before I embarked on this journey.

Some of us come to academia from years of community work that has propelled us to pursue theoretical or scholarly engagement. Yet activists who have spent years doing community-based work enter the academy and are often encouraged to shed that identity, start anew as researchers and scholars, and silo themselves off into discrete areas of knowledge production. Rather than pressuring you, as so many others will, to engage in the binary choice between being an activist or a scholar, I write to encourage you to keep your activist identity and training close to your heart while simultaneously entering this new world of academia. The academy has need for more researchers who identify as activist-scholars: faculty who undertake research and pedagogy in pursuit of social justice. In the following pages, I will share with you some of the lessons I have learned from my own transition from activism to the academy to activism-scholarship.

I should begin by introducing myself. Before entering the academy, I spent 20 years engaged in social justice work. I worked for years doing volunteer work (including, particularly, welfare rights work) at various social justice organizations before obtaining my MSW and becoming the Director at SAGE/Queens, an organization serving lesbian, gay, bisexual, and transgender (LGBT) senior citizens. After five years, I left SAGE/Queens and became the founding Executive Director of Queers for Economic Justice (QEJ), where I was on staff for six years before I left to begin a doctoral program in social work. I did much of this activism as a social worker engaged in feminist practice. Since entering academia, I have often reflected on what I learned in my feminist social work practice and how it informs my new practice as a feminist social work researcher. I believe activists from community organizations using feminist praxis have much to teach the social work academy about research, knowledge production, and practice.

Because there are so many feminisms, I want to identify the working definitions I use when I refer to feminist praxis or feminist research. Hesse-Biber (2012) explained that feminist praxis requires engaging with issues of power, authority, ethics, and reflexivity. Similarly, the editors of this text defined feminist research as being concerned with, among other things, the examination of power and authority, ethics, reflexivity, difference, and binary categories (Gringeri, Wahab, & Anderson-Nathe, 2010). When I refer to feminist praxis or research throughout this letter, I am referring to these feminist values.

In order to provide you with some context for my later comments, I want to begin this letter by explaining the ways in which these feminist principles informed my social work practice at community organizations. Then I will to try to prepare you for your new adventure by describing how the academic world of a researcher is often at odds with feminist tenets. I will present an overview of some of the challenges you can expect to confront in your transition from activism to academia. Because I think activists who enter the academy can help transform it, I will share some lessons I believe the academic world of social work can learn from your activism and from feminist community-based praxis. I hope this letter will help you bridge the world of activism and research and encourage you to become an activist-researcher.

Being an Activist

As community activists, we bring to our research and to our academic lives a commitment to social justice that is not merely rhetorical—it was demonstrated by our experiences engaging in social change work. It shaped our practice and now informs our research agendas. Consequently, it may be useful for me to share with you a little bit about my background in the social justice work that now drives my work as a feminist activist-scholar.

My Background: Feminist Research Principles Employed in Community-Based Practice

In 2003, I was part of a group of community activists who came together to build an organization that would address issues of queer poverty and represent the often-overlooked members of the queer community who are low-income. We were frustrated with a social movement rooted in "identity politics" that rarely addressed poverty or class as part of that identity. As we created the project that would become QEJ, we knew we wanted the organization built by people whose lives and identities reflected our mission and programs. We operated from a standpoint epistemology (Naples, 1998)—a position common for many groups based in identity politics. However, we knew that, too often, LGBT organizations engaged in the binary classification of gay and straight, where the only standpoint required for leadership was that of a gay or lesbian person. And, more often than not, the definition of gay or lesbian was an essentialized identity, with a default assumption of class privilege and white privilege. Even a cursory examination of the last 30 years of executive directors of LGBT organizations across the country illustrates that most gay rights organizations are led by middle-class or wealthy educated white gays and lesbians. In the identity politics that had been conceptualized by the movement, being gay or lesbian was sufficient to provide the legitimacy of insider status. Having the lived experiences of poverty or immigration or of being a person of color or transgender is not required in this dominant paradigm.

At QEJ, we had a different notion of insider status, and we were interested in leadership coming from standpoint positions that were more complicated than merely being gay or lesbian. For us the gay/straight binary had to be, as Burdge (2007) describes, challenged, eliminated, or expanded. We built an organization that was multiracial, multigender, and multiclassed, and in doing so embraced some of the principles of the intersectional lens put forth by Black feminism (Crenshaw, 1989). Intersectionality posits that identities such as gender, race, class, and others must all be examined simultaneously in order to understand women's experiences. Intersectionality addresses identity and social location. It focuses on structural barriers that are based on multiple forms of oppression, as well as on privileges based on simultaneous membership in other identity groups.

In order to take this intersectional approach to building the organization, we spent almost a year conducting meetings and recruiting queer community members and activists to work with us who possessed the skills we needed while also representing diverse race, gender, and class identities and backgrounds. We talked openly about our different class statuses and how that might affect our ability to work together. Collins (2008) argued that any feminist analysis must start with an examination of how differences are used to defend unequal power relations. Similarly, we knew we could not build an organization that challenged structural power if we did not begin by addressing the unequal power relations residing within the difference of our own queer lives and identities.

The board quickly decided we wanted to engage in policy work, community organizing, and leadership development (rather than providing direct services) and we would be committed to a broad vision of social justice (rather than a narrow vision of equality) and to changing structures and systems (rather than fighting for inclusion into unfair existing systems). These decisions share much in common with ethics central to feminist activist work and scholarship—an ethics concerned with rights, justice, duty, consequences, and concern for human relations (Preissle & Han, 2012).

Our board immediately adopted a consensus model of decision-making, deliberately taking a page from feminist organizations (Reineltl, 1994). We knew that democratic practices of majority rule render decision-making faster. Nevertheless, because we also understood the idea of the tyranny of the majority, we made a decision, rooted in the feminist value of attention to power (Presser, 2005), to challenge the default assumption of majority rule and assure that power was held equally by everyone on the board. We believed that consensus decision-making, although more time-consuming, created stronger group cohesion and more sustained, long-term commitment to the organization. In addition, the consensus model requires deeper conversations grounded in constant reflexivity and critical reflection, which are widely understood as essential components of feminist research (Daley, 2010; Speer, 2002) and which were vital parts of our feminist practice. As we began hiring staff, we decided that all employees would be hired at the same base salary rate, regardless of title or prior work experience. We were determined to recognize all work equally, rather than (re)creating a hierarchy. In writing about the issue of power in research, Presser (2005) explores the ways feminist scholars seek to eliminate hierarchies of knowledge construction. When feminist scholars challenge hierarchies, they are pursuing social justice goals. We were similarly committed to eliminating hierarchies, for similar reasons, even though we applied it in a different, non-research, context.

Throughout our work, we tried to ensure that as we built our organization we remained committed, at every turn, to the values and theoretical frameworks that brought us to this work in the first place. QEJ is not alone in these decisions: numerous radical queer organizations across the United States have centralized feminist principles such as reflexivity, examining differences, attending to power, and eliminating hierarchies (Arkles, Gehi, & Redfield, 2010; Currah, 2008; Jones-Yelvington, 2008; Mananzala & Spade, 2008; Pulliam & Mott, 2010; Richardson, 1999; Smith, 1999).

Being a Scholar

Coming from that background I found that academia was very different from my feminist activism. I expect you may feel the same way. In this section, I want to share with you some of the challenges you can expect to confront during your transition. It is intended as an overview, providing you with a general lay of the land, rather than an indepth exploration of any one issue.

Social Justice and Critical Theories

You probably already understand that social justice is a central tenet of social work. Indeed, it might be the very reason you chose the profession. Unfortunately, as you proceed through your course work, you may begin to feel that social work's commitment to social justice often remains rhetorical. One reason for this is that there are different definitions of social justice among the students and faculty. Some may feel that discussions of "diverse populations" address social justice concerns; for others these are just the tip of the iceberg and they require the inclusion of critical theories (such as anti-oppressive practice) that examine structural barriers to social justice. The type of social justice content included in your research agenda may vary depending on where you received your MSW, where you are getting your PhD, where your faculty was trained, and where you will be employed.

Despite social work education's claims of commitment to social justice, much of this content is presented in schools of social work in non-critical ways (Reisch, 2013). Course readings and lesson plans seldom probe deeply into the significance or implications of difficult and controversial social justice topics (Reisch, 2007, 2013). In addition, students and faculty often possess differing levels of commitment to any social justice content at all. I have spoken with many graduate students who feel that a social justice lens was not adequately infused throughout their course work. They did not merely refer to the lack of critical theory-based perspectives or anti-oppressive practice—they reported a shortage of any social justice-related theoretical base in the majority of their classes. Social justice content is often siloed off into the "diversity" or anti-oppressive practice classes, but not integrated into classes focused on research, program evaluation, human behavior, or administration. Research classes that assume social justice content is taught elsewhere run the risk of producing research that perpetuates inequality and oppression on already subordinated communities. As feminist activists, you will have to take up the often-unpleasant responsibility of challenging your research professors to address social justice issues throughout every step of your research training. In fact, if they do not have the training to do it themselves, you may need to help them address these issues. Be prepared to diligently bring articles to class, respectfully request changes to the assignments or reading lists, politely raise questions during presentations, and patiently challenge your fellow students. (Also be prepared to not be paid for doing that work.)

After years of doing social work practice informed by feminist critical theory, I was startled to enter academia and discover how much the social work discipline has embraced positivist dogma and rejected critical thought (Reisch, 2013; Reisch & Andrews, 2012). Feminisms, Marxism, critical race theory, queer theory, etc. are permitted but not required, nor even encouraged. In addition, often faculty is not equipped to support this kind of research or intellectual engagement. Instead, graduate social work education is often focused on professional training to do micro clinical training with a reliance on positivist approaches to research. Consequently, you may become frustrated that critical thinking is not centralized in the profession to the extent you had expected.

Despite social work education's inconsistent relationships with critical theories (and to social justice content), do not write off your entire institution.

You will find individual professors, as teachers or colleagues, who are engaged with these ideas. They may be hard to locate initially, but they are probably there. Find them. Learn from them and teach them. Debate ideas with them, do research with them, and write with them. Cling to them. They will help keep you centered and prevent you from feeling too isolated. This form of self-care is crucial to your ability to survive the academy. Remember, as Audre Lorde (1988) said, "Caring for myself is not self-indulgence, it is self-preservation, and that is an act of political warfare" (p. 131).

Professionalization

For years I engaged in activism that had me working side by side with community activists who lacked any formal education as social workers or advocates. In fact, one of the activists from whom I learned the most, and who remains one of my heroes, had been homeless for 20 years and lacked a high school diploma. When I decided to pursue my PhD in social work, I discovered a field that has become focused upon professionalization. This focus may be deeply troubling to those of you who, like me, have backgrounds in grassroots activism because it creates a hierarchical distinction between community-based workers and those who are more legitimized by their MSWs or PhDs. You may find yourself resistant to the distinction made between experts and community members that is implied by social work's pursuit of professionalization.

In addition, the Council for Social Work Education's shift to skill-based competencies and research funders' requirements of evidence-based practice (EBP) create a radically different environment from the community-based campaigns in which many activists work (Fawcett, Featherstone, Fook, & Rossiter, 2000). I spent a dozen years leading two start-up organizations that work with populations that had been previously completely unserved (as opposed to underserved). This meant that EBPs were neither desirable nor possible. There was no academically approved evidence upon which to make decisions because no programs had previously existed to serve these communities. With community members directing the work of QEJ, the people most impacted by the issues—not funders—determined which skills were considered most important for staff members to have. Consequently, the development of programs and the hiring of staff were designed in ways that do not align with the pretense of objectivity offered by EBP and expert-determined skill-based competencies. I spent the first two years of my doctoral studies baffled about how to translate my practice work to this academic audience. Relying upon EBP can stifle the creativity, originality, and entrepreneurship often found in community work. It can also result in the pursuit of best practices, rather than the pursuit of social change (Reisch, 2013).

As activists-turned-students, you can bring your practice experience into the classroom, sharing knowledge of new interventions developing from the communities in which you have worked. You can also resist the pressure to demand certainty and, instead, pursue creativity in your own research agenda. As a result, you can help academic researchers understand how they can benefit from relying less heavily upon EBP and, instead, putting EBP in conversation with untried innovations more often than is currently done.

Collaboration, Competition, and Independence

Another tension you may experience is between the collaborative nature of activism and the independent nature of American academic life. Certainly in academia, collaboration is encouraged, at least in theory. In some ways, it is more than merely theoretical. Research requires teams. Students are encouraged to have mentors. Faculties meet to discuss curriculum. These dynamics are most certainly collaborative. However, I can't shake the feeling that I am being retrained to shed my collaborative instincts and become more independent. For instance, you will be encouraged to "get your name out there" and carve out your own niche of scholarly pursuits and, indeed, solitary expertise. The expectation of autonomy in those pursuits feels much more aligned with the competition of the for-profit world than with the feminist practice and community organizing you may have done. For instance, although faculty are encouraged to work collaboratively, when they do collaborate on an article, the question of "first authorship" (rather than alphabetical listings of co-author) is evidence of the competitive and, ultimately, independent nature of scholarship.

This is not to say that there is no competition in feminist practice. As activists, many of us worked within 501(c)3 structures, where our organizations were in competition with allied groups for foundation dollars. In addition, occasionally there are turf wars between groups vying for credit for advocacy victories. Consequently, as activists we are often accustomed to dealing with a certain level of competition in our work. The competitiveness I experienced in my own practice was a regular feature of the larger context surrounding the work. It was not, however, embedded in the work itself. The work itself was collaborative in nature. Our ability to successfully survive the external competition (to get grants, to claim advocacy victories) was entirely dependent upon how successfully we worked together internally. Whatever competitions might exist beyond the work, the nature of the work itself is collaborative. Consciousness raising, community organizing, leadership development, public education, movement building—these are collaborative endeavors down to their DNA. Academic life is not structured that way. In academia, collaboration is possible, but it is not required. Sometimes it is treated with suspicion. I offer the following story as an illustration.

In my first year of doctoral studies, several fellow students and I were unhappy with our program for a number of reasons. We worked together to attempt to make some changes to it. We were told by several faculty members (as well as friends who are on faculty at other universities) to beware of organizing and working together too closely, lest we be accused of having a "groupthink" mentality. The faculty members who warned us did so out of genuine concern for our well-being and also share my feminist politics. Yet this warning was startling to me. As you know, in community organizing, the goal is to find common ground and then organize collectively from there. Here, in a graduate program of social work, I was given exactly the opposite message, despite the fact that collective action is in keeping with feminist theory (Gould, 1987) and with social work practice (Rothman, Erlich, Tropman, & Cox, 1995).

In my previous community work, putting my own ideas ahead of (or even separate from) those of the community would be cause for suspicion. When organizers disagree with members of the community, they are expected to discuss the points of contention and hash out their differences before arriving at a consensus that can be used to present a united front. As I mentioned earlier, even my Board of Directors processed their disagreements in order to make decisions using a consensus model that ensured that decisions were made with a cohesive voice, rather than representing merely the majority of voices. Here, in academia, I discovered that speaking collectively with a unified voice was cause for suspicion.

In addition to being antithetical to feminist principles, this mindset also leaves people (faculty, students, researchers) frequently feeling isolated. This isolation can negatively impact intellectual and material aspects of academic life, as people feel left to fend for themselves in everything from research and teaching to promotion negotiations. As feminist activists, we have the skills to help transform the culture of the academic institutions where we become employed from an ethos of individualism to one of collaboration. As you progress through your graduate work, think about ways in which you can build collaboration and community with other students. Here are five examples, drawn from my own experiences, which may be helpful: (1) Socialize together. Bowling, movies, cocktails, double-dates, or whatever floats your boat. It is just important to have friends who understand what you are going through. (2) Work together to develop and propose courses or reading groups that provide you with access to material you feel is missing from your program and which draws from the strengths of the classmates and teachers with whom you are collaborating. (3) Set up informal writing groups that meet regularly to give each other support and provide each other with deadlines that will motivate writing. (4) Support each other when you have grievances or concerns—even if it does not affect you directly, don't let your friends challenge the institution alone. (5) Share information (about classes, internships, jobs, requests for proposals, and opportunities to publish) with each other. Share the information even when it is awkward to do so (e.g., if one of you receives an invitation to submit something that was not extended to everyone). Not sharing information (regardless of the reason) fosters competition and distrust. This is probably the most important thing you can do to undermine the individualistic nature of academic life and the competition that it cultivates.

Despite my disappointment about how individualistic I have found academic life to be, the five examples listed above remind me of how my experience of being a doctoral student has also been deeply influenced by some collaborative experiences. I have learned much from the wonderful relationships and brilliant exchanges I have had with a handful of professors and with some fellow doctoral students (Abby Bandurraga, Miranda Cunningham, Thuan Duong, Sandy Leotti, Jennifer Muthanna, Meg Panichelli, and Christine Velez Klug). Sitting with them, debating ideas, learning research skills, and developing my teaching pedagogy is a privilege and luxury of academic life that I was not afforded in my practice. As activists, our work in the community often requires jumping into action without as much time as we would like to stop and reflect upon ideas. We often do not have the luxury to engage in the life of the mind. However, in my doctoral studies I spent so much time intellectually engaging with the above-named people that it is now often difficult to know from which of them some of my own ideas originated or were pushed into more exciting or nuanced directions. They have not merely helped me think through my research questions, but have also influenced my research agenda in ways that I am not always even aware of. Acknowledging my intellectual debt to them is not merely giving credit where credit is due, but it is also the recognition that life in the academy can sometimes be a sumptuously collaborative experience. You can expect similar relationships and inspirations.

While we are lucky to have these opportunities, you should understand that these intellectual partnerships often happen in informal settings. The structure of academia does not always support them and often actively works against them. The very concept of "knowledge creation" (a term used in the academy often) implies that individual scholars can generate new facts and theories on their own—as if whatever contributions we make are not building upon pre-existing facts and theories. Yet we are influenced by the work and ideas of countless others any time we make a claim at knowledge creation. In our activist work, our knowledge, politics, and values were indisputably shaped, at least in part, by those of our fellow activists. Academic life will expose us to many who similarly influence us through informal interactions. (Indeed, even as I offer this critique of knowledge creation, I am aware of how it has been informed by conversations with others.)

Of course, academic life does require some acknowledgment of our sources. Our writings acknowledge the published work we are building upon, certain research methods (e.g., grounded theory) require that knowledge is co-created, and universities and funders encourage collaboration. But none of these frameworks require us to acknowledge the many conversations, classes, or community experiences that may have influenced our thinking in the first place. Nor would it even be possible to do so, such is the vast array of influences we encounter that shapes our scholarship.

Yet researchers must still claim to generate knowledge. My practice work rarely required these particular types of arrogant claims. I was never asked to pretend we invented community-organizing strategies all on our own. It was quite the opposite—the strength of our actions was judged, in part, by how collaboratively we worked and by the number of people participating. Therefore, as you transition from an activism to research context, it may be uncomfortable finding the balance between acknowledging your influences and taking responsibility and credit for your own work in the way that academia requires.

The Relationship Between the Academy and the Community in Research[1]

When entering academia, it may appear, at first blush, that some of the tenets of feminist research are embraced by the academy. For instance, the general orientation in academia today is that connecting with community is sexy. We frequently see academics engaging in "public scholarship"—particularly in the humanities. Social science researchers, including (or, perhaps, especially) social work researchers, seem to have now embraced the community-based participatory research (CBPR) methods that originated in the popular education movement in Latin America (and in the work of Paulo Freire). In addition, funders increasingly want to see a Community Advisory Board included in proposals.

Unfortunately, you will soon discover that this interest in community work often plays out in problematic ways. Too often "public scholarship" ends up being little more than taking field trips and calling it "community work" or inviting a performance artist to share a campus stage for one night and then leave. Because of academic evaluation criteria, when universities partner with community groups on research projects, the community groups are frequently viewed as sources of obtainable data, rather than as true collaborators (Sudbury & Okazawa-Rey, 2009). Social work is not exempt from this dynamic.

Meanwhile, feminist researchers engaging in CBPR end up discovering that there is more lip service given to community-based work than there is actual support for it. This can be seen in tenure expectations, where researchers engaged in CBPR projects, which take longer to do, are punished for not yielding the same number of publications as more traditional researchers (Lowry & Ford-Paz, 2013). This means that when you become junior faculty, it will be harder for you to do CBPR and still meet your institution's tenure demands.

The pressure to raise funds for the university through government and foundation grants serves to stifle radical scholarship, as academics are "implicitly encouraged to gear their research agendas to improving governmentality or supporting industrial priorities rather than producing analyses that are critical of corporate and state power or engaging grassroots oppositional movements" (Sudbury & Okazawa-Rey, 2009, p. 5). I have seen this play out in our profession, where program evaluation has become an increasingly important source of revenue for social work schools. Certainly, program evaluation is an important endeavor, one that social work is uniquely qualified to lead. However, you may find yourself troubled by the way it has been elevated above activist scholarship, community-engaged research, or critical theoretical work because they do not generate similar funds. In addition, research about the effectiveness of social service programs often comes at the expense of researching the structural roots of the problems that necessitated those social service programs (Reisch, 2013). This can perpetuate a focus on the best way to cope with the problem, rather than the best way to eradicate it.

You may become troubled by another element of academic research: the ways in which community research is often co-opted by academia. Community Advisory Boards often end up as a mere token that allow academics to call something "participatory" or "community-informed," but which don't do anything to disrupt hierarchical power relationships between the academy, with its forms of academic knowledge production, and communities' experiences and knowledge. This is inconsistent with the values of feminist scholars (Presser, 2005).

Jay Rosen, an intellectual leader of the movement of public journalism, famously described sitting in a meeting with six academics and six journalists discussing polling data where the academics dominated the conversation with complicated statistical information and the journalists were shut out (Rosen, 1995). Fifteen years later, I found myself remembering Rosen's article as I attended a presentation by a professor who was co-presenting with an elder in an American Indian tribe. The faculty member emphasized the collaborative nature of their project but never actually let the elder speak. The information presented would have been richer had we been exposed to both of their voices.

The academy would benefit by taking more seriously the feminist praxis employed by those community-organizing groups that recognize the equal but different expertise brought to the table by the professional and the community member. Recognizing this equality of intellectual authority is in keeping with feminist research principles and would result in richer and more complicated findings (Intemann, 2012).

As activists, you may find the idea that the academy should connect with community is not merely problematic in its execution; it is also flawed in its very conception. It creates a binary distinction that assumes that no one in the academy is actually *from* the community. It presumes these are completely separate spaces without a dynamic relationship to each other. There is a disconnect between "legitimate" research (understood to only happen in the academy) and practice/activism/community work (believed to happen in communities that are "out there," separate from the university). There seems little room for the idea that there might be community members in the academy or academics engaged in community work. Your existence in the academy proves this untrue. Yet, what happens is that even when scholars have community-based experience and/or commitments these perspectives are often not integrated into theory-building, research, or pedagogy. This is because community knowledge (or personal experience or lessons learned from "practice" or "activism") is not considered legitimate and must be supported by the "academic" literature (Fawcett et al., 2000). This is difficult to do when many ideas from community practice are missing from academic literature.

I have colleagues who see this issue differently. They have encouraged me to consider the ways that types of critical and feminist research have created room and legitimacy for community knowledge. They point to critical ethnographies, performance ethnographies, autoethnography, and indigenous methodologies as examples. To an extent, I find this argument persuasive. Certainly these approaches bring community knowledge and practice into the academy and legitimize them to other scholars. This has allowed people like me to use those ideas in my own scholarship, and for that I am grateful. I am also encouraged to see scholars demanding that public scholarship be taken seriously by the academy (e.g., Santos, 2012). However, ultimately, community knowledge and practice is still not considered legitimate by the academy until it turns up in the scholarly literature. It is dependent upon the validation it gets when a critical feminist scholar brings it into the academy. This can be seen in the example of theorizing by the Combahee River Collective (1981). For decades, activists used their theories and built activist work upon it. Yet these theories did not turn up in the academic literature until Crenshaw's scholarship (Crenshaw, 1989). Only then did intersectionality become an academically valid theoretical framework.

As I begin my life as a scholar, I am trying to bridge the gap between queer activism and the academy. I intend to bring community and activist knowledge into academia. In my scholarly work thus far, I draw from gray literature (reports from non-profits and government agencies, organizational newsletters, newspaper articles, and activist blogs) almost as frequently as from academic journals. I justified this to my professors and editors by arguing that the scholarly literature has not kept up with recent developments as quickly as has the gray literature. Certainly, this is true. However, I am troubled by feeling pressured to offer that justification. Implicit in it is the academy's assumption that, were academic literature available, it would be a more desirable source of knowledge because it is more "legitimate." I question that assumption.

Yet, I know that I have already internalized this assumption. When given the choice between academic sources and gray literature, I chose to use academic sources to legitimize my work as a new scholar. Somewhere along the way I developed a voice in my head that tells me that I must prioritize knowledge from scholarly sources. I did this despite my own beliefs to the contrary.

I believe that gray literature is a perfectly valid tool for understanding the world. This is in keeping with the feminist principles of research that call for disrupting hierarchies in research, unsettling normative modes of knowledge production, and attending to power and authority (Collins, 2008; Gringeri et al., 2010; Presser, 2005). Feminism has always produced and referenced gray literature (Malina & Nutt, 2000). These kinds of writings have always served a crucial role in conveying women's knowledges and stimulating activism.

The significance of gray literature is now recognized beyond feminist circles (e.g., the publishers Campbell and Cochrane require the inclusion of gray literature in their literature reviews of healthcare issues), yet social work frequently lags behind on this issue, and much of social work scholarship continues to consider scholarly journals more valid than gray literature. Elevating the status of gray literature destabilizes the notion that scholarly writing is the only legitimate source of knowledge. This is of course inherently threatening to the academy. Yet, the academy would benefit from such realignment by having a wider array of perspectives and more up-to-date information from which to draw.

Being an Activist-Scholar

Upon entering academia, you may feel pressure to shed your activist identity and take on a new identity as a researcher and scholar. I certainly did. However, I am someone whose life, work, and scholarship are completely situated in community-based work. I am not interested in replicating the academy's problematic version of what it means to be in connection with communities. At the same time, I also recognize that power and privilege are attached to being in the academy. Being a scholar will allow me to pursue my intellectual interests and engage in a life of the mind that was not always possible in my activist work. It will allow me to teach, which I love. I know that despite my critiques, I want to be in the academy. I am now contemplating what it means to become an activist-scholar engaged in scholarship and pedagogy in the service of social justice. Sudbury and Okazawa-Rey (2009), and others, have argued against separating activism from scholarship and insisted that they can be combined. Rather than choosing between being an activist or an academic, I intend to be both.

My years doing community-based feminist social work practice guide how I approach my scholarship. I take the critical intersectional lens we used at QEJ as the epistemological starting point of my work. I continue to center the issue of classism as I study an identity-based social movement that seldom includes class as part of that identity. I continue to question the ways in which a lack of an intersectional lens has resulted in scholarship (as well as activism) that is often essentialist and which frequently positions white and middle-class as normative for LGBT communities.

There is a lot of exciting work, rooted in feminist values and an intersectional analysis, which is happening in queer communities across the country. Organizations led by transgender people, or queer people of color, or low-income LGBT people, are engaged in strategies that are quite different from the national gay rights organizations or the statewide equality groups. They also have very different objectives. Much of this work is absent from the academic literature and even less theoretical analysis of it exists. I have chosen to write about the things I know from activism that are not yet studied by the academy. This is the focus of my work.

My research agenda is constructed around the activism of amazing queer advocates and community organizations across the country. In addition, I build my work upon the writings of scholars (Cathy Cohen, Lisa Duggan, Roderick Ferguson, E. Patrick Johnson, Darren Rosenblum, etc.) who use the academy to cast a critical eye upon the mainstream gay rights movement. Finally, I take inspiration from queer activist-scholars (John D'Emilio, Martin Duberman, Kenyon Farrow, Marcia Gallo, Yasmin Nair, Urvashi Vaid, etc.) who straddle the insider/outsider divide to write about the queer movement, of which they have been a part. I see their work and become excited about the possibilities offered by the role of activist-scholar.

If more of us refuse to shed our activist identities in the academy, our roles as activist-scholars can enable the production of new forms of emancipatory scholarship and pedagogy. We can continue our work in social movement spaces as we simultaneously work in academia. Sudbury and Okazawa-Rey (2009) described how activist-scholars become "bilingual" as they become fluent in both academic and activist languages and cultures while engaging in intellectual exchanges between those two worlds. By participating in grassroots movements, activist-scholars build knowledge, collaborations and accountabilities that nourish and inform our research agenda.

Becoming an activist-scholar engaged in feminist praxis raises many questions. While our research could be useful to others, we must also remember that academia is littered with cautionary tales of communities that did not benefit from academic research. Like some of you, I was a feminist practitioner whose work was informed by academic principles and theories and I am now a feminist academic whose work is informed by practice methods and values. How can we work toward both spaces being transformed by our engagement—communities benefiting from the resources of the university as well as the university being transformed by the community? How can we bring our "real-world" (community-informed) knowledge into the classroom and into our research? How can we occupy that space without appropriating or co-opting community work? How can we occupy that space without replicating the usual power dynamic between researchers and community members? What is lost by bringing activist work into research? What is gained, by whom and how? How will the job market impact our work (e.g., how can I engage in community research with feminist queer activists of color if I end up at a school geographically removed from activism by feminist queers of color?)? How can researchers and the academy learn from community organizations using feminist praxis? How can we mobilize the privilege of our positions as academic researchers in service of radical movements? These questions are not often considered by activists or by researchers. However, we must wrestle with them if we are to be activist-researchers.

Note

1 These ideas were initially developed in conversation and collaboration with Gita Mehrotra. She has been generous about allowing me to pick her brain, but it is important to give her credit. In addition, this illustrates the tension I discussed about the value of collaborating. As Gita herself has observed, "ideas actually often develop in these dialogic and cooperative and collective ways and we can share 'credit' in this way."

References

Arkles, G., Gehi, P., & Redfield, E. (2010). The role of lawyers in trans liberation: Building a transformative movement for social change. *Seattle Journal for Social Justice, 8* (2), 579–641.

Burdge, B. (2007). Bending gender, ending gender: Theoretical foundations for social work practice with the transgender community. *Social Work, 52* (3), 243–250.

Collins, P. H. (2008). *Black feminist thought: Knowledge, consciousness and the politics of empowerment.* New York: Routledge.

Combahee River Collective. (1981). A black feminist statement. In C. Moraga & G. Anzaldua (Eds.), *This bridge called my back: Writings by radical women of color* (pp. 210–218). New York, NY: Kitchen Table Press.

Crenshaw, K. (1989). Demarginalizing the intersection of race and sex: A Black feminist critique of antidiscrimination doctrine, feminist theory and antiracist politics. *The University of Chicago Legal Forum,* pp. 139–167.

Currah, P. (2008). Stepping back, looking outward: Situating transgender activism and transgender studies—Kris Hayashi, Matt Richardson, and Susan Stryker frame the movement. *Sexuality Research & Social Policy, 5* (1), 93–105.

Daley, A. (2010). Reflections on reflexivity and critical reflection as critical research practices. *Affilia, 25* (1), 68–82.

Fawcett, B., Featherstone, B., Fook, J., & Rossiter, A. (Eds.). (2000). *Practice and research in social work: Post-modern feminist perspectives.* London: Routledge.

Gould, K. H. (1987). Feminist principles and minority concerns: Contributions, problems, and solutions. *Affilia, 2* (3), 6–19.

Gringeri, C. E., Wahab, S., & Anderson-Nathe, B. (2010). What makes it feminist? Mapping the landscape of feminist social work research. *Affilia, 25* (4), 390–405.

Hesse-Biber, S. (2012). Feminist research: Exploring, interrogating, and transforming the interconnections of epistemology, methodology, and method. In S.N. Hesse-Biber (Ed.), *Handbook of feminist research: Theory and praxis* (pp. 2–26). Thousand Oaks, CA: Sage.

Intemann, K. (2012). Putting feminist research principles into praxis. In S.N. Hesse-Biber (Ed.), *Handbook of feminist research: Theory and praxis* (pp. 495–510). Thousand Oaks, CA: Sage.

Jones-Yelvington, T. (2008). A half-dozen things that we are: Collective identity in intersectional LGBT/Queer social movement organizations: Part 1. *Theory in Action 1* (1), 23–47.

Lorde, A. (1988). *A burst of light: Essays.* New York: Firebrand Books.

Lowry, K.W. & Ford-Paz, R. (2013). Early career academic researchers and community-based participatory research: Wrestling match or dancing partners? *Clinical and Translational Science, 6* (6), 490–492.

Malina, D. & Nutt, D. (2000). Grey literature is a feminist issue: Women's knowledge and the net. *International Journal on Grey Literature, 1* (1), 18–27.

Mananzala, R. & Spade, D. (2008). The nonprofit industrial complex and trans resistance. *Sexuality Research & Social Policy, 5* (1), 53–71.

Naples, N.A. (1998). Towards comparative analyses of women's political praxis: Explicating multiple dimensions of standpoint epistemology for feminist ethnography. *Women and Politics, 20* (1), 29–54.

Preissle, J. & Han, Y. (2012). Feminist research ethics. In S. N. Hesse-Biber (Ed.), *Handbook of feminist research: Theory and praxis* (pp. 583–605). Thousand Oaks, CA: Sage.

Presser, L. (2005). Negotiating power and narrative in research: Implications for feminist methodology. *Journal of Women in Culture and Society, 30,* 2067–2090.

Pulliam, R. M., & Mott, M. (2010). allgo speaks: Reflections on intersectional organizing. *Affilia, 25* (4), 444–450.

Reineltl, C. (1994). Fostering empowerment, building community: The challenge for state-funded feminist organizations. *Human Relations, 47* (6), 685–705.

Reisch, M. (2007). Social justice and multiculturalism: Persistent tensions in the history of US social welfare and social work. *Studies in Social Justice, 1,* 67–92.

Reisch, M. (2013). Social work education and the neo-liberal challenge: The US response to increasing global inequality. *Social Work Education, 32* (6), 715–733.

Reisch, M. & Andrews, J. (2012). *The road not taken: A history of radical social work in the United States.* New York: Routledge.

Richardson, M. (1999). What you see is what you get: Building a movement toward liberation in the twenty-first century. In K. Kleindienst (Ed.), *This is what lesbian looks like* (pp. 210–219). Ithaca, NY: Firebrand Books.

Rosen, J. (1995). Public journalism: A case for public scholarship. *Change, 27* (3), 34–38.

Rothman, J., Erlich, J. L., Tropman, J. E., & Cox, F. M. (1995). *Strategies of community intervention: Macro practice.* Itasca, IL: FE Peacock.

Santos, A. C. (2012). Disclosed and willing: Towards A queer public sociology. *Social Movement Studies: Journal of Social, Cultural and Political Protest, 11* (2), 241–254.

Smith, B. (1999). Doing it from scratch: The challenge of black lesbian organizing. In K. Kleindienst (Ed.), *This is what lesbian looks like* (pp. 244–257). Ithaca, NY: Firebrand Books.

Speer, S. A. (2002). What can conversation analysis contribute to feminist methodology? Putting reflexivity into practice. *Discourse & Society, 13,* 783–803.

Sudbury, J. & Okazawa-Rey, M. (2009). *Activist scholarship: Antiracism, feminism and social science.* Boulder, CO: Paradigm.

4 Doing Profeminist Research with Men in Social Work

Reflections on Epistemology, Methodology, and Politics

Bob Pease

Introduction

In the late 1980s and early 1990s, I was involved in attempts to construct a profeminist activism in relation to gender inequality.[1] I had previously been involved in men's consciousness-raising groups in the 1970s and the 1980s. However, it was not until 1991 when I co-founded Men Against Sexual Assault that this consciousness raising moved into concerted activism against men's violence against women (Pease, 1997). Even in those early days, my sense was that work done by men with men against men's violence should be accountable to critical reference groups of women who worked in women's services.

Hence, my work with men has been explicitly profeminist. Profeminist perspectives (Connell, 2005; Hearn & Pringle, 2006; Pease, 2000a) locate men's lives in the context of patriarchy, hegemonic masculinity, and the social divisions between men. Profeminist approaches involve men in taking responsibility for their own and other men's sexism, and a commitment to work with women to end men's violence (Douglas, 1993). They acknowledge that men benefit from the oppression of women and draw men's attention to the privileges they receive as men and the harmful effects these privileges have on women (Thorne-Finch, 1992). Profeminism also recognizes that not all men benefit equally from the operation of the structures of domination. Issues of race, sexuality, class, disability, and age significantly affect the extent to which men benefit from patriarchy.

Consequently, I have always believed that the study of men and masculinities should focus on ways of working towards gender equality rather than focusing solely on the issues facing men and that it is important to locate the study of men in the context of feminist theories. Feminist theory began with a critique of masculinity and the study of men by men needs to incorporate these insights and the questions they raised about men as a gender. The "bottom line" is acknowledging the debt that masculinity theorists owe to feminist activism and theory and of articulating the power inequalities in personal and political life (Luck & Jackson, 1995).

I have argued elsewhere that the major task of critical studies on men should be part of a strategy for changing men's subjectivities and practices to contribute to a dismantling of patriarchy, and that we need to avoid the danger of the study of men being absorbed into the traditional academic framework without any explicit commitment to producing change (Pease, 2002). Thus, one of the purposes of critical studies on men should in my view be to inform profeminist activism among men in, for example, anti-violence work, countering sexist education in schools, antipornography campaigns, and gender equity struggles in workplaces. Masculinity academics should maintain strong links with feminist and profeminist activists and contribute to the development of political strategies for challenging the social relations of gender. Critical studies on men along with feminist theorizing can provide a theoretical basis for such activist work.

Constructing a Profeminist Epistemology in Researching Men

Messner (1990) argues that the key challenge in researching men and masculinities is to move beyond objectivism to a feminist standpoint. Standpoint epistemologies have been important in informing much profeminist research on men (Cowburn, 2007; Hearn, 2007; Pease, 2000a; Popoviciu, Haywood, & Mac an Ghaill, 2006). Such an approach is important in ensuring that the positioning of the researcher is acknowledged in the construction and implementation of research. Hence, knowledge is situated, embodied, and plurivocal, as opposed to being universal, abstract, and categorical (Halewood, 1995).

If masculinist research is based on notions of objectivity, whereby the male researcher purports to be an unbiased observer, it would seem that male researchers who want to do research differently would need to be self-reflexive about their positioning in relation to such concepts as gender, race, class, and geopolitical location. Such reflexivity is necessary to avoid both the male researcher's detachment and the universalizing of his experience (Sundberg, 2011).

While masculinist epistemologies are not inherently male, they are nevertheless connected to white straight academic men, because such men tend to regard objective knowledge as the only valid form of knowledge. Male researchers often do not think about how their structural and discursive positioning relates to their knowledge claims. Many are not likely to consider how being a white straight academic man will influence their scholarship and research (Halewood, 1995). As Morgan (1981) noted over 30 years ago, many male scholars find it difficult to take gender into account when doing research.

Some have raised questions about whether men can do research that undermines their material interests (Canaan & Griffin, 1990; Morgan, 1992). There have certainly been a number of feminist critiques of profeminist men's scholarship for failing to address men's privilege and power adequately (Ashe, 2007; Macleod, 2007; Robinson, 2003). Hearn (1994) has also raised the question about whether men could undertake an autobiographical critique of their own oppressor position within patriarchal society.

In the more traditional versions of standpoint theory, any research produced by members of dominant groups would lead to distorted understandings of social relations (Halewood, 1995). However, this is largely because the researchers' social positioning and embodiment were not acknowledged. If the male researcher does take account of his situatedness, he has the potential to develop a different standpoint from the traditional male perspective and hence adopt a different epistemological position.

Twenty-five years ago, Harding (1989) argued that men were potentially able to engage in self critique. I have noted previously (Pease, 2000b) that a standpoint entails both structural location and the discursive construction of subjectivity. This is what enables us to differentiate between a profeminist men's standpoint and traditional men's standpoints. May (1998) identifies four dimensions of a progressive male standpoint: knowledge that is based on personal experience, knowledge that is subjected to critical interrogations of that experience, a moral commitment to challenge oppression, and practical interventions that men can undertake.

A profeminist standpoint is informed by feminist epistemologies as well as antisexist frameworks about men and masculinities (Cowburn, 2007). Key characteristics of a profeminist standpoint entail knowledge of feminist critiques and a commitment to challenge patriarchy and male power (Cowburn, 2005). Enacting a profeminist standpoint that challenges white male heterosexual epistemology will require male researchers to understand and respond to key debates within antiracist, feminist, and gay literature, to engage in dialogues with women, to learn to speak and problematize their own whiteness, masculinity, and heterosexuality, which is too often obscured in universal claims (Ryder, 1991), and to ensure that their research is accountable to women.

Researching Profeminist Men's Lives

The preceding principles informed my PhD research on the pathways of profeminist men's involvement with feminism and the dilemmas they confronted in their personal relationships, their professional lives, and their politics. To address these issues, I invited self-defining profeminist men to participate in a collaborative inquiry group to examine how men who were supportive of feminism were responding to the feminist challenge through an exploration of their experiences and dilemmas of trying to live out their profeminist commitment. The aim was to explore the extent to which it was possible for men to reposition themselves in patriarchal discourses and to reformulate their interests in challenging gender domination (Pease, 1996).

Doing this research was when I first encountered memory work. In my search of the literature on memory work at that time, I was struck by the dearth of accounts of men using this method. Those accounts that were inspired by Haug's (1987, 1992) political project always focused on the internalized gender identities of the oppressed and not on the dominant and privileged group. What would it mean to use memory work to explore accommodations and resistances to privilege and social dominance?

I used the method to explore men's socialization into dominant attitudes and practices and to explore resistances to the dominant ideology. In the context of my project, we developed four memory work projects to explore aspects of internalized domination. These projects focused on father–son and mother–son relationships and experiences of homophobia and sexual objectification of women (Pease, 2000b, c, 2008).

This was emotionally a very powerful method. There were many times that men broke down and cried, as they read out their memories to the group and other men reported tears running down their face as they wrote the memories down in preparation for the meeting. What I found was that memory work enabled the participants to connect with their emotional histories and it provided an opportunity for us to examine the emotional and psychological basis of our relationships with women and other men. By asking men to reflect on their understandings of the ways in which they accommodated to or resisted the dominant constructions of masculinity, we were able to understand the ways in which new subjectivities could be created. The memory work made more visible the ways in which our masculinities were produced and it assisted us to identify some forms of resistance to dominant masculinities.

In addition to the memory work projects, I also organized dialogues with allies and opponents of profeminism. These dialogues contributed to the development of new spaces for the collective positioning of profeminist men's work in the ongoing public debates about masculinity politics. Among these dialogues, I arranged for conversations with feminist women and gay men to explore male privilege and heterosexual privilege respectively (Pease, 2000b). Because many heterosexual men are disconnected from the lived experiences of women and gay men, critical dialogue with these groups is essential to bring about changes in the relations of ruling as they pertain to research. To enable such a dialogue to take place, men need to understand their internalized domination (Pheterson, 1986) and recognize that their knowledge of women's subordination and gay men's oppression will only be partial. Heterosexual male researchers will also need to demonstrate an understanding that their knowledge and perception of the world are socially situated if they are to avoid oppressive practices in their encounters with women and gay men (Pease, 2000b).

The men in the collaborative inquiry group listened to women's suspicions about their work, their doubts about how men could overcome their dominant subjectivities, and why men would want to change. They also heard from the gay men about their reticence to engage in an open dialogue with straight men because of straight men's reluctance to acknowledge their heterosexual privilege and the concern that straight men's gay affirmative stance may marginalize gay men's voices. Due to the lack of trust and power inequality, these dialogues were difficult to conduct at times, but charting our way through them left me with some hope for the future of such conversations when researching straight men.

Listening attentively to the experiences of people who are oppressed is not easy for members of privileged groups (Johnson, 2006). In part, this is because it means relinquishing our perception of ourselves as knowers rather than listeners (O'Donnell, Lloyd, & Dreher, 2009). It can be quite destabilizing to have our dominance, knowledge, or expertise contested (Fellows & Razack, 1998).

Lloyd (2009) refers to listening as a precondition for democratic dialogue and believes that it entails an ethical responsibility on the part of the privileged. Listening across difference and inequality requires an attention to privilege and a preparedness to undo it. Dreher (2009) refers to this as "ethical listening." This involves not only the ability to understand the other, but also to be receptive to our own complicity with systems of privilege.

In my collaborative inquiry with profeminist men, I faced a number of dilemmas. The first dilemma I faced was whether, as a male author, I write about men in terms of "we" or "they." "We" in some contexts may imply a false community between men or suggest a connection with other men that I do not share. On the other hand, consistently referring to "they" implies a separation that denies my shared experience with other men and denies my own presence within my analysis. I chose, albeit with reservations, to write "we" when referring to both profeminist men and the men in the study and "they" when referring to men in general or men with whom I did not identify.

There was an additional dilemma related to my multiple voices in this research. As an active participant in the group and as a subject in my own research, my experiences, dilemmas, and memories were data and my ideas as they were formulated during the group process were part of the dialogues with the group and with the interlocutors. Notwithstanding my commitment to writing personally, to describe my personal memories and stories disclosed in the group process, I chose a pseudonym, giving myself, and my friends and family, the same degree of anonymity as the other participants. There was no need to separate myself out in the conduct of the research, as I allowed myself to be immersed within the group process. I retained my identity, though, when I was talking in the group as self-conscious actor in dialogue with other participants and interlocutors.

Thus, there were multiple senses of self in this research: first, there were memories and biographical experiences told through my pseudonym; second, there were dialogues with participants told through an "I" in the past tense; and third, there were the "I" as writer and interpreter of the research experiences spoken through the present tense. With each of these levels there were further multiple "I"s, as I moved between total immersion as a participant and as a self-conscious researcher-participant in the group process and I moved between disclosure of my personal self and scholarly narrator of the research experience. Undertaking research of this kind required a constant monitoring of subjectivities throughout all stages of the research process.

One of the purposes of the research was to produce a praxis of how men can change and the methodological approaches employed became some of the very strategies being sought. That is, memory work and the other methods used each represented pedagogical strategies for profeminist politics for men. Thus, in addition to theorizing men's subjectivities and shedding light on the insights about issues and dilemmas in profeminist men's lives, the research contributed to the development of these methodologies, both as research tools and as strategies for change in gender relations.

Researching Immigrant and Refugee Men

There is unstated presumption of whiteness in most of the men and masculinity literature. My own early writing about men and masculinity also took whiteness and the centrality of Western masculinity as a given (Pease, 1997). One step in the process of addressing this normativity of whiteness is to acknowledge that "the oppressions experienced by non-white men create different dilemmas centered around masculinity for each group" (Vecchio, 1998, p. 164). Indigenous men and immigrant men from culturally diverse backgrounds clearly do not benefit from patriarchy in the same way as other men (Flood, 1994/1995). White men thus need to recognize social difference and inequality in men's lives. In doing so, white profeminist men face a series of dilemmas and contradictions. Some of these dilemmas arise out of the relationship between feminism and antiracism and are influenced by the "debates about what is more important, the struggle against racism or the fight against sexism" (Bonnett, 2000, p. 128).

In addressing these issues, I have explored the impact of migration on the subjectivities and practices of men who are marginalized by racism in Australia (Crossley & Pease, 2009; wa Mungai & Pease, 2009; Pease, 2006, 2009). This project involved life history research with immigrant men who have migrated to Australia from four culturally diverse regions of the world: South Asia, Southern and East Africa, Latin America, and the Middle East. This research on structurally marginalized and subordinated men explores the contribution such men can make in changing dominant masculinities. I argued that a critical analysis of masculinities in Australia must begin with an analysis of how marginalized and subordinated masculinities are changing. Immigrant men are in contradictory positions in relation to dominance and subordination. By taking the standpoints of structurally marginalized groups of men as points of departure, the research removes hegemonic masculinity from the foreground in masculinity research.

By studying the experiences of men who are marginalized by class and race, I aimed to problematize some aspects of white hegemonic masculinity. Because white men use power over non-white men, I explore some of the ways that whiteness influences the construction of some masculinities (Robinson, 2003). I am also interested in how a critical examination of immigrant men's masculinities contributes to knowledge about gender-based inequalities in immigrant communities in Australia.

Many writers argue that migration provides women *and* men with the opportunity to transcend traditional sex roles (Kofman, Phizacklea, Raghuram, & Sales, 2000). It is said that it can "act as an escape route from oppressive patriarchal societies" (Boyle & Hiffance, 1999, p. 9). Others emphasize how "a new location provides a space in which gender relations can be renegotiated" (Willis & Yeoh, 2000, p. xv). In this view, domestic patriarchy is reliant upon support from its environment. Is patriarchal authority eroded by migration? Are men's patriarchal privileges diminished by the process of migration or is the "patriarchal bargain" simply renegotiated?

In undertaking this research, I have been mindful of the need to avoid the stereotyping of non-Western men as patriarchal and backward in gender terms, in contrast to more egalitarian white men (Bradley, 1996). I do not assume that immigrant men are "stuck in sexist traditional male roles while white educated middle-class men are forging a more egalitarian role" (Hondagneu-Sotello & Messner, 1994, p. 2000). Rather, I want to understand how gendered power operates in different immigrant communities so that strategies for engaging immigrant men in promoting gender equality can be responsive to culture, race, and ethnicity.

My research with immigrant and refugee men discovered that changes in identity and changes in gender roles had a major impact on these men's lives. Men's authority is undermined because of a change in their public status, with men being forced to take up employment well below their qualifications. Masculinity was associated with the provider role in all of the home countries of the participants in my study. The issue of being the sole provider was central to all of these men. When they migrate, men experience a threat to their ability to maintain the provider role and they experience challenges to their authority in the family At the same time, they endeavor to hang on to their traditional concept of masculinity and manhood in the face of the challenges they experience. The men experience marginalization in this culture and they have to contend with an increase in the status of women.

Clearly there are both limitations and dangers in this work. How can knowledge and understanding of marginalized men be used to decenter white male dominance rather than becoming a basis of white superiority? Moreton-Robinson (2000, p. 148) has written about how, in her view, white feminist academic women have incorporated cultural difference into their curricula but have failed to "challenge the subject position of middle-class white woman."

Some writers have also identified epistemological racism that exists in the research paradigms that dominate academic and scholarly research on race and ethnicity (Ladson-Billings, 2000). This racism is reinforced by "the social distance imposed by class and race relations when interviewers are white [and] middle-class and those being interviewed are not" (Anderson, 1993, p. 41). How can white middle-class researchers elicit an understanding of the experiences of those who are oppressed? How can we respect a perspective that is so different from our own? We must critically examine our own social locations. Injustice and inequality are easier to recognize than the privilege and power of the dominant racial and cultural group, which tends to remain normalized and unscrutinized (Anderson, 1993). The recognition of white race privilege in the relations of race is more difficulty than the recognition of the oppression of others (Frankenberg, 1993).

To address this issue, I have endeavored to write "against othering" (Krumer-Nevo & Sidi, 2012). That is, I have sought to ensure that the representation of the marginalized men does not further inscribe researcher privilege. This is done through the use of dialogue to express a variety of voices in the text and the use of reflexivity to make my own epistemological and methodological premises explicit.

Interrogating Straight White Male Privilege

In light of reflections on my research with immigrant non-white men, I have been refocusing my work on straight white middle-class men by more self-consciously exploring our privileged position in relation to women and other men. It is important to interrogate privileged social locations and find ways of undoing privilege (Pease, 2010). Carniol (2005) says that a critical consciousness of oppression *and* privilege is central to understand the ways our world views are shaped by our social positioning. This means, that to be truly reflexive, we must consider "our own complicity in systems of domination and subordination" (Strega, 2005, p. 229). Those of us who benefit from unearned privileges should interrogate the ways that our research practice may unwittingly reproduce the exploitative relationships we are challenging (Carey, 2004).

I have hence become interested in the construction and reconstruction of privileged subjectivities. Towards this end, I have recently completed a book (Pease, 2010) where I have been exploring the construction of Eurocentrism, class elitism, hegemonic masculinity, white supremacy, heteronormativity, and ableism as six intersecting sites of privilege.

Increasingly, one of the genres for interrogating privilege has been personal accounts of coming to terms with one's unearned entitlements. That is, the authors engage in critical interrogations of their own complicity in systems of privilege which benefit them. Individual authors talk about the ways in which various forms of privilege have functioned in their lives. Using this autoethnographic approach, in the book I talk about being challenged by women about my entitlement as a man. Being in a relationship with a feminist woman in the 1970s, I was forced to confront some of my experiences of male privilege. My partner would come home from women's consciousness-raising meetings and challenge my limited participation in housework and my over-commitment to paid work at the expense of our relationship. I had to work out what these challenges would mean, not only for my personal relationship, but also for my chosen career of social work and my political activism on issues of social justice. As a socialist who was involved in community politics in relation to housing, unemployment, and health issues, I found it relatively easy at the intellectual level to see the justice of the feminist claims and my own complicity in the oppression of women. At the emotional level, I was deeply threatened by it. In my writings about gender, I have always inserted myself in the text and grounded the ideas in my own experiences as a man.

I also write about my developing awareness of white privilege. I was 13 years old when my older brother formed a relationship with an Aboriginal woman in Australia. When my parents became aware of this relationship, they became outraged and disowned him as a son. It would take some years before they were able to begrudgingly accept my brother's partner as a part of the family. Even then, though, they needed to exceptionalize her, to see her as different from other Aboriginal people so that their views about Indigenous Australians were not disrupted by getting to know her as a person.

Encountering my parents' racism as a child was deeply shocking to me. No less so was the connection it would give me into the Aboriginal world of city slums and rural reserves where many Aboriginal people lived. As I connected with some aspects of urban and rural Aboriginal culture in Australia, I developed a consciousness of being white. In my teens I did not have an awareness of how this experience of whiteness represented privilege. And while I was very critical of what I saw as the racist attitudes of my parents, the experience did not in itself lead me to a consciousness of my own internalized racism. All of this would come much later.

Although the book is not a memoir, it has elements of memoir woven into the exploration of privilege. I have tried to illustrate the interrogation of privilege with my own experience. Of course first-person accounts such as this generate some anxiety, as you increase your own vulnerability. When I first disclosed vignettes from my personal experiences in published writing, I felt very anxious. In some instances, those who knew me well felt that I had made myself too vulnerable at times.

Critics argue that autobiographical sociology is self-indulgent and inappropriately introspective (Mykhalovskiy, 1996). However, ideally in such writing, the reader does not just learn about the individual author. Rather, through the experiences of the author, the reader learns something about the wider society. When it works well, autoethnography inspires readers to critically reflect upon their own life experiences within a sociocultural context (Spry, 2001).

As a teacher, I know that sociologically informed personal stories are powerful ways to talk to students about patterns or privilege and oppression. I have used personal stories to illustrate aspects of the social construction of dominant forms of masculinity, white supremacy, and heteronormativity.

Given that I am interested in writing as a form of political engagement, and that writing a book about privilege is itself an expression of privilege, I want to explore the politics of the use of personal experience in my writing.

One of the rationales of writing personally is that it is situated (Willard-Traub, 2007). When we write autobiographically, we illuminate our subject position as a writer. Generally, when white straight men write they do so as a form of objective truth. The point of view of men in dominant groups has led to the view of Western thought as universal. Our ways of knowing and seeing the world inscribe a particular form of epistemological dominance—what Ryder (1991) calls "epistemological imperialism."

This is particularly so when we define the experiences of others rather than talking about ourselves. I believe that it is fundamentally important that academics keep issues of power, privilege, and positionality at the forefront of our analysis (Johnston & Goodman, 2006). We all need to recognize the multiple subjectivities we inhabit and to locate ourselves in relation to privilege and oppression in our lives. Those of us who are most unmarked, white, heterosexual, middle-class, able-bodied men, need to understand how our subjectivities are constructed (Pease, 2012).

Thus, when straight white men write, it too is socially situated and partial. Naming it as such undermines its claim to universality. However, in articulating our positionality, and in demonstrating reflexivity about it, we need to be clear that this does not erase our power and privilege. The academic memoir is shaped by institutional privilege (Franklin, 2009). If it is to have progressive potential it must unmask and interrogate that privilege and explore how dominant identities are constructed. There are dangers here as well that we need to engage with.

We must be aware of privileged speaking positions. What does it mean when profeminist men who challenge patriarchy are listened to more than feminist women who challenge patriarchy? It has been argued that this is a way of using privilege to challenge privilege. Men are likely to be perceived by other men as more credible and thus they will be listened to more. However, this can in fact reinforce those barriers that prevent women from having their own voices heard. When feminist colleagues and I have presented papers together on men's responsibility for challenging men's violence, I have been concerned when my voice has been given more credibility than theirs.

I am also conscious that when I write or talk about white privilege as a white academic, it is likely to carry more credibility than if a non-white person raises these issues. This is one of the consequences of privilege: the views of the privileged are more likely to be listened to. There is power in speaking from the dominant position, in part because I benefit from the privileges that I critique.

There is also the question of where autobiographical writing sits within the wider context of global inequalities. What does it mean to spend so much time on writing style when global capitalism is expanding across the world? How does personal writing style illuminate our critiques of power, privilege, and oppression? We need to locate our discussions about representation in the text in the context of new imperialism and neo-liberalism (Bourgois, 2002).

Notwithstanding the tensions and dangers that I have discussed, I believe that politically conscious autobiographical writing has something important to contribute to social justice struggles. Being critical about the structures of privilege and oppression in the world can sit alongside writing in a personal voice. In fact, interrogating privilege from within requires it. The transformation of oppressive structures will mean that privileged individuals will need to be willing to forgo and challenge their privileges. Autobiographical writing about privilege provides an insight into the extent to which that is possible (Pease, 2012).

Conclusion

While I make no claims that my research methodology in any of these projects is feminist, I was inspired by feminist principles in constructing my methodologies. Wadsworth and Hargreaves (1993) suggested that the methodological approaches of feminism will be relevant to men who are seeking to transform subordinating practices, whilst Maguire (1987) also encouraged men to use participatory research to uncover their own modes of domination of women.

When there was a view that feminist methods could be read off from feminist epistemologies, the issue of whether men could use these methods to research men's lives was contentious (Kremer, 1990). While the idea of feminist methods would later be challenged, the articulation of feminist methods did open up important discussions about the relationship between methods, epistemology, and purposes of the research.

It is also now clear that quantitative methods are not inherently positivist and patriarchal and that qualitative methods are not necessarily feminist or emancipatory. However, just as feminists have been very interested in women's experience and subjectivity, it is important for profeminist male researchers to give greater attention to their own subjectivity and the subjectivity of the men in their studies. Hence, while men should not necessarily be deterred from using quantitative methods if they are appropriate to their specific research project, qualitative and ethnographic methods such as collaborative inquiry, life history interviews, ethnography, autoethnography, and memory work are more likely to encourage male researchers to focus on subjectivity. The interrogation of masculine subjectivities is important in any research with men that aims to challenge gender inequality.

Note

1   I use the language of profeminism to articulate men's support for a feminist perspective. I believe that men should not call themselves feminists both because feminism is grounded in women's experiences of patriarchy and because I believe that there are dangers in men appropriating women's work. I recognize, however, that some men committed to feminism may not necessarily share this distinction.

References

Anderson, J. (1993). Studying across difference: Race, class and gender in qualitative research. In J. Stanford II & R. Dennis (Eds.), *Race and ethnicity in research methods* (pp. 39–52). Newbury Park, CA: Sage.

Ashe, F. (2007). *The new politics of masculinity: Men, power and resistance.* New York: Routledge.

Bonnett, A. (2000). *Antiracism.* London: Routledge.

Bourgois, P. (2002). Ethnography's troubles and the reproduction of academic habitus. *Qualitative Studies in Education, 15* (4), 417–420.

Boyle, P. & Hiffance, K. (Eds.). (1999). *Migration and gender in the developed world.* London: Routledge.

Bradley, H. (1996). *Fractured identities: Changing patterns of inequality.* Cambridge: Polity Press.

Canaan, J. & Griffin, C. (1990). The new men's studies: Part of the problem or part of the solution? In J. Hearn & D. Morgan (Eds.), *Men, masculinities and social theory* (pp. 206–214). London: Unwin Hyman.

Carey, L. (2004). Always, already colonizer/colonized: White Australian wanderings. In K. Mutua & B. Swadena (Eds.), *Decolonizing research in cross-cultural contexts* (pp. 69–86). Albany, NY: State University of New York Press.

Carniol, B. (2005). Analysis of social location and change: Practice implications. In S. Hicks, J. Fook, & R. Pozzuto (Eds.) *Social work: A critical turn,* pp. 153–165). Toronto: Thompson Educational Publishing.

Connell, R. (2005). *Masculinities.* Sydney: Allen and Unwin.

Cowburn, M. (2005). Confidentiality and public protection: Ethical dilemmas in qualitative research with adult sex offenders. *Journal of Sexual Aggression, 11* (1), 49–63.

Cowburn, M. (2007). Men researching men in prison: The challenges for profeminist research. *The Howard Journal, 46* (3), 276–288.

Crossley, P. & Pease, B. (2009). Machismo and the construction of immigrant Latin American masculinities. In M. Donaldson, R. Hibbins, R. Howson, & B. Pease (Eds.), *Migrant men: Critical perspectives on masculinities and the migration experience* (pp. 115–134). New York: Routledge.

Douglas, P. (1993). Men equals violence: A profeminist perspective on dismantling the masculine equation. Paper presented at the Second National Conference on Violence, Australian Institute of Criminology, Canberra, 15–18 June.

Dreher, T. (2009). Listening across difference: Media and multiculturalism beyond the politics of voice. *Continuum: A Journal of Media and Cultural Studies, 23* (4), 445–458.

Fellows, M. & Razack, R. (1998). The race to innocence: Confronting hierarchical relations among women. *Journal of Gender, Race and Justice, 1,* 335–352.

Flood, M. (1994/1995). Men difference and racism. *XY: Men, Sex, Politics, 4* (4), 19–21.

Frankenberg, R. (1993). *White women, race matters.* Minneapolis: University of Minnesota Press.

Franklin, C. (2009). *Academic lives: Memoir, cultural theory and the university today.* Athens: University of Georgia Press.

Halewood, P. (1995). White men can't jump: Critical epistemologies, embodiment and the praxis of legal scholarship. *Yale Journal of Law and Feminism, 7* (1), 1–36.

Harding, S. (1989). Is there a feminist method? In N. Tuana (Ed.), *Feminism and science* (pp. 17–32). Bloomington: Indiana University Press.

Haug, F. (1987). *Female sexualisation: A collective work of memory.* London: Verso.

Haug, F. (1992). *Beyond female masochism: Memory work and politics.* London: Verso.

Hearn, J. (1994). Critical studies on men. *International Association of the Study of Men Newsletter, 1* (1), 8.

Hearn, J. (2007). Methods, methodology and research. In M. Flood, J. Gardiner, B. Pease & K. Pringle (Eds.), *International Encyclopedia of Men and Masculinities* (pp. 433–438). Abingdon, Oxon: Routledge.

Hearn, J. & Pringle, K. (2006). *European perspectives on men and masculinities.* New York: Palgrave.

Hondagneu-Sotelo, P. & Messner, M. (1994). Gender displays and men's power: The "new man" and the Mexican immigrant man. In H. Brod & M. Kaufman (Eds.), *Theorizing masculinities,* (pp. 200–218). Thousand Oaks, CA: Sage.

Johnson, A. (2006). *Privilege, power and difference* (2nd ed.). New York: McGraw-Hill.

Johnston, J. & Goodman, J. (2006). Hope and activism in the ivory tower: Freirian lessons for critical globalization research. *Globalizations, 3* (1): 9–30.

Kofman E., Phizacklea, A., Raghuram, P., & Sales, R. (2000). *Gender and international migration in Europe.* London: Routledge.

Kremer, B. (1990). Learning to say no: Keeping feminist research methods for ourselves. *Women's Studies International Journal, 13* (5), 463–467.

Krumer-Nevo, M. & Sidi, M. (2012). Writing against othering. *Qualitative Inquiry, 18* (4), 299–309.

Ladson-Billings, G. (2000). Racialised discourses and ethnic epistemologies. In N. Denzin & Y. Lincoln (Eds.), *Handbook of Qualitative Research* (2nd ed.) (pp. 257–277). Thousand Oaks, CA: Sage.

Lloyd, J. (2009). The listening cure. *Continuum: A Journal of Media and Cultural Studies, 23* (4), 477–487.

Luck, M. & Jackson, D. (1995). The exploration of men and masculinities from an anti-sexist perspective. *International Association of the Study of Men Newsletter, 3* (2), 5.

Macleod, C. (2007). The risk of phallocentrism in masculinities studies: How a revision of the concept of patriarchy may help. *Journal for the Theory of Social Behaviour, 32* (1), 41–60.

Maguire, P. (1987). *Doing participatory research: A feminist approach.* Amherst, MA: University of Massachusetts.

May, L. (1998). A progressive male standpoint. In T. Rigby (Ed.) *Men doing feminism* (pp. 337–354). New York: Routledge.

Messner, M. (1990). Men studying masculinity: Some epistemological issues in sport sociology. *Sociology of Sport Journal, 7* (2), 136–153.

Moreton-Robinson, A. (2000). *Talkin' up to the white woman: Indigenous women and feminism.* St. Lucia: University of Queensland Press.

Morgan, D. (1981). Men, masculinity and the process of sociological inquiry. In H. Roberts (Ed.), *Doing feminist research* (pp. 83–113). London: Routledge.

Morgan, D. (1992). *Discovering men.* London: Routledge.

wa Mungai, N. & Pease, B. (2009). Rethinking masculinities in the African diaspora. In M. Donaldson, R. Hibbins, R. Howson, & B. Pease (Eds.), *Migrant men: Critical perspectives on masculinities and the migration experience* (pp. 96–114). New York: Routledge.

Mykhalovskiy, E. (1996). Reconsidering table talk: Critical thoughts on the relationship between sociology, autobiography and self-indulgence. *Qualitative Sociology, 19* (1), 131–151.

O'Donnell, P., Lloyd, J., & Dreher, T. (2009). Listening, path building and continuations: A research agenda for the analysis of listening. *Continuum: A Journal of Media and Cultural Studies, 23* (4), 423–439.

Pease, B. (1996). Reforming men: Masculine subjectivities and the politics and practices of profeminism, PhD Thesis. La Trobe University, Melbourne.

Pease, B. (1997). *Men and sexual politics: Towards a profeminist practice.* Adelaide: Dulwich Centre Publications.

Pease, B. (2000a). *Recreating men: Postmodern masculinity politics.* London: Sage.

Pease, B. (2000b). Reconstructing heterosexual subjectivities and practices with white middle-class men. *Race, Gender and Class, 7* (1), 133–145.

Pease, B. (2000c). Beyond the father wound: Memory-work and the deconstruction of the father–son relationship. *Australian and New Zealand Journal of Family Therapy, 21* (1), 9–15.

Pease, B. (2002). *Men and gender relations.* Melbourne: Tertiary Press.

Pease, B. (2006). Masculine migrations. In A. Jones (Ed.) *Men of the global south: A reader* (pp. 343–348). London: Zed Books.

Pease, B. (2008). Mothers and sons: Using memory-work to explore the subjectivities and practices of profeminist men. In M. Ewing, A. Hyle, J. Kaufman, & D. Montgomery (Eds.), *Dissecting the mundane: International perspectives on memory-work* (pp. 133–150). New York: University Press of America.

Pease, B. (2009). Immigrant men and domestic life: Renegotiating the patriarchal bargain. In M. Donaldson, R. Hibbins, R. Howson, & B. Pease (Eds.), *Migrant men: Critical perspectives on masculinities and the migration experience* (pp. 79–95). New York: Routledge.

Pease, B. (2010). *Undoing privilege: Unearned advantage in a divided world.* London: Sage.

Pease, B. (2012). Interrogating privileged subjectivities: Reflections on writing personal accounts of privilege. In M. Livholts (Ed.), *Emergent writing methodologies in feminist studies* (pp. 71–82). New York: Routledge.

Pheterson, G. (1986). Alliances between women: Overcoming internalised oppression and internalised domination. *Signs: Journal of Women, Culture and Society, 12* (1), 146–160.

Popoviciu, L., Haywood, C., & Mac an Ghaill, M. (2006). The promise of post-structuralist methodology: Ethnographic representation of education and masculinity. *Ethnography and Education, 1* (3), 393–412.

Robinson, V. (2003). Radical revisionings? The theorizing of masculinity and (radical) feminist theory. *Women's Studies International Journal, 26* (2), 129–137.

Ryder, B. (1991). Straight talk: Male heterosexual privilege. *Queen's Law Journal, 16,* 287–312.

Spry, T. (2001). Performing autoethnography: An embodied methodological praxis. *Qualitative Inquiry, 7* (6), 706–732.

Strega, S. (2005). The view from the poststructural margins: Epistemology and methodology reconsidered. In L. Brown & S. Strega (Eds.), *Research as resistance: Critical, indigenous and anti-oppressive approaches* (pp. 199–235). Toronto: Canadian Scholars' Press.

Sundberg, J. (2011). Masculinist epistemologies and the politics of fieldwork in Latin Americanist geography. *The Professional Geographer, 55* (2), 180–190.

Thorne-Finch, R. (1992). *Ending the silence: The origins and treatment of male violence against women.* Toronto: University of Toronto Press.

Vecchio, K. (1998). Dismantling white male privilege within family therapy. In M. McGoldrick (Ed.), *Revisioning family therapy* (pp. 159–175). New York: New York University Press.

Wadsworth, Y. & Hargreaves, K. (1993). *What is feminist research?* Melbourne: Action Research Issues Association.

Willard-Traub, M. (2007). Scholarly autobiography: An alternative intellectual practice. *Feminist Studies, 33*, 188–206.

Willis, K. & Yeoh, B. (Eds.) (2000). *Gender and migration.* Cheltenham: Edward Elgar.

Section 2

Theory in Research

5 Operationalizing Intersectionality in Feminist Social Work Research

Reflections and Techniques from Research with Equity-Seeking Groups

Wendy Hulko

While constructive use of self is a core social work skill and social location is a key concept in social work education, it can be argued that feminist social work academics are encouraged to acknowledge their subjectivity and account for their social location more deliberately and routinely than other social work educators and researchers. Feminists seek to embody praxis by enacting our theoretical commitments (de Vault, 1999; Gringeri, Wahab, & Anderson-Nathe, 2010; Lather, 1991; Wahab, Anderson-Nathe, & Gringeri, 2012), or at least ensuring that theory and practice are in conversation with one another. Praxis has been defined as "reflection and action upon the world in order to transform it" (Freire, 2001, p. 51) and is often diagrammed with a bidirectional arrow between theory and action, or knowing and doing. As such, building capacity to engage in feminist social work research is best accomplished through an experiential approach that involves socially locating oneself, continually "asking the other question," trying to effect social change, and other activities explicitly connected to feminist theory, i.e., that make the personal political. Feminist social work research responds to Lather's (1991) call for more theoretically informed research methods: "we who do empirical research in the name of emancipatory politics must discover ways to connect our research methodology to our theoretical concerns and political commitments" (p. 172). This includes adopting theoretical innovations arising from third- and fourth-wave feminism, including the disruption of binaries associated with queer feminism and intersectionality (Baumgardner, 2011; Gringeri et al., 2010; Marinucci, 2010).

In this chapter, I aim to demonstrate the application of an intersectionality and interlocking oppressions paradigm to feminist social work research based on my experiences doing research with equity-seeking groups[1] and teaching research to Bachelor of Social Work (BSW) students and community members. To illustrate the integration of knowing and doing, I discuss a number of techniques and tools consistent with an anti-oppressive feminist approach, drawing on examples from several implicitly or explicitly feminist research studies conducted on my own or in collaboration with others over the past decade. In focusing specifically on theory and its application to research methods, this chapter addresses the need for more critical engagement with theory in social work and demonstrates ways to design research grounded in critical theory, two of the issues raised by the editors. Further, it concentrates on a topic—intersectionality—in need of attention within feminist social work research (Wahab et al., 2012). The overall aim of this chapter is to demonstrate the value of feminist social work research, including the ways in which focused application of a theoretical framework like intersectionality and associated methodological techniques can shift research relationships and change the knowledge creation process. In the following sections, I provide an overview of the theoretical foundation to my work and the five research studies drawn on in this chapter, discuss phases of the research process and methodological tools consistent with "doing research differently," present numerous examples of operationalizing intersectionality in feminist social work research,[2] identify the connections to feminist theory, and conclude with future directions for feminist social work research.

Intersectionality as Integral to Feminist Social Work Research

Intersectionality refers to the ways in which socially constructed categories like gender, race, sexual orientation, and age interact with one another to produce relations of domination and subordination and the effect this has on individuals marked as having more than one marginalized social status. In my case, the referents are my gender (woman) and sexual orientation (bi-queer). The assumption underpinning this theoretical proposition is that the social location of individuals influences their "actions, choices, and outcomes" (Murphy, Hunt, Zajicek, Norris, & Hamilton, 2009, p. 7). Yet, as Anthias (2013) notes, "it is important to be sensitive to the relationships between social categories, rather than presuppose them" (p. 14) and to acknowledge that categories "exist within spatial and temporal contexts and are emergent rather than given and unchangeable" (p. 8; see also Hulko, 2009a). The connection between individual experiences and social structures is taken for granted in intersectionality theorizing, with both structure and agency or the micro and macro levels being implicated (Hill Collins, 2000). This suggests why intersectionality has become a key concept in social work practice, education, and research (Murphy et al., 2009), a discipline that seeks to make "personal troubles public issues" (Carniol, 2010; Wright Mills, 2000).

Theorists and researchers adopting an intersectional lens avoid isolating a particular aspect of a person's identity or prioritizing one form of oppression over another and instead consider various facets of a person's social location and treat oppressions (and sometimes privileges) as interactive and mutually reinforcing (Hulko, 2009a). Intersectionality theorizing was developed by critical race scholars and Black feminists, including the Combahee River Collective (1977), who demanded that their lives as Black lesbian women be considered holistically; Kimberly Crenshaw (1989), who coined the term intersectionality and identified accidents that occur at intersections where marginalized identities meet; Patricia Hill Collins (2000), who conceptualized the matrix of domination depicting the interlocking nature of oppression; and Richard Delgado (2011), whose creative method of counter-storytelling can be seen in many of the intersectional tales told in the past 20 years. Intersectionality has been integrated into feminist social work scholarship, often with the additional naming of unearned privileges as an integral part of challenging oppression (Brotman & Kraniou, 1999; Clark, Drolet, Arouse, Walton, Tamburro, Mathews, Derrick, Michaud, & Armstrong, 2009; Hulko, 2009a; Mehrotra, 2010; Murphy et al., 2009). This arises from the recognition that subordination is accompanied by domination, i.e., if there are disadvantaged groups, then there are privileged ones as well; and members of social groups are differentially located, i.e., individuals can be subject to both disadvantage and unearned privilege depending on the social groups to which they belong.

Feminist methodology seeks to "reveal the locations and perspectives of (all) women" who have been overlooked in research, with the explicit goal being "excavation and inclusion" (de Vault, 1999, p. 30); use methods that change the power dynamics in research relationships and avoid harm to women; and achieve social change through the process and outcomes of research (de Vault, 1999; Morris, 2007). According to Murphy and colleagues (2009), research must meet three criteria to be recognized as having adopted an intersectionality approach: (1) two or more categories of oppression must be investigated; (2) the data collected in relation to these categories must be analyzed in a way that goes beyond sample description; and (3) intersectionality must be a main theme, i.e., appear throughout the article or study (p. 56). Intersectionality is particularly compatible with methodologies that view reality as socially constructed and that try to draw out the uniqueness of individuals (e.g., case study), build theory about basic social processes (e.g., grounded theory), and/or facilitate spaces for the voices of disempowered groups (e.g., feminist and anti-oppressive research). Intersectionality scholars are social justice-oriented or interested in doing research and creating theory that effects social change (Hill Collins, 2012; Morris, 2007).

My approach to intersectionality involves considering privilege as well as oppression, thus I do not restrict my research to working with people who inhabit multiple sites of marginalization or oppression, which was the original intent of intersectionality as a concept (Crenshaw, 1989) and remains the dominant approach in intersectionality theorizing (Hankivsky, 2011; Hill Collins, 2012). I also refrain from expanding the list of social identity categories to include outcomes such as addictions or social desirability characteristics like attractiveness. When teaching students about intersectionality and interlocking oppressions, I provide an overview of the development of this type of theorizing, distinguishing

between the various theorists and identifying contributions and limitations, present the various models or diagrams used to depict intersectionality and interlocking oppressions, demonstrate the construction of
a social location diagram (Figure 5.1), and require students to socially
locate themselves—often with the assistance of a diagram. Further, I make
extensive use of data from my own research and social location diagrams
of former students to make explicit the connections between theory and
practice. After an indepth introduction such as this, if the BSW or MEd
students that I teach suggest that people who are "fat" or "ugly" should be
considered oppressed groups, I refer them to Iris Marion Young's (1990)
five faces of oppression and ask them whether any of the groups they have
named have been subject to exploitation, marginalization, powerlessness,
cultural imperialism, and/or violence (Carniol, 2010; Hulko, 2009a). This
approach shifts away from "social preference"—"a fondness, predilection,
or inclination toward a favored group"—and towards "privilege," defined
as "any entitlement, sanction, power, and advantage or right granted to a
person or group solely by birthright membership in a prescribed group
or groups; [which results in] the oppression of a nonprivileged group"
(Black & Stone, 2005, p. 245).

Black and Stone (2005) identified the following domains as the most
frequently cited in the literature and theoretically robust: race/ethnicity,
gender, sexual orientation, age, socioeconomic status, differing degrees of
ableness, and religious affiliation. These are the same social identity categories in the social location diagrams that I draw (Figure 5.1) when teaching

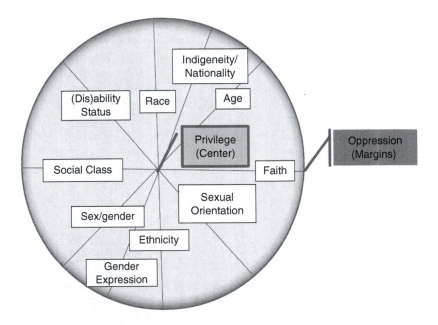

Figure 5.1 Social location diagram.

students about intersectionality and interlocking oppressions—albeit with race and ethnicity separated; recently I started adding lines for gender expression and Indigeneity or nationality to distinguish these social divisions from sex/gender and race and ethnicity respectively. This diagramming will be addressed further in the section on sampling for diversity, below.

The advantages of operationalizing intersectionality in research with equity-seeking groups are that it makes visible the invisible, honors voice and subjectivity, links micro (subjective experiences) with macro (social structures), and embraces the complexity and messiness of life. This is consistent with the goals of feminist social work research. In this chapter, I aim to avoid potential weaknesses in the application of intersectionality to research such as a lack of conceptual clarity and specificity in its use, through clearly articulating the theoretical and epistemological underpinnings of my research and demonstrating specific ways that an intersectional approach can alter the process of doing research with equity-seeking groups and the knowledge that we can create together.

Overview of Five Research Projects with Equity-Seeking Groups

The following research studies are drawn on in this chapter: (1) grounded theory research into the experiences of older people with dementia and intersectionality using interviews, participant observation, and photography with eight older people (average age of 77 years) and 50 members of their social worlds (Hulko, 2009b, 2011); (2) an exploratory study of aging in Cuba through interviews in Spanish and photography with 12 older Cubans (average age of 61 years) from equity-seeking groups (women, Afro-Cubans, sexual minorities) living in Havana (Hulko, 2013); (3) feminist research using interviews and focus groups with 14 lesbian or bisexual women and seven transgender persons under the age of 30 (average of 20.5 years) or over the age of 50 (average of 56 years) on identifying as a sexual and/or gender minority and finding community in a small city or rural community (Hulko, forthcoming; Hulko & Hovanes, forthcoming); (4) grounded theory research on views of memory loss and memory care in later life through a series of sharing circles and interviews with 21 First Nation Elders (average age of 69.7 years), including four older women experiencing memory loss, and two community members (Hulko et al., 2010); and (5) community-based research on culturally safe dementia care (CSDC) that involved a series of roundtables with 35 Secwepemc[3] Nation Elders to develop teaching tools for nurses, followed by an educational intervention, before and after which the nurse participants[4] were evaluated. These studies will be shown to exemplify elements of feminist social work research identified by the editors (Gringeri et al., 2010), although only one was identified as feminist research. Each study met the three criteria outlined by Murphy and colleagues (2009), although the two Indigenous research projects focused less on analyzing the diversity within the sample.

Doing Research Differently as a Feminist Social Work Researcher

"Doing research differently" or taking an anti-oppressive approach to research addresses the ways in which one does research rather than pre-scribing the topic or focus of the research, as "anti-oppressive research is not methodologically distinctive, but epistemologically distinctive" (Potts & Brown, 2005, p. 282–283). Given the relationships between "ways of know-ing," "ways of doing" and "ways of being" (Wilson, 2008), anti-oppressive researchers are often drawn to questions that are best answered through the use of qualitative methods of data collection and analysis. This does not preclude the use of quantitative methods by feminist social work researchers and others concerned with social justice; in fact, mixed methods research can have a powerful effect on decision-makers and the public. The statisti-cal research of the Canadian Centre for Policy Alternatives on poverty levels is one example, as Potts and Brown (2005) note; however, "there is an epis-temological difference between such social justice research, grounded in reclaiming positivism and . . . anti-oppressive research" (p. 260).

A key part of the doing of research is a researcher's relationships with research participants and other research partners like their co-investigators, advisory committee members, and research staff (Clark et al., 2009; Frisby & Creese, 2011; Van de Sande & Schwartz, 2011). In these relationships, the researcher is expected to be transparent, authentic, and open; this means rejecting the myth of objectivity, acknowledging one's subjectivity, and socially locating oneself (Absolon, 2011; Anderson-Nathe, Gringeri & Wahab, 2013; Brown & Strega, 2005; Kirby, Greaves, & Reid, 2006; Kovach, 2010; Letherby, 2003; Reid, Brief, & Le Drew, 2009; Wilson, 2008). This undoubtedly poses challenges for some researchers. Consider this: if your participants see you as white, middle-class, straight, able-bodied, majority ethnic, *and* they are wrong about any of these things (e.g., you have an invis-ible disability and/or are queer), then do you correct them? Personally, I disclose my identity as a bi-queer woman—an insider—when doing research related to sexual orientation and/or gender expression, i.e., with my com-munity, and do not mention this when doing research with First Nation Elders. In the latter case, it is vital that I acknowledge my identity as an outsider rather than an insider or an outsider-within (Hill Collins, 2000; Tuhiwai Smith, 2012). This call to identify pertains more to my relation-ship to land and territory (Absolon, 2011; Kovach, 2010; Wilson, 2008) as a third-generation Canadian of Scottish and Scandinavian ancestry who was born and raised on Coast Salish territory and now resides in Shuswap terri-tory than it does to my marginalized social status as a bi-queer woman, how-ever. Disclosing my sexual orientation could hinder recruitment and data collection in research with Elders due to the legacy of residential schools, i.e., the attribution of deviancy to same-sex relationships, and by extension to gender transgressions. Thus, the group(s) with whom one does research and the degree to which epistemic privilege is shared places a limit on the authenticity and subjectivity that can be expressed by feminist social work researchers. The situation above could be faced by an Indigenous researcher who identifies as Two-Spirit (or does not identify as such yet is Indigenous and a sexual minority and/or gender transgressive), which lends support to the idea of troubling the binary of insider/outsider (Gringeri et al., 2010) in feminist social work research. If "deeper conversation" is the goal, then one could "name it [social group membership] and let it stand" (Anderson-Nathe et al., 2013, p. 289), as in the editors' example of presenting oneself as both religious and queer.

Becker (1966) argues that research is never a neutral enterprise and that we always take sides, yet these sides are rarely those of the research participants. Researchers need to be accountable to funding bodies, employers, colleagues, professional associations, and ethical review boards, and this can prevent them from taking the side of research participants. Yet, doing research with equity-seeking groups—with populations that have been harmed by research in the past—calls us to identify whose side we are taking or for whose benefit we are seeking to conduct a piece of research (Tuhiwai Smith, 2012). That is, if there is a disagreement over when and how to share research results, e.g., community forum, peer-reviewed article, professional conference, then will the researcher side with the university, funding body, or with the community? Another way of looking at this is the need for researchers to respond to the "terms of engagement" (Stalker, 1998) that research participants might establish. Researchers need to consider the possibility of requests for involvement in data analysis, consent before publication of results, and/or ongoing contact once the research has finished, for example.

Clearly power is a key element of doing research differently in terms of how we use—and avoid abusing—power in our relationships with participants and collaborators (Brown & Strega, 2005; Frisby & Creese, 2011) and is a key concern in feminist social work research (Wahab et al., 2012). Anti-oppressive researchers believe that there should be "no research without relationships" and suggest approaching research relationships "as if we may be in relationship with people for life" (Potts & Brown, 2005, p. 263). Researchers need to determine if this is a "term of engagement" to which they can agree and then negotiate degrees of inclusion and collaboration. In doing research with First Nation communities, the weight of history, i.e., past harms done by researchers, is omnipresent and thus research should be participatory or collaborative at all times (Absolon, 2011; Kovach, 2010; Tuhiwai Smith, 2012; Wilson, 2008) and seek to abide by the principles of ownership, control, access and possession (Schnarch, 2004; see also Van de Sande & Schwartz, 2011, pp. 82–83). Another "term of engagement" proposed by an older lesbian woman participating in the queer project and to which I agreed on behalf of myself and my research assistant was to conduct an interview with her in the lounge area of a restaurant and to have a drink with her during the course of the interview.

Building on this overview of my theoretical and methodological approach, I now discuss the following six methodological strategies and tools associated with doing research differently and which are clearly informed by feminist theory: (1) being reflective and reflexive; (2) sampling for diversity and equity; (3) getting good data; (4) facilitating voice in data collection and analysis; (5) sharing ownership and control; and (6) disseminating results with an eye to social change. I will address each of these in turn and offer specific examples to show how to enact ontological and epistemological principles such as these.

Being Reflective and Reflexive

As feminist researchers are well aware, research is not value-neutral:

> research methodologies and methods have been developed by people who see the world in particular ways, and every time a research tool is used, a researcher needs to be aware that it contains the perspectives of those who created it. Being responsive to [this] is the essence of reflexivity (Kirby et al., 2006, p. 19).

Feminist social work research—or "research beyond the mainstream"—requires "intersubjectivity" and "critical reflection or reflexivity" (Kirby et al., 2006, p. 7). Subjectivity is essential to feminist research, as noted in the introduction, and acknowledging one's social location and attending to ways in which it could impact the research is a means of demonstrating this. Further, an awareness of the sociocultural and political economic context of research (D'Cruz & Jones, 2004) in general and in relation to a specific study is essential. Questions that can aid in understanding the sociopolitical context include: (1) who are the relevant actors/stakeholders? (2) why is this project relevant? and (3) how can this research make a difference?

Reflexivity requires researchers to take stock of their influence on the research process through means such as a reflexive journal (Kirby et al., 2006) and to act on these reflections by changing the data collection methods based on feedback from participants. In Hulko et al. (2010), one community requested family and community members be invited to join an Elders' sharing circle in order to learn first-hand the Elders' views on dementia. Our amendment request to the university's research ethics committee was approved, and this enabled us to allow non-participants to attend (i.e., to have access to data) and to video-tape in case there was a crowd. While only two community members attended (participant and observer), it was important to the community that we responded to their request and adapted our research design to be more reciprocal (Kovach, 2010; Varcoe et al., 2011; Wilson, 2008).

Sampling for Diversity and Equity

When first operationalizing intersectionality in my doctoral research on dementia and intersectionality, I struggled to avoid the pull towards essentialism or reducing the participants to their marginalized social statuses in order to construct a "diverse" sample. My sense was that the actual participants themselves, as a group, should represent various social locations, rather than different mathematical configurations of the variables of race, ethnicity, class, and gender. That said, I did play with different algebraic formulas in an effort to devise a "diverse sample" (Figure 5.2), which I later viewed as an expression of my positivisitic hangover.

I was able to reject this process of essentializing the participants as people with its ostensible goal of simplifying complexity or managing diversity once I came up with an alternate method more in line with my research aims that could result in a diverse sample. This new approach called for the selection of people who lay at different points on the axes of oppression and privilege, based on their race, ethnicity, class, and gender. In this way, similar or shared social locations, ranging from multiply privileged to multiply oppressed, rather than individual characteristics, formed the basis upon which the sample was stratified. Based on the information known about the participant's sex/gender, race, ethnicity, age, disability status, social class, sexual orientation, faith, gender expression, and Indigeneity or nationality, together with an awareness of historical and contemporary patterns of exclusion and inclusion, dots are placed along each axis (Figure 5.1). A dot

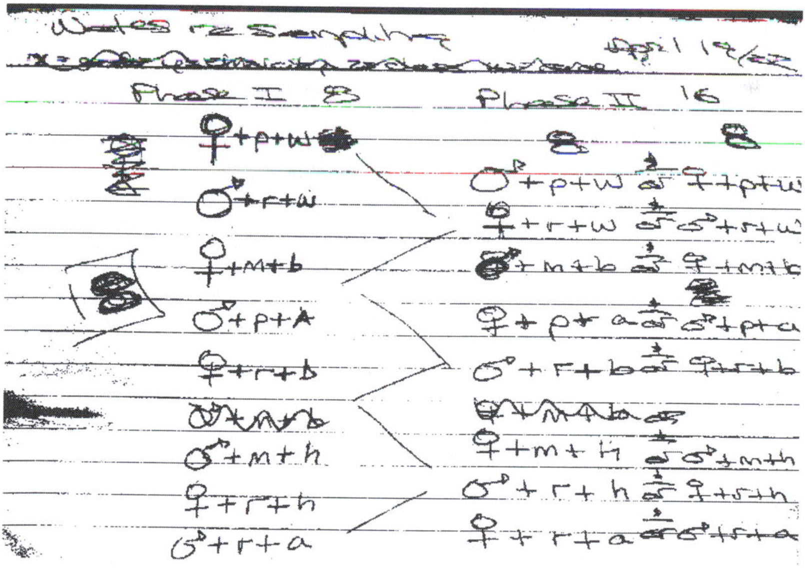

Figure 5.2 Sampling for diversity–algebraic or essentialist approach. (Taken from reflexive journal for PhD research, April 19, 2002.)

in the center represents privilege and one at the outside indicates marginalization or oppression and participants are located along the continuum, creating a visual representation of their social location (Figure 5.3).

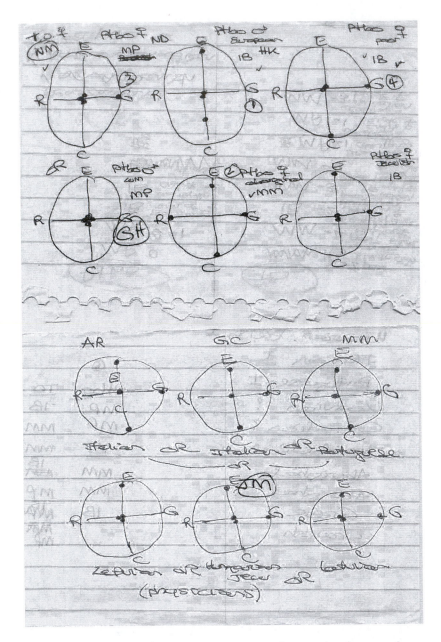

Figure 5.3 Sampling for diversity—continuum or intersectional approach.

The example given in Figure 5.3 is from my doctoral research (Hulko, 2009b, 2011), during the course of which I developed this approach to sampling for diversity. Such a relativist or continuum approach is undoubtedly an expression of my queer feminism (Baumgardner, 2011; Marinucci, 2010; Mehrotra, 2010), as it rejects binaries and acknowledges that gender is not dichotomous, for example. This method has informed recruitment in subsequent research projects, particularly when recruitment is ongoing, and also has been an effective teaching tool.

Getting Good Data or Asking What You Really Want to Know

The question of to what extent you name or label people is one with which intersectionality scholars and other critical social science researchers grapple. In Hulko (2009b, 2011), I asked open-ended questions like "when you think of yourself, what image comes to mind?" and "how would others describe you as a person?" in an effort to have participants self-identify. This line of questioning did not result in very good data—not as good as when I asked direct questions, which aligns with Bowleg's (2008) advice about "asking precisely what you want to know."

As a result of these experiences, I recommend starting with a vague self-identifying-type question and then following up with a more specific/direct one later, as well as probing intersectionality throughout the interview. This satisfies Murphy and colleagues' (2009) second criterion. Examples from three different research studies demonstrate the impact on the data of asking or not asking research participants direct questions about their social location. First, in Hulko (2013), the following question was posed[5] after general questions about aging in Cuba and being Cuban and resulted in rich data:

> Does being a [woman, Afro-Cuban, lesbian] make a difference in any way? How? Give me an example please.

In discussing the situation of women in Cuba, an older lesbian woman, who was an economist, quickly identified herself as a feminist—"of course women in Cuba and in the world have always been below, in relation to men"—and then introduced the notion of intersectionality:

> That is to say that the problem of women, as women, is that they are always underneath and with such a tremendous load! But if you're old . . . there is one thing you would have if you are a woman, are old, and you're Black. It is almost as if [you should] cut your veins! But if on top of this, you're old, female, Black and lesbian, with this you already closed the cycle [of life] . . . Because the fact that you are lesbian or gay, or black or old, you have to defend your race, defend your sexual choice, and defend your age (individual interview, February 2008, author's translation).

This is an example of the data that can be elicited when asking directly about intersectionality. In contrast, my American colleague had not asked a question about social location or intersectionality in his earlier interviews with older Cubans, thus we were unable to combine our data sets to the extent we had hoped prior to my data collection.

The second example comes from the queer research project. Below is a series of specific questions asked in interviews and focus groups with lesbian and bisexual women and transgender persons in order to elicit their views on intersectionality. As can be seen, we started with one vague and two general questions to allow for self-identification and then asked more specific questions and introduced a greater number of social identities.

> When you think of yourself in relation to sexuality and gender, what comes to mind?
>
> How does sexual orientation relate to your image of yourself?
>
> What about gender (expression)?
>
> How do other aspects of your identity affect this image? i.e., "race," class, ethnicity, faith, age, Aboriginal ancestry, (dis)ability/health status, marital status, geographic location.
>
> There are a number of factors which might impact on your experience of developing an identity and finding community. One of these is living in a small city or rural area. How has this affected you? What other aspects of your identity have made a difference? How so?

As we asked direct questions and also probed responses of the participants that hinted at social location, we gathered rich data on intersectionality, some of which challenged the premise of intersectionality that identities are indivisible and not hierarchically ordered (Hulko & Hovanes, forthcoming). Here is one quote from a transgender youth with a disability that indicates the strength of the data we received on "talking intersectionality":

> The only thing I have ever been called is retard . . . I am [disabled[6]] so they assume that I am mentally handicapped because of that . . . Well I am still afraid, even groups like this [queer youth group] because I am sure we all identify in the same sort of sense even if it is not exactly the same, but I [am] still a minority being [disabled] and all, like no matter where I go, even if it is a group like this, I am always scared I'm going to be judged for being [disabled]. And if I am in a place where there [are] enough people [who are disabled] I can be judged for being a girl looking like a guy (focus group) (Hulko & Hovanes, forthcoming, p. 18).

These examples illustrate how operationalizing intersectionality in feminist social work research can generate knowledge grounded in lived experiences that actually challenges and thereby extends theorizing about the dynamics of privilege and oppression.

Facilitating Voice in Data Collection and Analysis

I have found visual methods to be an extremely effective way to facilitate voice and inclusion in data collection when doing research with equity-seeking groups, having used both photography and photo elicitation (PE) in conjunction with third-party questioning (Allan, 2001). PE is simply introducing a photograph into an interview or focus group discussion and asking questions about it (Harper, 2002), as it is believed that "images evoke deeper elements of human consciousness than do words" (Harper, 2002, p. 13). PE can elicit more or different information (Wenger, 2002), empower children and persons with disabilities (Prosser & Loxley, 2008) and make it "safer" to answer sensitive questions about aging, disability, service use, and care practices, for example (Allan, 2001; Wenger, 2002). This reflects the goals of facilitating voice and inclusion and sharing power set by feminist researchers (de Vault, 1999; Morris, 2007).

In the dementia and intersectionality research project, I introduced a deck of image cards and asked participants to pull out the person most similar to and most different from themselves. Their responses were fascinating (Figure 5.4) and suggested their social locations played a role in their very different descriptions of the same older white woman grocery shopping.

"Hard life I would think . . . She looks weary, tired, she's well enough, good coat. [pause] Probably doesn't have anyone to love her or look after her or . . . The basket's sort of got [a] fair bit in it for a person of her age . . . " – Multiply privileged participant

". . . and here's old mama, I like, I like that picture. Oh, I like this picture, she looks happy man. She one of those happy-go-lucky ladies boy, oh yeah, oh yeah. Oh, happy about life, with what she's doing, she's shopping." – Participant marginalized due to race & class & privileged due to gender & ethnicity

[in Tagalog] "I don't know . . . I don't know, maybe somebody, sometimes a person who is poor [gestures someone walking] . . . with like newspaper for example, and they stealing, and take it." – Multiply marginalized participant

"Ohh, she's an old one . . . Yeah . . . Well, the way she dresses and . . . that looks like an old hat, a young person would not dress like that." – Participant marginalized due to gender & ethnicity & privileged due to race & class

Photo, Health Canada, © Minister of PWGSC, 2001.

The reproduction of the photos in Figures 5.4–5.6 is not an official version of the materials reproduced, nor were they made in affiliation with or with the endorsement of Health Canada. For information on copyright and permission to reproduce, see http://publications.gc.ca/collections/Collection/H88-3-30-2001/html/disc_s_e.htm

Figure 5.4 Responses to image of older white woman shopping.

These markedly different responses to the same picture demonstrate how our social location and our values and beliefs can influence what we see in a photo and the value we place on the person so depicted. Used in this way, PE can be a very useful tool for soliciting views of people that are both different from and similar to the respondent. Two more examples demonstrate the ways in which PE in combination with third-party questioning can enable people from equity-seeking groups to voice their experiences and views.

Figure 5.5 illustrates the use of PE and third-party questioning with the most cognitively impaired of the participants in the same project. "Ester Hernandez" was a working-class South Asian woman initially not recommended for inclusion due to her dementia and lack of English; she proved able to communicate with the assistance of an interpreter and the use of PE, however. This can be seen in the dialogue accompanying Figure 5.5, during which Ester identifies the South Asian women as "outsiders . . . because they are not born in Canada," surprising the interviewer with her insight into patterns of inclusion and exclusion.

The final example is from the Secwepemc views on dementia study in which two photos of First Nation Elders—a close-up of a female Elder (Figure 5.6) and a male Elder with a hide he had tanned—were used to prompt discussion of memory loss. For one of the female Elders with dementia who had been unwilling or unable to discuss how memory loss impacted her own life, the image of the female Elder led her to speak of ways in which her engagement in cultural activities like berry picking and making bannock (a kind of bread) could be impacted by memory loss in spite of there being neither berries nor bannock in the photo.

Int: What do you think life is like for this woman here?

EH: This woman?

Int: Mm-hmm.

EH: I think maybe that **they are outsiders**.

Int: They're which?

EH: Outsiders.

Int: Outsiders?

EH: Yeah, maybe.

Int: Why are they outsiders?

EH: **Because they are not born in Canada**.

Photo, Health Canada, © Minister of PWGSC, 2001.

Figure 5.5 Response to image of older South Asian woman with Asian care aide.

Well, she looks like she is down in the country too. And she likely goes and pick[s] berries and she might forget her way back from there. Looks like, [she] cooks for quite a few, she might forget cooking, making bread [bannock] one day or something when she was supposed to" – Female First Nation Elder with memory loss

Photo: Health Canada/Santé Canada

Photo, Health Canada, © Minister of PWGSC, 2001.

Figure 5.6 Response to image of older Indigenous (or First Nations) woman.

Sharing Ownership and Control

This section mainly deals with the ethics of doing research and suggests ways to shift the power imbalance inherent in research relationships so that research is more collaborative and meaningful for the participants. An initial step is viewing the attainment of informed consent as a process (Dewing, 2007) and introducing ways to increase participant understanding of and control over this process. This could include meeting with participants to discuss the project in advance of seeking consent and/or collecting data; showing pictures of the data collection process (e.g., an interview); demonstrating equipment to be used and indicating how to stop the recording mechanism; and inviting participants to select their own pseudonyms. In Hulko (2013), I adopted what I termed "participatory photography," seeking permission to take photos in advance and asking for suggestions on what to photograph, showing images to participants immediately after taking them and getting their permission to keep/use them, and providing copies of the images to the participants when feasible.

In collaborative research with Secwepemc Nation Elders over the past six years, sharing ownership and control is of paramount importance and this, as well as other strategies discussed up to this point, is reflected throughout the research process. For example, with both the initial grounded theory research and the community-based research that followed, we negotiated research agreements with participating communities in advance of applying for approval from university and health authority ethical review committees, established research advisory committees on which Elders serve (two on the first and four on the second), and took our direction from the Elders (see Clark et al., 2009, for discussion of similar strategies).

Disseminating Results With an Eye to Social Change

There is tremendous potential to shift power relations and celebrate diversity and difference in the dissemination phase through facilitating the voice of participants, sharing results with participants in plain/accessible language, publishing in multiple genres and forums in order to reach the broad audience of people who may benefit from having the information (De Vault, 1999; Fine et al., 2000; Kirby et al., 2006), and involving participants as co-authors. Fine et al. (2000) suggest that we can facilitate voice though the use of long narratives, underplaying hegemonic voices, and creating room for counter-hegemonic narratives. For me this has meant using quotes from persons living with dementia, although it may seem to be "word salad"; giving more narrative space to multiply oppressed persons with dementia than to multiply privileged ones; and stressing the voices of persons with dementia over those of their significant others and the literature (Hulko, 2009b).

At a minimum, researchers should prepare key findings and implications of the research in an accessible format and share this with all of the research participants. Whether oral or written, this may require leaving out some findings and/or rewording key phrases so as not to cause discomfort for the participants. This was the case with the Secwepemc views on dementia study, after which we were advised to remove any mention of residential schools from the one-page flyer, although Elders had identified this as a cause of dementia and most of the participants were residential school survivors (Hulko et al., 2010; see http://irsss.ca/irsss/). We were told that we could speak and write about residential schools in academic and professional venues, yet should not bring this back to the community as it could cause re-victimization. Moreover, discussing residential schools should be accompanied by ceremony—before and after—as many Elders did not survive residential schools and their spirits may be disturbed by evoking this traumatic period in Canada's recent history.

Co-authoring and co-presenting with research participants is another way to disseminate results with a view to social change, particularly when working with persons with low levels of literacy and formal education, such as First Nation Elders or minority ethnic older adults and those who are cognitively impaired, like persons with dementia, as it positions members of equity-seeking groups as meaning-makers and knowledge creators. I had the opportunity to co-present with both of the Elder advisors to the research mentioned above; they took turns traveling with me to other cities, provinces, and the United States. We assisted with a two-day training session for Aboriginal home care workers, gave a 90-minute colloquium to researchers and graduate students, attended a two-day academic conference, and facilitated a 90-minute workshop for healthcare practitioners. This was impactful not only for the Elders, but also for those who took part in each of these learning opportunities. This was made possible by shifting research funds away from researchers and toward Elders, receiving support from organizations (e.g., Interior Health, T'Kemlups te Secwepemc) to which research partners belonged, and requesting support for Elders to accompany researchers from external organizations when asked to speak to their staff.

Conclusion

This chapter discussed the following methodological strategies and tools associated with doing research differently and consistent with feminist social work research: being reflective and reflexive; sampling for diversity and equity; getting good data; facilitating voice in data collection and analysis; sharing ownership and control; and disseminating results with an eye to social change. Numerous examples from five research studies with equity-seeking groups were provided to demonstrate the ways in which intersectionality can be operationalized in feminist social work research. I argue that using strategies arising from and/or consistent with a solid theoretical framework like intersectionality and interlocking oppressions can ensure an ontologically coherent process and epistemologically sound results in research with equity-seeking groups.

Feminist methodology seeks to highlight the voices and experiences of women through recruiting women as opposed to or in addition to men (de Vault, 1999; Letherby, 2003) and employing methods like counter-storytelling (Delgado, 2011; Delgado & Stefancic, 2001), while critical feminist social work research aims to disrupt binaries like men and women and to embrace intersectionality (Wahab et al., 2012), which necessarily makes research more complex. Thus the latter is an extension of feminist methodology and is more reflective of recent articulations of feminism—queer, border, intersectional—as well as the longstanding importance of praxis to the discipline of social work. As the research featured in this chapter has shown, application of an intersectionality and interlocking oppressions theoretical framework to the research process can aid in making categories like insider/outsider and men/women more complex and result in quite different understandings of the social world. The purpose of research is to generate knowledge and, if we want knowledge to resonate with people from equity-seeking groups—even if it challenges what we believe about a social phenomenon such as dementia, as in the research with Secwepemc Elders, or a theoretical construct like intersectionality, as in the research with queer women—then we need to adapt our methods (Lather, 1991) and move beyond describing a sample as diverse when it is not composed entirely of "majoritarian"[7] women and men to actually analyzing the role that such diversity plays. This would ensure that theory and practice are in much closer dialogue and that, when social change occurs, it reflects the desires of people from equity-seeking groups.

Acknowledgments

This chapter and my approach to "doing research differently" began with my doctoral dissertation on dementia and intersectionality and evolved into this manuscript through a further eight years of conducting research with equity-seeking groups and teaching undergraduate students, community-based researchers, and practitioners how to do research. For their encouragement and critical questioning, I want to thank all my students in past BSW research and MEd diversity courses at Thompson Rivers University, members of my various research teams, and participants in the 2011 Intersectionality Spring Learning Institute, where I presented some of these ideas. The research discussed in this chapter was funded by the following sources: Michael Smith Foundation for Health Research, Interior Health, Thompson Rivers University, Social Sciences and Humanities Research Council of Canada, Women's Health Research Network, the BC Rural and Remote Health Research Network, and the University of Stirling Alumni Association.

Notes

1 Equity-seeking groups include the four "designated groups" named in federal (Canadian) Employment Equity legislation (Aboriginal Peoples, Persons with a Disability, Women, and Members of Visible Minorities: http://laws-lois.justice.gc.ca/eng/acts/E-5.401/index.html) in addition to sexual and/or gender minorities and other groups who are also subject to workplace discrimination and victimization.
2 I use feminist social work research and antioppressive research interchangeably as the latter is largely associated with social work (see Brown & Strega, 2005) and more explicitly concerned with "complexifying" the category of women and avoiding positioning the sex/gender system as primary.

3 This is a First Nation in the Interior of British Columbia, Canada.
4 Although 33 nurses were enrolled in the CSDC study and completed the pre-tests, only 15 completed the educational intervention and post-tests.
5 The questions were asked (and answers given) in Spanish, which I have omitted for ease of reading.
6 The participant referred to his specific disability, which has been masked to ensure anonymity.
7 This is another way of saying "mainstream" or dominant group in critical race theory; it counterposes "the majority" to "the minority" and indicates that the former imposes its values and beliefs on the latter through majority rule. In contrast to counter-storytelling, majoritarian storytelling is "the master narrative" often construed as history (Delgado, 2011; Delgado & Stefancic, 2001).

References

Absolon, K. (2011). *Kaandossiwin: How we come to know.* Halifax, NS: Fernwood.

Allan, K. (2001). *Communication and consultation: Exploring ways for staff to involve people with dementia in developing services.* Bristol, UK: The Policy Press.

Anderson-Nathe, B., Gringeri, C., & Wahab, S. (2013). Nurturing "critical hope" in teaching feminist social work research. *Journal of Social Work Education, 49* (2), 277–291.

Anthias, F. (2013). Intersectional what? Social divisions, intersectionality and levels of analysis. *Ethnicities, 13* (1), 3–19.

Baumgardner, J. (2011). *F'em!: Goo goo, gaga, and some thoughts on balls.* Berkeley, CA: Seal Press.

Becker, H. (1966). Whose side are we on? *Social Problems, 14* (1–4), 239–247.

Black, L. L. & Stone, D. (2005). Expanding the definition of privilege: The concept of social privilege. *Journal of Multicultural Counseling & Development, 33* (4), 243–255.

Bowleg, L. (2008). When black + lesbian + women = black lesbian woman: The methodological challenges of qualitative and quantitative intersectionality research. *Sex Roles, 59,* 312–325.

Brotman, S. & Kraniou, S. (1999). Ethnic and lesbian: Understanding identity through the life history approach. *Affilia, 14* (4), 417–438.

Brown, L. & Strega, S. (Eds). (2005). *Research as resistance: Critical, Indigenous and anti-oppressive approaches.* Toronto: Canadian Scholars' Press.

Carniol, B. (2010). *Case critical: Social services and social justice in Canada* (6th ed.). Toronto: Between the Lines.

Clark, N., Drolet, J., Arnouse, M., Walton, P., Tamburro, P., Mathews, N., Derrick, J., Michaud, V., & Armstrong, J. (2009). "Melq'ilwiye" coming together in an intersectional research team—Using narratives and cultural safety to transform Aboriginal Social Work and Human Service field education. *Pimatisiwin: A Journal of Aboriginal and Indigenous Community Health 7* (2), 291–315.

Combahee River Collective. (1977). *The Combahee River Collective statement.* Retrieved September 3, 2012 from http://zinelibrary.info/files/Combahee3.pdf.

Crenshaw, K. W. (1989). Demarginalizing the intersection of race and sex: A Black feminist critique of antidiscrimination doctrine, feminist theory and anti-racist politics. *University of Chicago Legal Forum,* 139–167.

D'Cruz, H. & Jones, M. (2004). *Social work research: Ethical and political contexts.* Thousand Oaks, CA: Sage.

De Vault, M.L. (1999). *Liberating method: Feminism and social research*. Philadelphia: Temple University Press.

Delgado, R. (2011). Rodrigo's reconsideration: Intersectionality and the future of critical race theory. *Iowa Law Review, 96*, 1247–1288.

Delgado, R. & Stefancic, J. (2001). *Critical race theory: An introduction*. New York: New York University Press.

Dewing, J. (2007). Participatory research: A method for process consent with persons who have dementia. *Dementia, 6* (1), 11–25.

Fine, M., Weis, L., Weseen, S., & Wong, L. (2000). For whom? Qualitative research, representations and social responsibilities. In N.K. Denzin & Y.S. Lincoln (Eds.), *Handbook of qualitative research* (2nd ed.) (pp. 107–131). Thousand Oaks, CA: Sage.

Freire, P. (2001). *Pedagogy of the oppressed* (30th Anniversary ed.). New York: Continuum.

Frisby, W. & Creese, G. (2011). Unpacking relationships in feminist community research: Cross-cutting themes. In G. Creese & W. Frisby (Eds.), *Feminist community research: Case studies and methodologies* (pp. 1–24). Vancouver: UBC Press.

Gringeri, C., Wahab, S., & Anderson-Nathe, B. (2010). What makes it feminist? Mapping the landscape of social work feminist research. *Affilia, 25* (4), 390–405.

Hankivsky, O. (Ed.). (2011) *Health inequities in Canada: Intersectional frameworks and practices* (pp. 198–220). Vancouver: UBC Press.

Harper, D. (2002). Talking about pictures: A case for photo elicitation. *Visual Studies, 17* (1), 13–26.

Hill Collins, P. (2000). *Black feminist thought: Knowledge, consciousness, and the politics of empowerment* (2nd ed.). New York: Routledge.

Hill Collins, P. (2012). Looking back, moving ahead: Scholarship in service to social justice. *Gender & Society, 26* (1), 14–22.

Hulko, W. (2009a). The time and context contingent nature of intersectionality and interlocking oppressions. *Affilia, 24* (1), 44–55.

Hulko, W. (2009b). From 'not a big deal' to 'hellish': Experiences of older people with dementia. *Journal of Aging Studies, 23*(3), 131–144.

Hulko, W. (2011). Intersectionality in the context of later life experiences of dementia. In O. Hankivsky (Ed.), *Health inequities in Canada: Intersectional frameworks and practices* (pp. 198–220). Vancouver: UBC Press.

Hulko, W. (2013, November). *'Es un privilegio ser Cubano': Las perspectivas de los adultos mayores que son miembros de los grupos en búsqueda de la equidad sobre el envejezimiento en Cuba*. Paper presentation at the Women in the 21st Century IX International Conference, Havana, Cuba.

Hulko, W. (forthcoming). Being queer in the small city. In C. Walmsley & T. Kading (Eds.), *Power and possibility in the small city*. Vancouver: UBC Press.

Hulko, W. & Hovanes, J. (forthcoming). Intersectionality in the lives of LGBTQ youth: Identifying and finding community in small cities and rural communities. *Journal of Homosexuality*.

Hulko, W., Camille, E., Antifeau, E., Arnouse, M., Bachynksi, N., & Taylor, D. (2010). Views of First Nation Elders on memory loss and memory care in later life. *Journal of Cross Cultural Gerontology, 25*, 317–342.

Kirby, S., Greaves, L., & Reid, C. (2006). *Experience, research, social change: Methods beyond the mainstream* (2nd ed.). Peterborough, Canada: Broadview Press.

Kovach, M. (2010). *Indigenous methodologies: Characteristics, conversations, and contexts*. Toronto: University of Toronto Press.

Lather, P. (1991). *Getting smart: Feminist research and pedagogy with/in the postmodern.* New York: Routledge.

Letherby, G. (2003). *Feminist research in theory and practice.* Buckingham, UK: Open University Press.

Marinucci, M. (2010). *Feminism is queer: The intimate connection between queer and feminist theory.* London: Zed Publishing.

Mehrotra, G. (2010). Toward a continuum of intersectionality theorizing for feminist social work scholarship. *Affilia, 25* (4), 417–430.

Morris, M. with Bunjun, B. (2007). *Using intersectional feminist frameworks in research: A resource for embracing the complexities of women's lives.* Ottawa: Canadian Research Institute for the Advancement of Women.

Murphy, Y., Hunt, V., Zajicek, A. M., Norris, A. N., & Hamilton, L. (2009). *Incorporating intersectionality in social work practice, research, policy, and education.* Washington, DC: NASW Press.

Potts, K. & Brown, L. (2005). Becoming an anti-oppressive researcher. In L. Brown & S. Strega (Eds.), *Research as resistance: Critical, Indigenous and anti-oppressive approaches* (pp. 255–286). Toronto: Canadian Scholars' Press.

Prosser, J. & Loxley, A. (2008, October). *ESRC National Centre for Research Methods review paper: Introducing visual methods.* Southampton, UK: National Centre for Research Methods.

Reid, C., Brief, E., & LeDrew, R. (2009). *Our common ground: Cultivating women's health through community based research.* Vancouver: Women's Health Research Network.

Schnarch, B. (2004). Ownership, control, access, and possession (OCAP) or self-determination applied to research: A critical analysis of contemporary First Nations research and some options for First Nations communities. *Journal of Aboriginal Health, January,* 80–95.

Stalker, K. (1998). Some ethical and methodological issues in research with people with learning difficulties. *Disability & Society, 13* (1), 5–19.

Tuhiwai Smith, L. (2012). *Decolonizing methodologies: Research and indigenous peoples* (2nd ed.). London: Zed Books.

Van de Sande, A. & Schwartz, K. (2011). *Research for social justice: A community-based approach.* Halifax, NS: Fernwood.

Varcoe, C., Brown, H., Calam, B., Buchanan, M., & Newman, V. (2011). Capacity building is a two-way street: Learning from doing research in Aboriginal communities. In G. Creese & W. Frisby (Eds.), *Feminist community research: Case studies and methodologies* (pp. 210–232). Vancouver: UBC Press.

Wahab, S., Anderson-Nathe, B., & Gringeri, C. (2012). Joining the conversation: Social work contributions to feminist research. In S. Hesse-Biber (Ed.), *Handbook of feminist research* (pp. 455–474). Los Angeles: Sage.

Wenger, C. (2002). Interviewing older people. In J.F. Gubrium & J.A. Holstein (Eds.), *Handbook of interview research: Context and method* (pp. 259–278). Thousand Oaks, CA: Sage.

Wilson, S. (2008). *Research is ceremony. Indigenous research methods.* Halifax, NS: Fernwood.

Wright Mills, C. (2000). *The sociological imagination* (40th anniversary ed.). Oxford: Oxford University Press.

Young, I.M. (1990). *Justice and the politics of difference.* Princeton, NJ: Princeton University Press.

6   Intersectional Feminism and Social Work Responses to Homelessness

Carole Zufferey

In this chapter, I reflect on the complexities of intersectionality when researching social work responses to homelessness. I argue that social work responses to homelessness are influenced by gendered, white, Western, and middle-class discourses, which are embodied and performed by social workers in their professional practice. As a white, Western, middle-class social work educator and practitioner, I continually question how my gender, class, and whiteness shape my worldview, grant me particular privileges, and inform my own professional social work practice in the area of homelessness (Zufferey, 2012). These questions contribute to my interest in researching how homelessness and social work responses to homelessness are constituted by gender, race, class, and power relations. An intersectional feminist approach is a useful lens for examining the complex and intersecting power dynamics in social workers' responses to homelessness. However, the "doing" of intersectional feminist research in the Australian context is complicated and contested.

I began exploring and thinking about the notion of intersectionality during an earlier research project on the perspectives and identities of Aboriginal and non-Aboriginal people who experience homelessness (Zufferey & Kerr, 2004). I completed this research in 2001 while I was a social work practitioner in the field of homelessness in Adelaide, South Australia. This was my initial engagement with how experiences and perceptions of home and homelessness were influenced by diverse racialized, classed, and gendered social identities. These social categories of disadvantage are embodied, interactional, relational, and embedded in social structures and normative social work practices, despite the central aim of social work, which is to be inclusive of diverse client groups and diverse service providers working in the field of homelessness. This raised some dilemmas for me about being a white, Western, and middle-class social worker exploring other people's lives. When researching homelessness in Australia and as a social work practitioner in the field of homelessness, I became quite conscious of the intersecting discriminatory influences of class, gender, and racial background on social work responses to homelessness. Feminist intersectionality offered a means by which research on social policy and practice approaches to homelessness could be more responsive to the interrelationships of gender, race, class, sexuality, relationship status, age, health status, ethnicity, and other social divisions (Damant et al., 2008).

Social work is frequently questioned for being ethnocentric because social work is a culturally and historically embedded activity that exists within white institutions, unequal social relations, and taken-for-granted dimensions of power (Briskman, 2003; Pease, 2010; Quinn, 2003; Walter, Taylor, & Habibis, 2011). This creates tensions for me related to researching social work in Australia within a predominantly white and racist society and with predominantly white social work participants. However, intersectional theorists have also pointed to the importance of researching whiteness and the masculinity of majority groups, to include all members of society and to question the "imagined normality" of the majority (Christensen & Jensen, 2012, p.112). This "majority inclusive" principle points to the need to research the discourses and lived experiences of privileged populations (such as social workers) and how these privileges shape daily interactions within unequal power relations (Christensen & Jensen, 2012; Frankenberg, 1993). This inspired me to conduct research on the experiences of privileged populations, which in this context was social workers employed in the field of homelessness (Frankenberg, 1993). As well, feminist social work research tends to focus on feminism as an approach that is "by, about and for women" (Wahab, Anderson-Nathe, & Gringeri, 2012, p. 459). While this is valuable in understanding the experiences of women and giving voice to marginalized and disadvantaged women, involving both men and women as subjects in research enables researchers to examine the embodiment and constructions of both masculinity and femininity (Connell, 2002; Pease, 2011). Therefore, a component of my PhD study explored how gender and power are constituted in the lives and work of both male and female social workers, employed in policy and frontline practice responses to homelessness in Australia. This chapter particularly reflects on the complexities and tensions I experienced as a feminist researcher engaging with intersectional theory when researching social work responses to homelessness in Australia (see also Zufferey, 2009). Next, to contextualize social work and homelessness in Australia, I briefly examine Australian feminist, social work, and social policy contexts.

The Australian Context

Australian feminist authors, such as Lake (1999) and Summers (2002), argue that feminist activism in Australia occurred within dominant and normative assumptions of masculinity. Summers's (2002) classic book *Damned Whores and God's Police. The Colonisation of Women in Australia* discusses how women from working-class backgrounds were constructed as "whores" and middle-class women, who often volunteered as "social workers," as "God's police." Feminist activism has made important social, political, and economic gains for most women. However, both feminism and social work have been criticized for being dominated by white, Western, and middle-class discourses (Leonard, 1997; Moreton-Robinson, 2009; Orme, 2003). An analysis of "whiteness" and white privilege has been invisible in "mainstream" social work and feminism, as they struggle to incorporate notions of power and diversity (Kemp & Brandwein, 2010). Social workers have also been criticized for adapting to the contemporary neo-liberal context that focuses on individual responsibility and for neglecting its activist roots (Gordon & Zufferey, 2013; Zufferey, 2008). Furthermore, the contemporary Western-based curricula in social work education continue to raise questions about whose values, traditions, practices, and knowledges are being privileged (Holtzhausen, 2011; Roberts & Smith, 2002). The production of knowledge in academia has also been contained within normative, predominantly white, masculine, and middle-class institutionalized structures (Dill & Kohlman, 2012).

In the Australian context, the sense of belonging and home enjoyed by Australian colonizers and migrants is based on the "dispossession of the original owners of the land" and the denial of the rights of Indigenous peoples (Moreton-Robinson, 2003, p. 23). Aboriginal Australians are the most disadvantaged group in Australia on a wide range of socioeconomic indicators such as health, income, education, employment, and housing. Social work has been criticized for being involved in "racist, patronizing and unjust practices" that continue to disadvantage Aboriginal communities (Green & Baldry, 2008, p. 389). Social work academics, policy makers, and practitioners have been slow to engage with Indigenous knowledges and "theorizing," and in acknowledging white race privilege (Briskman, 2003). Despite this, according to Australian census and service data, Aboriginal and Torres Strait Islander people are overrepresented in the Australian homelessness statistics. Aboriginal Australians are four times more likely to experience homelessness than non-Indigenous Australians; twice as likely to sleep rough, or in improvised dwellings and shelters; their rate of home ownership is a third compared to two-thirds for non-Indigenous Australians; and they are ten times more likely to live in overcrowded housing conditions (Australian Institute of Health and Welfare (AIHW), 2011). These statistics point to the need to examine homelessness from a multilevel analysis that is inclusive of the historical effects of racism, Indigenous dispossession, and colonization in Australia.

Furthermore, the main cause of women's homelessness is (gendered) domestic and family violence, and Indigenous women experience up to 38 times the rate of hospitalization compared to other females for spouse/domestic partner-inflicted assaults (Al-Yaman, Van Doeland, & Wallis, 2006). In 2011, the Australian census data identified 105,237 people as experiencing homelessness, which was just under 49 out of 10,000 people, that is, one in every 200 Australians (Australian Bureau of Statistics (ABS), 2012; Homelessness Australia, 2012). The proportion of females who reported being homeless in the census increased from 43% in 2006 to 44% in 2011 (Homelessness Australia, 2012). However, 51% of people staying in homelessness-supported accommodation and 57% of people staying in other temporary lodging (such as hotels/motels on vouchers) were females (Homelessness Australia, 2012). Passaro (1996, p. 2) argues that women who are homeless are more likely to be assisted by services if the woman performs her femininity according to dominant gendered paradigms, as "dependent, frightened and vulnerable." As well, unequal gender and power relations and the responsibility of perpetrators (who are predominantly men) are rarely examined in Australian homelessness policies (Zufferey, 2009). Therefore, community "attitudes within the context of familial, organisational, community and social norms which support violence against women" are left unquestioned (Pease & Flood, 2008, p. 547).

Social policy and practice responses to homelessness are a microcosm of dominant gendered power relationships that operate at a broader societal level. Despite the emergence of violence against women in the Australian political domain since the 1970s (Weeks & Gilmore, 1996), policy and practice responses to social problems such as homelessness have been criticized for being gender-neutral and "reductionist and incremental" (Manuel, 2006, p. 164). Current policy definitions, implementation, and contracting processes are narrow and prohibitive, frequently leading to contracting services for prescribed "one size fits all" strategies, which are presumed to produce required outcomes, such as "housing the homeless" (Horsell, 2006; Zufferey & Kerr, 2004). Social policy also conceptualizes "home" as a place of "safety and security" and homelessness is characterized as "residential instability" and "rooflessness" (Tomas & Dittmar, 1995, p. 493). This assumes that housing is the solution and homelessness is the problem, ignoring diverse and contested meanings and experiences of home and homelessness (Somerville, 1992). The paradox for many women is that, whilst "home" should be a place of safety, violence in the home is the main reason for their homelessness. However, "gender-blind" policy and legislation continue to ignore or neutralize gender and women's experiences of homelessness (Phillips, 2006). Policy responses to homelessness are rarely linked to (unequal) gendered power relations, nor do they always acknowledge that domestic and family violence is generally perpetrated by men.

Historically, Australian government policies have not focused on gendered inequalities and community responses to homelessness and domestic violence but on individual responsibility and "the family" as a site for intervention. Conservative national government policies in Australia during the Howard years (1996–2007) explicitly promoted de-gendered, pro-family, neo-liberal, and socially conservative values (Murray & Powell, 2009; Oberin, 2009; Phillips, 2006). Whilst there continue to be women's policy units and sections within Australian government bureaucracies, the emphasis on policy mainstreaming and gender-neutral policies means that "women's policy issues" can be invisible or reduced to a "risk" factor in social policy problem analysis (Phillips, 2006). Therefore, policy and practice responses to homelessness can reinforce deep-seated community values that maintain unequal gender and power relations, by not addressing important gendered issues that cause homelessness for women and children. This gendered analysis of the policy and practice context of homelessness set the scene for intersectional feminist research on social work and homelessness in Australia. Next, I provide a very brief overview of my Australian social work research.

Researching Social Work and Homelessness

When researching social work responses to homelessness in Australia I asked social workers how they thought their practices, in the homelessness policy area or "frontline" service delivery, were influenced by their cultural background, gender, and class. This study used a qualitative methodology, involving face-to-face, semi-structured interviews, which enabled an indepth analysis of the influences on social work practice in the field of homelessness. I interviewed a total of 39 social workers employed in homelessness services in Adelaide, Melbourne, and Sydney, Australia. People employed in homelessness services may call themselves "social workers" but not be university-trained in "social work." To set the parameters for this research, only social workers who were professionally trained and eligible for membership of the Australian Association of Social Workers (AASW) were invited to participate in this research. Furthermore, out of the 39 social work participants, 19 worked in a "not for profit" or non-government organization, 13 worked for government services (such as hospitals, mental health, drug and alcohol services), and seven worked as policy or project workers in state, local government, and advocacy services. A total of eight participants were employed in gender-specific services such as male (three participants) and female residential accommodation or health services (five participants). The social workers interviewed worked across diverse organizational settings and the influence of neo-liberal sociopolitical and organizational contexts was evident in the findings (Zufferey, 2008).

The influences of gender, age, experience, cultural background, and class on the processes of personal and professional identity construction can be invisible (Holstein & Gubrium, 2000). It is therefore important to make visible the demographics of the sample group. The sample group consisted of ten men and 29 women, which is reflective of the gender differences of practicing social workers in Australia (Lewis, 2004; McCormack, 2001, p. 68). The majority of the group were over 30 years old and had more than five years' post-qualifying experience. The findings indicated that, in general, social workers were aware of the often invisible influences of power, gender, class, and cultural background on their practices as social workers in the field of homelessness. The diverse and intersecting influences on social workers in the field of homelessness included personal experiences of oppression related to gender, class, migration, and "being a refugee," as well as variable commitments to professional values and practices, such as feminist social work approaches to homelessness (Zufferey, 2009).

The cultural and family backgrounds of participants were diverse, and included identifying as being "European Australian," Latvian, Polish, Chilean, Greek, Italian, Lebanese, and Yugoslavian, as well as "Anglo Australian," such as Irish and English. However, the sample was predominantly white and of Anglo/Celtic origin; only ten participants were of European origin, and two were from South America and Asia. These 12 participants discussed the significant influence their refugee and family migration experiences had on their social work practice. Three participants spoke of their own or families' experiences of being oppressed because of their refugee status and cultural background and how this influenced their practice and empathy as social workers. For example, one worker from a refugee background spoke of her experiences of being abused because of her cultural background and constructed as the "other" due to racial differences. She said that this gave her empathy with marginalized population groups such as "homeless people": "I was an outsider when I arrived . . . I know about outsiders who are homeless people . . . I'm a wog . . . I was abused as a child as a wog" (Interview 15).

Another social worker, whose family were refugees because they "fought for social justice and human rights" in their country of origin, said that, since being a young person, the refugee community has helped each other:

A big part of my life . . . fighting for social justice and human rights . . . helping refugees . . . doing community work without even being paid for it . . . that has continued on and that is what comes through my work at the moment [with homeless people]. (Interview 35)

This highlights how cultural and racial background influences social workers' engagement with the social justice values of social work and their responses and commitments to working in the field of homelessness. The research findings of this study, which examined how social workers themselves embody and perform gender, power, and class relations in their responses to homelessness, have been reported elsewhere (Zufferey, 2009).

I analyzed the research data using an intersectional thematic analysis, which identified and reported patterns and "meaningful essences" within the interviews (Braun & Clarke, 2006; Morse, 2008). This intersectional analysis combined Connell's (2002) theories of gender, masculinity, and femininity, and feminist intersectionality (Zufferey, 2009). Connell's (2002) framework of gender relations include: production relations (sexual divisions of labor), emotional relations (such as emotional attachments, heterosexual dominance, and emotional labor), symbolic relations (such as the social meaning and appearance of gender), and power relations (such as gender and power in social work institutions and social work practice).

These dimensions interrelate discursively to constitute power relations and gender identities. Discursive construction refers to how language or discourses define knowledge, are related to context, and embody power relations (Burr, 1995; Franzway, 2004).

Intersectionality is the overarching theory that enables the analysis of diverse and intersecting influences on social workers' responses to homelessness. Intersectional feminism has emerged as a theoretical perspective for recognizing multiple layers of disadvantage, examining how power relations and social categories of gender, race, class, religion, sexuality, age, and other markers of identity intersect, to constitute social meaning and practices in "everyday life" (Christensen & Jensen, 2012; Gressgård, 2008; Manuel, 2006). Drawing on intersectionality theory to examine how gender, power, and class intersected in the data (Zufferey, 2009) offered a complex understanding of how power operates variously and diffusely in people's lives, moving the analysis beyond hierarchies of disadvantage. The intersectional feminist approach complicates the social work response to homelessness by examining the discursive constructions and heterogeneity of people's lives, including the lives of "homeless people" and social workers, without disregarding the material reality and "risk" of homelessness due to socioeconomic positions of power.

When conducting my analyses of the data I wanted to move beyond "individualized politics" (Nixon & Humphreys, 2010) that focus entirely on interrelated identity categories such as gender, class, and ethnicity in social workers' personal and professional identities. Social relations are complex. Multiple identities intersect and are influenced by social structures, organizations, and social institutions, the processes of identity construction, as well as cultural symbols and discursive representations of social problems (Winker & Degele, 2011). Therefore, in retrospect, my analysis was consistent with Winker and Degele's multilayered intersectional analysis, which examines social structures, constructions of identities, and symbolic representations of social issues. This involves socially locating and positioned social work and homelessness within organizational contexts and social institutions that are unequal, multilayered, dynamic, and complex. For example, in social work organizational contexts, dichotomous powerless/powerful identities are constructed in client–worker relationships, which engage with symbolic representations of social work and homelessness in the media (Passaro, 1996; Webb, 2000; Winker & Degele, 2011). This was evident when I examined print media representations of homelessness that framed constructions of homelessness as a social problem to be "fixed" by service providers such as social workers (Zufferey & Chung, 2006). However, social workers are involved in resisting as well as supporting dominant social institutions and inequalities. This challenges "one size fits all" policies often inadvertently used in policy-making decisions, which are often criticized by people who experience homelessness and frontline social workers (Winker & Degele, 2011; Zufferey, 2008, 2009, 2012; Zufferey & Chung, 2006; Zufferey & Kerr, 2004).

Critically Examining Intersectional Categorical Complexities

Feminist social work research informed by intersectionality enables social workers to recognize, examine, reflect on, and address complex and multiple layers of "oppression," including race, ethnicity, culture, gender, class, sexuality, age, and ability (Dill & Kohlman, 2012). However, the complexities involved in designing an intersectional feminist research project and applying an intersectional analysis can be overwhelming and difficult to articulate. The challenges posed by engaging in intersectional research related to categorical complexities, researching and constructing multiple axes of social division and the contested theorizing of intersectional analysis (Christensen & Jensen, 2012; McCall, 2005; Winker & Degele, 2011).

Despite my assertion of the merits of intersectionality, a number of questions were raised for me about the categorical complexities involved in doing intersectional feminist research. These complexities relate to whether the research is anti-categorical, intra-categorical, and inter-categorical (Christensen & Jensen, 2012; McCall, 2005). An anti-categorical focus examines how concepts, terms, and categories are constructed, problematizing the process of categorization, which aligns with post-structural feminist understandings. For example, I am currently researching intersectionality and meanings of home and homelessness by examining the dynamic interplay between gender, race, class, and age in shaping notions of belonging and connections to home, to deconstruct dominant policy definitions of home and homelessness. Intra-categorical research takes identity categories into account but acknowledges that identities are fluid and multiple, tending to focus on "neglected points of intersection" and on individuals at the micro level (McCall, 2005; Winker & Degele, 2011). For example, when I asked social workers about the influences on their personal and professional identities, this focused on the individual social worker and how she or he embodied power, gender, class, and cultural relations (Zufferey, 2009). Inter-categorical research examines the relationship between different categories and "multiple inequalities between socially constructed groups," which is also often used in quantitative research (McCall, 2005; Winker & Degele, 2011, p. 53). This approach focuses on the relationship between categories where existing categorical differences are predefined and can be used to document and measure inequality across multiple dimensions and how categories and inequalities change over time. Intersectional research involves a macro political analysis of the structural positioning of social groupings (Winker & Degele, 2011). For example, in 1977 the Combahee River Collective promoted a "Black Feminist Statement," which outlined women's political, sexual, and economic oppression, marking the beginning of intersectionality work

(Kemp & Brandwein, 2010). Critical race theorists (such as Crenshaw, 1990; hooks, 2000) have emphasized how Black women's experiences of oppression are located in the interconnections of gender, race, and class. However, Yuval-Davis (2012, p. 48) cautions us against constructing "hierarchies of oppression" and calls for a dialogue between people from different positionings (Collins, 1990), which would be an ideal process when designing intersectional research projects.

A second dilemma in designing intersectional feminist research related to deciding what actual social categories are going to be focused on in the research study and why. Should I examine gender, ethnicity, race, religion, class, age, sexuality, ability, physical location, or other social division? The endless list of potential categories can be overwhelming and researchers can under-theorise key historical markers of social inequality such as class, race, and gender (Yuval-Davis, 2006), or conflate these categories (Bryant & Hoon, 2006). As Gressgård (2008) asks: "Could it be that the terminology of intersectionality, which includes the key concepts 'complexity' and 'multiplicity,' actually obscures more than it reveals, when it comes to dealing with difference?" (p. 1). When designing intersectional research, what categories do I privilege and what categories do I make invisible? How do social work researchers continue to construct and essentialize what inequalities do or do not matter, constituting who remains "at the margins"? In retrospect, I have tended to focus on commonly examined categories such as power, gender, class, and culture, rendering invisible other neglected social categories, such as sexuality, religion, age, disability, geographical location, places, and spaces (McDowell, 1999).

Another dilemma in doing intersectional research relates to how complexities are reported and analyzed. Intersectionality involves researchers thinking simultaneously at the level of structures, dynamics, and subjectivities (Carbin & Edenheim, 2013). My intersectional research is multidimensional, examining social structures, diverse constructions of identities, and symbolic representations of social work and homelessness (Winker & Degele, 2011). Social categories such as class, race, and gender are ontologically different, with variable effects at a structural and identity level (Christensen & Jensen, 2012). These social categories cannot be treated as independent and are always mutually constitutive (Christensen & Jensen, 2012; Phoenix & Pattynama, 2006). However, when analyzing "difference" it is difficult for social work researchers to resist constructing additive, compounding ideas of disadvantage, given that the purpose of social work has historically been related to empowerment and addressing injustice affecting socially disadvantaged groups (AASW, 2010). Christensen and Jensen (2012) argue that a life story narrative analysis can examine "the complex process of identification and positioning," by focusing on both "actual information" about social structures and institutions, as well as how social categories intersect in the "discursive construction of meaning" (p. 114). Feminist social work researchers who engage in intersectional research have to take into consideration these complexities when designing and analyzing their research projects.

Conclusion

Carbin and Edenheim (2013) argue that "today intersectionality is no longer just a metaphor. It is presented as *the* feminist theory" (p. 13). Social work researchers using intersectional theory negotiate this complex terrain to find a way of researching social issues that suits their personal and professional values and the aims of the study they wish to pursue. Social work authors Murphy, Hunt, Zajicek, Norris, and Hamilton (2009) note that intersectionality provides a holistic and systems-focused perspective, which is consistent with social work's commitment to social justice. Despite the complexities discussed in this chapter, I have found that intersectionality is useful for examining how social identity categories and structured power and gender relations interplay to constitute social work responses to homelessness. Social workers' personal and professional identities are embodied and constructed within interrelated and diverse institutionalized discourses. Both structural and individual considerations influence social workers' engagement with the social justice values of social work, informing activist responses to inequalities, such as homelessness. Further intersectional research is indicated, which examines other axes of social division in more depth, to include a theorizing of Indigeneity, sexuality, ability, and age, in the research area of social work and homelessness.

References

Al-Yaman, F., Van Doeland, M., & Wallis, M. (2006). *Family violence among Aboriginal and Torres Strait Islander peoples.* Australian Institute of Health and Welfare (AIHW), Canberra, pp. 54–55. Retrieved 21 July 2011 from http://www.aihw.gov.au/publication-detail/?id=6442467912.

Australian Association of Social Workers (AASW). (2010). *Code of ethics.* Retrieved 10 March 2012 from http://www.aasw.asn.au/document/item/740.

Australian Bureau of Statistics (ABS). (2012). *Census of population and housing: estimating homelessness* (2011). ABS Catalogue no. 2049.0. Canberra: Commonwealth of Australia.

Australian Institute of Health and Welfare (AIHW). (2011). *Housing and homelessness services: Access for Aboriginal and Torres Strait Islander people.* Catalogue no. HOU 237. Canberra: AIHW.

Braun, V. & Clarke, V. (2006). Using thematic analysis in psychology. *Qualitative Research in Psychology*, 3, 77–101.

Briskman, L. (2003). Indigenous Australians: Towards postcolonial social work. In J. Allan, B. Pease, & L. Briskman (Eds.), *Critical social work* (pp. 92–106). Crows Nest, NSW, Australia: Allen and Unwin.

Bryant, L. & Hoon, E. (2006). How can the intersections between gender, class and sexuality be translated to an empirical agenda? *International Journal of Qualitative Methods*, 5 (1), 1–12.

Burr, V. (1995). *An introduction to social constructionism.* London: Routledge.

Carbin, M. & Edenheim, S. (2013). The intersectional turn in feminist theory: A dream of a common language? *European Journal of Women's Studies* Published online 20 May 2013 DOI: 10.1177/1350506813484723.

Christensen, A. & Jensen, S. (2012). Doing intersectional analysis: Methodological implications for qualitative research. *Nordic Journal of Feminist and Gender Research, 20* (2), 109–125.

Collins, P. H. (1990). *Black feminist thought: Knowledge, consciousness, and the politics of empowerment.* New York: Routledge.

Connell, R.W. (2002). *Gender.* London: Polity Press.

Crenshaw, K. (1990). Mapping the margins: Intersectionality, identity politics, and violence against women of color. *Stanford Law Review, 43,* 1241–1299.

Damant, D., Lapierre, S., Kouraga, A., Fortin, A., Hamelin-Brabant, L., Lavergne, C., et al. (2008). Taking child abuse and mothering into account: Intersectional feminism as an alternative for the study of domestic violence. *Affilia, 23,* 123–133.

Dill, B.T. & Kohlman, M.H. (2012). Intersectionality. In S. Hesse-Biber (Ed.), *Handbook of feminist research* (pp. 154–171). Los Angeles: Sage.

Frankenberg, R. (1993). *White women, race matters: The social construction of whiteness.* Minneapolis: University of Minnesota Press.

Franzway, S. (2004). *Sexual politics and greedy institutions.* Melbourne: Pluto Press.

Gordon, L. & Zufferey, C. (2013). Working with diversity in a neoliberal environment. *Advances in Social Work and Welfare Education, 15,* 20–30.

Green, S. & Baldry, E. (2008). Building indigenous Australian social work. *Australian Social Work, 61* (4), 389–402.

Gressgård, R. (2008). Mind the gap: Intersectionality, complexity and 'the event'. *Theory & Science, 10,* 1–16.

Holstein, J. A. & Gubrium, J. F. (2000). *The self we live by: Narrative identity in a postmodern world.* New York: Oxford University Press.

Holtzhausen, L. (2011). When values collide: Finding common ground for social work education in the United Arab Emirates. *International Social Work, 54* (2), 191–208.

Homelessness Australia. (2012). *Sector briefing: 2011 Census night homelessness estimates,* 13 November 2012, 1–10.

hooks, b. (2000). *Feminist theory: From margins to center.* Boston: South End Press.

Horsell, C. (2006). Homelessness and social exclusion: A Foucauldian perspective for social workers. *Australian Social Work, 59* (2), 213–225.

Kemp, S. & Brandwein, R. (2010). Feminisms and social work in the United States: An intertwined history. *Affilia, 25* (4), 341–364.

Lake, M. (1999). *Getting equal. The history of Australian feminism.* Sydney: Allen and Unwin.

Leonard, P. (1997). *Postmodern welfare: Reconstructing an emancipatory project.* London: Sage.

Lewis, I. (2004). Gender and professional identity: A qualitative study of social workers practicing as counsellors and psychotherapists. *Australian Social Work, 57,* 394–407.

Manuel, T. (2006). Envisioning the possibility for a good life: Exploring the public policy implications of intersectionality theory. *Journal of Women, Politics and Policy, 28* (3–4), 173–203.

McCall, L. (2005). The complexity of intersectionality. *Signs: Journal of Women in Culture and Society, 30* (3), 1771–1800.

McCormack, J. (2001). How many social workers now? A review of census and other data. *Australian Social Work, 54,* 63–72.

McDowell, L. (1999). *Gender, identity and place. Understanding feminist geographies.* Oxford: Polity Press.

Moreton-Robinson, A. (2003). I still call Australia home: Indigenous belonging and place in a white postcolonizing society. In S. Ahmed, C. Castaneda, A. Fortier, & M. Sheller (Eds.), *Uprootings/regroundings: Questions of home and migration* (pp. 23–40). Oxford: Berg Publishers.

Moreton-Robinson, A. (2009). *Talkin' up to the white woman.* St Lucia, Australia: University of QLD Press.

Morse, J. (2008). Editorial: Confusing categories and themes. *Qualitative Health Research,* 18, 727–728.

Murphy, Y., Hunt, V., Zajicek, A.M., Norris, A.N., & Hamilton, L. (2009). *Incorporating intersectionality in social work practice, research, policy, and education.* Washington DC: National Association of Social Workers (NASW) Press.

Murray, S. & Powell, A. (2009). What's the problem? Australian public policy constructions of domestic and family violence. *Violence Against Women, 15* (5), 532–552.

Nixon, J. & Humphreys, C. (2010). Marshalling the evidence: Using intersectionality in the domestic violence frame. *Social Politics, 17* (2), 137–158.

Oberin, J. (2009). Homelessness and violence against women in Australia: The road home or blind alleys? *Parity, 22* (10), 17–19.

Orme, J. (2003). 'It's feminist because I say so!': Feminism, social work and critical practice in the UK. *Qualitative Social Work, 2* (2), 131–153.

Passaro, J. (1996). *The unequal homeless: Men on the streets, women in their place.* New York: Routledge.

Pease, B. (2010). *Undoing privilege: Unearned advantage in a divided world.* London: Zed Books.

Pease, B. (2011). Men in social work: Challenging or reproducing an unequal gender regime? *Affilia, 26* (4), 406–418.

Pease, B. & Flood, M. (2008). Rethinking the significance of attitudes in preventing men's violence against women. *Australian Journal of Social Issues, 43* (4), 547–561.

Phillips, R. (2006). Undoing an activist response: feminism and the Australian government's domestic violence policy. *Critical Social Policy, 26* (1), 192–219.

Phoenix, A. & Pattynama, P. (2006). Intersectionality. *European Journal of Women's Studies, 13,* 187–192.

Quinn, M. (2003). Immigrants and refugees: Towards anti racist and culturally affirming practices. In J. Allan, B. Pease & L. Briskman (Eds.), *Critical social work* (pp. 75–91). Crows Nest, Australia: Allen and Unwin.

Roberts, T.L. & Smith, L.A. (2002). The illusion of inclusion: An analysis of approaches to diversity within predominantly white schools of social work. *Journal of Teaching in Social Work, 22* (3), 189–211.

Somerville, P. (1992). Homelessness and the meaning of home: Rooflessness or rootlessness? *International Journal of Urban and Regional Research, 16* (4), 529–538.

Summers, A. (2002). *Damned whores and God's police. The colonisation of women in Australia.* Ringwood, Victoria, Australia: Penguin Books.

Tomas, A. & Dittmar, H. (1995). The experience of homeless women: An exploration of housing histories and the meaning of home. *Housing Studies, 10* (4), 493–513.

Wahab, S., Anderson-Nathe, B., & Gringeri, C. (2012). Joining the conversation: Social work contributions to feminist research. In S. Hesse-Biber (Ed.), *Handbook of Feminist Research* (pp. 455–474). Los Angeles: Sage.

Walter, M., Taylor, S., & Habibis, D. (2011). How White is social work in Australia? *Australian Social Work, 64* (1), 6–19.

Webb, S. (2000). The politics of social work: Power and subjectivity. *Critical Social Work, 1,* 1–10.

Weeks, W. & Gilmore, K. (1996). How violence against women became an issue on the national policy agenda. In T. Dalton, M. Draper, W. Weeks, & J. Wiseman (Eds.), *Making social policy in Australia* (pp. 141–153). St. Leonards, Australia: Allen and Unwin.

Winker, G. & Degele, N. (2011). Intersectionality as multi-level analysis: Dealing with social inequality. *European Journal of Women's Studies, 18* (1), 51–66.

Yuval-Davis, N. (2006). Intersectionality and feminist politics. *European Journal of Women's Studies, 13* (3), 93–209.

Yuval-Davis, N. (2012). Dialogical epistemology: An intersectional resistance to the "Oppression Olympics." *Gender & Society, 26,* 46–64.

Zufferey, C. (2008). Responses to homelessness in Australian cities: Social worker perspectives. *Australian Social Work, 61* (4), 356–370.

Zufferey, C. (2009). Making gender visible: Social work responses to homelessness. *Affilia, 24* (4), 382–393.

Zufferey, C. (2012). 'Not knowing that I do not know and not wanting to know': Reflections of a white Australian social worker. *International Social Work,* published online 17 May 2012 DOI: 10.1177/0020872812436624.

Zufferey, C. & Chung, D. (2006). Representations of homelessness in the Australian print media: Some implications for social policy. *Just Policy, 42,* 33–38.

Zufferey, C. & Kerr, L. (2004). Identity and everyday experiences of homelessness: Some implications for social work. *Australian Social Work, 57* (4), 343–353.

7 Borderlands as a Critical Feminist Perspective in Social Work Research

K. D. Hudson

Critical feminisms seem to have an occasional and contested home in social work research (see Gringeri, Wahab, & Anderson-Nathe, 2010). As an epistemological and theoretical perspective that tiptoes around disciplinary boundaries and thresholds of acceptability/acceptance, there are perhaps few more fitting frameworks for characterizing the estranged relationship between critical feminism and social work research than the "borderlands." In fact, borderlands have emerged as a necessary conceptual and interpretive tool in my work largely due to the ways my biographical landscape and epistemic politics intersect with a general failure of the field to seriously take up certain paradigmatic imperatives related to the lived experience. In this chapter, I will introduce one conceptualization of a borderlands framework for social work research. An experimental, hybrid feminist theoretical and epistemological framework, a borderlands perspective has enabled me to approach my work with a multidisciplinary set of tools, allowing for contributions to social work knowledge and knowledge building at multiple levels.

As I will further explore in this chapter, the genealogy of a borderlands perspective is largely grounded in the work of Latino/a scholars, Chicana feminists, and philosophers from the global South. In the Council on Social Work Education's (CSWE) 2007 report from *Taskforce on Latinos/as in Social Work*, the authors explored and began to explain the underrepresentation of Latina/o faculty in social work. This report named ideological dislocation, or "the lack of fit between the academic value base and one's personal orientation," as an obstacle facing Latinos/as, who in 2004 comprised approximately 5% of social work faculty across rank and type of program (CSWE, 2007, pp. 17–18; Le-Doux, 1996). The underrepresentation of Latino/a social work faculty has remained steady over the past 20 years, and, according to the CSWE report, there are no strong indications that there will be a dramatic change in the near future.

The lack of representation of Latino/a scholars and other scholars of color, as well as other minoritized scholars, such as feminist, indigenous, queer, and trans* scholars in social work faculty positions, is part of a broader set of issues facing ideological and epistemological departures from positivism and (what author bell hooks and others might call) the "imperialist white supremacist heteropatriarchical" norms of the academy. However, the problem is also in the standard and often singular solution to the "diversity problem," namely the recruitment and retention of traditionally underrepresented faculty. These efforts may help address the lack of structural diversity, but they give no promises of addressing the problems of ideological isolation and paradigm disagreement, which may marginalize the perspective of some scholars across and beyond particular identity groups. For example, some queer and of color-identified academics fit, and are socialized to fit, comfortably within dominant paradigms of social work research. In this chapter, I hope to provoke feminist social work scholars to consider the ideological deserts that are most prevalent and relevant to their work and context, and to consider the importance in creating ideological havens for diverse perspectives, knowledges, and relationships to social work research.

With this in mind, I will first discuss my perspective as a critical feminist social work scholar. Specifically, I explore limitations I acknowledged and considered when constructing a borderlands framework, as well as the commitments I wanted to center and uphold in my work. Next I will introduce a recent study about community belongingness and well-being that I conducted with queer-identified, mixed-race adults as an example of an application of a borderlands framework. Following that, I will present the theoretical "pool" from which I draw and reflect on how each theory serves a particular purpose as heuristic tools and analytic resources. Included in this theoretical pool are: (1) borderland epistemology, which considers the relationship between knowledge and colonization, and the emergence of hybrid knowledges (Mignolo, 2000); (2) transnational feminism, providing insights into systems of dominance and resistance, with specific attention paid to interstitial power configurations, discontinuity, and flexibility (e.g., Mohanty, 2003; Swarr & Nagar, 2010); (3) Chicana feminism, purposed to think of the body and sexuality as subversive tools (e.g., Anzaldúa, 1987; Hurtado, 2003); and (4) postcolonial studies, positioned to shift voice, context, and power, and to explore "other" possibilities (e.g., Alexander, 2008).

Concluding this chapter, I will engage in a nascent discussion of how a borderlands framework might promote the critical feminist agenda of giving attention to and resisting oppressive, colonial gestures of social work research and practice, including giving voice to voiceless subjects, ensuring authority of the researcher/practitioner, and rescuing disempowered clients (Deepak, 2012). I also discuss specific methodological and analytic features of my work resulting from a borderlands framework. Finally, I will suggest that such a framework stretches feminist theory in social work to consider epistemological standpoints and worldviews from what Gloria Anzaldúa called a "perspective from the cracks" between worlds (in Keating, 2005).

Arriving at a Borderlands Framework

Since the beginning of my formal education in social work, I have been both fascinated and perplexed by articulations of sameness and differences in intentionally diverse spaces, and by the idea that talking about multiple identities and oppression could be a transformative moment that enhances collaborative efforts for social change. However, a reliance upon dichotomous, binary thinking—privilege–oppression, insider–outsider, service provider–client, white–of color, gay–straight—was both apparent and problematic for me as someone committed to mixed-race, queer, and trans* communities as both a member and an ally. This brought me to my interest in liminality and, in particular, borderlands and other in-between spaces. As a feminist scholar continually engaged in discourses related to race, gender, and sexuality, both personally and professionally, I wanted my work to disrupt "business as usual" in research in communities—especially queer of color communities—and alter social work's relationship with those discourses, particularly around mixedness and queerness. Specifically, I looked toward the borderlands of these experiences and explored how they are negotiated and embraced within the context of community.

Community Borderlands: A Study

The overall purpose of the study for which I developed a borderlands framework was to explore experiences of community belonging and well-being from a queer-mixed perspective. In 2011, I conducted an interview-based study with a sample of 12 mixed-race and queer-identified individuals in an urban area in the western United States with the goal of better understanding how collective experiences of community and well-being might overlap, diverge, and shift in concert with intersecting experiences of mixedness and queerness. Due to the high level of variance within experiences of race, gender, and sexuality, a critical component of this project was the epistemological and theoretical framework within which it was imagined. This framework, which is reflective of my personal worldview, positionality, and standpoint, guided the development of the study and my interpretive lens.

The following review of the theoretical background starts with the epistemological origins and extends through specific theoretical concepts that serve as useful analytic tools in my work and, as I suggest here, in critical feminist social work scholarship broadly. This borderlands framework was uniquely conceptualized for the purpose of looking at the experiences of queer-identified mixed-race individuals' experiences in community, blending borderland epistemology, transnational and Chicana feminisms, and postcolonial studies. This instance of theoretical pluralism was consistent with this project's intent to consider and disrupt multiple borders and boundaries, including those around disciplinary traditions, as well as to use the best theoretical tools available to explore the lived experience of community borderlands.

Flexible, Theoretically Pluralist Approaches

Over the last several years, especially with the emergence of intersectionality theorizing, a number of scholars have identified theoretical pluralism as an often useful and sometimes necessary theoretical approach (Borden,

2010; Mehrotra, 2010). Stemming from a feminist of color and social constructionist perspective, theoretical pluralism and its sister concept bricolage follow in the tradition of making creative and resourceful use of theory (Denzin & Lincoln, 2000; Hill-Collins, 1990; Hurtado, 2003; Kincheloe, 2001). In my work, I employ the type of theoretical pluralism and bricolage that calls for using the theoretical tool you need when you need it. Theoretical pluralism and bricolage can be contentious practices, particularly when they challenge very well-maintained (and vigorously patrolled) disciplinary boundaries or when they are employed in a way that promotes superficial interdisciplinarity (Kincheloe, 2001). These practices are also contentious because multiple paradigms with differing epistemological and/or ontological bases are brought together, as is often the case in theoretically informed social work literature that is intended to communicate ideas across diverse audiences. However, as Kincheloe argues, theoretical pluralism and bricolage are also useful tools for multiperspectival knowledge production, translation, and application across disciplinary boundaries. As such, the epistemological and theoretical perspectives from which I drew to inform this study were adapted and applied beyond their original intended purpose; I found it necessary to pay attention to original context and selected those theories that offered novel insight into the topic of this study and contributed most abundantly to a better understanding of the lived experience.

The theoretical framework reviewed in this section is broadly framed within a borderland epistemology, borrowing from previous work of feminist scholars, such as Gloria Anzaldúa (1987) and Sandra Harding (1998), who argue for "academic atrocities" such as inconsistency and contradiction to exist within scholarly spaces. Utilizing the theoretical pluralist approach discussed above, I selected a cohort of theoretical perspectives to inform my study and to further develop a borderlands perspective. Primarily, these included liberatory theoretical frameworks from transnational feminisms and postcolonial studies because of the insights they offer into lived experiences of race, gender, and sexuality, and their relationships with systems of dominance and collective resistance. Drawing from these perspectives allowed for distinctive imaginings of community borders and belongingness that pay particular attention to ambiguity, discontinuity, and flexibility, and the ways in which these experiences inform material realities, hardships, and triumphs.

This section begins with a brief discussion of borderland epistemology, a metatheoretical perspective on the meaning of knowledge and knowledge production that is grounded in the idea of symbolic borders and rooted in the disentanglement of knowledge valuation and domination. The subsequent sections offer a description of: (1) transnational feminism, emphasizing the intersectional lens extended from this body of work; (2) Chicana feminism (specifically borderland-*mestizaje* feminism) and the queer framework generated from this frame of reference; and (3) critical postcolonial studies, particularly the ideas of third space, third scenario, and otherness. These concepts lend unique strengths and opportunities for discussing community borderlands and the ways they are experienced and expressed. Because each body of work from which this study drew is voluminous and nuanced, this section is not intended to be an exhaustive review of the literature. Rather, the following section will describe the essential elements of each body of work as they relate to my research around queer-mixed experiences of/in community.

Borderland Epistemology

Broadly stated, borderland epistemology is primarily concerned with demystifying relationships between systems of knowledge and of colonization, and how these relationships emerge historically and contemporarily. It critically looks at processes that protect the dominant position of Western knowledge, inhibit the sovereignty of indigenous ways of knowing, and result in the emergence of hybrid knowledges. Specifically, borderland epistemology considers physical and symbolic borders to be sites where the intimacies of epistemology and coloniality can be unraveled and explored. In his work, Latin American philosopher Walter Mignolo (2000, 2007) uses the term "border thinking" to describe the process of interrogating the interconnectedness of coloniality/epistemology and the exploration of borderland spaces. Mignolo posits both symbolic and physical borders as both "knowers" and "places of knowing." My work follows in this tradition by exploring borders related to the body, community, and knowledge, as expressed in narrative accounts of queer-mixed lived experiences, belonging, and wellness. As I have discussed in previous writing, I think about these borderlands (of bodies, communities, and knowledge) as dynamic spaces that are created, crossed, occupied, and policed from within as well as from outside, both individually and collectively (Hudson, 2012). I incorporate a borderlands perspective in order to help better understand multiple and contradictory experiences of community and belonging, and how we keep each other and ourselves well.

Borderland epistemology also centers the ways in which historical conditions (such as processes of colonization), as well as contemporary conditions (such as neoliberal globalization), have reshaped traditional knowledges into hybrid or in-between forms that have been, at times, systematically denied and hidden, and at other times misused and exploited. I extend this epistemic shift by challenging the "exclusivity of insight" claimed by dominant discourses (Appiah, 1991); I do this by looking to lived experiences and practiced lives at what some frame as "troubled and troubling" intersections (Kumashiro, 2001; Ratcliffe, 2005), or to lived experiences that challenge dominant narratives and disrupt traditional notions of being racialized, gendered, and sexualized. These lived experiences may draw and define boundaries differently than Western knowledge that, within the context of neoliberal globalization, displaces knowledge gained through spatial, lived experiences of the body and replaces it with aspatial, corporate-produced, and market-driven forms of knowledge (Carter, 2010).

There are many nuances, disagreements, and contradictions among scholars who draw upon and contribute to borderland epistemology, making a comprehensive review of the literature difficult; the current agenda of borderland scholars is far-reaching and diverse. One of the reasons for this divide is the wide applicability of the border and borderlands as a conceptual tool. Another reason is a general divergence in thinking around the value of empiricism versus theory. In addition, there is disagreement regarding the wider application of border theory beyond the United States–Mexico border (Naples, 2010). For example, some scholars, such as Vila (2003), have criticized conceptual, metaphoric adaptations of border theory. "For scholars doing border studies from the Mexican side of the line, it is difficult to see the border as mere metaphor, as the epitomized possibility of crossings, hybrids, and the like" (Vila, 2003, as cited in Naples, 2010, p. 514). However, the theoretical contributions of border theorists in cultural studies fill in theoretical gaps faced by social scientists doing empirical work not only along the United States–Mexico border, but other bordered spaces where material realities could only be explained through first understanding the complexity of relationships across and within bordered spaces. Particularly useful to my work is borderland theory's reach into racialized, gendered, and sexualized spheres through underscoring the significance of their processes of overlap and convergence.

While some disciplinary focuses remain at measuring outcome-related characteristics of United States—Mexico border populations, other scholars continue to develop conceptual and metaphoric ideas of the border. Within the social and health sciences, borderland scholarship remains primarily focused on demographic trends and health-related outcomes of those who live at physical borders. Recently, however, borderland frameworks have been used within an emergent body of qualitative social science and health science research; for example, Bathum and Baumann (2007) explored newly developed connections to communities, as well as existing connections, that are maintained by recent Latina immigrants. A borderlands framework has also been used as a reflexive framework in research; for example, Hernandez-Wolfe (2011), a Latina health researcher, drew from borderland epistemology to describe how her experiences in the field, as well as in academia, reflect multiple borderland positions. This kind of shift reinforces the feminist origins of borderland theories and their practical purposes. Naples (2010) highlighted borderland theory's unique capacity to link scholarship and activism, emphasizing the value of "contemporary feminist and queer border studies that link local struggles with cross-border organizing against violence against women, labor rights, and sexual citizenship" (p. 1). Therefore, borderland epistemology—when considering its queer, feminist, and critical realist roots/applications—grounded my work in a social justice agenda concerned with upholding and extending certain social welfare values, such as self-determination and social justice, while remaining critical of its limitations through engaging in an iterative, reflexive process.

Transnational Feminism

Transnational feminism has a legacy of seeking out in-between, liminal, or borderland spaces in order to work through and across them in a collective resistance to systems of dominance and oppression. Thus, it is a critical framework for liberatory social welfare scholarship, practice, and education (Moosa-Mitha & Ross-Sheriff, 2010). One major contribution of transnational feminism is a focus on the intersectionality of identities and embodied experiences of race, gender, and sexuality within specific contexts (e.g., historic, political) and on multiple scales (e.g., social, spatial). I see my work as framed within these very contexts, and I extend this critique to lived experiences across intersecting identities that are sometimes situated within and across bordered spaces and scales. As a transnational feminist project, this work is also invested in the translation of theoretical projects into action taking "on the ground," the interrogation of power relations in knowledge production, and the ongoing self-reflection and self-critique of academics engaged in collaborative practices (Swarr & Nagar, 2010).

Intersectionality

An intersectional approach allows for the exploration of lived experiences in order to make sense of various discontinuities within borderland spaces (Hernandez-Wolfe, 2011), such as multiple identities and (simultaneous) experiences of connection/disconnection, visibility/invisibility, and the local/global divide. A transnational feminist perspective considers identities to be flexible, situational, relational, and co-constructed, partially in relation to community. While the concept of intersectionality has notable roots in Black feminism and Women of Color feminisms and is grounded primarily in the intersectionality of multiple identities and oppressions, it is also important to pay attention to the intersectionality of space, imagined broadly and ambitiously: the creation and collision of physical and psychic spheres, and the maintenance of socio-spatial boundaries. In my work specifically, I have looked to and beyond intersectionality to explore the deployment of community to name and locate experiences of belonging and wellness of individuals whose experiences of race, gender, and sexuality engage with and contradict multiple dominant discourses simultaneously. An intersectional approach to exploring and claiming community borderland spaces may serve to disrupt racialized, gendered, heterosexualized, and classed spaces (Oswin, 2008; Puar, 2002) by looking from the perspective of "people moving in and out of borders constructed around co-ordinates of differences of power" with the intention of speaking "of, from, and across [. . .] identities and develop[ing] narratives of plurality, fluidity, as an always emergent becoming" (Bromley, 2000, p. 2; Hall, 1994). Consequently, I support an emerging scholarly agenda within social work to understand "how interconnected systems of inequality operate on multiple levels to affect marginalized people" (Mehrotra, 2010, p. 419), and I strive to hold the field of social work accountable to its commitment to explore lived experiences of privilege and oppression (CSWE, 2008).

Scale

A feminist conceptualization of borderland spaces relies as much on a critical consideration of the intersectionality of space as it does on the concept of "scale." Recent feminist scholarship by geographers has illustrated that attention to scale "allows us to understand the nuanced ways in which neocolonial relations of power and political economic structures of domination and subordination combine to shape gendered politics of inequalities, difference, and resistance" (Nagar, 2000, p. 685). Transnational feminism lends an eye to issues of power at multiple scales: challenging binaries and focusing on interdependencies; conceiving of cultural forces that construct borders; and ultimately seeking social justice (Nagar, Lawson, McDowell, & Hanson, 2002). Binary-dependent scales, such as the local–global divide, are socially constructed, and "social relations are in fact played out across scales rather than confined with them" (Kelly, 1999, pp. 381–382). I extend this argument by applying the notion of scale to multiple binary expressions (self–other, insider–outsider, oppressor–oppressed), and centering the idea that social relations played out across scales and also between them, highlighting interstitial configurations of power. This means reaching beyond binary divides and allowing for multiple power positions within, between, and across identities.

Borderland-Mestizaje Feminism and the Closeness of Queer Theory

Another area of feminist thought grounded in the exploration and utilization of borderlands for academic theorizing, personal reflection, and collective action is Chicana feminism. Foundational Chicana feminist literature conceptualized the border as a liminal space that generates and resolves conflict; it is situated both physically and symbolically between domination and resistance, but it is also a "home" with the power to restore and transform (Anzaldúa, 1987; Hurtado, 2003; Moraga & Anzaldúa, 1981). Gloria Anzaldúa, a poet and cultural theorist, was instrumental in the articulation of a Chicana feminism. Particularly with her foundational work on border identities during the 1980s, the work of Anzaldúa represents a hybrid genre of hybrid spaces. A number of scholars, particularly feminists of color, have advanced and continue to advance Anzaldúa's work, as her

conceptualization of borderlands is one that has proven to be an endur-
ing poetic and politic within a number of disciplines. Anzaldúa (1987)
conceived of borderlands as liminal spaces between races/ethnicities/
cultures, genders, and sexualities that produce epistemic resources for
resisting dominating culture and creating new knowledges—an "open
wound . . . that bleeds" (p. 25), yet also a place with potential for healing
and liberation on multiple scales—personal, familial, communal, national,
and political. As I have asserted in previous writing (Hudson, 2012) and
continue to explore, such transformation can occur through the recovery
of knowledges related to the lived experiences of community—the ways we
care for each other, resist together, preserve and celebrate collective memory, and hold each other accountable—especially within those communities marginalized within dominant ideological landscapes.

Born out of and located within the family of Chicana feminist
approaches, Borderland-*Mestizaje* Feminism (BMF) pays attention to relationships between the physical body and its desires, the physical and spiritual environment, and lived experiences in generating valuable knowledges.
Moraga and Anzaldúa (1981) conceptualized this approach as a way of theorizing "in the flesh," centering how "the physical realities of our lives—our
skin color, the land or concrete we grew up on, our sexual longings—all
fuse to create a politic born out of necessity" (p. 23). Working within a
BMF framework allows us to "rethink, deconstruct, and reconstruct new
and hybrid ways to know, be, and become" (Saavedra & Nymark, 2008,
p. 263). In line with a BMF framework, this study considered the body and
sexuality, and how they intersect with race, ethnicity, and gender, as perhaps two of the most "subversive and anticolonial" *herramientas* (tools) to
recover bodies that have been "scarred and split" by colonialism and other
systems of oppression (p. 266). A BMF framework disrupts and decenters
the "Western clinical sterilized approach to theory, research, and practice"
(p. 267); I apply this framework through affirming those experiences that
fall outside of normative ways of being, being together, and caring for one
another. Life at and within borderlands allows for a kind of openness to
contradiction, deviance, fierceness, and beauty that comes from surviving
together, transcending adversity, and loving unaffectedly.

Queer Framework

As is true with many critical and feminist epistemological standpoints, BMF
is a bricolage of a number of perspectives and frameworks that, according to
Saavedra and Nymark (2008), "use, embody, and borrow from queer, feminist, postmodern, postcolonial, and poststructuralist scholarship and epistemologies" (p. 262). As such, "queerness" in particular is a key element of this
study. Rather than drawing from traditional "queer theory" literature, which
largely stems from a white, gay male tradition, this project emphasizes the
intersections and coarticulations of race, gender, and sexuality, and employs

BMF as a queer framework. In line with a larger body of literature, in this study, "queerness becomes a topic and a resource for investigating the way group boundaries are created, negotiated, and changed" (Denzin, Lincoln, & Smith, 2008, p. 26). This is accomplished through centering the subjective experiences of the body (its racialization, gender socialization, and sexualization) and belongingness, which allows for the interrogation and deconstruction of racial, gendered, and racialized subjects, boundaries, and norms (Denzin et al., 2008). My use of queer theory also disrupts binaried systems, including the heterosexual–homosexual divide and other reductive conceptualizations of socio-spatial organization. As Oswin (2008) notes, "Once we dismiss the presumption that queer theory offers only a focus on 'queer' lives and an abstract critique of the heterosexualization of space, we can utilize it to deconstruct the hetero/homo binary and examine sexuality's deployments in concert with racialized, classed, and gendered processes," as well as (trans)nationalized, global, capitalist, diasporic, and migratory processes (p. 100). This framework can be used to disrupt normative conceptualizations related to race, gender, and sexuality, and to construct an alternate perspective that is partial, polyvocal, and contradictory—one that collects histories of place, connectedness, and struggle.

Critical Postcolonial Studies

Critical postcolonial theory is centered around shifting voice, context, and theory in order to better understand lived experiences (Alexander, 2008). This borderlands framework follows a critical postcolonial perspective through centering the voices and perspectives of queer-identified mixed-race individuals (shifting voice); by focusing on the everyday lives and lived experiences of queer-mixed folks, while holding on to and making ties to larger social systems, contexts, and histories (shifting context); and finally, contributing to a critical postcolonial (and transnational/Chicana feminist) perspective through reconstructing "other" possibilities that can serve as praxis for transformation of future social welfare scholarship, education, and practice (shifting theory). Postcolonial theory and social work have at least two very important values in common: self-determination and social justice. Yet, until recently, postcolonial theory has been largely missing from social work research, teaching, and practice (Deepak, 2012). By focusing on intersecting global systems, such as imperialism, militarization, migration, and capitalism, postcolonial perspectives allow us to pay attention to and resist various colonial gestures articulated by social work research and practice—by "giving voice" to voiceless subjects, ensuring the authority of the researcher/educator, and rescuing disempowered clients (Jones & Jenkins, 2008). This perspective lends critical social welfare scholars tools to identify and dismantle oppressive and disempowering relations created through the research process, many of which parallel social welfare practice, and offer alternative ways of thinking and doing.

Third Space, Third Scenario, and Otherness

Postcolonial theory has offered the social work profession and social work education, in particular, the concepts of third space and third scenario. These concepts, put forward by different theorists, are similar in their central thesis and usage. In the section that follows, I will briefly outline several key definitions and discuss their utility for this project through an umbrella term of the "third." "Third space" refers to an unpredictable and changing hybrid space located on the border between two domains (Bhabha, 1994). Third space is also thought of as an ambiguous location where meaning and representation have no fixed origin or destination. Like Anzaldúa's *mestizaje*, third space seeks to move beyond the "either/or" binary. Similarly, the "third scenario" (Hall, 1994) refers to a "non-binarist space of reflection" that reimagines and transforms ideas of plurality and difference (in Bromley, 2000).

> The dilemma we experience is of both attempting to situate this scenario and also refusing to confine it to a knowable location. It is not a liberal, multicultural space in which several cultures are juxtaposed with their essentialized frontiers intact—the space of demographic plurality, but instead is a space that is in constant transition (Bromley, 2000, p. 6; Hall, 1994).

The construct of the "other" is also a central tenet of postcolonial theorizing that has relevance to feminist social work research. "Postcolonial studies is built around the concept of otherness—as both a point of departure and critique that has the potential of opening spaces of critical discussion about how we construct self and other . . . and the resulting devastations of such differentiation" (Alexander, 2008, pp. 106–107). These ideas of the third, described above, offer the field of social work conceptual tools for resisting othering processes and binary dependence. The third also allows us to consider real and imagined geographies of social space—specifically, otherness, hybridity, and borderland communities (Saldívar, 2006) and, as Juanita Heredia (2009) writes, engage in a "decolonizing process through writing and relocating subaltern cultures" (p. 5). As such, this study intended to situate communities that are in constant transition, that undermine forces that discipline migrating and moving bodies that live, connect, and create social bonds within, across, and beyond borders.

Points of Departure

Borderlands may prove to be an underutilized yet ample framework from which to reimagine, retheorize, and reapproach social work research, thus situating social work scholarship and research as suitable sites for intervention. As such, a borderlands framework may create opportunities for both thinking and doing in social work research. Features of this framework that I invite readers to consider include: (1) theoretical pluralism in the creative and resourceful use of feminist theory and the challenging of disciplinary boundaries (Kincheloe, 2001); (2) a focus on lived experiences and practiced lives; (3) queerness as a resource for investigating experiences, group boundaries, and norms (Denzin & Lincoln, 2000); (4) attention to intersectionalities and in-between spaces/times, multiple identities, and interlocking systems of oppression (e.g., Mehrotra, 2010); (5) appreciation of transitions, hybrid cultures, and social positions (e.g., Anzaldúa, 1987; Keating, 2005); (6) commitments to activist scholarship and bridging scholarship with organizing efforts (e.g., Swarr & Nagar, 2010); and (7) borderlands as a mode of self-reflection, incorporating multiple positionalities of the researcher (e.g., Hernandez-Wolfe, 2011). Below I outline specific methodological and analytic choices I made, and will continue to make, in my research that have emerged from this framework.

Methodological Considerations

I used flexible inclusion criteria for participation in the study. In my recruitment materials, for example, I used intentionally inclusive language, acknowledging the varying and sometimes creative ways queer-mixed folks have come to identify. I did not exclude any potential participants based on my assumptions of what "counted" as a mixed or queer experience. Also, and with approval from the Institutional Review Board, I allowed participants the option to be identified in the study using their name of choice, including their legal name or a pseudonym. Names hold intimate and intrinsic value in mixed, queer, and trans* communities; names can be one of a few markers of personal and social identity, family history, and heritage, and can reflect one's understanding of oneself in the social world. Participants were informed of the potential risk of choosing their legal name or name of choice; some participants chose a pseudonym, and I did not disclose which participants did so. By doing so, I allowed participants to claim their stories and own their experiences, providing an alternative to the invisibility attributable to the requisite use of pseudonyms, a "nameless presence" suffered most specifically in the context of immigration and diaspora (Sullivan, 2001, p. xvi). It also allowed participants to represent their story with names they might not usually use but have always wanted to try on, names that people only in their communities know them by, names that bended and played with readers' assumptions about the speaker.

Analytic Adjustments

I analyzed interview data in a way that understood participants' stories as counternarratives of race, gender, and sexuality, for which dominant discourse is steeped in binary, inflexible, and dislocated understandings of mixed, queer, and trans* experiences. I accomplished this, in part, by refusing to involve the study participants in a traditional, population-based research approach. As such, this study benefited from avoiding the all too predictable path of theorizing on identity and engaging in the reification of a dominant queer-mixed cultural script. By doing so, I hoped to avoid essentialist and reductive conclusions about mixed-race and queer identity, identity politics, and social issues. In this vein, rather than considering race, gender, and sexuality as individuals' possessions, in my work, I saw race, gender, and sexuality (as well as their correspond-ing, intersecting identities) as dynamic, contested, and relational pro-cesses. Specifically, I looked toward the borderlands of these experiences and explored how they were negotiated and embraced within the context of community. By engaging a borderlands framework, I was also able to understand liminality, rather than identity, as a useful heuristic to explore how individuals shaped and nurtured senses of self, communities, and other spaces of belonging that are in between (see Gallego, 2002). In the sense that the liminal self and liminal space are "always becoming," liminality can be helpful in understanding the experiences of those "who look in from outside while looking out from inside to the extent that both inside and outside lose their defining contours," or, in other words, the state in which borders of belonging become blurred (Hall, 1994, as cited in Kavoori, 2007, p. 55).

Ethical Considerations

Finally, this work raised significant ethical tensions for me as a social work researcher that compelled me to consider the ways in which engaging in this research reinforced processes of othering and in-betweenness. I grap-pled with the extent to which this study contributed to a body of knowledge and the extent to which it contributed to a "postcolonial perspective and queer theory [. . .] grounded in Whiteness. Each [. . .] committed to res-cuing the silenced other" (Denzin et al., 2008, p. 25). Either in intent or as a consequence, research on otherness is conflictively positioned between "voicing" and exploitation, and has become an issue I have had to grapple with in an academic space that is personally delicate and sacred. While I intended this research to "speak truth" and "shed light," the unknown, yet somewhat predictable, consequences of creating an avenue for dominant groups to access others' knowledge remain. As Jones and Jenkins (2008) wrote, "the imperialist resonances are uncomfortably apt" (p. 480). I con-tinue to look for ways to engage with this tension through personal reflec-tion, consultation with peers, and openly acknowledging and dialoguing with study participants/community members about the sometimes cruel and contradictory contexts of academic research, and the ways in which we could do better work within and for our communities. This includes considering participatory opportunities, participants' rights to data, and sustainable, action-oriented products for communities to be ethical imperatives.

Future Research

A borderlands framework lends itself well to ongoing, critical reflexivity by encouraging social work scholars to engage in a number of practices. One practice is to advance a social justice imperative that critically engages with the field's investment in narrating oppression, allowing for participants' agency in self-definition while maintaining a structural analysis of privilege and oppression. Another practice is to acknowledge "outsider-within" experiences in social work research (Daniel, 2007), and to create opportunities in social work scholarship for those who are usually the subject, or supposed beneficiary of research, to engage in the knowledge-building process. Not only might this practice allow for social welfare scholars to continue to better conceptualize, grasp, and work towards liberatory and anti-oppressive goals, it also would allow the field to reinvest in asking better questions and to think more complexly about how systems of dominance and oppression are played out in practice settings, as well as in our own scholarship and teaching.

While research from a borderlands perspective may point to implications for social work practice with "diverse" populations and community configurations, the purpose of this work need not be to fashion better services for "diverse" individuals and their communities, as is common in social work research. For example, the borderlands framework I developed in this study did not lead to suggestions that people who identify as queer and mixed race need a specific type of social service—or social services at all. Nor did the study promote a list of skills to improve cultural competency among service providers. (I do believe, however, this area will always remain in need of constant critical evaluation.) Rather, the purpose of this work was to look to the queer-mixed perspective as an equitable partner in knowledge building. I situated this study within a larger body of critical feminist work by problematizing the idea that some (other) people are best suited to be recipients/beneficiaries of research rather than active contributors to a body of knowledge—a position that may, ultimately, improve work towards an inclusive and liberatory practice.

A borderlands framework is also generous in its applicability. In my work so far, I have conceptualized borderland experiences of race, gender, and sexuality as being primarily reflected in mixedness, queerness, and gender nonconformity. However, borderlands are home to many more experiences than those alone. Borderlands frameworks may be suitable for research looking at intersections with other experiences, for example, transracial/transnational adoption, children in foster care, queer parenthood, people with disabilities, the 1.5 generation and immigrant families, detained and incarcerated individuals, as well as the dilemmas and contradictions faced by activist scholars

(Hames-Garcia, 2009). In fact, and as I continue to learn and be reminded, research on mixedness and queerness is not separate from research on diaspora, migration, violence, intimate and familial relationships, or possibly any other phenomena imaginable. A borderlands approach can help social work scholars, students, and practitioners to more critically and holistically approach practice concerned with multiple client systems, including multi-, inter-, and trans-racial, immigrant, and queer/trans*-affirming families, organizations, and institutions, by looking at the intersections of and experiences of in-between races, genders, sexualities, abilities, and other identities, as well as in-between places, memories, and disciplines. Borderlands can also be a space for critical self-reflection, as well as opportunities for equitable collaborative research and practice relationships within communities. These opportunities create avenues for ongoing reflection on the pool of theory from which we draw and the ways we can grow and continually appraise our use of theory, as well as prompt reconsideration of the way theory intersects with and informs personal/political commitments and multiple ideological imperatives for critical feminist social work research.

References

Alexander, K.B. (2008). Queer(y)ing the postcolonial through the West(ern). In N. K. Denzin, Y. Lincoln, & L. T. Smith (Eds.), *Handbook of critical and indigenous methodologies* (pp. 101–133). Thousand Oaks, CA: Sage.

Anzaldúa, G. (1987). *Borderlands: The new mestiza = La frontera.* San Francisco: Spinsters/Aunt Lute.

Appiah, A. (1991). Is the post- in postmodernism the post- in postcolonial? *Critical Inquiry, 17,* 336–357.

Bathum, M. E. & Baumann, L. C. (2007). A sense of community among immigrant Latinas. *Family & Community Health, 30* (3), 167–177.

Bhabha, H. K. (1994). *The location of culture.* London: Routledge.

Borden, W. (2010). *Reshaping theory in contemporary social work: Toward a critical pluralism in clinical practice.* New York: Columbia University Press.

Bromley, R. (2000). *Narratives for a new belonging: Diasporic cultural fictions.* Edinburgh: Edinburgh University Press.

Carter, L. (2010). The armchair at the borders: The "messy" ideas of borders and border epistemologies within multicultural science education scholarship. *Science Education, 94,* 428–447.

Council on Social Work Education. (2007). *Taskforce on Latinos/as in Social Work: Final Report to the Council on Social Work Education Board of Directors.* Alexandria, VA: Council on Social Work Education.

Council on Social Work Education. (2008). *Educational policy and accreditation standards.* Alexandria, VA: Council on Social Work Education.

Daniel, C. (2007). Outsiders-within: Critical race theory, graduate education and barriers to professionalization. *Journal of Sociology and Social Welfare, 34* (1), 25–42.

Deepak, A. C. (2012). Globalization, power and resistance: Postcolonial and transnational feminist perspectives for social work practice. *International Social Work, 55* (6), 779–793.

Denzin, N. K. & Lincoln, Y. S. (2000). *Handbook of qualitative research.* Thousand Oaks, CA: Sage Publications.

Denzin, N. K., Lincoln, Y. S., & Smith, L. T. (2008). *Handbook of critical and indigenous methodologies.* Los Angeles: Sage.

Gallego, M. M. (2002). The borders of the self: Identity and community in Louise Erdrich's *Love Medicine* and Paule Marshall's *Praisesong for the Widow.* In J. Benito & A.M. Manzanas (Eds.), *Literature and Ethnicity in the Cultural Borderlands* (pp. 145–158). Amsterdam: Rodopi.

Gringeri, C. E., Wahab, S., & Anderson-Nathe, B. (2010). What makes it feminist? Mapping the landscape of feminist social work research. *Affilia, 25* (4), 390–405.

Hall, S. (1994). Cultural identity and diaspora. In P. Williams & L. Chrisman (Eds.), *Colonial discourse and post-colonial theory* (pp. 392–403). Hemel Hempstead: Harvester Wheatsheaf.

Hames-Garcia, M. (2009). Three dilemmas of a queer activist scholar of color. In J. Sudbury & M. Okazawa-Rey (Eds.), *Activist scholarship: Antiracism, feminism, and social change* (pp. 149–166). Boulder, CO: Paradigm Publishers.

Harding, S. G. (1998). *Is science multicultural? Postcolonialisms, feminisms, and epistemologies.* Bloomington, IN: Indiana University Press.

Heredia, J. (2009). *Transnational Latina narratives in the twenty-first century: The politics of gender, race, and migrations.* New York: Palgrave Macmillan.

Hernandez-Wolfe, P. (2011). Decolonization and "mental" health: A mestiza's journey in the borderlands. *Women and Therapy, 34* (3), 293–306.

Hill-Collins, P. (1990). *Black feminist thought: Knowledge, consciousness, and the politics of empowerment.* Boston: Unwin Hyman.

Hudson, K. D. (2012). Bordering community: Reclaiming ambiguity as a transgressive landscape of knowledge. *Affilia, 27* (2), 167–179.

Hurtado, A. (2003). Theory in the flesh: Toward an endarkened epistemology. *International Journal of Qualitative Studies in Education, 16* (2), 215–225.

Jones, A. & Jenkins, K. (2008). Rethinking collaboration: Working the indigene-coloniser hyphen. In N. K. Denzin, Y. S. Lincoln, & L. T. Smith (Eds.), *Handbook of critical and indigenous methodologies* (pp. 471–486). Thousand Oaks, CA: Sage.

Kavoori, A. P. (2007). Thinking through contra-flows: Perspectives from post-colonial and transnational cultural studies. In D. K. Thussu (Ed.), *Media on the move: Global flow and contra-flow* (pp. 55–58). London: Routledge.

Keating, A. (2005). *Entre mundos/among worlds: New perspectives on Gloria E. Anzaldúa.* New York: Palgrave Macmillan.

Kelly, P. F. (1999). The geographies and politics of globalization. *Progress in Human Geography, 23* (3), 359–400.

Kincheloe, J. L. (2001). Describing the bricolage: Conceptualizing a new rigor in qualitative research. *Qualitative Inquiry, 7* (6), 679–692.

Kumashiro, K. K. (2001). *Troubling intersections of race and sexuality: Queer students of color and anti-oppressive education.* Lanham, MD: Rowman & Littlefield Publishers.

Le-Doux, C. (1996). Career patterns of African-American and Hispanic social work doctorates and ABDs. *Journal of Social Work Education, 32,* 245–252

Mehrotra, G. (2010). Toward a continuum of intersectionality theorizing for feminist social work scholarship. *Affilia, 25* (4), 417–430.

Mignolo, W. (2000). *Local histories/global designs: Coloniality, subaltern knowledges, and border thinking.* Princeton, NJ: Princeton University Press.

Mignolo, W. (2007). DeLinking. The rhetoric of modernity, the logic of coloniality and the grammar of decoloniality. *Cultural Studies, 21* (2–3), 449–514.

Mohanty, C. T. (2003). *Feminism without borders: Decolonizing theory, practicing solidarity.* Durham, NC: Duke University Press.

Moosa-Mitha, M. & Ross-Sheriff, F. (2010). Transnational social work and lessons learned from transnational feminism. *Affilia, 25* (2), 105–109.

Moraga, C. & Anzaldúa, G. (1981). *This bridge called my back: Writings by radical women of color.* Watertown, MA: Persephone Press.

Nagar, R. (2000). Religion, race, and the debate over Mut'a in Dar es Salaam. *Feminist Studies, 26* (3), 661–690.

Nagar, R., Lawson, V., McDowell, L., & Hanson, S. (2002). Locating globalization: Feminist (re)readings of the subjects and spaces of globalization. *Economic Geography, 78,* 257–284.

Naples, N. A. (2010). Borderlands studies and border theory: Linking activism and scholarship for social justice. *Sociology Compass, 4* (7), 505–518.

Oswin, N. (2008). Critical geographies and the uses of sexuality: Deconstructing queer space. *Progress in Human Geography, 32* (1), 89–103.

Puar, J. (2002). A transnational feminist critique of queer tourism. *Antipode, 34* (5), 935–946.

Ratcliffe, K. (2005). *Rhetorical listening: Identification, gender, whiteness.* Carbondale, IL: Southern Illinois University Press.

Saavedra, C. M. & Nymark, E. D. (2008). Borderland-Mestizaje feminism: The new tribalism. In N. K. Denzin, Y. S. Lincoln, & L. T. Smith (Eds.), *Handbook of critical and indigenous methodologies.* Thousand Oaks, CA: Sage.

Saldívar, R. (2006). *The borderlands of culture: Américo Paredes and the transnational imaginary.* Durham, NC: Duke University Press.

Sullivan, Z. T. (2001). *Exiled memories: Stories of Iranian diaspora.* Philadelphia, PA: Temple University Press.

Swarr, A. L. & Nagar, R. (2010). *Critical transnational feminist praxis.* Albany, NY: SUNY Press.

Vila, P. (2003). The limits of American border theory. In P. Vila (Ed.), *Ethnography at the border.* Minneapolis, MN: University of Minnesota Press.

8 Myths and Monsters

Challenging Assumptions of Poor Working-Class Motherhood through Feminist Research

Victoria Foster

Legend

> *Once upon a time there was a she-monster. She lived submerged 20,000 feet under the sea, and was only a legend, until one day the scientists got together to fish her out. They hauled her ashore and loaded her on trucks and finally set her down in a vast amphitheatre where they began their dissection. It soon became evident that the creature was pregnant. They alerted security and sealed all the doors, being responsible men and unwilling to take chances with the monster's whelps, for who could know what damage they might do if unleashed on the world . . . Suniti Namjoshi (1993, p. 31)*

This chapter focuses on the ways in which a feminist approach to research can challenge hegemonic understandings of poor working-class mothers. Enmeshed relations between knowledge and power, hegemonic, "common–sense" understandings, and the state's involvement in families' lives form an oppressive net, which has long held such women in its snare. For the past several decades, feminist research has provided a means of unraveling these affairs and examining the invisible bonds that continue to constrain large sections of the population. The chapter explores how feminisms have shaped my work in terms of knowledge production and in challenging commonly held assumptions. This ethnographic research with poor working-class mothers at a Sure Start program in the United Kingdom provides an illustrative example.

The myth of poor working-class women has historical roots and the chapter begins by stressing the importance of acknowledging the fact that such women, particularly in their role of mothers, have long been maligned. Like the she-monster in the opening poem, they have held a horrible fascination, and concern has often focused on the need to prevent offspring from being infected with the same deviant characteristics that afflict the mother. This is of particular import for social workers since social work has historically centered on interventions with impoverished women and their families. Such women are regularly demonized for their failure to conform to middle-class norms, and contact with social services tends to be both unwelcome and punitive.

The chapter provides an outline of the recent policy turn in the United Kingdom in order to look at the continuation of a particular ideology and also to provide context to the feminist participatory research project at Sure Start. My discussion of this Sure Start research addresses three significant areas: the design of the study; the everyday interactions that took place during the study; and the process of disseminating the research findings. I consider how such an approach can provide an alternative picture of working-class motherhood.

In this chapter, I also incorporate discussion of Gramsci's concept of hegemony. I suggest that this can be employed as a means of understanding the diffuse and pervasive ways that myths surrounding working-class mothers are woven through our social and cultural lives. Although Gramsci's work has long fallen out of fashion, it has made a significant contribution to feminism and I examine how it can be fruitful when thinking about the aims of a feminist research process. I conclude by arguing that, in order to make the positive changes for women and society that feminist research strives to do, and to remain free of those constrictive bonds, we need to be aware of our own everyday actions. We need to make a commitment not to replicate hierarchies of power, however small and insignificant they may seem.

Echoes of the Past

The dichotomy of the good/bad mother has been in existence for many, many years, with the verdict of "bad mother" overwhelmingly falling on the poor working class (earlier known as the "residuum" class or the "underclass"). This is perhaps unsurprising given the "dreadful historical continuity to the abuse of the poorest and their presentation as something 'other' and inferior" (Jones & Novak, 1999, p. 100). This abuse is "essential" in order for wealthy societies to be able to accept poverty and the persistence of stark inequalities. In terms of mothering, those who do not meet normative expectations of this role "are inevitably positioned as the deviant 'other' and considered to be unfit to parent" (Wilson & Huntington, 2005, p. 61). Yet these norms are, for the most part, based on middle-class families and are out of reach for the poor working classes. Here the female subject has long been considered problematic, "in need of surveillance and regulation" to contain the "disruption and unruliness which is seen to stem from the very biology of the body of Woman" (Smart, 1992, p. 7). It is the reproduction of destitution and deviance that has historically been most feared by the state, professionals, and the public. Pressure has been on to ensure that the transformation of the problem mother happened "before her progeny inherited her fecklessness" (Starkey, 2000, p. 551).

Pervasive and fluid hegemonic practices have ensured that the poor working-class mother has long been monitored and managed by the state, professional health and social care workers, and the public. This is significant in terms of the Sure Start initiative discussed below, which arguably provides a further means of surveillance of this group. It is also significant in terms of knowledge production and what is accepted as "truth." Claims to scientific truth have the effect of legitimating the profound inequalities of our social world. Such knowledge is "constitutive of relations of *ruling* as well as of relations of *knowing*" (Stanley, 1990, p. 10). Its powerful discourse has ensured that the profession of modern scientific medicine gained its "hegemonic position" (Abbott & Wallace, 1998, p. 19), and positivism also informs the knowledge base of social work.

Carey and Foster (2013, p. 255) discuss the complex, heterogeneous ways by which "ideology and discourse can permeate our thoughts, values, prejudices and actions" in social work practice. One significant way that this takes place is through the profession's adoption of scientific methods, from its early years through to a recent surge of interest in "evidence-based" practice. Social work developed alongside sophisticated improvements in gathering data on populations that meant that "the necessary precision for specifying culprits and victims [could] be deployed" (Smart, 1992, p. 12). The state's involvement in family life was justified as it became seen as something to be known, surveyed, and monitored (Abbott & Wallace, 1998). Identified as "culprit," the problem mother was an ideal target for the social worker whose training in "scientific" knowledge, notably psychology (Carey & Foster, 2013), provided legitimating fuel for the moralizing intervention that would take place within the family setting, "the place where social problems arose and where they could be prevented or overcome" (Abbott & Wallace, 1998, p. 30). Social work has always reflected the dominant attitudes of society towards the impoverished and has also played a significant role "in the shaping and legitimating of those beliefs" (Jones & Novak, 1999, p. 80), to the extent that it can be argued that "the whole system of modern social work is founded upon the classed construction of inadequate mothering" (Smart, 1992, p. 24).

Sure Start, Evaluation, and Ideology

The need to break cycles of deprivation is echoed in recent UK social policy surrounding the family. This describes the social investment approach of the recent (1997–2010) Labour government, who indeed saw today's children as the country's future citizens. The current Coalition government is also committed to ending child poverty, and the state's gaze remains on the family unit (in particular the mother) as playing a significant role in this. Wiegers (2002) finds child poverty discourse problematic because, she asserts, it serves:

> to make the structural causes of poverty less visible; to encourage a response motivated by pity for the helpless child alongside a mentality of blaming adults/mothers; and to displace women's issues generally and women's poverty specifically (pp. 91–2, as cited in Lister, 2006, p. 329).

Clarke (2006, p. 718) observes that within this discourse the child is seen in the dyadic relationship with the mother. Here the mother is "all powerful" and the child is "passive and vulnerable." Through focusing on the promotion of particular kinds of maternal behavior, and blaming and punishing those who do not conform, structural divisions of class, gender, and "race" are neglected.

The Sure Start initiative was announced in 1998 as a means of working with young children and their families to reduce social and health inequalities. Compatible with other social investment approaches, such as Head Start in the United States and Canada, the significant amount of money promised to the program demonstrated the government's dedication to this initiative. Sure Start local programs (SSLPs) were rolled out in waves of about 70 at a time, until over 500 existed nationwide.

The poorest wards in the country were targeted first, in line with the social investment approach. Targeted, as opposed to universal, initiatives are geared to meet the state's priorities, "particularly in terms of reinforcing the responsibilities of parents to raise 'suitable' children" (Fawcett, Featherstone, & Goddard, 2004, p. 14).

SSLPs, each containing 400–800 children under the age of five, had considerable autonomy over the services provided. They typically included baby groups and toddler groups with much emphasis on learning through play and on healthy eating. There was often focus on promoting breastfeeding and smoking cessation for mothers. Parenting classes were generally provided and so were day trips and family events. SSLPs were required to evaluate aspects of this work and were allocated monies to do so. The Sure Start research that I was involved in was funded through an Economic and Social Research Council (ESRC) CASE award,[1] which meant that the SSLP where I was based contributed to the research funding. This took place between 2003 and 2006 in an ex-mining town in a particularly impoverished area of north-west England at one of the first SSLPs in the country. It aimed to capture local people's attitudes towards the program and their experiences of parenting in such a socially and economically disadvantaged area. It also investigated why significant numbers of families who were eligible to access the Sure Start program were not doing so. I received further funding in 2008 to carry out more research in this area and look at the "lasting legacy" of the initial project.[2]

Whilst there was considerable freedom in designing and carrying out this local research, it would always be overshadowed by "official" work by the National Evaluation of Sure Start (NESS). This large-scale evaluation was launched at the start of the Sure Start initiative and a team of researchers based at Birkbeck College, London produced a series of high-profile reports over the years. Subject matter included economic perspectives, characteristics of Sure Start catchment areas, and longitudinal research into impact (NESS Research Team, 2010, 2011, 2012). These researchers are considered "official spokespersons" of the initiative, contributing to public debate and policy development. Such high-profile evaluations contribute to "the construction of particular discourses that structure particular ways of working" (Broadhurst, Mason, & Grover, 2007, p. 446). Rather than being "an objective activity involving the collection of 'hard' evidence," evaluation is "always ideological because . . . it is central to the construction of practice" (p. 447).

Gramsci and Feminist Research

If the Sure Start initiative and its evaluation can be seen as ideological, then it is useful to look at how Gramsci's concept of hegemony "extends and enriches the notion of ideology" (Eagleton, 2007, p. 115). It also "lends this otherwise somewhat abstract term a material body and political cutting edge" (p. 115). The myth of the deviant poor working-class mother is maintained through a complex hegemonic apparatus, transmitted through social policy and practice, television programs, and newspaper articles (Foster, 2009), as well as being constantly renewed through day-to-day actions, thoughts, and speech. Gramsci understood that civil society was a particularly effective mechanism for maintaining authority because "it blurs the distinction between political authority and everyday life. What takes place in our homes, in our leisure activities or in the shops seems, for the most part, apolitical" (Jones, 2006, p. 48). It is this "lived, habitual social practice" (Eagleton, 2007, p. 115) that is key and must encompass "the unconscious, inarticulate dimensions of social experience as well as the workings of formal institutions" (Eagleton, 2007, p. 115).

In order to challenge this diffuse power, which, through this social practice, comes to be seen as "common sense," it is necessary to disrupt the process of normalization (Foster, 2009). For Patti Lather (1991) (as cited in Kenway, 2001, p. 59), feminism is a prime example of the forms of mobilization that Gramsci advocated "as an organic part of the struggle to transcend everyday life." His work on hegemony, counter-hegemony, and a war of position all made an "immense contribution" to feminism (Ledwith, 2008, p. 687), in spite of the fact that the picture of his relations to women, reflecting gender stereotypes of the time, "is not a rosy one" (Holub, 1992, p. 191). It was Gramsci's concept of hegemony which "turned the key to the personal as political," argues Ledwith (2008, p. 687).

The triumph of hegemony is in the fact that so much of its transmittance is unconscious and inarticulate. It makes it incredibly difficult to fathom how or when this is happening. Social workers, teachers, or researchers are no more likely to be enlightened than anyone else, particularly in terms of their relationship to "an ideological state apparatus and exploitative materialist Capitalist society" (Carey, 2011, p. 8). Indeed, their role and status mean that they are inclined to be "more ideologically impregnated." The knowledge constructed through social research has the potential to sustain hegemonic depictions of its subjects and add further to oppression, whether this process is conscious or not. Lynch (2000, p. 89) is clear that "research which is not oriented towards transformation effectively reinforces inequality by default."

Strengths of feminist approaches to research include a commitment to challenging the status quo in order to seek social justice and to improve the position of women in society (Daly, 2000). Feminist research recognizes that social inquiry is without doubt a *political* process; it can never be about detached truth seeking, even though claims to notions of objectivity and value neutrality persist. Decisions about the choice of subject matter undertaken, the source of funding, and the methodology employed are all unavoidably, inevitably political in that they are influenced by relations of power. Research is also political in that "its findings can be construed as relevant to the making of decisions about the way people live" (Oakley, 1992, p. 301).

Gramsci's work has fallen from favor with feminists, since its height of popularity in the 1980s (Kenway, 2001), replaced with concerns of cultural identity and difference (Ledwith, 2008). "The politics of recognition" have triumphed over "the politics of redistribution" (Fraser, as cited in Kenway, 2001, p. 60). However, it can still be useful to refer to some of these ideas when carrying out a feminist research project, not least in terms of the connection with the understanding that the personal really is political. This theme runs through the following discussion of the Sure Start research, which is divided into three sections. First, the rationale for the research design is set out, with discussion incorporating issues of methodology and method. Second, everyday interactions that took place through the research project are highlighted in order to illustrate the ways that these can reflect and transmit dominant ways of thinking. Third, the dissemination of the findings is discussed, this process being crucial in order to effect change.

Research Design

A feminist participatory research methodology was employed at the Sure Start program. This is not necessarily a typical approach to feminist research, but it is a sympathetic one and one which is suited to the context because of its concern with redressing the power balance between researcher and researched. Participatory research shares feminists' commitment to "ways of knowing that avoid subordination" (Humphries, 2000, p. 181), to valuing the experiences of research participants, and to making visible the hidden forces of oppression. Having the luxury of time—two years—to undertake the field work meant that it was possible to use a range of ambitious methods. A team of six working-class women, all mothers of young children attending the Sure Start program, were recruited and trained so that they could be fully involved in carrying out the research, from structuring questions and collecting data through to the analysis and dissemination of the findings. A door-to-door questionnaire survey ($n = 72$) was carried out in order to look at why those families who were eligible to access Sure Start were not doing so. Indepth interviews ($n = 27$) took place with mothers of pre-school children accessing the program as well as with volunteers and members of staff.

The project also involved larger numbers of the local community through setting up a range of arts-based groups, including creative writing, short film making, drama, and visual art, which were attended by mothers, as well as grandmothers, of children attending the Sure Start program. Over the course of the two years, participants produced work describing their experiences of motherhood and poverty, and their interactions with Sure Start. These data not only supplemented the interview and questionnaire data, they also provided an aural and visual means of narrating research findings to a community which has low literacy levels (see Foster, 2012a, b, 2013 for more information on these arts-based methods).

In feminist research, whilst qualitative inquiry is often, but not always, favored, there is no one preferred method. Methods, like the methodology, should be tailored to the specific context of the research and, as Du Bois (1983, p. 110) notes, should have the desired effect of opening up "our seeing and our thinking, our conceptual frameworks, to new perceptions that actually derive from women's experience." However, it is important to acknowledge that such experiences are often bound in layers of assumption that may warrant unraveling. Because of this, there was an element of "consciousness raising" involved in the project; this centered on challenging the attitudes of the mothers involved in the research to "poor parenting" because the nature of hegemony means that they too were implicated in perpetuating these myths (see below). Knowledge is an important aspect of a counter-hegemonic force and by creating "many small revolutions" and "many small changes in relationships, behaviours, attitudes and experiences" we are close to Gramsci's notion of a "war of position" (Lather (1991), as cited in Kenway, 2001, p. 59).

At the same time, there are evident limitations to the research and what it can expect to achieve. Gillies and Alldred (2002, p. 45) are wary of research that claims to "empower" or "enlighten" its participants. This, they say, can be "simplistic and patronising," not least because much feminist research is led by middle-class women on behalf of the working class. Moreover, a research project is unlikely to directly change the material conditions of women's lives. Whilst I was genuinely committed to this participatory way of working, there is also no doubt that it was politically expedient and helped me to gain the funding for the project. Service user involvement was beginning to grow in popularity at this time and parental involvement was an extremely important and innovative aspect of SSLPs. Local programs had, to some extent, been shaped by local people through consultation in order to foster a sense of ownership by local communities (not a wholly successful project). The SSLP where the research was carried out also involved parents on its partnership board. Given that the Sure Start initiative is arguably underscored by an assumption that working-class parents lack competence, there is an interesting tension between parents as being "capable, reflective and aware of their own and their children's needs and able to articulate these needs effectively" (Clarke, 2006, p. 717) and the targets for the program which are "built on an assumption of deficits in parenting and parental ignorance" (Clarke, 2006, p. 717). Examples of how these tensions played out in the SSLP are discussed below.

Everyday Interactions

Feminist research has political aims and in the Sure Start research these centered round challenging stereotypical representations of working-class mothers and acknowledging some of the ideology behind the Sure Start initiative. Whilst the findings from the project were important in terms of achieving these aims, the research *process* also lent itself to paying attention to our own everyday practices and interactions with others. Fernandes' (2003, p. 19) discussion of the perceived gap between theory and practice is relevant here:

> In practice we live, indeed we enact, what seem like abstract concepts such as justice, structural oppression, social change and transformation in every moment of our lives, in every relationship, from the most mundane interactions we engage in with strangers in supermarkets to the most intimate relationships we have with loved ones to the most public interactions we have in work, school, society, the world.

This is also fitting with Gramsci's concept of hegemony; it is the daily, habitual, unnoteworthy actions that transmit something much more powerful.

The day-to-day tensions between staff and parents at the Sure Start program, particularly those parents who were involved in a voluntary capacity with the SSLP, were a recurrent theme throughout the project. This was not aided by the fact that, true to the ideology of the initiative, the staff at the SSLP saw their mission as "improving" families, as the following exchange between a member of the research team and a member of staff illustrates:

Researcher (Sure Start parent):	Erm, okay, Sure Start. What do you see Sure Start's main purposes as being?
Staff member [without pausing]:	Helping parents to become better parents.

This aim was at odds with parents' perceptions of the SSLP's purpose. They were much more likely to discuss the fact that the program had provided opportunities for them to make friends, alleviating the isolation they had previously felt. It had also enabled their children to mix with others, and provided activities and meeting spaces to "get them out of the house." Whilst this might have improved parents' and children's quality of life, it was material conditions that prevented them from doing this prior to the arrival of the SSLP. For example, the local park was inaccessible due to hazards of discarded needles used for injection drugs, and broken glass littering the ground. There were no playgroups or children's activities in the locality. Poor public transport links and the fact that few families had their own transport meant that they remained cut off from surrounding areas.

The area had a poor reputation and it became quickly apparent that Sure Start staff viewed the mothers attending the SSLP as "other." They frequently voiced their concerns about local parents' behavior, the ways they interacted with their children, and their eating, drinking, and smoking habits. They spoke of particular families as being "nice," implying that others were not nice, and echoing the age-old "deserving" and "undeserving" poor debate. The following extract is from an interview I conducted with a middle-class, senior member of staff who (unprompted) is reflecting on the spending habits of people in the Sure Start catchment area. The "chip shops" (short for "fish and chip shops") referred to are a British phenomenon where a hot meal—often a meat pie and chipped potatoes or chipped potatoes and gravy—can be purchased relatively cheaply. It is stodgy food high in saturated fat, so not considered to be a healthy option:

> Well, I think within a sort of mile radius of here, there are three or four chip shops. And those chip shops are busy every time I go past them. Now [where I live] there's one chip shop and it's changed hands three or four times because it's just done so poorly. People don't go to it. Certainly not at lunchtime, 'cause there's nobody around at lunchtime . . . And I can't afford to eat my lunch out every day and I work five days a week. So I find that's quite amazing as well, the way people spend their money. I'm far more careful with mine and I think I've probably got more of it [she drives an expensive new car and has just returned from a long holiday overseas], but it is a strange thing.

While such musings were rarely intended to be hostile towards the families concerned, but rather demonstrate puzzlement at the way others live their lives, they do underscore the myth that people living in poverty are doing so because of the individual, poor choices that they make. The structural causes of poverty remain hidden.

The Sure Start mothers on the research team conducted the bulk of the interviews, and had one of them interviewed this staff member (rather than me, a middle-class woman) the resultant conversation is likely to have been different. It is interesting, yet hardly surprising, that the members of the research team also, at times, demonstrated opinions on "responsible" mothering that mirrored Sure Start's ideology and that were often at the expense of other women. This was also the case in Hey and Bradford's (2006) research at a different Sure Start program. I did frequently gently contest the opinions of the research team, particularly in the regular research meetings we held to discuss the progress of the project. Prior to data collection, the view was expressed by the research team, as by the Sure Start staff, that mothers who did not engage with the SSLP did not care about their children (interestingly, fathers' role in this process was never the focus of attention). Through the questionnaire survey, we met a large number of these women and learned of the diversity of issues that stopped them from bringing their children to Sure Start activities. These ranged from debilitating mental and physical health problems through to simply being too busy tending to other aspects of their life, often prioritizing spending time with extended family. This discovery increased the compassion of the research team. The door-to-door nature of the survey meant that we were visiting people's homes, and many of them were in very poor condition. To begin with, some members of the research team were scathing about this, but through our discussions, opinions shifted. At the end of the project one participant noted:

> [The research has] changed my attitude as well—I don't judge people as much. Like if their house is a bit dirty and things like that, there's always a reason—I used to think they were just scruffy! Where now, I probably still comment like, but I don't do it as much—not as bad. 'Cause there's always a reason, like, why things are bad.

I made the decision not to directly challenge the member of staff about her attitudes expressed during our interview to the poverty experienced by families accessing Sure Start. Nor did we (the research team) challenge similar views that were articulated by other members of staff on separate occasions. Staff members already found the research project quite a threatening one, worried about what we might say about the SSLP and their ways of working. We decided that the more suitable way of challenging assumptions about local people's lives and parenting abilities was through the presentation of the research findings. We worked together to design ways of doing this that would engage and inspire rather than intimidate.

Dissemination

The dissemination of our findings from the Sure Start research took a number of forms, including a research report, presentations to the management board and papers at academic conferences (which the research team delivered with me). Here the focus is on the arts-based presentation of findings that took place over the course of an afternoon in a local community venue. Invitations were issued to local families, Sure Start workers, local professionals, councillors, and academics. The turnout was high for such an event, with around 70 people in the audience. The afternoon comprised a showcase of artwork, readings of poems, and screenings of short films that had all been created during the course of the research project by mothers or grandmothers of children attending the SSLP. We (myself and a group of Sure Start mothers) also performed two short plays based on data from the interviews.

One of the main themes of the work presented included the devotion of mothers to their children. The poems in particular conveyed this sentiment in often very moving ways. This chimes with Oakley's (1997, p. xxvi) understanding that what helps mothers living in poverty to cope with their situation is the "strength of the bonds they have with their children." They want the very best for them and would work hard to ensure that their needs were met. It is ironic, then, that the attention the Labour government paid to ensure that parents be "responsible" failed to recognize that "[m]ost parents are acutely aware of their responsibilities to their children, even though they may differ in the ways they carry these out" (Williams, 2004, p. 419).

Positive aspects of living in the local area were highlighted. One mother spoke in an interview about how she found that the Sure Start initiative placed too much emphasis on "the state of your house . . . whether it looks like a shed or whatever," when "there's other things that can be counted that have more of a wealth that you can't see." This feeling was reflected in colorful collages that, through layers of tissue paper and paint, depicted images that their creators deemed important to them: a garden gate leading to their home; a family meal; a familiar skyline; a smiling baby. The short films emphasized both these themes, portraying vivid snapshots of family life (Foster, 2009). Happy, if raucous, scenes showed mischievous children and chaotic homes; more sober voiceovers comprised mothers telling stories of difficulties that they had overcome in their lives, including drug misuse. The plays captured stories told to us through the research interviews, particularly concerning mothers' varied interactions with the Sure Start program and their desire to do the best for their children (Foster, 2013).

The presentation of findings not only celebrated relationships between mothers and children, it also drew attention to the achievements of the research team. The event was warmly received by its audience and a number of its members were moved to tears by the performances and the stories told, as one Sure Start worker reports:

> I found the presentation today very moving (can't believe I couldn't stop crying!). I've been a member of staff in the program virtually from the beginning and am so happy to see the parents who helped me settle in on that stage today with loads of confidence, etc, etc. The videos were excellent as others maybe do not fully understand their lives.

Another staff member commented on the abilities of the participants in the research:

> Excellent to see all the talents and strengths of people in the community, who often I see during my work hours, to see another side to their lives was fantastic.

Emmel (2004, p. 8) states that there is "clear evidence of those who are excluded being treated as the 'other'; individuals who are perceived to have neither the capacity nor the capability to achieve." This, he points out, is one of the mechanisms that perpetuate social exclusion. Countering such assumptions was perhaps the greatest achievement of the research project. Maguire (1996, p. 38) discusses the impact this can have:

> In the sharing of successes, however small and micro, we gain courage and encouragement to learn by doing. Feminism includes joyful affirmation and celebration of our strengths and successes, even redefining success in an increasingly isolating and alienating world.

The research findings received remarkably less attention of those produced by the National Evaluation of Sure Start team in their role as "the selected and designated 'official' evaluators of the Sure Start program" (Broadhurst et al., 2007, p. 446). In this role they can be seen as "powerful spokespersons . . . who have privileged access to networks of dissemination." It was their work, focusing predominantly on measurable outcomes, which was frequently reported in newspapers and contributed to the development of policy and practice. Reports included economic perspectives, characteristics of Sure Start catchment areas, and longitudinal research into impact (NESS Research Team, 2010, 2011, 2012). Whilst potentially useful, the NESS research does not challenge current ideology around working-class motherhood and can thus help to "construct and sustain particular practices" (Broadhurst et al., 2007, p. 444). The findings of our project were less politically influential but they, and the feminist research process itself, did impact in small but significant ways on people's ways of thinking about mothering in poverty. Ideally, as Maguire (2001) points out, feminist research should be about transformation on a personal as well as structural level.

Conclusion

Fernandes (2003, p. 56) points out that there is a certain irony in the fact that the feminist goal of making women visible "may lead feminists to overlook the invisible everyday practices we engage in as we negotiate our lives, our jobs and our activist endeavours." The personal really *is* political, despite the fact that this well-known feminist slogan has "for the most part not been understood in terms of its deepest ethical implications" (p. 55). Revisiting Gramsci can help this understanding. As Johnson (2007, p. 95) articulates, his work on counter-hegemony remains "a strategic resource" when there is still so much to achieve in terms of social justice.

In recent UK social policy and practice, as historically, women's poverty has gone largely unremarked, despite the focus on lifting children out of poverty. Labour's early-years interventions, including Sure Start, were "predicated on the assumption that at least part of the problem is the parenting skills of poor parents, that is, poor parenting rather that parenting in poverty" (Levitas, 2004, p. 49). The merit of parenting ability is judged on archetypal middle-class behaviors (Gewirtz, 2001), which is particularly unjust given the refusal to recognize poverty "and the stress, ill-health and poor living conditions associated with it" (Gewirtz, 2001, p. 374). Emphasis is placed on cultural practices (Clarke, 2006), such as reading to children, structured play, clean and safe homes (difficult to achieve when houses are riddled with damp and mold), and attendance at nursery.

The research discussed in this chapter aimed to gently challenge these assumptions and practices amongst its participants and its varied audiences. Contemporary feminism is "a particularly fruitful place" for exploring such broad questions of social justice (Fernandes, 2003, p. 12). As Stanley (1990) asserts, feminism is not merely a perspective (way of seeing) or an epistemology (way of knowing), it is also "an ontology, or a way of being in the world" (p. 14). Without the commitments outlined here, particularly in terms of recognizing power relations in the research process and the reproduction of power through everyday speech and actions, there is a danger that academic research will only perpetuate exploitation, oppression, and injustice. Research findings can be used to justify and strengthen the status quo, particularly when those findings are grounded in "science." Conquergood (2002) states that there is "no contest" between such objective knowledge and local, community-based knowing. It is, he says drolly, "the choice between science and old wives' tales" (p. 146). It is ironic then that state-sanctioned, "rational" accounts of poor-working class mothers only serve to strengthen the myth of their monstrousness, as they retell the story that such women need surveillance and intervention to avoid transmitting their problems to their offspring and to wider society. Maguire (1996, p. 31) raises the following "profound" challenge: if one is to know the world differently then one should, in one's approach to life, "act and be differently" in the world. By giving consideration to our everyday behaviors and interactions with others we can help to ensure that we are not reproducing the inequalities and exclusions that we speak out against.

Notes

1 Funded through an ESRC CASE award. Grant reference: PTA-033-2003-00024.
2 Funded through an ESRC postdoctoral fellowship award. Grant reference: PTA-026-27-1870.

References

Abbott, P. & Wallace, C. (1998). Health visiting, social work, nursing and midwifery: a history. In P. Abbott & L. Meerabeau (Eds.), *The sociology of the caring professions* (2nd ed.) (pp. 20–53). London: UCL.

Broadhurst, K., Mason, C., & Grover, C. (2007). Sure Start and the "re-authorization" of Section 47 child protection practices. *Critical Social Policy, 27* (4), 443–461.

Carey, M. (2011). Should I stay or should I go? Practical, ethical and political challenges to "service user" participation within social work research. *Qualitative Social Work, 10* (2), 224–243.

Carey, M. & Foster, V. (2013). Social work, ideology, discourse and the limits of post-hegemony. *Journal of Social Work, 13* (3), 248–266.

Clarke, K. (2006). Childhood, parenting and early intervention: A critical examination of the Sure Start national program. *Critical Social Policy, 26* (4), 699–721.

Conquergood, D. (2002). Performance studies: Interventions and radical research. *The Drama Review, 46* (2), 145–156.

Daly, M. (2000). Feminist research methodology: The case of Ireland. In A. Byrne & R. Lentin (Eds.), *(Re)searching women: Feminist research methodologies in the social sciences in Ireland* (pp. 60–72). Dublin: Institute of Public Administration.

Du Bois, B. (1983). Passionate scholarship: notes on values, knowing and method in feminist social science. In G. Bowles & R. Duelli Klein (Eds.), *Theories of women's studies* (pp. 105–116). London: Routledge and Kegan Paul.

Eagleton, T. (2007). *Ideology: An introduction.* London: Verso.

Emmel, N. (2004). Comments on tackling social exclusion: taking stock and looking to the future: a response. *ESRC Research Methods Programme: Working paper no. 8.* Retrieved from http://www.ccsr.ac.uk/methods/publications/documents.

Fawcett, B., Featherstone, B., & Goddard, J. (2004). *Contemporary child care policy and practice.* Houndmills: Palgrave Macmillan.

Fernandes, L. (2003). *Transforming feminist practice: Non-violence, social justice and the possibilities of a spiritualized feminism.* San Francisco: Aunt Lute Books.

Foster, V. (2009). Authentic representation? Using video as counter-hegemony in participatory research with poor working-class women. *International Journal of Research Approaches, 3* (3), 233–245.

Foster, V. (2012a). What if? The use of poetry to promote social justice. *Social Work Education, 3* (6), 742–755.

Foster, V. (2012b). The pleasure principle: employing arts-based methods in social work research. *The European Journal of Social Work, 15* (4), 532–545.

Foster, V. (2013). Pantomime and politics: The story of a performance ethnography. *Qualitative Research, 13* (1), 36–52.

Gewirtz, S. (2001). Cloning the Blairs: New Labour's program for the re-socialisation of working-class parents. *Journal of Education Policy, 16* (4), 365–378.

Gillies, V. & Alldred, P. (2002). The ethics of intention: Using research as a political tool. In M. Mauthner, J. Birch, & T. Miller (Eds.), *Ethics in qualitative research* (pp. 32–52). London: Sage.

Hey, V. & Bradford, S. (2006). Re-engineering motherhood? Sure Start in the Community. *Contemporary Issues in Early Childhood, 7* (1), 53–67.

Holub, R. (1992). *Antonio Gramsci: Beyond Marxism and postmodernism.* London: Routledge.

Humphries, B. (2000). From critical thought to emancipatory action: Contradictory research goals? In C. Truman, D.M. Mertens & B. Humphries (Eds.), *Research and Inequality* (pp. 179–190). London: UCL Press.

Johnson, R. (2007). Post-hegemony? I don't think so. *Theory, Culture and Society, 24* (3), 95–110.

Jones, C. & Novak, T. (1999). *Poverty, welfare and the disciplinary state.* London: Routledge.

Jones, S. (2006). *Antonio Gramsci.* London: Routledge

Kenway, J. (2001). Remembering and regenerating Gramsci. In *Feminist engagements. Reading, resisting and revisioning male theorists in education and cultural studies* (pp. 47–66). New York: Routledge.

Lather, P. (1991). *Getting smart: Feminist research and pedagogy with/in the postmodern.* New York: Routledge.

Ledwith, M. (2009) Antonio Gramsci and feminism: the elusive nature of power. *Educational Philosophy and Theory, 41* (6).

Levitas, R. (2004). Let's hear it for Humpty: Social exclusion, the Third Way and cultural capital. *Cultural Trends, 13* (2), 41–56.

Lister, R. (2006). Children (but not women) first: New Labour, child welfare and gender. *Critical Social Policy, 26* (2), 315–335.

Lynch, K. (2000). The role of emancipatory research in the academy. In A. Byrne & R. Lentin (Eds.), *(Re)searching women: Feminist research methodologies in the social sciences in Ireland* (pp. 73–104). Dublin: Institute of Public Administration.

Maguire, P. (1996). Proposing a more feminist participatory research: knowing and being embraced openly. In K. De Koning & M. Martin (Eds.), *Participatory research in health: Issues and experiences* (pp. 27–39). London: Zed Books.

Maguire, P. (2001). Uneven ground: Feminisms and action research. In P. Reason & H. Bradbury (Eds.), *Handbook of action research* (pp. 59–69). London: Sage.

Namjoshi, S. (1993). *Feminist fables.* North Melbourne: Spinifex Press.

NESS Research Team (2010). *The impact of Sure Start Local Programmes on five year olds and their families.* London: DfES. Retrieved from http://www.education.gov.uk/publications/RSG/AllPublications/Page1/DFE-RR067.

NESS Research Team (2011). *National evaluation of Sure Start local programs: An economic perspective.* London: DfES. Retrieved from http://www.education.gov.uk/publications/RSG/EarlyYearseducationandchildcare/Page2/DFE-RR073.

NESS Research Team (2012). *The impact of Sure Start Local Programmes on seven year olds and their families.* London: DfES. Retrieved from http://www.education.gov.uk/publications/RSG/EarlyYearseducationandchildcare/Page2/DFE-RR220.

Oakley, A. (1992). *Social support and motherhood.* Oxford: Blackwell.

Oakley, A. (1997). Introduction. In C. Gowdridge, A.S. Williams, & M. Wynn (Eds.), *Mother courage: Letters from mothers in poverty at the end of the century* (pp. xv–xvii). London: Penguin Books.

Smart, C. (1992). Disruptive bodies and unruly sex: the regulation of reproduction and sexuality in the nineteenth century. In C. Smart (Ed.), *Regulating womanhood: Historical essays on marriage, motherhood and sexuality* (pp. 7–32). London: Routledge.

Stanley, L. (1990). An editorial introduction. In L. Stanley (Ed.) *Feminist praxis: Research, theory and epistemology in feminist sociology* (pp. 3–19). London: Routledge.

Starkey, P. (2000). The feckless mother: Women, poverty and social workers in wartime and post-war England. *Women's History Review, 9* (3), 539–557.

Wiegers, W. (2002). *The framing of poverty as "child poverty" and its implications for women.* Ottawa: Status of Women Canada.

Williams, F. (2004). In and beyond New Labour: Towards a new political ethics of care. *Critical Social Policy, 24* (3), 406–427.

Wilson, H. & Huntington, A. (2005) Deviant (m)others: The construction of teenage motherhood in contemporary discourse. *Journal of Social Policy, 35* (1), 59–76.

Section 3

Treatment of Binaries in Research

9 Feminist Research in the Absence of Gender

Exploring Intersubjectivity in Practice, Purpose, and Representation

Ann Curry-Stevens

For the last six years, I have conducted community-based participatory research with the Coalition of Communities of Color in Multnomah County in Portland, Oregon. We sought to document racial disparities in the region and press policy makers and elected officials to improve racial equity. We have released a total of seven major research reports, with significant impacts on local discourses on racial equity, and have positively affected local policy practices and policy outcomes. The implicit goals of our research were to transfer lived experiences of inequality and understandings of the magnitude of institutional racism into a form of knowledge that could persuade policy makers that the issues are urgent and solutions are available. The Coalition initiated this research project as its leaders continued to be marginalized in policy practice—rarely invited to policy tables, or invited late and in tokenistic roles, rarely passing the "raised eyebrows" test (as in, "how bad do you say it is?") on the severity of challenges facing the community. From their position, a university partnership offered the chance of putting an evidence base underneath their issues. From my position as an academic, and specifically an academic who identifies as white, it offered a chance to be useful to the community and to build a research project that held the possibility of influencing policy.

This research was not framed as explicitly feminist. Most often, I frame it as anti-racist scholarship, anti-oppressive or critical research, and its approach as "community-based participatory action research" (combining community-based participatory research (CBPR) and participatory action research). With the invitation to consider writing for this text, I dug more deeply into what I consider to be feminist scholarship. Beyond a focus on women and gender, feminist research is also founded on key principles surrounding ethics, reflexivity, engagement in social change, close tending to dynamics of power and authority, and efforts to address subjectivities brought about by varying social locations (Gringeri, Wahab, & Anderson-Nathe, 2010). The way the Coalition and I have navigated these issues is deeply feminist, and draws in pronounced ways from feminist scholars in spite of not centering gender.

Feminist Research in the Absence of Gender

Key ethics I have sought to enact are those of solidarity (whereby I am led by the political sensibilities of the Coalition and endeavor to make their struggles my own) and respectful recognition (Rossiter, 2005, para. 38), which draws heavily on the "politics of recognition" (Fraser & Honneth, 2003, p. 7) as an enactment of social justice in scholarship. Recognition is advanced by these studies, as they bring visibility to the communities of color and compel the policy community to understand local struggles and priorities for action. My personal research ethos is also tied to respectful recognition and solidarity—to use the privilege I have to align with the communities' issues and priorities, and remain committed to creating a rendering of their experiences in a way that built their power and influence. In my view, theirs is an important form of knowledge demanding the utmost respect, as the work on the uniqueness of feminist knowledges developed by Belenky, Clinchy, Goldberger, and Tarule (1997) confirms. The knowledge of marginalized communities must be amplified—not treated suspiciously, as it tends to be when positivist and post-positivist researchers confirm that the "objective" researcher and his/her research practices generate knowledge. The larger context of racism (and, in Belenky et al.'s work, patriarchy) imbues a form of knowledge that I bridged by deep listening, and enacted (in reflection) "listening as a very active and demanding process" (p. 37). Akin to "bearing witness," as articulated in Finn and Jacobson (2008), socially just engagement requires "speak[ing] out about the suffering of others . . . making the connections between personal pain and structural violence" (pp. 236–237). To position myself in a neutral or objective stance to their lived experiences would have been an act of disaffirmation and disavowal of the realities of racism and white privilege. Rather, a stance of believing honors the community's experience. It required me to reject the semi-objective research stance to which I had been acculturated, an action that was essential to a productive working relationship. This reflects, I hope, Rossiter's assertion of the need for a "responsible epistemic practice" (1996, p. 33) in order to ensure that knowledge is viewed as situated and context-laden.

I connect solidarity and respectful recognition to advanced ethics, stretching well beyond the conventions of Institutional Review Boards. My ethic in working across racial and institutional differences required me to adopt and enact the following principles: solidarity, a stance of believing, implicating myself in relations of domination, implicating my institution (as one of higher education that fails local communities of color time and again), and sharing power in the decisions made throughout and following the research. To have neglected these principles would have violated "respectful recognition" and enacted trespass on the community. These principles remained aspirations of my work, though they are breeched during the research and in its representation (as in this text and in Curry-Stevens, 2012).

The praxis enacted in this research reflects that asserted by Gringeri et al. (2010): "Feminist research challenges contemplative spectator research by virtue of being openly political, connected, and involved in liberatory actions" (p. 393). Our research goals were both implicitly and explicitly political: the former illustrated how the reports raised the visibility of communities of color, and the latter was illustrated in the reports' policy recommendations asserting the need to accurately understand racial disparities in every institution, to build action plans to eliminate disparities, to advance both the knowledge claims and the resource claims of communities of color, and to name racism and white privilege.

Our process also illustrated a political praxis, as we committed to power sharing throughout the research project and rebalanced formal power arrangements in favor of the Coalition when I took missteps in the middle of the work (Curry-Stevens, 2012). The Coalition held the power of having initiated the work, implicitly supporting their ability to also cancel or modify the research project. They certainly could have severed the working partnership with me and recruited an alternative researcher—they maintained primary ownership of the project itself. Their role and influence were substantive: the research questions were established in partnership, the methods were selected primarily by the Coalition, the review of drafts and final editorial roles were led by the Coalition, and the dissemination process occurred in public and political venues (city council, state legislative offices, newspaper editorial boards) with Coalition leaders taking leading roles and following up to leverage influence to address racial disparities. From initiation to systems change outcomes, the central focus on power is evident within this research project, as it is a vehicle for building the power of communities of color in both process and outcome. This embodies, I suggest, the perspectives articulated by Gringeri et al. (2010).

Intersubjectivity and Opportunities to Resist Imperialism

Turning now to the ways in which I navigated issues of power and difference, and how I endeavored to address the subjectivities embedded in "researcher" and "researched," I draw from the second- and third-wave feminist insights embedded within the fundamentals of power at a deeply constructivist level: those of self and other, of the process of "othering," of subject and object, and the binaries on which these relationships are constructed. I consider these elements more fundamental, and thus potentially more important to the power hierarchies within the research process. I have been interested in these themes for the last few years, as I notice the oppression that exists within the very foundation of the research process—that of the subject/object construction. I am excited to follow these themes throughout my own research, offering them up to expose, to trouble, and simultaneously affirm with ambiguity.

Considerable damage to a community's integrity can be wrought by othering through researching "down" social locations. The violation embedded in such research provides a justification for why the Coalition gave priority to a CBPR approach, which rejected the inquiry of the academic researcher into the lives of marginalized communities. Instead, we adopted a foundation that supported multiple research relationships—up, down, and lateral.

The "subject/object" divide is often considered from a post-modern perspective that emphasizes positivist challenges to the creation of the subject. The reach of this challenge is significant, with the "death of the subject" and the "death of the author" suggested as outcomes. Feminist writers amplify the ways that patriarchy has infused the creation of the subject in limiting, exclusionary, and oppressive ways (Benhabib, Butler, Cornell, & Fraser, 1995). The appeal of such analysis is its cohesive, theoretically robust critique of the subject/object divide. When I follow this trail for long, however, I end up down a rabbit hole of critique, with growing divergence from the methodological choices that I made with the Coalition in this research. Essentially our research is structural and post-structural research, and aligned with the feminist forms of standpoint epistemologies, highlighting the larger institutional injustices and the more mezzo and micro procedures and practices that are oppressively enacted on communities of color while simultaneously benefiting white communities. Post-modern critiques of the subject trouble the very construction of this research as it leads to the erosion of binaries, and a deep challenge to research that is based on binaries—as is the case with my research work.

Pulling myself out of the rabbit hole (with assistance from Ben Anderson-Nathe), I simply honor the contribution of post-modern scholars that deeply troubles and ultimately rejects binaries, and assert that my pragmatic and politically engaged scholarship requires me to locate the research in relatively untroubled ways within binaries. An "easy out" for me is to let the reader discern whether my treatment of this divergence is acceptable. We retained a binary construction of people of color and whites in our research, and further disaggregated to detail specific communities of color. If this results in a violation of critical feminist constructs, and renders the work no longer aligned with third-wave feminism, then so be it. Our political agenda of catalyzing action on institutional racism takes priority.

I notice a parallel here with conventional complaints about postmodernism that it unsettles knowledge (even the tacit and lived knowledges of marginalized communities) to such a degree that movement forward is so complicated as to not happen. As Razack positions her own scholarship:

> I . . . keep a modernist eye on domination. Who is dominating whom is not a question I reply to with the answer that we are all constructed simultaneously as dominant and subordinate. While we are all simultaneously dominant and subordinate, and have varying degrees of privilege and penalty, this insight is not the most relevant when we are seeking to end specific hierarchies at specific sites . . . such a response amounts to a statement that race does not matter, an outright denial of the impact of white supremacy on the lives of people of color (1998, p. 161).

My effort is similar: to remain respectful of the challenges anti-essentialism brings to my research work, to affirm the value of its contributions as a vehicle through which to understand the unease I experience in writing about "they" as subjects under the researcher's gaze, and to maintain the pragmatic resolution of this when we wrote as the collective "we"—here positioning myself as (inauthentically) part of the communities of color whose experiences we detailed.

Formulating the Research Questions

I am not a person of color—I am white, relatively affluent, and a beneficiary of the omnipresent societal, discursive, institutional, and historic advantages that come my way as a result. What does this mean for the research process? First, it means that I come to academia with a lot of bells and whistles on my résumé; born partially of effort but mostly the result of hiring practices that favored my forms of expertise—professional credentials, academic degrees, authored works, and an ability to volunteer in relevant service areas. I did not come into the role of principal investigator with a lived experience of racism nor the daily reminders of unfair and inequitable education, employment, or banking practices. What did I know about racism? Almost nothing. And of the urgency borne of seeing these same systems harming my children and community? Nothing.

At first, I did not navigate deep weakness in my experience well. I knew I needed to be cautious of the subjectivity that positioned me as "researching down" the power hierarchies (Stanley & Wise, 1983), and that the ignorance embedded in my lived experience was prone to morphing into arrogance in an assumption that I could understand the lives of "other" (Hobgood, 2000). The dangers of constructing the research whereby I as principal investigator was researching an oppressed "other" were deeply problematic.

These dynamics have long been identified by feminist scholars who understood the violation conducted by men who spoke for women, pathologizing features of women's reactions to injustice, and typifying (and limiting) our social, political, and economic roles. Says Butler (1990), "the effort to include 'other' cultures as variegated amplifications of a global phallogocentrism constitutes an appropriative act that risks . . . self-aggrandizing [and] . . . colonizing" (p. 13). When research is conducted in ways that ignore the social construction of gender through the lens of the male researcher, violations occur. Feminist researchers applied that same critique to their own positionality in researching "other."

Considering the challenges in "researching down" across class differences, Reay (1996) amplifies the potential for "exploitation implicit in mixing up one's own personal history with very different working-class experiences" (p. 65). Using Said's (1993) terminology, orientalized feminists have extended this analysis into the violations to communities of color by occidental researchers (Mohanty, 1991; Smith, 1999; Spivak, 1988). Said's (1993) work on the imperial basis of orientalism is a prime example of the damage done to an entire race of people through the construction of "other" by occidental researchers that implicitly (and, more historically, explicitly) justify conquest, and "our right to direct the rest of humanity" (Harmand, 1910, as cited in Said, 1993, p. 17).

Conditions in my own research with the Coalition of Communities of Color were ripe for the risk of trespass and imperialism. The construct of "trespass" within the research relationship draws from Rossiter's heightened attention to this dynamic within the social work relationship. Drawing from Orlie (1997), Rossiter determines that "trespasses are the harm brought to others by our own participation in the governing ways of envisioning and making the world" (Orlie, 1997, as cited by Rossiter, 2000, p. 151). She concludes that our professional knowledges must be troubled for how they reinforce ruling relations of power:

> In view of the loss of innocence of professional knowledge, and our understanding of the ways power and knowledge ground governmentality, the option that offers us freedom is the exercise of thinking and acting politically to uncover the trespasses that accompany the good we do. (p. 160)

When I considered how I might navigate this trespass, we decided to fundamentally rework the research question, which also demanded that we revise our research objectives, in spite of these having been stipulated in our grant application:

> Why is this initiative needed? There are four reasons. The first is that at every step in the causal chain in health outcomes, people of color are overrepresented among people in poverty, juvenile justice, without education, experiencing trauma, in unaffordable housing, less likely to live in safe neighborhoods and unlikely to be reunified with their families quickly if they go into child welfare services. They are also underrepresented among those who have access to culturally specific mental health and counseling services. (Curry-Stevens & Coalition of Communities of Color, 2008, p. 5)

In this framing, the community itself is portrayed as "object" of study. Implicitly, the researcher is simultaneously constructed as "subject." In an intentional act to deconstruct the "object" positioning of communities of color, I forwarded a heightened focus on whiteness and the experiences of white populations throughout the research. By bringing my subjectivity into focus, I suggested to the Coalition the importance of centering whiteness in the work, by comparing the experiences of communities of color with those of the "white, not Hispanic" community. The Coalition supported this suggestion. As a result, every analysis and display in the collected works scrutinizes whiteness. This is an intentional act of resistance. We opted not to compare the experiences of communities of color to that of "total" population data. Intentionally, we used what Said (1993, p. 66) called "contrapuntal reading" that emphasizes the importance of side-by-side comparisons to highlight injustice. This juxtaposition approach simultaneously amplifies the experiences of privilege and oppression, and advances social justice in a profoundly logical way, since systems of oppression and domination are mutually constructed. The experiences of the white community are laid out beside the experiences of communities of color.

While these studies are not explicitly about white privilege, they bring whiteness into focus and highlight the injustices of white privilege across 28 systems and institutions. The correlated benefit is that the research transitions away from "researching down" to intersubjective research, which in this case is about the researcher both studying across and down, and the Coalition members studying across (one's own communities) and "up" into white communities.

The benefits of studying "up" are numerous, including the opportunities to rectify the invisibility of powerholders (Aguiar, 2012), to deconstruct the myths of meritocracy (Aguiar, 2012; Vodde, 2001), and to challenge the policy landscape that ignores the undue influence of elites (Aguiar, 2012). The cautions of earlier writings from Puwar (1997) on researching "up" have been largely navigated through the advent of CBPR. As multiply identified researchers (with the community included), her cautions about issues of suspicion and discomfort in the relational rapport of data collection can be (and were) navigated by a team of researchers whose composition can be customized to ensure that at least one member shares the identity of the participants.

While my research with the Coalition uses conventional binaries of racial identity, the form of "othering" decried by feminist and critical scholars is not in evidence. Conventional relations of domination adhere to the construct of white as superior and communities of color as inferior (Butler, 1990; Wright, 1997). Our writing clearly implicates white racial identity as problematic and dynamics of whiteness as ethically suspect due to the relentless manifestations of advantage that are illustrated in the texts. By extension, the privileged white group is implicitly "othered" as it is homogeneously profiled on the winning end of many unjust systems. In this sense, our research has added the study of whiteness to the study of racial disparities—a lateral subjective position—as opposed to researching "down" the ladder of socially constructed identities. We foregrounded this subjectivity, and with the subjectivities of our communities of color, we co-created an intersubjective stance as it interrogates both the researcher's and the Coalition's communities.

There have been numerous positive outcomes of the research in the policy arena, in profile and influence for the Coalition, and in discourse. To begin, the conventional racial discourse in the United States centers the black/white binary. Our work has expanded across several communities of color, as an array of communities of color contributed to the undertaking (African, African American, Native American, Asian and Pacific Islander, Latino and Slavic, with intention to integrate the Middle Eastern community in an upcoming research effort). In the words of a Coalition member, the work has helped to unite "our black and brown brothers and sisters" as a community and as an advocacy group. This is a key political gain, for communities of color on their own are a small percentage of the total population, with the largest being 12% (Latino) and the smallest being less than 1% (Pacific Islander), but together the community sits at close to one-third of Multnomah County's population. Working together across communities of color has built both social and political capital and enacted solidarity that unites advocacy efforts.

Another discourse gain is in raising the visibility of racial disparities, which previously required leaders of color to defend their need to join policy dialogues and to advance policies that would reduce disparities. As determined in a 2013 evaluation, "discourse gains continue to be pronounced in the area of awareness of racial equity. It is increasingly rare for public sector leaders to be unaware of the prevalence of racial disparities in their sector" (Curry-Stevens, 2013, p. 6). Recently a leading racial equity advocate told me that the impact of this work was in the millions of dollars, simply because abundant time had been saved justifying the need to focus on racial equity—time that now could be directed to finding solutions to disparities (Jones, personal communication, 2013).

That said, the research has fallen short of Krumer-Nevo and Sidi's (2012) caution against objectification. Though the research did not intend to objectify, there is an implicit and persistent message of misery across the research reports, compelling one coalition to publicly implore, "we are not our disparities" (Ramirez, personal communication, 2013). It is possible that communities of color are now more likely to be perceived as damaged and miserable. Given that the research reports were intended to detail the disparities facing communities of color and to amplify the injustices behind these data, we gave relatively scant attention to the strengths and assets of the communities, with the exception of their abilities to withstand adversity. While we did not formally discuss this, when we received feedback about the need for more attention to strengths in the work, we added a few sentences rather than expansively reworking the reports.

Fundamentally, the targets of the reports were policy leaders. The Coalition believed that it could generate a stronger imperative to act by portraying the fullness of distress as opposed to the ability to survive distress. If we had added a stronger complexity about experience, the policy community's gaze would be diffused across issues. By keeping the work structurally oriented and framed by binaries, we hoped to catalyze change.

Pathways of resistance, stories of achievement, and creative expressions of the communities' vitality may help rebalance how communities of color are perceived and minimize their objectification. These stories are needed to affirm communities of color for their fullness. How one lives with adversity, how one might thrive and how one might also be defeated—including the impacts of community building and the ways in which community groups have supported their members—could be important to resist the portrayal of communities of color as largely victims of injustice. Such work would ease the overlying binary emphasis (as oppressed) with which communities of color have been painted in these research reports.

I still support how we constructed the original research reports. Heavy emphasis on a binary construction of identity has, however, created a possible impact of objectifying and homogenizing local communities of color, and also of white communities. But these constructions are resistive in their formulation—for communities of color to be seen to have a shared identity, and for whites to have their identity troubled and foregrounded as unjustly benefiting from inequity.

This formulation is not overly aligned with post-modern sensibilities, but such was not our intention. The Coalition sought to build visibility and influence, and concretely build an evidence base for their advocacy work. Simultaneously, we formalized tacit knowledge and challenged dominant discourses prevalent in the region.

Dominant discourse has shifted as a result of the research reports and the political attention that the work has garnered. The region has a longstanding prideful embrace as being a progressive enclave of the United States. These reports have challenged this identity, as racial inequities are pronounced and in many situations worsening. As well, inequities are worse than King County, home to Seattle, just 160 miles to the north. There is grudging acknowledgement that Portland "nice" has willfully ignored the needs of communities of color in policy, in governance, and in political will. Power has also shifted towards communities of color in gaining seats at policy tables and in gaining ground on the influence of mainstream service providers. Concrete policy gains have manifest and significant undertakings are underway to address institutional racism and disparities in a few arenas, most notably in education. In light of these gains, it would be hasty to conclude that we should have addressed the overly homogenizing profile of communities of color or the growing literature on anti-essentialism (Brown, 2012; Kumsa, 2007). Essentialism is a problematic construct across social work research and practice, including that of anti-oppressive practice (which has typically emphasized a binary construction of identity as either oppressed or privileged, with a requisite nod to intersecting and interlocking oppressions), but to resist this construction would have left us in a bind. If we had rejected the binary construction of racial identity, we would have lost touch with the experience of racism and white privilege with which the majority of communities of color identify. To have advocated an anti-essentialist framework in this research project would have been paramount to denying racism.

I look forward to the contributions of anti-essentialism in the years to come, and now I advocate that a structuralist approach to identity and racial disparities and inequities was essential for moving an advocacy agenda forward. This is admittedly an imperfect resolution; portraying communities of color as damaged cannot possibly be ideal. I hope that the contributions outweigh the eventual negative results of such positioning. I look forward to further contemplation on the intersections of "recognition" and "redistribution," as have been articulated by Fraser and Honneth (2003). If justice is advanced without respectful recognition, then can we claim it as justice?

Representation of the Community

The Coalition of Communities of Color decided early in the research process that it would co-author these reports and that its members wanted the representation of their experiences to be told with the "we" voice, precluding (obviously) that the story would be told about "them" or profiling their communities as "they." This allowed the reports to be owned by the community—formally as authors of the work, culturally as the writing is about "we," and discursively as the texts center the self-identification of the community and simultaneously research "up" to implicate whiteness. This issue can benefit, however, from additional critical self-reflection on my behalf, as an author who writes about "we" when I do not belong to the communities profiled in the reports (except as white, but that is not the usage of the term "we").

Consider the heightened sensibilities of voice and authorship and the conventions of dominant culture scholarship. What dominant discourse underlies the framework of "we" writing about "they" or "them"? I am now much more sensitive to this discord and the likely violation embedded here. The very language distances and objectifies. When the academic "we" write about the community "them," "we" seem entitled to portray "them" in ways that are not troubled, except voluntarily by the researcher who has been exposed to the critique of dominant research culture. Rossiter (2007) decries that the person who is synthesizing (researching) others' lives falls out of sight, performing what she calls the "god trick" (Haraway, 1988, cited on p. 24) through which the other's life appears to emerge from nowhere, and is believed to exist as an objective reality, a stance she calls the "hallmark of domination: the gaze from nowhere" (p. 24). Social work writing about the lives of clients and their communities, and in fact the majority of writings about the lives of others, has been filtered by someone else (the "we" or "I" that is the researcher) but our subjectivities—be they inaccuracies, biases, or social constructions—are invisible unless the researcher voluntarily discloses them. This is the nature of Rossiter's (2001) eschewal of social workers' innocence. Such constructions of the self and other, and of "we" and "they," do damage. Boundaries of language amplify the divides between "we" and "they," precluding a common identity. They ripen the potential for "othering" and for rendering othered groups as inferior (or at the very least objectified), and provide, as they have always done, the justification for hierarchy and oppression. Foucault's reflection (1980) on how discourses amplify relations of domination provides insight: the "we/they" binary is both constituted through the daily navigations of power relationships (in this case the writing of a research report) as well as being reflective of pre-existing social divides. These divides within discourse and culture amplify divides in social, economic, and political distance between groups of different statures and identities.

At the same time, fertile spaces exist for challenging these divides and resistive possibilities might merge to blur the we/they binary. If we could narrow these boundaries and see ourselves as a greater part of a collective whole, we might become more invested in the collective wellbeing of all of us. The social construction of language constitutes and legitimates considerable power imbalances. Advancing Foucault's vision for language to reconstitute social relations is a worthy change effort. It begins, in my opinion, in the research language of "subject/object" and extends to the research writings that are "we/they" and "us/them," or, perhaps more poignantly, simply that of "they" and "them," for in fact, the "we" part typically disappears in research writings.

What would it take to blur the boundaries—social, political, and economic—between "we" and "they"? Consider what feminist theorists have said about the objectification that is embedded in the categories of the "us/them" binaries. Wright's work on how we represent the "other" (1997) suggests that the research process is prone to imperialism, but that it can be rectified if informed by post-modern sensibilities and a more ambiguous relationship with "truth." She goes further to etch out a space for a more privileged researcher by suggesting that we each hold degrees of separation from epistemic "knowing" and that, at an individual level, all are fundamentally challenged in knowing and therefore being able to accurately define another. I ask, however, if this focus is part of a race to innocence (Fellows & Razack, 1998) that advances researchers' entitlement to study areas of interest, as long as trespass is not excessive.

Weiner-Levy and Queder (2012) emphasize that identity differences impact researchers' affinity or remoteness from the community and their culture. This challenge is minimized, though, by shared identity. Research remains, as I suggest to my students, an act of trespass that strips us of our innocence in the research relationship. Weiner-Levy and Queder state, "being an integral part of the society one studies does not guarantee automatic entrance, trust or acceptance" (p. 1164), although insider status can lessen the social distance that the more privileged researcher needs to navigate. Insider-based research (or researching laterally) has been the typical response to the imperialist construction of research. I suggest that intersubjectivity might look distinctly different—and that intention to break away from the "subject/object" construction embedded in the majority of research undertakings might be reconfigured in creative and evocative ways.

Our decision to write with the "we" voice ends the othering that occurs when communities are written about as "they" and "them." It is an imperfect solution as it is inauthentic for the white researcher, but the decision advances the likelihood of community ownership and embrace of the product.

Retrospective on the Decision to be Sole Author

Telling this research story has been complicated. I initially attempted to write it to avoid the subject/object divide and referred to "we" as both the subject and object of the text. I could not navigate this successfully, as I am the sole author. I still wanted to uphold my commitment to intersubjectivity, adhering to the same forms of resistance evident in the research reports. I could not accomplish this with integrity, as speaking in the "we" construct was inauthentic and inappropriately possessive as I was claiming membership in a group to which I did not belong. I now turn to unpack the writing of this text as sole author, and unpack my decision to write this alone, and assess the degree to which this was an act of trespass and paternalism, and whereby I return to a stance of subject that enacts domination over my community partners. I dig into this process in an effort to explore how I have trespassed.

When I look more deeply at the absence of power sharing in this text (as I am sole author), I wonder about the way I am enacting privilege. My first reaction is that my Coalition partners are not likely to be interested in such a chapter. They are busy and this is work that will primarily benefit an academic audience as opposed to their racial equity advocacy. But have they ever said such a thing? A few have indicated their lack of interest in speaking at academic conferences. I have kept such requests minimal—it feels like such an infringement on their free time, and an act of disrespect to the urgency of their advocacy priorities. There are many things I would love from my community partners—their participation in strategic planning for the School of Social Work, joining advisory committees for a new center on racial equity, visiting classrooms to share their work, providing input on grants, reviewing research reports, joining working groups to develop new research, and the list can go on. I minimize these requests to one or two a year.

On the surface, my choice can be interpreted as an act of paternalism, but that does not reveal enough of the issue. Digging deeper, when I center my own analysis of dynamics, I get to reserve the choice of how to both look back and how to plan for moving forward. I get to shape the story of this research partnership. While this might look like it protects me, it also reserves for me the space to be more deeply critical of myself and my stance within the research. Quite honestly, some Coalition members (when I have discussed a critical reviewing of difficult times in the partnership) are prone to giving me a "pass," citing these moments as unimportant. So too I anticipate they would respond to the critiques embedded in this text.

I recall a student a few years ago stating that she, as a community-identified research collaborator, was offended by the research writings about partnership and analysis of research dynamics. How researchers interpret dynamics tends to be one-sided and alternatively self-flagellating and self-aggrandizing. Binaries of "good" and "bad" practices tend to fill up pages on this issue. These types of texts, at the same time, are what students and some researchers want to read and what journals ask for us to write. They want to learn what we have learned in these processes, and particularly like to read about the mistakes we have made, wanting to see the humility involved in making mistakes and being willing to share this publicly. While I think this is partly about "seeing" research as more than its products, it is also about interpreting the scholarship's trustworthiness. Such interest is about believing that respectful research is about how one navigates unexpected issues of power and issues of use of self as a researcher.

I am aware too that the dimensions of this work are not very accessible. Subjectivities, epistemologies, the social construction of knowledge: these are dense constructs. But that seems like a defense. I think I can find ways to render these topics accessible to community members by talking about decision making, influence, the ways their communities are talked about in the research reports, and what this implicitly says about mainstream communities, including the researcher.

That said, and I am noticing this really late in the process, the Coalition membership is not monolithic. It is not a uniform group, and there are some for whom an academic future is possibly of interest, increasing the likelihood of interest if I were to issue an invitation. To presume uniformity is a trespass itself. It would have taken more time to write such a chapter with others, though I am certain it would ultimately be stronger. I do face challenges with collaborative work as so much of my work is in partnership that sometimes I seek opportunities to work in solitude. Such a desire might also have influenced my choice.

As I get close to a commitment to open this up with Coalition members, my throat constricts and quite literally my heart jumps a beat. I am nervous. My fears? That I will be told that I take up too much space, that I am not taking advantage of the opportunity to mentor new scholars into this role, and that I am not replacing myself fast enough. And that my failure to act is selfish and harmful to the community. At the same time, I compensate for my anticipated shortcomings by promising much, by taking on too many roles. And money cannot help but get in the way. My salary is not sufficient to pay for a decent quality of life, and I have depended on some contracts to provide for my family. If I need to get out of the way, I need to find other work. But that is not quite true—and as a Coalition colleague likes to chide me, we would be fine with less money.

Ultimately, I wonder if my rendition—even of these paragraphs—is an implicit effort to render myself innocent of the power seized by solo authoring this text. I am certainly aware that I write articles on the Coalition products and its research practices in a co-authored manner. But the retelling of the research process has remained mine. Right now, I am navigating the complexity of implicating myself as trespass in that their community's voice is heard only through me, at the same time as what seems equally true of honoring their priorities and the urgent need to put available energies into advocacy work.

I hope I am interrupting the automatic impulse towards innocence and "troubl[ing] the moment of gratification" (Rossiter, 2005, para. 12) that lets social workers ignore the trespass that has led to deeming ourselves useful. In the context of this research, it means that I remain open to considering that my decision to exclude Coalition partners from reflections on dynamics of the research relationship is an act of trespass, even if I have an abundance of good reasons for this decision.

The best I can seem to do is to allow both to be accurate. What does this say about me? I think I have spent too long in the contemplative practices of reflexivity and side-stepped the risk of shared contemplation. Consequently, I have denied the challenges of creating a learning community that can learn and grow together through alternative opinions.

And as I close this section, I make a dedication to being unsettled. I resolve to invite engagement on reflections concerning the process of the research and ways we have sacrificed authenticity, side-stepped conflict, and misstepped or trespassed over respectful recognition and complexity. The space for ambiguity and complexity needs to surface. I commit to reject handy frames that negate the interest and priority of community in dialogue on process and in conventionally academic topics. Voice in all areas needs to be shared.

Summary

My research partnership with the Coalition of Communities of Color has been fertile in both knowledge building and social change. Interrogating four aspects of the research endeavor and the preparation of this chapter explores pathways through which imperialism and anti-imperialism infuse the research project, highlighting opportunities to reject one of the most insidious violations of research: that of the "subject/object" construction embedded in research design. I have explored alternatives, albeit imperfect ones: the decisions to research up, down, and laterally within the same research project. This was achieved by implicating whiteness in the research agenda, and thus providing the principal investigator with a subject position that included researching up. Simultaneously, it also provided the community research partners with the opportunity of researching up, and thereby provided an abundance of research findings that included the illogic and immorality of white privilege.

Second, the expertise of community members infused the analysis of the research, and it rejected the typical role-defined boundaries suggesting the academic researcher would determine the reach of the research and, by extension, the advocacy agenda. In our project, the wisdom, understanding, and vision of Coalition members determined how far this work could have impact, and have characterized it from start to end. I urge researchers to never narrow expectations, to remain open to community insights at whatever level they appear, and to guard against their own bias and acculturation as researchers.

Third, the community's empowerment, agency, and influence are maximized when every practice that others, objectifies, and typifies "them" (noticing here the incongruence of my own words in this text with my aspirations) is resisted. Our decision to represent the community as "we" instead of "they" is an act of resistance, although it renders the lead author as inauthentic in implying she is a member of communities of color. There is simultaneously and insidiously a real possibility that my inclusion in the collective "we" is an act of dominance, where I speak possessively as part of a community that I do not own. This makes my head spin for its complexity and for uncertainty that it brings in finding a space of integrity on which to stand in this work.

Fourth, the rendition of all research stories is an act of trespass, one that risks compromising the respectful recognition of community partners. When undertaken in the solitude of the researcher's mind, it is particularly ripe for trespass. While many reasons may exist for not inviting research partners into dialogue on such reflections, the academic scholar needs to trouble such decisions and understand that this, too, is an act of imperialism, even if the project itself is anti-imperial and intersubjective.

I close this work convinced of the importance of discovering pathways to advance intersubjectivity and resisting the "subject/object" imperial constructs embedded in the research relationship. I look forward to future dialogues in the years to come.

References

Aguiar, L. (2012). Redirecting the academic gaze upward. In L. Aguiar & C. Schneider (Eds.), *Researching amongst elites: Challenges and opportunities in studying up* (pp. 1–28). Surrey, UK: Ashgate.

Benhabib, S., Butler, J., Cornell, D., & Fraser, N. (1995). *Feminist contentions: A philosophical exchange*. New York: Routledge.

Belenky, M., Clinchy, B., Goldberger, N., & Tarule, J. (Eds.). (1997). *Women's ways of knowing*. New York: Basic Books.

Brown, C. (2012). Anti-oppression through a postmodern lens: Dismantling the master's conceptual tools in discursive social work practice. *Critical Social Work, 13* (1), 34–65.

Butler, J. (1990). *Gender trouble: Feminism and the subversion of identity*. New York: Routledge, Chapman and Hall.

Curry-Stevens, A. (2012). The end of the honeymoon: CBPR, positional privilege and working with community coalitions. *American International Journal of Contemporary Research, 2* (7), 92–101.

Curry-Stevens, A. (2013). *Evaluation report: Coalition of Communities of Color's "Infrastructure to fortify disparity reduction" at the close of the Kaiser Permanente Community Foundation grant*. Portland, OR: Unpublished.

Curry-Stevens, A. & Coalition of Communities of Color (2008). Making people of color count in policy making (grant application). Unpublished.

Fellows, M. L. & Razack, S. (1998). The race to innocence: Confronting hierarchical relations among women. *Journal of Gender, Race and Justice, 1* (2), 335–352.

Finn, J. & Jacobson, M. (2008). *Just practice: A social justice approach to social work.* Peosta, Iowa: Eddie Bowers.

Foucault, M. (1980). *Power/Knowledge.* Brighton, England: Harvester.

Fraser, N. & Honneth, A. (2003). *Redistribution or recognition? A political-philosophical exchange.* New York: Verso.

Gringeri, C., Wahab, S., & Anderson-Nathe, B. (2010). What makes it feminist?: Mapping the landscape of feminist social work research. *Affilia: Journal of Women and Social Work, 25* (4), 390–405.

Haraway, D. (1988). Situated knowledges: The science question in feminism and the privilege of partial perspective. *Feminist Studies, 14* (3), 575–599.

Hobgood, M. (2000) *Dismantling privilege: An ethics of accountability.* Cleveland, OH: The Pilgrim Press.

Krumer-Nevo, M. & Sidi, M. (2012). Writing against othering. *Qualitative Inquiry, 18* (4), 299–309.

Kumsa, M. (2007). Encounters in social work practice. In D. Mandell (Ed.), *Revisiting the use of self: Questioning professional identities* (pp. 87–104). Toronto: Canadian Scholars Press.

Mohanty, C. (1991). Under western eyes: Feminist scholarship and colonial discourses. In C. Mohanty, A. Russo, & L. Torres (Eds.), *Third world women and the politics of feminism* (pp. 51–80). Bloomington: Indiana University Press.

Orlie, M. (1997). *Living ethically, acting political/y.* Ithaca, NY: Cornell University Press.

Puwar, N. (1997). Reflections on interviewing women MPs. *Sociological Research Online,* 2(1). Retrieved from http://www.socresonline.org.uk/2/1/4.html.

Razack, S. (1998). *Looking white people in the eye: Gender, race, and culture in courtrooms and classrooms.* Toronto, ON: University of Toronto Press.

Reay, D. (1996). Insider perspectives or stealing the words out of women's mouths. *Feminist Review, 53,* 57–73.

Rossiter, A. (1996). A perspective on critical social work. *Journal of Progressive Human Services,* 7(2), 23–41.

Rossiter, A. (2000). The professional is political: An interpretation of the problem of the past in solution-focused therapy. *American Journal of Orthopsychiatry, 70* (2), 150–161.

Rossiter, A. (2001). Innocence lost and suspicion found: Do we educate for or against social work? *Critical Social Work, 2* (1), 1–5.

Rossiter, A. (2005). Discourse analysis in critical social work: From apology to question. *Critical Social Work,* 6(1). Downloaded from http://www1.uwindsor.ca/critical socialwork/discourse-analysis-in-critical-social-work-from-apology-to-question.

Rossiter, A. (2007). Self as subjectivity: Toward a use of self as respectful relations of recognition. In D. Mandell (Ed), *Revisiting the use of self: Questioning professional identities* (pp. 21–34). Toronto: Canadian Scholars Press.

Said, E. (1993). *Culture and imperialism.* New York: Vintage.

Smith, L. (1999). *Decolonizing methodologies: Research and indigenous peoples.* London: Zed Books.

Spivak, G. (1988). Can the subaltern speak? In C. Nelson & Grossberg, L. (Eds), *Marxism and the interpretation of culture* (pp. 271–313). London: Macmillan.

Stanley, L. & Wise, S. (1983). *Breaking out: Feminist consciousness and feminist research.* New York: Routledge, Chapman & Hall.

Vodde, R. (2001). De-centering white privilege in social work education: Whose job is it anyway? *Race, Gender and Class, 7* (4), 139–160.

Weiner-Levy, N. & Queder, S. (2012). Researching my people, researching the "other": Field experiences of two researchers along shifting positionalities. *Quantity and Quality, 46* (4), 1151–1166.

Wright, C. (1997). Representing the "other": Some thoughts. *Indian Journal of Gender Studies, 4* (1), 83–89.

10 Precarious Positioning

Tensions in Doing *Siiqqee* Feminist Social Work Research

Martha Kuwee Kumsa

Cover Stories

Sometimes I position myself as a feminist social work researcher, a feminist researcher in social work, or a researcher in feminist social work. I often play with such puzzles of my precarious positioning as I slip in and out of discourses but here is my first caveat: feminism, social work, and research are just three pieces of the puzzle that do not describe me wholly or solely. They leave out too many pieces of my life to give me any comfort. My *siiqqee* feminism is one such piece left out and rendered invisible. My second caveat: unlike the jigsaw, all my pieces do not fit together perfectly to solve the puzzle at the end and give the one prefect product, the *Truth*. There are myriad ways of putting the pieces together, giving many products, many truths. Sometimes these discursive pieces are not even meant to fit together, so there are all forms and shapes of holes and clefts and cracks and crevices in the product. My third caveat: this fitting together is an ongoing process; so there really is no final product, just tentative works in progress. Sometimes the pieces are not even solid fragments that fit or don't fit together; they are just fragile threads and fabrics woven together in various ways.

In this chapter, I will reflect on the tensions I encounter in doing my *siiqqee* feminist social work research. Often when scholars write about research, the focus is on the research question(s), the conceptual and methodological frameworks, and the findings. The ontological and epistemological tensions, the intricate socio-political processes, and the intimate personal struggles out of which the research questions emerge rarely get acknowledged. And this mystifies research. In this chapter, I will demystify research by focusing on ordinary life events and personal circumstances from which my research topics emerge. Highlighting these struggles is particularly important in feminist research because of its origin in grassroots movements and women's political activism and because of its commitment to social change and transformation. In my reflections, then, I wish to highlight that feminist research is activist research emerging from women's everyday struggles. Please bear with me as I walk you through my struggles and discursive tensions through which I formulate my research questions and conduct my research.

Essence and Contingency

A feminist social work researcher does not just drop from the sky. S/he is born and raised in some family and community among a people of some culture in some land. I, for one, was born and raised an Oromo woman in Ethiopia. *A woman is born. No! A woman is made! Man makes history. No! History makes man! We create culture. No! Culture creates us. We speak language. No! Language speaks us!* Whirls of nature/nurture, agency/structure, modern/postmodern, and structural/poststructural binaries swirl around me. *They sweep me off my feet and twirl me around and around. My head is spinning. I'm dizzy. Stop it! I shout at the top of my lungs:* A feminist social work researcher creates herself! She does so in the crucible of historical, political, social, economic, cultural, spiritual processes.

I contest the either/or essentialist/constructionist binary and declare my preference for interactional spaces of mutual constitution and mutual transformation (Ahmed, 2000). I may not be free of my context but I can imagine a radically different world from within its constraints—and struggle to make that imagined world a reality. I am who I am because of *and* in spite of all the encounters in my life. My *siiqqee* feminism is such an encounter. Let me story it here the way I remember. *Remember? No! Re-member! No, it's both!* My *siiqqee* feminist story is not something tucked away, something that I reach into the past and retrieve. It is what I stitch together now, in my needs of this moment and for the purposes of this chapter. Yet, I stitch it together from bits of discursive threads and fabrics strewn throughout the 59 years of my life.

Reflexive Research

I call myself a reflexive researcher to claim that I am simultaneously embodied by and embedded in discourses. Therefore, I am not a neutral observer doing objective research. What I bring into the study knowingly or unknowingly, in terms of values and beliefs or even my simple likes and dislikes, shapes the research I do. Moreover, my stories are constitutive parts of the data and are entered into interpretive analysis as data. That means data are not just some readymade material that I go out and *gather* from out there; they are also what I bring into the process of mutual constitution. This recognition makes me a reflexive researcher precariously positioned in webs of power relationships and discursive practices. As a positioned researcher, then, sharing where I am coming from with equally positioned readers constitutes ethical research. Hiding my positioned agenda behind the guise of objectivity and neutrality is unethical in my view.

Unfortunately this view of reflexivity is not widely shared in social work research. For example, I came of age and cut my political teeth in the great revolutionary era of liberation movements, including women's liberation and anti-colonial national liberation struggles. I was soaked to my bones in second-wave feminism and I bring these stories to my social work classes. I talk about the tumultuous '60s with so much enthusiasm and how I draw my inspirations from it in my feminist research. Social work students look at me as though I were from another planet. Some don't know that history of feminism; some just don't see the connection between feminism and social work; others strongly dis-identify with that face of feminism because they were taught it was misguided and destructive. How can we recenter critical feminist social work research in this context of invisibility? Others have begun the inquiry (Gringeri, Wahab, & Anderson-Nathe, 2010; Wahab, Anderson-Nathe, & Gringeri, 2012). My work builds on these beginnings and elaborates on my *siiqqee* feminist social work research.

My Feminist Social Work Research

I discern my feminist social work research as multilayered and reflexive. I understand reflexivity as a hotly contested concept (Pillow, 2003). By claiming multilayered reflexivity, however, I mean to blur the binary and underscore the inseparable relationality between researcher(s) and the research topic, between researchers and the researched, between conceptual and methodological frameworks, between particularity and commonality, between time and space, between past and future in this' *now* of time, between *there* and *here* in this nick of space, and between the known and unknown/unknowable in the production of knowledge. I also mean to emphasize the inherent discomfort in blurring these binaries.

In the following sections, I story the tensions in my reflexive encounters of doing my *siiqqee* feminist social work research, specifically focusing on the tensions between identity and difference and between local and global issues of equity and justice. To help me think through these tensions, I organize my processes into three symbolic/cultural themes: *Intala Aayyaa* [Mother's Daughter], *Iyya Siiqqee* [The *Siiqqee* Scream], and *Godaansa Siiqqee* [the *Siiqqee* Trek]. These themes emerged from my first feminist social work research which brought to light *siiqqee* feminism as my contribution to knowledge. In the first section, *Intala Aayyaa*, I provide the epistemological, socio-cultural, and spiritual foundations of *siiqqee* feminism. In *Iyya Siiqqee*, I story the tensions through which identity politics shaped my first research. In *Godaansa Siiqqee*, I engage the tensions through which the politics of difference shaped my subsequent research projects.

Intala Aayyaa [Mother's Daughter]

The opening words of a paper published from my first feminist social work research state that:

> Women's struggle against domination and oppression has taken different forms that vary across time and culture. For Oromo women of precolonial times, the form was a collective struggle through building

the *siiqqee* solidarity. *Siiqqee* is a stick symbolizing a socially sanctioned set of rights exercised by Oromo women. This paper uses a historical feminist perspective to explore what *siiqqee* is, what rights it symbolized, what sanctions it enforced, what factors contributed to its decline, how it is practiced by contemporary Oromo women, and the prospects for reviving the *siiqqee* principles on a new basis. (Kumsa, 1997, p. 115)

The overarching finding of this study suggests that, as a group, women and girls were seen as *halagaa* [strangers/outsiders] in the pre-colonial Oromo society and, as such, they were protected by the laws of *muka laaftuu* [soft wood]. As its name suggests, this law is stipulated to protect vulnerable groups because of their structural liminality. In the patrilineal Oromo society, girls were seen as *halagaa* in their communities of birth because they would soon be given away in marriage. Women were seen as *halagaa* in their communities of marriage because, not being born there, they would come from somewhere else. Not belonging anywhere, then, females were seen as the floating glue that holds together the various communities.

This bonding role of women parallels the broader spiritual bonding role of *safuu* in Oromo cosmology (Kumsa, 1997, 2013). *Safuu* is the power of *Waaqa* [God] that holds together everything and everyone in the cosmos in a well-balanced egalitarian order. Deriving from this broader egalitarian balance of *safuu*, pre-colonial Oromo society governed itself by integrating many layers of checks and balances into an egalitarian holistic system called *gadaa*. In *gadaa*, women's rights and wellbeing were protected by the *siiqqee* institution. Girls' rights were protected by the *Addooyyee* sisterhood paralleling the *siiqqee* institution (Kumsa, 2013). *Gadaa* and *siiqqee* maintained the male–female checks and balances within the larger cosmic order of *safuu*. Pre-colonial Oromos believed that society would collapse if *safuu* was lost. Therefore, both men and women considered it their sacred duty to maintain the male–female balance in order to maintain the overall checks and balances of *safuu*.

Siiqqee is the stick a girl receives as a gift on her wedding day through a blessing ceremony. The mother holds one end of the *siiqqee* as she chants blessings and the daughter holds the other end repeating *haa ta'u* [akin to amen] after every chant. In this ritual, *siiqqee* signifies the mother–daughter bond. However, there are also several broader socio-cultural and spiritual meanings to *siiqqee* rituals beyond this bond of the mother–daughter dyad. First, such gift giving and blessing rituals are the oath females take to remind each other of the matriarchal reign of *Akkoo Manooyyee* [Grandma *Manooyyee*], the legendary Oromo matriarch whose egalitarian rule touched all Oromos. It is storied that power-greedy men overthrew her sweet rule, distorting her story and debasing her character. To this day, *Akkoo Manooyyee* is laughed at and ridiculed to satirize and regulate women (Wako, 2003). Quietly contesting this caricature, then, women use every *siiqqee* ritual to remember the glorious matriarchy of their grandmother, *Akkoo Manooyyee*, and to pass her memory on to next generations of females. Secondly, *siiqqee* symbolizes the mother and broader female ties between all mothers and daughters. Thirdly, standing for the universal mother, *siiqqee* also symbolizes the broader female ties among all *halagaa* females in all communities. Finally, at a more profoundly spiritual level, *siiqqee* represents the spirit of *Ateetee*, the female deity (Kumsa, 2013; Østebø, 2009; Qashu, 2009).

In effect, then, *siiqqee* represents the image of the mother—and all women call each other *Intala Aayyaa* [Daughters of a Mother]. If her rights are violated or her wellbeing is hurt in any way, a woman grabs her *siiqqee*, goes out of the house, raises her *siiqqee* and screams:

> *Intala Aayyaa dhageettee?* [Mother's Daughter, have you heard?!]
> *Oduun si geettee?* [Did the news reach you?!]

This is called *iyya siiqqee* [the *siiqqee* scream]. Upon hearing the *siiqqee* scream of their sister, all women grab and raise their own *siiqqees* in solidarity and come out screaming:

> *Eeyee dhagahee!* [Yes, I've heard!]
> *Oduun na gahee!* [The news did reach me!]

If a woman raises her *siiqqee* and screams, it means the cosmic balance of *safuu* is upset and everyone, women and men alike, must interrupt everything they are doing because *safuu* must be restored before any normal life activity can resume. Women consider it their sacred duty to restore *safuu* and, with their raised *siiqqees*, they gather under a *qilxuu* tree [a type of oak tree symbolizing the generic female]. They listen to the current violation, recount past infringements, quote the law of *muka laaftuu* [soft wood] invoked at the time, and pass their verdict. Also considering it their sacred duty to restore *safuu*, men send respectable elders immediately to hear the women's *siiqqee* verdict and fulfill their demands. If not, the *siiqqee* women vow to leave the community. They vow to cross the river and go on *godaansa siiqqee* [the *siiqqee* trek]. Here, vowing to cross the river has a deeper spiritual meaning because water symbolizes the very source of life. By vowing to cross the river, then, women are affirming their readiness to die and sacrifice their lives in order to restore the disrupted *safuu*. The consequences of the *siiqqee* trek are hefty because neighboring communities also consider it their sacred duty to restore *safuu* to the extent that they would declare war on the community that failed or delayed to fulfill the women's *siiqqee* demands.

Iyya Siiqqee [Siiqqee Scream]: The Politics of Identity

It is fall 1991. I just arrived in Canada. I am in a democracy, escaping ten years of imprisonment and torture in Ethiopia. Here I can express my views freely. I scream from the rooftop: I am Oromo! I am feminist! I am revolutionary! Workers of all countries unite! We have nothing to lose but our chains! These national boundaries are nothing but state-woven lies to keep us apart! Women of all countries unite! (Rowbotham, 1972). I let out my *iyya siiqqee* [siiqqee scream] to reach my Western *Intala Aayyaa* [daughters of my mother]. A resounding silence! Some willful deafness and some obliviousness. *Oromo? What is it?* For goodness' sake, this is the identity I was tortured for! I was ready to die for it! And people don't even know it? To add insult to injury, every time I project Oromo, the discursive mirror on the wall reflects back Black. What? So I am now Black too? I never knew myself as Black. *Workers of all countries unite? Sorry, here workers negotiate with the state. They perfect the art of negotiation, not revolution.* What? Am I dreaming then? *Women of all countries unite? Where are you from? There is no monolithic woman here!* Really? Am I from Mars, then? I want to pull out my hair! I want to scream! But what's the use of screaming if no one hears (Spivak, 1988)? My world is turning upside down. My truths are becoming untruths.

The global sisterhood of second-wave feminism is no more. *Intala Aayyaa* is no more. Feminists have forgotten that we were once sisters, daughters of a mother. Third-wave feminism is in a painful fragmentation. Women may be disappearing into identity politics but feminist scholarship is giving me eye-opening *aha* moments of profound learning. In *The Burning Times* (National Film Board of Canada, 1990), I learn how people went on witch-hunting rampages and killed nine million women across Europe and North America in just 300 years. *Aha!* It is this force that massacred and colonized women at home that was unleashed in my part of the world! In the three centuries when men were hanging and burning women at the stake in Europe and North America, Oromos were enjoying the egalitarian male–female checks and balances of *gadaa* and *siiqqee*. Look what colonialism destroyed! Three hundred years later, look where we are at and where we are heading!

Social work research is quiet on these profound and inseparable interconnections between the local and the global and the past and the future. *It is stifling me!* In another *aha* moment, bell hooks (1981, 1984) speaks to me intimately when she describes how leaders of the Black liberation movements of the 60s assigned women to the subservient domestic role of breeding warriors for the revolution. *Aha!* That is the role the leaders of Oromo liberation assign to women in practice, although they preach women's emancipation. Reclaiming our forefathers' *gadaa* is like a sacred mission for them but they were not hot about reclaiming the equally egalitarian *siiqqee* of our foremothers.

Black men do not acknowledge sexism and White women do not acknowledge racism so Black women must find a space of their own from which to speak and demand to be heard. In their turn Black women do not acknowledge heterosexism so Black lesbians must find a different space. I see identity struggles as central for the social justice work of social work.

These are marginalized groups struggling for equality and justice, the very centerpiece and *raison d'être* of social work. Radical feminist theories from the margins of North America populate my thinking (Anzaldúa, 1990; Hill Collins, 1990; hooks, 1981, 1984; Lorde, 1984; Moraga & Anzaldúa, 1981). *Gender, race, class, and sexuality are inseparable!* they seem to sing in chorus. I slip into these discourses of interlocking oppressions and hang on to them like a lifeline.

The oppression and subordination of women result from historical and political processes that hide women's knowledge, experiences, and strategies of resistance. We need to reclaim these from obscurity and rewrite women's history from their own perspective. I'm fired up by all this. Some of the truths I was robbed of are being thrown back at me in bits and fragments but the distinct set of truths and experiences of Oromo women is missing from this beautiful array of women's voices. It is missing even from the literature on the so-called Third World feminism.

Sojourner Truth's powerful question is now my question: *Ain't I a woman?* Yes, I am a woman! Oromo women are women too! Identity politics does not take away from womanhood: it opens it up and imbues it with texture. Yes, we are all women, but we are women in so many different ways. And we struggle against our subordination in very different ways. Discourses of feminist standpoint speak to me intimately (Harding, 1987; Hill Collins, 1990). If knowledge is always partial due to its production within specific historical political contexts, then the most *authentic* knowledge is that which comes from oppressed people's struggle against subordination.

My first feminist social work research question is birthed through this intense labor of identity politics. I look back to the roots of my foremothers' *authentic* knowledge in order to see ahead. I want to know their forms of subordination and strategies of resistance and how this shifts over space and time. I focus on a specific symbol of Oromo women's resistance and solidarity: *siiqqee*. I seek deeper symbolic meanings of *siiqqee* within the history and culture of the people who crafted and practiced it. My research questions are simple: What does *siiqqee* mean? How did Oromo women use *siiqqee* in pre-colonial times? How did they use it after colonialism? What does *siiqqee* mean to contemporary Oromos? How can the principles of *siiqqee* resistance and solidarity be revived in the current context of Oromo women's struggle for liberation?

My first feminist social work research unveils Oromo women's epistemology, political strategies of resistance, and beautiful history of solidarity. It draws on these deep wells of *siiqqee* institution and puts Oromo women on a par with their sisters and other oppressed peoples of the world, telling their stories, transforming their stigmatized identity, and claiming equal rights and their rightful place in history. Immersed in revolutionary discourses of progress, I had not been able to see these intimate links between contemporary Oromo women's struggles and the deep wells from which they draw—until feminist identity politics brought it to light. The remainder of my journey, then, is to stretch this horizon of learning and contribute to the transformation of the broader society where social relations are renegotiated on the basis of equal rights. I tell myself that the goal of feminist social work research is not to collect dust on the shelves of the ivory tower but to facilitate such transformation of social relations based on the equal worth of the unique standpoint of every group. I present my findings at conferences. I circulate in various feminist circles and take my *siiqqee* feminism to social work classes.

Enthused by the *siiqqee* message of solidarity, feminists of various stripes quickly pick me up and sniff me but they put me down as quickly. Alas! The critique of my *siiqqee* feminism is too deficient for some and too sharp-tongued for others, too essentialist for some and too hollow for others. For some it is too simplistic, usable only in simple societies. My *siiqqee* feminism is also too multilayered to fit into any one category of feminism. It contests patriarchy hotly but it does not fit into radical feminism. It takes on both culture and economy but it does not wholly belong in socialist feminism. It critically engages racism but it does not neatly fit into Black feminism. It tackles nested hierarchies of global power but it is not Third World feminism, postcolonial feminism, or transnational feminism. The uncontainable excesses left outside of these circles are many-directional and fluid and I encounter intense tensions as identity threatens to dissolve into difference. Whichever circle I enter in search of identity, I find differences and from wherever I move away because I am different, I deeply long to go back to belong. Identity becomes difference turned inside out. To soothe my wounds of alienation and precarious positioning, I shrink back into my own circle of Oromo women where I deeply feel I belong. Indeed, standpoint theory (Harding, 1987; Hill Collins, 1990) asserts that we share the same historical reality that sets us apart from everyone else in the world.

Godaansa Siiqqee [Siiqqee Trek]: The Politics of Difference

Oromo women have been hurt and violated. Their communities have been ruptured and forcibly displaced. *Safuu* has been lost. Women have raised their *siiqqees* and screamed. They have gone on *godaansa siiqqee* [the *siiqqee* trek] and crossed the ocean as refugees in search of solidarity and justice. They now seek to restore the intricate checks and balances of *safuu* in their new countries of dwelling and in their homeland. As an Oromo woman, I have seen *safuu* lost in my homeland. I have seen my truths turn into untruths and drag me through hell. I have screamed with my raised *siiqqee* and crossed the ocean in search of justice, only to find that the discourses have shifted. The truths I believed have become untruths once again. The promise of liberal humanism that lured me to the West has become a mere illusion. I learn that the claim of equality in my identity politics is flawed as it is based on a flawed assumption of identical humanity.

There is no such thing as identical humanity. Humans are all different. No such thing as identical womanhood either. Women are all different. Liberal claims of humanity, equality, and inclusion only serve as a smokescreen for the further margin-alization and exploitation of oppressed groups. The very foundation of identity politics and equal worth is being shaken to its core. I plunge into the politics of difference headfirst. *We are all different! We are all unique!*

My head spins with the churning multiplicity of the discourses of difference. The era of 'I demand inclusion because I am like you and equal to you' is over. I hear people chanting: 'I refuse to be included for being like you! I refuse equality for being identical with you! I am not like you! I don't want to be like you! I demand equity because I am different from you!'

So identity turns into difference and equality into equity. Conceptually, I enjoy riding these tensions but living the bitter reality is a different matter altogether. I cannot enjoy the innocent warm and fuzzy feelings of belonging any more because there is no innocence, not even among my most intimate group of Oromo women. Discovering my difference from Black and White women is difficult but bearable, but discovering difference where I assume ultimate identity, homogeneity, and belonging is very painful. Worse still, what is excruciating is not just my discovery of difference but the horrifying agony of my exposed privilege. There is no innocent difference that is not infused with inequities of power. As a woman who used the discourses of liberation to weave my identity as a liberated liberator, I have always pointed outwards to oppressors, away from myself. But who is a better reflexive mirror for my liberated liberator identity than those I am out to liberate? This identity crumbled on me when an Oromo woman pointed to me and said in no uncertain terms: *You are oppressor too! You don't speak for us!* (Kumsa, 2007/2011). As anti-oppressive feminist, being called out as oppressor by one of my very own hurt me more than anything in the world had ever hurt me!

The lessons I glean from the shattered assumptions of my feminist benevolence of liberating others prompt me to unpack my social work assumptions of helping others. Once sacred and lofty, *liberation* and *help* are now dirty words in my mouth. I need to critically engage their innocence and make visible the atrocities that happen in the guise of *help* and *liberation*. Many innocent helpers rush to rescue poor traumatized refugee women who have come to *us* fleeing from their war-torn homelands. They speak out against these women's miserable Third World status within the affluent spaces of the First World. They speak out against the racism, sexism, and xenophobia of others without implicating themselves in these intricate webs of power relations and examining how they are constructed as helpers and how their help re-traumatizes refugees. As a refugee who has been re-traumatized by such innocent help and as a feminist researcher who has traumatized others by my benevolent practices of anti-oppression, I seek to make visible the discursive practices that construct the innocence of help and the benevolence of anti-oppression. I situate feminist social work as a child of the liberal nation-state and position its innocent help within the discursive practices of the *caring* nation-state (Kelly, 2001; Pratt, 2005). I situate the rhetoric of protecting vulnerable women and children within masculinist discursive practices of both the global colonial family of nations and local anti-colonial national liberation struggles.

Intense tensions between local and global processes threaten to tear me apart. Yes, globalization has created a global village for those who can travel with ease, but it has left most Oromo women stuck in their local dwellings and cut off from intimate families flung and dispersed around the world. Globalization conceals the incredible multiplicity of their losses—loss of home and homeland, loss of familiar connections, loss of nationhood in the struggle for a liberated homeland, loss of anticipated democracy and freedom in the new land, loss of imagined friends and support systems in the new land, loss of status, loss of dreams and desires for good life—hopes raised and dashed. As others argue, such overwhelming multiplicity of losses turns into the loss of loss itself (Butler, 2003; Frost & Hoggett, 2008). Once the loss is lost, the root cause of it is also lost while the oozing wounds persist. In an ironic discursive twist of the loss of loss, perpetrators become rescuers, colonizers become liberators, and oppressed women turn against each other in anger and tear each other up. While all these do shed light on Oromo women's realities, however, such exclusive focus on loss, vulnerability, and victimization obscures the women's incredible resistance and subversive agencies.

There is little doubt in my mind that the experiences of Oromo refugee women resettled in the West and their wrestling with webs of local and global relations of power offer a rich site for feminist research and theorizing. But who researches whose life and who theorizes whose experiences (hooks, 1984)? This becomes an intricate ethical issue of power for me when I position myself as reflexive researcher and my positioning becomes even more precarious. I do share these multiplicities of loss with other Oromo women but I cannot represent them as *our* collective experiences. My friend's voice rings in my ears over and over again like roaring thunder: *You are oppressor too! You don't speak for us!* As other researchers also find, there is a crisis of representation, a crisis of truth, of who can accurately represent whose reality, of who can speak on whose behalf and in whose voice (Ahmed, 2000; Lather, 1993; Spivak, 1988).

Every woman experiences this shared reality in ways that are unique to her. How can I shed light on the uniqueness of a woman's experiences without losing our shared realities? How can *I* highlight *our* differences without dissolving into difference and, as Ahmed (2000) argues, without the *I* dissolving into the *we?* How can I do ethically responsive research that makes visible the local and global forces beating down on Oromo women without reducing them/us to mere victims? How can I acknowledge embodied discourses and shed light on our embodiedness while also honouring the subversive agencies of women? As Pillow (2003) would ask, how can I develop strategies of holding myself accountable to the struggles, self-representations, and voices of Oromo women?

In my current research projects, my research questions and reflexive strategies emerge from these intense struggles in the politics of difference. I want to make sense of *how* Oromo women are embodying and coping with the multiplicities of loss. I want to understand *how* they/we are engaging local and global webs of power relations. These *how* questions help me make sense of processes and discursive practices rather than rigid structures but they do not address issues of agency or representation. I cannot interpret women's realities from my precarious positioning in multiple circles of partial belonging. That would perpetuate the new re-colonization of simultaneous particularization and universalization. A way out of this no-way is to look at women's practices in the here and now and make multiple linkages to the multiplicity of contradictory global and local discourses swirling around us and churning inside us. Performance-based approaches (Hamera, 2011; Pelias, 2008; Pollock, 2007; Visweswaran, 1994) resonate with these intense struggles and offer possibilities of interrogating the live processes of *how* women engage conflicting discourses.

Some Oromo women in the diaspora, including myself, have created a grassroots movement of reclaiming our foremothers' ancient spirituality as part of broader Oromo grassroots movements of creatively engaging contemporary recolonization (Kumsa, 2013). We are passionately researching and reclaiming our foremothers' heritage. We are performing the *lost* rituals of our ancestors in the generative spaces of the Oromo diaspora. Here is a fertile place to explore performance and the *Ateetee* birth rituals offer a site of a particular performance. Here, there are little ethical concerns around inviting participants or representing them because each woman is simultaneously a participant and a researcher. The rituals are performed only upon the invitation of the woman who gives birth, the *Haadha Ateetee* [Mother (of) *Ateetee*]. It is her unique *Ateetee* where she invites only those she wants and determines which rituals she wants performed. As a result, no two *Ateetee* performances are the same. I find a comfortable home in this self-initiated subversive self-study that demystifies the very notion of research (Absolon, 2011; Smith, 1999). The processes of researching and sifting through and reinterpreting reclaimed materials all demystify the notion of data analysis. As both audiences and performers, we share our findings with each other through mundane talks, stories, poetry, songs, dances, and fragments of remembered ancient lyrics and rituals. And this demystifies the notions of research findings, dissemination, and conference presentations. This project is literally a creative process of birthing our foremothers' spiritualities in our own unique contexts performatively—by repeating them in unrepeatable novel ways.

Indeed, the comfort I draw from this project is that its processes seem to address the ethical issues of power, agency, voice, and representation, at least partially. However, as a woman circulating in the worlds of women's grassroots movement and academia, these same issues remain sites of hot contestations, ongoing struggles, and painful encounters for me. I have also been a witness to the many tears women shed, tears of the painful exclusion of their spiritual practices both by religious and secular community elders. Indeed, contradictory discourses and conflicting practices are not just out there; they also scream from deep within our bones.

While such transformative relations of subversive research are profoundly rewarding for me, these rewards come with a hefty price tag to my academic performance. How can I present these stories when there is no innocent representation? Inescapable issues of power and privilege stare me in the eye. For whom do I write? Who is my audience/reader? Writing for/with the women who perform *Ateetee* leaves the work within the group. Writing for outsiders necessarily involves representation, which cannot be innocent and must come from my unique positioning. Even with untroubled innocence, however, my stories, writings, and works from these marginal spaces get trashed by gatekeepers of scholarly journals, thus eroding my confidence and exacting huge costs to my academic career in the world of publish or perish. Also, my subversive research fails miserably in attracting research funds in a world where research grants determine who the *good* and *capable* researcher is. I have yet to find that magical balance where my grassroots activism and academic works blend without coopting each other. Perhaps these intense conflicts will remain ongoing tensions that I have to ride on an ongoing basis.

Deploying multilayered reflexivity from my multiple precarious positioning to interpret our exilic performances of birth rituals opens up several transformative possibilities (Kumsa, 2009, 2013). First, these performances transpose time and space where ancient ancestral rituals from *there* and *then* are not only reborn in the *here* and *now* of time–space compression but *there* and *then* also become *here* and *now* through broader spiritual connections. Second, global processes of recolonization, euphemized as globalization, forcefully uproot Oromo women from their ancestral homeland and fling them into exile. In these performances, women subvert globalization and hang on to ancestral rituals and through these rituals to their homeland. Third, processes of localization slot them into marginal categories of gender, race, class, religion, ethnicity, nationality, and citizenship. In these performances, however, women transform conditions of their marginality into spaces of subversive agencies, providing each other with solidarity, care, and support. Fourth, these performances make visible the hidden but inseparable interconnections between global and local processes (Ahmed, 2000; Kaplan, 1994). By celebrating motherhood and creating spaces of self-empowerment in these performances, women simultaneously embrace and subvert masculinized spaces of both global neocolonial family of nations and local anticolonial national liberation struggles (Kumsa, 2009; Liu, 1994). They make visible the inseparable interconnectedness of these seemingly opposing global/local processes as male-centered nation-building projects whether they come in colonial, neocolonial, or anticolonial forms.

Isn't that ironic that diaspora, the supposedly barren space of loss and despair, is also such a fertile space of transformative possibilities? I have been immensely intrigued by how most of us who are now researching and actively reclaiming our indigenous ancestral spiritualities in the diaspora are also the very ones who had rejected them as heathen and backward while we were in our homeland. Both Western and Eastern blocs of the Cold War binary of modernism (Davidson, 1992; Fanon, 1963; Young, 1990, 2001), both religious and secular discourses of colonization marked our ancestors' indigenous spiritualities as heathen and backward and targeted them for destruction. As good children of progress, we embodied these discourses and played instrumental roles in the destruction of what we saw as our ancestors' *paganism* and *backwardness*. By attacking their worldviews and ways of life, we practically displaced and exiled them in their own homeland.

It is only in the space of our own displacement and exile, a space where we become the newest settlers in the new lands stolen from other indigenous peoples, that we are able to connect the dots and look at the horrifying continuity of global colonialism, albeit through its radical discontinuity. It is in exile that we can see the linkages between discursive practices that displace us from our homeland and those that emplace us in the miserably marginal spaces of our new countries. Researching and embracing *Ateetee* is our way of subverting our conditions of homelessness and staying connected to home; it is our way of making home out of exile (Kumsa, 2013). For me, this is finding identity in difference. Seeking out and nurturing difference through each woman's unique *Ateetee*, I come to identity. This time difference becomes identity turned inside out. Seeking identity, I find difference and seeking difference, I find identity.

Safuu: Back to Identity through Difference

Let me conclude this chapter by opening it up to some of the lessons I learnt and the further questions I gleaned from the critical explorations of my precarious positioning in various circles of belonging and in feminist social work research. I will touch on three salient themes: positioning *siiqqee* feminism, restoring ruptured *safuu*, and ongoing tensions.

Positioning Siiqqee Feminism

The way I have embraced and articulated it through decades of researching and exploring, *siiqqee* feminism is one among many feminisms. It signifies intimate interconnectedness and solidarity among women while also honoring and nurturing differences and unique experiences. Beyond the intimate relationships among women, *siiqqee* also signifies broader intimate interconnectedness among various individuals and groups, communities and societies, among living and non-living beings, among flora and fauna, and among all beings in the cosmos. This intimate interconnectedness of everyone and everything, known as *safuu* in Oromo cosmology, is fundamental to the principles of *siiqqee* solidarity. In the contemporary context, I see *safuu* as the fundamental glue that holds together everyone and everything in this glocalizing world and in the entire cosmos. And the fundamental glue in *safuu* that holds everything together is the principle of egalitarian checks and balances.

Restoring Ruptured Safuu

Safuu has been lost and Oromos are in desperate struggle to restore it. *Siiqqee* feminism is part of this struggle, seeking solidarity with feminists and other oppressed groups. I see *safuu* as being lost in the entire glocalizing world. The egalitarian checks and balances holding together the entire cosmos are ruptured. Law of *muka laaftuu* [soft wood] that is supposed to protect vulnerable groups is lost. The gap is widening between the haves and have-nots of the world. The cosmos is in pain. The environment is hurting. The flora and fauna are in pain. *Haadha Dachii* [Mother Earth] is screaming with her *siiqqee* raised. *Ateetee* is screaming with her *siiqqee* raised. Oromo women have raised their *siiqqee* and crossed the ocean screaming. The lost checks and balances of *safuu* must be restored for the sake of all cosmic beings. As *halagaa* [strangers] not belonging anywhere, women are the floating glue that holds together the various communities and entire societies. As strangers in others' lands, exiles are the floating glue that bonds and holds together the entire glocalizing world. They tell their warring governments: 'you are hurting my family out there!' Exiles are like *siiqqee* women on trek. Oromo women double up as both, strangers at home and strangers abroad. They are screaming for solidarity to restore *safuu*, the ultimate holding glue that bonds and holds together the entirety of the cosmos. The cosmic egalitarian balance of *safuu* must be restored for life to continue.

Ongoing Tensions

This chapter is inspired by the desire to recenter feminisms in social work research and can be seen as one way of recentering a feminism. However, I am torn apart by the tension between my desires to recenter and decenter *siiqqee* feminism. For me this is an ongoing tension that breeds other equally intense tensions like identity and difference, unity and multiplicity, local and global. In terms of identity and difference, at this point in my explorations, I cannot see any category of identity that does not open up into differences and no category of difference that does not seek identity. I cannot eschew difference in search of identity. Nor can I embrace difference and eschew identity. Homogenizing difference is oppressive and getting lost in difference feeds into dividing practices that serve the status quo to continue blissfully. In terms of unity and multiplicity, feminists have asked if it is enough to call it feminisms instead of feminism or if there is something more fundamental that needs to shift.

I hope this chapter has shown that multiplicity is not enough, that *there are many of us and we are all different* does not reach deep down and touch profound issues of inequity and injustice infused in the multiplicities of these positions. Acknowledging and working through privileged positions is especially hard, at least for me. My privilege comes with responsibility for those marginalized by it. That is why liberating others needs to come home to liberating self. This constitutes another ongoing tension between personal liberation and social transformation. Also, in this intimately interconnected glocalizing world, there is no global issue that is not also local and no local issue that is not also global. Oromo women have crossed multiple identity boundaries. They have crossed the ocean and come to the West screaming. Their *siiqqees* remain raised. Their screams continue. Will feminist social work researchers see this as *their* own glocal issue? Will they scream with them in solidarity? Will they participate in restoring *safuu?*

References

Absolon, K. E. (Minogiizhigokwe). (2011). *Kaandossiwin. How we come to know.* Halifax: Fernwood Publishing.

Ahmed, S. (2000). *Strange encounters: Embodied Others in post-coloniality.* London and New York: Routledge.

Anzaldúa, G. (1990). *Making face, making soul/haciendo caras: Creative and critical perspectives by women of color.* San Francisco: Aunt Lute Foundation Books.

Butler, J. (2003). Afterword: After loss, what then? In D. Eng & D. Kazanjian (Eds.), *Loss: The politics of mourning* (pp. 467–473). Berkeley and LA: University of California Press.

Davidson, B. (1992). *The Black man's burden: Africa and the curse of the nation-state.* New York: Times Books.

Fanon, F. (1963). *The wretched of the earth.* New York: Grove Press.

Frost, L. & Hoggett, P. (2008). Human agency and social suffering. *Critical Social Policy, 28* (4), 438—460.

Gringeri, C., Wahab, S., & Anderson-Nathe, B. (2010). What makes it feminist? Mapping the landscape of social work feminist research. *Affilia, 25* (4), 390–405.

Hamera, J. (2011). Performance ethnography. In N. K. Denzin & Y. S. Lincoln (Eds.), *The Sage handbook of qualitative research* (pp. 317–330). Los Angeles: Sage.

Harding, S. (1987). *Feminism and methodology.* Buckingham: Open University Press.

Hill Collins, P. (1990). *Black feminist thought: Knowledge, consciousness and the politics of empowerment.* Boston: UnwynHyman.

hooks, b. (1981). *Ain't I a woman? Black women and feminism.* Boston: South End Press.

hooks, b. (1984). *Feminist theory: From margin to center.* Boston: South End Press.

Kaplan, C. (1994). The politics of location as transnational feminist practice. In I. Grewal & C Kaplan (Eds.), *Scattered hegemonies: Transnational feminist practices* (pp. 137–152). Minneapolis: University of Minnesota Press.

Kelly, P. (2001). Youth at risk: Processes of individualization and responsiblization in the risk society. *Discourse, 22* (1), 23–33.

Kumsa, M. K. (1997). The siiqqee institution of Oromo women. *Journal of Oromo Studies, 4* (1&2), 115–152.

Kumsa, M. K. (2007/2011). A resettlement story of unsettlement: Transformative practices of taking it personally. In D. Baines (Ed.), *Doing anti-oppressive practice: Social justice social work* (pp. 229–248). Halifax and Winnipeg: Fernwood Publishing.

Kumsa, M.K. (2009). Soothing the wounds of the nation: Oromo women perform-ing Ateetee in exile. In C. Korieh & P. Okeke-Ihejirika (Eds.), *Gendering trans-formations: Gender, culture, race, and identity* (pp. 87–100). New York: Routledge.

Kumsa, M. K. (2013). *Songs of exile: Singing the past into the future.* Kitchener, Canada: Duudhaa Publishing.

Lather, P. (1993). Fertile obsession: Validity after poststructuralism. *The Sociological Quarterly 34* (4), 673–693.

Liu, L. (1994). The female body and nationalist discourse: The field of life and death revisited. In I. Grewal & C Kaplan (Eds.), *Scattered hegemonies: Transnational feminist practices* (pp. 37–62). Minneapolis: University of Minnesota Press.

Lorde, A. (1984). *Sister outsider: Essays and speeches.* Toronto: Crossing Press.

Moraga, C. & Anzaldúa, G. (Eds). (1981). *This bridge called my back: Writings by radical women of color.* New York: Kitchen Table: Women of Color Press.

National Film Board of Canada (1990). *The burning times.* Montreal: National Film Board of Canada.

Østebø, M. (2009). Wayyuu—Women's respect and rights among the Arsi-Oromo. In S. Ege, H. Aspen, B. Teferra, & S. Bekele (Eds.), *Proceedings of the 16th International Conference of Ethiopian Studies* (pp. 1049–1060). Trondheim.

Pelias, R. J. (2008). Performance inquiry: Embodiment and its challenges. In J. G. Knowels & A. L. Cole (Eds.), *Handbook of the arts in qualitative research* (pp. 185–194). Los Angeles: Sage.

Pillow, W. (2003). Confessions, catharsis, or cure? *International Journal of Qualitative Studies in Education, 16* (2), 175–196.

Pollock, D. (2007). The performative "I". *Cultural Studies ↔ Critical Methodologies, 7* (3), 239–255.

Pratt, A. (2005). *Securing borders: Detention and deportation in Canada.* Vancouver: University of British Columbia Press.

Qashu, L. (2009). Arsi Oromo society viewed through its wedding music. In S. Ege, H. Aspen, B. Teferra, & S. Bekele (Eds.), *Proceedings of the 16th International Conference of Ethiopian Studies* (pp. 1235–1248). Trondheim.

Rowbotham, S. (1972). *Women, resistance and revolution.* London: Random House.

Smith, L. T. (1999). *Decolonizing methodologies. Research and indigenous peoples.* London and New York: Zed Books.

Spivak, G. (1988). Can the subaltern speak? In C. Nelson & L. Grossberg (Eds.), *Marxism and the interpretation of culture* (pp. 271–313). Chicago: University of Illinois Press.

Visweswaran, K. (1994). Betrayal: An analysis in three acts. In I. Grewal & C. Kaplan (Eds.), *Scattered hegemonies: Transnational feminist practices* (pp. 90–109). Minneapolis: University of Minnesota Press.

Wahab, S., Anderson-Nathe, B., & Gringeri, C. (2012). Joining the conversation: Social work contributions to feminist research. In S. Hesse-Biber (Ed.), *Handbook of Feminist Research* (pp. 455–474). Los Angeles: Sage.

Wako, F. (2003). Contesting marginality in jest: The voice of Borana women in oral tradition. *Journal of Oromo Studies, 10* (1–2), 91–118.

Young, R. (1990). *White mythologies: Writing history and the West.* London: Routledge.

Young, R. (2001). *Postcolonialism: An historical introduction.* Oxford: Blackwell Publishers.

11 Troubling the Binary

A Critical Look at the Dualistic Construction of Quantitative/Qualitative Methods in Feminist Social Work Research

Sandra M. Leotti and Jennifer S. Muthanna

Introduction

This chapter seeks to trouble the accepted construction of the qualitative/quantitative divide in social work research. We begin by positioning our discussion within our own experiences, as well as within the larger context of feminist social work in the academy, or lack thereof. We proceed to reflect on how, traditionally, due to their epistemological and ontological assumptions, feminist theories and values have been aligned with qualitative methods and we consider how this has resulted in a lack of discussion regarding how and when quantitative research methods might be used by feminist social work researchers. Ultimately, we believe social work research will benefit from re-engaging with feminist theories—in both qualitative and quantitative methods. We recognize that feminist activists use quantitative research to further their aims, bolster their agendas, inform their practice, and affect social change. As a tension exists between feminist activism and the academy (the "ivory tower" critique still holds sway), it is difficult to locate the research and achievements of feminist activists within peer-reviewed journals. As a result, dominant social work discourse often assumes that feminist social work researchers do not utilize quantitative methods; thus, the false qualitative/quantitative dichotomy is reified. This dichotomy excludes the many potential and useful ways quantitative methods could be used to further feminist goals of social justice and change. This chapter, thus, presents how quantitative methods might be used by feminists in ways that are epistemologically meaningful and grounded in theory. To clarify, we differentiate between quantitative research that is explicitly feminist in its epistemology, methodology, and goals and quantitative research that is purported to be feminist insofar as it is simply research "about women." To us, the latter is positivistic research masquerading as feminist research.

We conclude by wondering what might happen should the dominant binary be subverted. We posit that one's research method ought to be determined by the research questions posed and operationalized with respect to the researcher's values and goals. The distinction ought not to be around the use of quantitative or qualitative methods, but rooted in ontological and epistemological choices. This holds significant implications for social work education in terms of how we train students to understand, utilize, and engage in research.

Framing Our Perspectives

We come to this work as social work doctoral students frustrated by the superficiality and limitedness of feminist theories in our education and research. We explicitly position ourselves and our work within critical feminist frameworks. One white and one brown, we identify as women, students, social workers, scholars, educators, and reluctantly, researchers. We recognize and embrace the politically laden nature of each of these contested terms. These labels are unfinished aspects of our identities and have brought us joy and despair, relief and frustration, and embody contradictions on multiple levels. Our perspectives presented in this chapter are partial and shifting and are embodied by and within our identities.

Although each of us is drawn more toward qualitative inquiry, we have worked on quantitative social work research projects and have been disappointed by the lack of engagement with issues around epistemology, framing, ethics, and representation. We assert that these are not just issues for qualitative research, feminist or otherwise, and that such standards for rigor ought to be applied to quantitative research. In our education, we have come to learn that qualitative research is not judged or viewed as adequate without attention to these issues, yet quantitative research is typically evaluated solely based on findings and "gold standard" methods with little consideration to these other central concerns. We believe this is problematic and driven by the reified binary between quantitative/qualitative.

We find the debates and struggles that are centered around quantitative versus qualitative and which have dominated our social work education (though we surmise this experience is far from unique or isolated) to be empty and exhausting. This has, in part, contributed to the intellectual despair we feel as budding social work researchers and scholars. We are weary of the positivist and normative voices that define what "good" social work research is and of lapping up the intellectual crumbs we get as feminists in the social work academy. We come to this project because we ask and expect more of social work and of ourselves as feminist social work scholars. Furthermore, we believe that "what it means to do feminist research" is not just about choice of method; rather, many of the values and agendas that drive feminist research can and should be used in quantitative research as well. Thinking about how to break down and through the qualitative/quantitative binary allows us to engage in the act of knowledge production in a way we find useful and meaningful.

Marginalized Voices in Social Work Research

Despite its rich history in social work, feminisms are largely absent in the academy and contemporary practice and research (Barretti, 2011; Gray & Boddy, 2010; Kemp & Brandwein, 2010; Swigonski & Raheim, 2011). Regardless, scholars are highlighting the relevance of feminist thought and arguing for its application in social work education and research (Freeman, 1990; Gringeri, Wahab, & Anderson-Nathe, 2010; Moosa-Mitha & Ross-Sheriff, 2010; Orme, 2003) and emphasizing feminisms' compatibility with social work values and ethics (Barretti, 2011; Collins, 1986; Gray & Boddy, 2010; Sands & Nuccio, 1992). We draw on these ideas when conceptualizing the diverse ways in which feminist thoughts can be integrated into social work research.

This chapter begins from the understanding of feminisms as evolving epistemological and theoretical frameworks with no one universal definition (Collins, 1986; Dominelli, 1996; Freeman, 1990; Gringeri et al., 2010; Kemp & Brandwein, 2010; Rupp & Taylor, 1999). The terrain of feminisms, not unlike that of social work, is multiple, shifting, and contested.

As others in this edition, we seek to disrupt the dominant ideology in social work that *a* feminist theory exists. We believe this reductionism has resulted in the reluctance of those who could or would identify with feminisms to do so. As a result, feminisms have been dismissed in a wholesale fashion as being "irrelevant" or "unnecessary" and feminist scholars and researchers have been alienated within academia and by prospective funders.

The lack of nuance and depth around discussions of feminisms in social work education leads to a simplistic and dualistic framing of methods in feminist social work research. This construction is more complex, however, as binary discourse occurs on multiple fronts simultaneously. For example, in social work discourse, positivist/post-positivist = traditional/modernist = objective = quantitative while anti-positivist = feminist/critical/interpretive/post-modernist = subjective = qualitative. Whether we additionally contend that the former is rooted in subjugation and social control while the latter is aimed at emancipation and social change depends on our epistemologies. We recognize that this is an incredibly nuanced conversation and are not naïve enough to suggest that we can exhaustively address the question of how quantitative methods came to rest primarily in the domain of positivist epistemologies. Instead, we explore some of the most critical aspects of this divide and locate this discussion in a social work context.

Breaking Down the Binary

In beginning to address the question of how quantitative methods based in positivist epistemologies have become the accepted methods in social sciences, we first must explore and elucidate key concepts. This is central in exploring the ways in which language and discourse shape the research process. Too often, the quantitative/qualitative debate assumes a shared understanding of the issues and neglects to operationalize definitions or deconstruct epistemological assumptions. In an effort to subvert this tendency, we endeavor to consider: quantitative/qualitative and methods/methodology.

Quantitative and Qualitative

Oftentimes, the quantitative/qualitative debate is framed as being paradigmatic in nature (Howe, 1992; Sale, Lohfeld, & Brazil, 2002; Smith & Heshusius, 1986). Although this is an interesting conversation to be had, we argue that qualitative and quantitative methods are not paradigms or epistemologies in and of themselves, rather they are mere tools of measurement (or procedures) that are imbued with paradigmatic characteristics when expressed through one's research methodology.

Although we do not see quantitative and qualitative methods as paradigmatic in themselves, neither do we "de-epistemologize" them. To be explicit, we believe epistemology is a core issue for researchers; however, we do not believe certain methods inherently embody epistemology. Additionally, we recognize that both quantitative and qualitative research traditions are historically rooted in Enlightenment thought. Without engaging around the "thinking" of research, as Smythe (2005) calls it, both risk being based in objectivist epistemologies (i.e., positivism/post-positivism).

Jayaratne and Stewart (2008) contend that "[q]uantification, in a strict sense, only refers to the transformation of observations . . . into numbers" (p. 49). They caution that while, historically, quantitative research has obscured the experiences of marginalized groups, logically it need not always be used in such a manner. Denzin and Lincoln (2005) further assert that quantitative studies concern themselves with the causal relationships between variables and are remiss in considering process. While this may be true within a hegemonic context, we believe this argument imbues quantitative *techniques* with inherent epistemological underpinnings. It is this conflation that is problematic as it reifies a poorly constructed binary. Howe (1992) contends that the quantitative/qualitative debate has been unfolding for several decades, but that it has "evolved from one about the incompatibility of . . . techniques and procedures to one about the incompatibility of . . . fundamental epistemological assumptions" (p. 236). He goes on to suggest that using positivism as "a foil" (p. 237) forces anti-positivists to define their positions negatively and in opposition to positivism.

Lawson (1995) states that the coupling of feminist with qualitative is "historically produced and not necessary or inevitable" (p. 451). Although this historical association makes sense, we believe this binary positioning of methods distracts from deeper issues regarding epistemology and knowledge production. A narrow allegiance to qualitative methods reinforces the quantitative/qualitative binary and obscures the fact that what "makes it feminist" is not to be found in the method used, but rather the attention to research processes (Lawson, 1995). As Giddings (2006) states, "an effect of maintaining the binary positioning is to make methodological diversity invisible and hide the dominant positioning of scientific positivist research" (p. 199). Further, such dualism excludes the use of quantitative methods (which have the potential to promote certain types of social change) among feminists, confines the types of questions being asked by feminists, and reinforces the faulty hegemonic notion that qualitative methods are "unscientific" or less rigorous. Hence, it is crucial to dislodge the discussion from being one of quantitative versus qualitative to one in which we critically examine how our epistemological locations can shape and strengthen our research, regardless of method.

Methods and Methodology

Again, the terms "methods" and "methodology" often are used interchangeably. This results in confusion and reifies the notion that some methods are inherently inconsistent or incommensurate with the researcher's epistemology. We urge a discrete and uncomplicated differentiation of the terms. We defer to Harding (as cited in Jayaratne & Stewart, 2008) who defines "methods" as "particular procedures used in the course of research" (p. 48). In this way, "methods" refers to tools or techniques such as interviews, surveys, or questionnaires. Methodology, however, refers to the "theory of how research is carried out or the broad principles about how to conduct research and how theory is applied" (Jayaratne & Stewart, 2008, p. 48). Therefore, it's possible to use feminist, hermeneutic, or positivistic methodologies. Strega (2005) makes the case that "the epistemological foundation of methodology prescribes what good research involves, justifies why research is done, gives a value base to research, and provides ethical principles for conducting research" (p. 211). Thus, all vital aspects of a research endeavor are forged from epistemological assumptions and commitments, not in choice of methods (Denzin & Lincoln, 2005).

When constructed in this way, it is clear how the positivist/feminist debate is not the same as the quantitative/qualitative debate. Somehow, though, quantitative methods became the purview solely of positivism and were deemed incommensurate with feminisms and/or critical, interpretative, constructivist paradigmatic traditions. How did this come to pass and, more importantly, how is this continuously reified?

Hegemony and Quantitative Research Methods

How quantitative research methods came to be entrenched in positivism hinges on the conflation of method, methodology, and epistemology and the uncritical manner in which these terms are used interchangeably. The emphasis in dominant social sciences on realist ontological and positivist epistemological foundations has produced a strong reliance on concepts such as objectivity, neutrality, detachment, and value-free methods; thus, quantitative analysis has been utilized and deemed the most rigorous and scientifically sound (Giddings, 2006; Moosa-Mitha, 2005; Sale et al., 2002).

Much has been said about the damaging and colonizing nature of dominant social sciences research. "Second-wave" feminist epistemological criticisms of positivist methodologies are well understood and, perhaps, account for the predominant use of qualitative methods by feminists (Cohen, Hughes, & Lampard, 2011; Scott, 2010; Undurraga, 2010). These criticisms include the predominance of an androcentric bias in traditional research; the impossibility of objectivity; the treatment of subjects as objects; the hierarchical nature of traditional research relationships; the marked absence of women from research as both subjects and scholars; and the problematic veil of neutrality (thus, not using research results to create social change) (Haraway, 2008; Harding, 2006; Hughes & Cohen, 2010; Jayaratne & Stewart, 2008; Lawson, 1995).

In contrast, feminist research is explicitly political, seeks to eliminate hierarchy, claims subjectivity within researchers and participants, and centralizes gender (Fonow & Cook, 2005; Gringeri et al., 2010; Jayaratne & Stewart, 2008; Moosa-Mitha, 2005; Olesen, 2005). As feminist principles are in tension with the ontological and epistemological foundations of dominant social sciences, the focus of feminist critiques historically has been on quantitative research; thus many feminists have aligned themselves with qualitative methods. Jayaratne and Stewart (2008) caution against assuming there is a "natural" alignment between feminisms and qualitative research techniques. They argue that this is the result of essentialist thinking and that it unnecessarily limits feminists' evaluations and critiques of research procedures and methodologies. Again, the conflation of epistemology and method obscures the fact that simply utilizing a qualitative method is not adequate criteria for calling research "feminist." In addition, contemporary feminist theorists and researchers increasingly distinguish between qualitative methods and feminist approaches.

Toward a Shifting Discourse

We note and do not discard historical criticisms of dominant positivist social sciences. However, we think it is a mistake to completely and outrightly dismiss quantitative methods as decisions around quality of research should not be based solely on one's choice of methods.

Lawson (1995) calls for researchers to take seriously "the ways that we . . . mark the knowledge that we produce" (p. 452) regardless of method. She states that both quantitative and qualitative research have the potential to mask as much as they expose, if essentialized concepts of gender are employed and feminist values are not attended to in the process. We agree and, as others before us, see the potential in harnessing quantitative methods in new ways so as to use quantification to document existing social conditions with an end to bringing about change in the political arena (Crocker, 2010; Lawson, 1995; Scott, 2010). This can be seen around a variety of issues that were ignored historically or went unrecognized until feminists began documenting the depth and prevalence of issues such as domestic violence, sexual harassment, and the gender pay gap (Crocker, 2010; Scott, 2010).

Many scholars point to the emancipatory potential of quantitative research (Harnois, 2005; Lawson, 1995; Payne, 2007; Scott, 2010; Spierings, 2012; Undurraga, 2010). It is particularly useful in uncovering and describing relations of power, various consequences of unequal power relations, and patterns of inequality. Although we agree with the post-modern/post-structural understandings of power as diffuse and of meaning as discursive (Wendt & Boylan, 2008), we also acknowledge the very real material manifestations of oppression and unequal power relations. Lawson (1995) contends that quantitative methods can be useful for addressing certain questions regarding the material reality and less suited for questions about identity and subjective experiences. One's choice of methods should be guided and driven more by research questions than by a devotion to a particular methodological approach (DeVault, 1996; Lawson, 1995; Payne, 2007; Scott, 2010). Moreover, statistics have the ability to "enable and constrain policy development" (Crocker, 2010, p. 272) and/or to shape larger common understandings around social issues. Therefore, it is crucial that feminists have a place at the "counting table" in order to raise public awareness and direct policy development in line with feminist concerns. Crocker (2010) argues that, "when feminists count we need to consider the constitutive role of our statistics and the policies that emerge from them" (p. 272).

Additionally, gender scholars in a number of fields outside of social work, particularly sociology and geography, are utilizing and expanding intersectional perspectives in quantitative research (Harnois, 2005; Lawson, 1995; McCall, 2005; Spierings, 2012). Such research calls to attention multiple variables, asks questions regarding difference, and is carefully contextualized so as to avoid essentialist assumptions embedded in generalizations and inferential thinking. Scott (2010) purports that

> there is very limited data that can support statistical analysis of the multiple, intersecting and complex patterns of inequalities that cross the gender, class, age and ethnic boundaries. However, analysis of this kind, although still in its theoretical and methodological infancy, is important because it can illustrate the ways different bases of discrimination and inequality interact, depending on the context. (p. 225)

Feminist social worker researchers can and should have a place in this development. Quantitative research, as long as it is robust feminist social science, has a place and power, particularly in regard to the feminist goals of social change (Hughes & Cohen, 2010; Lawson, 1995; Payne, 2007; Undurraga, 2010). Given social work's and feminists' commitment to praxis, the potential for using quantitative research to achieve emancipatory ends cannot be ignored. In order to do so, however, we urge the deconflation of method and epistemology. We contend that a failure to do so not only reifies the assumption that feminists do not use quantitative research, but that our inattention makes us complicit in perpetuating problematic hegemonic binaries. Therefore, it is essential that feminist researchers (and others with critical epistemologies) become conversant in and comfortable using quantitative research methods.

The strength of feminist research is found in its willingness to look beyond the pragmatics of research and into the epistemology and processes that drive and shape it. Doing so asks researchers to locate themselves in their work, questioning values, assumptions, power, and privilege, and to make these things transparent so as to better judge the quality of their research process and interpretation. The importance of situating ourselves, our biases, and processes so readers can make their own decisions regarding claims made in our analyses cannot be understated in feminist research, regardless of method. Additionally, the subsequent dichotomous positioning of methods reifies those gendered binaries deeply entrenched in modernity by associating "the binary of qualitative and quantitative with a dualistic structuring of female/male; soft/hard; intuitive/rational; art/science and so forth" (Hughes & Cohen, 2010, p. 189). This serves to distract from the real issues regarding epistemology and knowledge production. As Jayaratne and Stewart (2008) contend, "the focus of feminist dialogue on 'methods' and particularly on qualitative versus quantitative methods, obscures the more fundamental challenge of feminism to the traditional 'scientific method'" (p. 53). In this, feminists, like positivists, are prone to policing the boundaries of what "counts" as knowledge. Like Giddings' (2006) hope-based critique of mixed methods research, we fear that without adequate attention to reflexivity, epistemological dilemmas, political goals, and lenses of analyses and interpretation, feminist quantitative research can easily become veiled positivism, just as "qualitative" can become a "'catch all' for non-positivist inquiry" (p. 199). So the question remains, regardless of method, how do we incorporate feminist perspectives and values into the research process?

Feminist Epistemologies: Tension and Discord

We would be remiss if we did not acknowledge the tensions that exist between feminist epistemologies. While feminists can (and should) use quantitative methods, the methodology enacted will vary considerably. Those feminist researchers who identify as post-positivists will be more aligned to positivist constructions of objectivity (i.e., while "true" objectivity may not be possible, the intention is to approach it as closely as possible); critical or post-modern feminist researchers will conceptualize and embrace "objectivity" as "situated knowledge" (Haraway, 2008, p. 348). Haraway writes that "feminist objectivity is about limited location and situated knowledge, not about transcendence and splitting of subject and object. It allows us to become answerable for what we learn how to see" (p. 248). In this sense, there is a real disconnect between post-positivist feminist research epistemologies and critical feminist research epistemologies. The former may be employed by those feminist researchers who identify with the "second-wave" feminist movement and/or are aligned with liberal feminism. To this end, post-positivist feminist researchers will be constrained by hegemonic constructions of objectivity in their quest for equality. On the contrary, post-modern or critical feminist researchers have sought to redefine "objectivity" in a fundamental and transformative way so that equity and emancipation might be achieved (Haraway, 2008). Given the differing goals of equality and equity, we wonder whether the tension that exists between post-positivist feminist researchers and post-modern/critical feminist researchers is insoluble. That is, on some level, these epistemologies are incommensurate. While this pondering may be unsatisfactory to some, we suggest that our energies are best directed at strengthening and increasing the visibility of the work of post-modern/critical feminist researchers so that the hegemonic "ideal" in research can be challenged and disrupted.

Locating Feminist Quantitative Research

Scholars have found that much research labeled as "feminist" lacks explicit engagement with feminist theories, ideas, and debates regarding the topic material or methodological issues (Cohen et al., 2011; Gringeri et al., 2010; Orme, 2003). Additionally, despite the utility and historical use of quantitative methods in feminist activism, discussions of how feminist epistemologies might inform contemporary quantitative research are difficult to locate.

In a systematic review of articles published in "gender, women's studies, feminist, and other women-oriented journals," Cohen et al. (2011) found that an "explicit discussion of the relationship between feminism and method does not [therefore] comprise a common part of published research" (p. 576) and that those that explicitly claimed feminism were least likely to use quantitative methods. Only two out of 109 articles using solely quantitative methods explicitly claimed feminism in reference to their methodological choice. Conversely, articles claiming transformative justifications for methodological choice were more likely to be quantitative in nature. Gringeri et al.'s (2010) review of social work research supports the claim that those with explicitly feminist epistemologies are more likely to gravitate toward qualitative methods. Cohen et al. (2011) found that reflexivity was unlikely to be a part of quantitative articles, despite claiming a feminist orientation. In a review of major feminist research textbooks,

Undurraga (2010) found a stark lack of attention regarding how to engage effectively in quantitative research; however, in the few chapters that dealt with quantitative methods, rich and useful discussions regarding how to engage in quantitative research in a way that is consistent with feminist values and agendas were provided.

Undurraga (2010), like others (DeVault, 1996; Mason, 1997), argues that there is no one "feminist method" and that we should shift our focus to look at how methods (whether they be quantitative or qualitative) are used and how they are, or are not, used in a manner that is consistent with feminist values. That is, she suggests we consider methodology over methods. Further, she calls on feminists to consider the types of questions they are (or are not) asking, if the tendency is to rely solely on qualitative methods. Additionally, Ryan and Golden (2006) note that "quantitative research seems largely to avoid the issue of how social boundaries are defined, contested, and negotiated" (p. 1192). Given that reflexivity is increasingly recognized as a core component of rigorous feminist research (Daley, 2010; Gringeri et al., 2010; Olesen, 2005), such findings speak to the need for the "development and legitimation of a more reflexive quantitative discourse" (Cohen et al., 2011, p. 583). Cohen and colleagues suggest that this discourse should include epistemological discussions regarding the justification of methods on the basis of goals (political and social change), reflection on the process and context of research(ers), and "critical approaches to the choice of statistical measures and techniques" (p. 583). Such reflexivity allows us to situate knowledge construction within a larger context as well as within the context of the self.

From the findings cited above, one can surmise that feminists are perhaps unprepared to adequately engage in and with quantitative research, thus reinforcing the notion that feminists can only do qualitative work. We, however, feel that it is a call to the larger academy and field of feminists to expand our notions of what it means to do research and infuse that into our writing and pedagogy in order to more adequately equip feminists to engage with various methods and questions. This calls for extensive change in the discourse and practices of both feminists and quantitative researchers. We recognize the feat of this, particularly in a field such as social work, that seemingly resists feminisms. However, we contend that such a shift has immense possibility for the transformation of science and the academy.

(Re)conceptualizing Feminist Quantitative Research: Possibilities

Audre Lorde (1984/2007) said that, "the master's tools will never dismantle the master's house" (p. 112). We take this assertion to heart when grappling with the social construction of knowledge and the deep epistemological issues around feminists' use of traditional tools in social sciences. The tensions and contradictions are abundant and not to be taken lightly. Still, we believe it is a mistake to locate the master in a dichotomous position of "power over." In line with Foucault's later work, we believe that notions of power as being solely centralized are misleading and incomplete (Rose, 2000). Thus, we propose reclaiming these tools in order to use them in new ways. As Blanchard (2002) says:

> we'll realize that those tools didn't belong to the master, after all. Well, they didn't belong to him all by himself. They are our tools, too. And they have been so all the time. And that is one way that we gain agency, by adapting the tools we have rather than by reinventing the wheel; although the wheel is reinvented along the way. (p. 256)

We wonder, in a field such as social work that is ethically rooted in social justice, how is it that quantitative research has been constructed and accepted as apolitical and atheoretical? We find this question particularly poignant given that quantitative research is currently the dominant research method in social work. In line with Blanchard's (2002) assertion, we believe that feminist epistemological assumptions can reshape the use of quantitative methods to be more in line with the goals and vision of the profession. As Jayaratne and Stewart (2008) state, "procedures commonly used in quantitative research which are inconsistent with feminist values can be altered without abandoning the quantitative strategies which can beneficial to feminists" (p. 46). For feminist social work researchers, this concern is relevant to what Fine (1992) calls the "central contradiction" (p. 206) between being a social science researcher and a feminist with an explicitly social justice-driven, activist agenda.

Interrogating the Dispassioned Scientist

Similar to the findings of a lack of reflexivity in feminist quantitative research (Cohen et al., 2011; Ryan & Golden, 2006), we find that in dominant social work research, ethics and positioning oneself in the research are often not seen as part of the "real" research, let alone part of an ongoing process.

Considering our own experiences on quantitative research projects, we observe that, despite the slippery ethical terrain of these projects and the loaded nature of the topics, research team members were never expected to engage in reflexive questions regarding our own roles in the process (including biases, positioning, engagement with participants, and interpretations) or with epistemological concerns. We find the lack of explicit engagement with reflexivity in quantitative research, particularly that labeled as feminist, disturbing as it renders us (as researchers) invisible, disguises power processes, distorts and misrepresents the actual words, perspectives, and experiences of participants, and obscures the contested nature of science and knowledge (Fine, 1992). As many before us have asserted, our voices are not disembodied carriers of objective truth; our results carry with them the baggage of our social and political positioning and analytic choices.

Fine (1992) notes the importance of engaging with epistemological dilemmas involving questions such as, "What makes this research? When does intervention stop and reflection begin? How do I/we 'know' what I/we 'know'? What are our grounds for disproof? What are the limits of collaboration? And what are the bases for shared censorship?" (p. 230). Additionally, Crocker (2010) draws attention to the importance of questions regarding how data should be analyzed, how interpretations and theoretical extrapolations are made and/or rejected, what findings should be used for, as well as "our place in the web of governmental power" (p. 273) when engaging with feminist quantitative research for social justice aims. Lastly, reflexivity can guide us in disrupting traditional research relationships. We think it is crucial to interrogate our role as "researcher" and consider our obligations to participants, as feminists, social workers, and fellow humans.

By engaging in such processes we refuse invisibility for ourselves and our participants and, thus, reveal the partiality of knowledge claims as well as the power and authority embedded in the research process. Instead of "editing out," we seek to edit ourselves back in. We ought to explicitly position the "self" (the political self, social self, and professional self) and connect our work to larger socio-political structures. These reflexive processes should draw attention to how certain research questions, processes, and interpretations win out over others and make visible the ways in which researchers guide and influence analyses and findings (Fine, 1992; Hughes & Cohen, 2010; Lawson, 1995; Undurraga, 2010). This "interrogation of the practices that construct knowledge" (Daley, 2010, p. 69) makes transparent the process of moving from data analysis to theoretical conclusions, which is perhaps, although often neglected, especially crucial in quantitative work when engaging in complex statistical analyses that can be misleading and misunderstood. The reality of social sciences is that, quantitative or qualitative, we only get a partial picture. Reflexivity can provide insight into the process and experience of doing not only qualitative, but also quantitative, research (see Browne, 2008, as an example) and thus shatter the scientific veil of objectivity and neutrality.

Interrogating Tensions Embedded in Techniques

We assert that the boundaries and assumptions guiding dominant social sciences research and feminist research are and should be open to contestation. As it stands, feminists, alongside positivists, reinforce a rhetoric of binaries within academic social research. That is not to say that the tensions feminists have historically pointed to are not real and valid; rather it calls attention to the ways in which certain discourses are uncritically produced and reproduced in research. There may be very real places of discomfort for feminists who engage in quantitative research. As Lawson (1995) states, "there may be considerable tensions in learning how to count differently—from a feminist, relational ontological position" (p. 455). Yet still, entrenching binary methodological lines has created a less than useful tendency for researchers to take certain forms of "evidence" seriously while neglecting others. Rather than dismiss the potentiality or usefulness of any one type of method, perhaps it would be more fruitful to expose these tensions and engage with them.

Browne (2008) does such a thing in discussing her quantitative research on sexualities. By exposing decision-making processes in her research, she calls attention to how everyday judgments in regard to question formulation, measurement construction, coding, and negotiating academic and community priorities are not value-neutral. Lawson's (1995) assertion that "reworking counting along feminist lines involves understanding how our acts of counting are embedded in fields of power" (p. 455) supports this claim. In Browne's (2008) discussion, she engages with the very real dangers and difficulties involved in relying on "particular hegemonic understandings of gendered and sex categories" (p. 19) while concurrently trying to theoretically deconstruct them. This type of reflexive work does not erase the fixed (and often essentialized) categories used, but it does open them to interpretation. Her work calls attention to the ways in which we can use categories and quantitative methods to further community goals while simultaneously problematizing them. She argues that instead of doing away with quantitative research because of these tensions, the tools of queer theory can be used to deconstruct it to "reveal its/their social, economic, epistemological, ontological, and methodological (re)formations and contexts" (p. 14).

Browne (2008) goes on to argue for the importance of methodological reflexivity in order to expose the spaces where the research process was adjusted and negotiated along epistemological lines. She states,

> In addition, whilst I contested the existence of only three genders (male, female, and trans) and four sexualities, I referred to multiple categories rather than contesting the existence of these categories themselves. This was because the nature of the questionnaire required boxes that could be ticked. I seek to emphasize, that this process whilst it fixed particular identities and categories had moments of disruption that were potentially transgressive but these were recuperated and solidified into particular products of research. Focusing mainly on the recuperated categories hides the queer moments that were introduced into the research process (for example the delinking of gender, sexualities, and behaviors). Perhaps then, such moments of interference can be read as important because they contest and render visible the illusion of fixed categories. (p. 13)

As Fine (1992) so aptly puts it, "[t]he problem is not what we tailor but that so few researchers reveal how we do this work" (p. 218).

Reflections and Take-Away Thoughts

Having been through the process of researching and writing this chapter, we concluded that it would be appropriate and helpful to reflect on the experience. Also, we did not want to leave readers with a sense of hopelessness about the future of feminist research or what role they might play. Indeed, we recognized that we are privileged to be able to engage in this discussion and to affect the thoughts of others.

One of our first discussions after finishing this chapter was about the irony of what we'd written. As self-identified feminists, we are committed to the idea of praxis and wanted to actualize this through our chapter. However, the language used in our writing is jargon-laden and could (rightfully) be accused of being inaccessible (or worse, irrelevant) to those outside of academia. When we discussed this further, we recognized the importance of drawing together our thoughts in such a way that makes them accessible to social work students, practitioners, academics, and researchers alike. We also thought it necessary to explore possibilities for combating frustration and despair. That is, looking back at our doctoral experiences, what would we have done differently? Looking forward as academics and researchers, what might we challenge ourselves to do?

It is our experience that academia has its own hegemonic form of socialization. When we realized that ours had normalized the conflation of "method" and "epistemology," we were both humbled and outraged. We recognize the importance of those instructors, friends, and colleagues we've had (or worked with) who have nurtured our critical analyses and pushed us to challenge dominant constructions within the social work academy; this has been crucial in our development as feminist social work researchers. To prospective and current students, we urge you to seek out and cultivate relationships like these—they will keep you afloat and engaged when all else fails!

We encourage our readers to challenge the use of the word "feminism" and to educate others as to why a shift to the word "feminisms" is preferable. When we accept the word "feminism," we tacitly endorse the notion that a myriad of diverse theories can be distilled or reduced into a single representative theory. This is at odds with post-modern epistemology which values multiple voices and focuses on difference.

Yet again, this assertion is not without its own set of tensions as we must find ways to work collectively across, in solidarity with, and/or in alliance with theoretical differences in order to affect large-scale change. Additionally, when reductionism is employed in feminisms, it serves the dominant interests and alienates and renders invisible those who already are marginalized.

We wonder how our experiences and discussions in doctoral classrooms might have been different (not better or worse, just different) had we asked our instructors and classmates to operationalize and epistemologize the terms used. For example, whenever the term "quantitative research" was used, we could have asked, "Are you referring to quantitative research methods or positivist epistemology?" or "How might these quantitative research methods have been used differently if the researchers had situated themselves within feminist epistemologies?" Though this appears to be of trivial significance, we are certain that this small act of resistance would have disrupted what Steinmetz (2005) refers to as epistemological unconsciousness in the academy. It also would have led to the abandonment of exhausting and fruitless debates about the merits (or superiority) of quantitative research methods over qualitative research methods, when, in truth, the debates were fueled by incommensurate epistemologies.

These debates are neither nebulous nor esoteric. The ramifications that students might feel disengaged, silenced, or discounted are real and troubling. This serves as a call to social work educators to more fully integrate and engage with the philosophy of science in methods classes. Re-engaging questions of epistemology, as opposed to just methods, opens up more possibilities for research and for feminists. Additionally, the question of how to utilize quantitative methods from a feminist perspective is a core epistemological question for many. For those from realist ontological positionings, it is a question of validity. Thus, feminists will need to take the lead in developing new standards of rigor for feminist quantitative research.

Like scholars before us, we believe that feminist assertions are "transformative for social work theory and practice" (Swigonski & Raheim, 2011, p. 10) and that there should be greater integration into social work education, practice, and research (Collins, 1986; Gringeri & Roche, 2010; Orme, 2003). The decision to engage in or call one's research feminist does not erase epistemological issues or ensure an unproblematic, liberating process. Rather, the decision comes loaded with epistemological accountability. This has very real implications for educating social work practitioners and scholars, as well as for the lived realities of people outside of academia. As Orme (2003) asserts, "struggles to understand how others come to experience, know and make sense of the world is core to social work practice" (p. 132).

References

Barretti, M. A. (2011). Women, feminism, and social work journals 10 years later. *Affilia, 26*, 264–277.

Blanchard, M. L. (2002). Poets, lovers, and the master's tools: A conversation with Audre Lorde. In G. E. Anzaldúa & A. Keating (Eds.), *This bridge we call home* (pp. 254–257). New York: Routledge.

Browne, K. (2008). Selling my queer soul or queerying quantitative research? *Sociological Research Online, 13* (1), 11.

Cohen, R. L., Hughes, C., & Lampard, R. (2011). The methodological impact of feminism: A troubling issue for sociology? *Sociology, 45*, 570–586.

Collins, B. G. (1986). Defining feminist social work. *Social Work, 31*, 214–219.

Crocker, D. (2010). Counting woman abuse: A cautionary tale of two surveys. *International Journal of Social Research Methodology, 13*, 265–275.

Daley, A. (2010). Reflections on reflexivity and critical reflection as critical research practices. *Affilia, 25* (1), 68–82.

Denzin, N. K. & Lincoln, Y. S. (2005). Introduction. In N. K. Denzin & Y. S. Lincoln (Eds.), *Handbook of qualitative research* (3rd ed.) (pp. 1–32). Thousand Oaks, CA: Sage.

DeVault, M. L. (1996). Talking back to sociology: Distinctive contributions of feminist methodology. *Annual Review of Sociology, 22* (1), 29–50.

Dominelli, L. (1996). Deprofessionalizing social work: Anti-oppressive practice, competencies and postmodernism. *British Journal of Social Work, 26*, 153–175.

Fine, M. (1992). *Disruptive voices: The possibilities of feminist research*. Ann Arbor, MI: University of Michigan Press.

Fonow, M. M. & Cook, J. A. (2005). Feminist methodology: New applications in the academy and public policy. *Signs, 30*, 2211–2236.

Freeman, M. L. (1990). Beyond women's issues: Feminism and social work. *Affilia, 5*, 72–89.

Giddings, L. S. (2006). Mixed-methods research: Positivism dressed in drag? *Journal of Research in Nursing, 11*, 195–203.

Gray, M. & Boddy, J. (2010). Making sense of the waves: Wipeout or still riding high? *Affilia, 25*, 368–389.

Gringeri, C. E. & Roche, S. E. (2010). Beyond the binary: Critical feminisms in social work. *Affilia, 25*, 337–340.

Gringeri, C. E., Wahab, S., & Anderson-Nathe, B. (2010). What makes it feminist? Mapping the landscape of feminist social work research. *Affilia, 25*, 390–405.

Harding, S. (2006). *Science and social inequality: Feminist and postcolonial issues.* Chicago: University of Illinois Press.

Haraway, D. (2008). Situated knowledge: The science question in feminism and the privilege of partial perspective. In A. M. Jaggar (Ed.), *Just methods: An interdisciplinary feminist reader* (pp. 346–352). Boulder, CO: Paradigm Publishers.

Harnois, C. E. (2005). Different paths to different feminisms? Bridging multiracial feminist theory and quantitative sociological gender research. *Gender & Society, 19*, 809–828.

Howe, K. R. (1992). Getting over the quantitative-qualitative debate. *American Journal of Education, 100*, 236–256.

Hughes, C. & Cohen, R. L. (2010). Feminists really do count: The complexity of feminist methodologies. *International Journal of Social Research Methodology, 13*, 189–196.

Jayaratne, T. E. & Stewart, A. J. (2008). Quantitative and qualitative methods in the social sciences. Current feminist issues and practical strategies. In A. M. Jaggar (Ed.), *Just methods: An interdisciplinary feminist reader* (pp. 44–57). Boulder, CO: Paradigm Publishers.

Kemp, S. P. & Brandwein, R. (2010). Feminisms and social work in the United States: An intertwined history. *Affilia, 25*, 341–364.

Lawson, V. (1995). The politics of difference: Examining the quantitative/qualitative dualism in post-structural feminist research. *The Professional Geographer, 47*, 449–457.

Lorde, A. (1984/2007). *Sister outsider: Essays and speeches by Audre Lorde*. Berkeley, CA: Crossing Press.

Mason, S. (1997). Social work research: Is there a feminist method? *Affilia, 12*, 10–32.

McCall, L. (2005). The complexity of intersectionality. *Signs, 30*, 1771–1800.

Moosa-Mitha, M. (2005). Situating anti-oppressive theories within critical and difference-centred perspectives. In L. Brown & S. Strega (Eds.), *Research as resistance: Critical, indigenous and anti-oppressive approaches* (pp. 37–72). Toronto, ON: Canadian Scholars' Press.

Moosa-Mitha, M. & Ross-Sheriff, F. (2010). Transnational social work and lessons learned from transnational feminism. *Affilia, 25*, 105–109.

Olesen, V. (2005). Early millennial feminist qualitative research: Challenges and contours. In N. K. Denzin & Y. S. Lincoln (Eds.), *Handbook of qualitative research* (3rd ed.) (pp. 235–278). Thousand Oaks, CA: Sage.

Orme, J. (2003). It's feminist because I say so! Feminism, social work and critical practice in the UK. *Qualitative Social Work, 2*, 131–153.

Payne, G. (2007). Social divisions, social mobilities and social research: Methodological issues after 40 years. *Sociology, 41*, 901–915.

Rose, N. (2000). Government and control. *British Journal of Criminology, 40*, 321–339.

Rupp, L. J. & Taylor, V. (1999). Forging feminist identity in an international movement: a collective identity approach to twentieth-century feminism. *Signs, 24*, 363–386.

Ryan, L. & Golden, A. (2006). "Tick the box please": A reflexive approach to doing quantitative social research. *Sociology, 40*, 1191–1200.

Sale, J. E. M., Lohfeld, L. H., & Brazil, K. (2002). Revisiting the quantitative-qualitative debate: Implications for mixed-methods research. *Quality & Quantity, 36*, 43–53.

Sands, R. G. & Nuccio, K. (1992). Postmodern feminist theory and social work. *Social Work, 37*, 489–494.

Scott, J. (2010). Quantitative methods and gender inequalities. *International Journal of Social Research Methodology, 13*, 223–236.

Smith, J. K. & Heshusius, L. (1986). Closing down the conversation: The end of the quantitative–qualitative debate among educational inquirers. *Educational Researcher, 15* (1), 4–12.

Smythe, E. (2005). The thinking of research. In P. Ironside (Ed.), *Beyond method: Philosophical conversations in healthcare research and scholarship* (pp. 223–258). Madison, WI: The University of Wisconsin Press.

Spierings, N. (2012). The inclusion of quantitative techniques and diversity in the mainstream of feminist research. *European Journal of Women's Studies, 19*, 331–347.

Steinmetz, G. (2005). The epistemological unconscious of US sociology and the transition to post-Fordism: The case of historical sociology. In J. Adams, E. S. Clemens, & A. S. Orloff (Eds.), *Remaking modernity: Politics, history, and sociology* (pp. 109–157). Durham, NC: Duke University Press.

Strega, S. (2005). The view from the poststructural margins: Epistemology and methodology reconsidered. In L. A. Brown & S. Strega (Eds.), *Research as resistance: Critical, indigenous, and anti-oppressive approaches* (pp. 199–236). Toronto, ON: Canadian Scholars' Press/Women's Press.

Swigonski, M. E. & Raheim, S. (2011). Feminist contributions to understanding women's lives and the social environment. *Affilia, 26*, 10–21.

Undurraga, R. (2010). How quantitative are feminist research methods textbooks? *International Journal of Social Research Methodology, 13*, 227–281.

Wendt, S. & Boylan, J. (2008). Feminist social work engaging with poststructural ideas. *International Social Work, 51* (5), 599–609.

Section 4

Engagement with Methodology

12 Collage as Reflexivity

Illustrations and Reflections of a Photovoice Study with Sex Workers

Moshoula Capous-Desyllas

As a feminist social work researcher, activist, and artist, I implemented photovoice method with women working in diverse aspects of the sex industry. The purpose of this project was to understand sex workers' needs and aspirations through their own artistic self-representation, to provide opportunities for group dialogue, and to engage in community education and activism through art. My research involved a synthesis of critical feminist theoretical values with arts-based approaches to social work research. In this chapter, I use the art medium of collage as a form of reflexivity to illustrate my research process of using photovoice method with sex workers. Collage as reflexivity allows for spontaneity in the research process that gives rise to possibilities and new discoveries; new ways of seeing, knowing and experiencing the world; and a platform for engaging in social justice work.

Synthesizing Critical Feminism and Arts-Based Research

A central feature of arts-based research is the subjective and reflexive presence of the researcher through his or her creativity/artistic ability. In line with a critical feminist lens, reflexivity is a key aspect in the research process, challenging the researcher to make transparent values and beliefs that inform actions, thoughts, and interpretations throughout the research process. Similarly, arts-informed research incorporates strong reflexive elements that indicate the presence and signature of the researcher. Reflexivity in arts-based research forces a researcher to take a step back and look introspectively from a new perspective provided by the artistic medium itself, increasing the potential for a deeper self-analysis (Weber & Mitchell, 2004). It can offer new ways of revisioning issues that are simply not possible through descriptive linear language. Using arts-based inquiry serves to "counteract the hegemony and linearity in written texts, to increase voice and reflexivity in the research process, and to expand the possibilities of multiple, diverse realities and understandings" (Butler-Kisber, 2008, p. 268). Merging a critical feminist lens with arts-based approaches to research provides the opportunity for deconstructing dualistic relationships that can be perpetuated in research, such as researcher/participant, layperson/expert, artist/audience, and art/science. It also has the potential to unsettle stereo-types, challenge dominant ideologies and hegemonic ways of representing knowledge, build bridges across differences, promote understanding, foster empathetic connections, and raise critical consciousness.

Finding my Visual Voice

As I reflect on how my research project manifested, I am reminded of my journey, fraught with fear, excitement, uncertainty, doubt, hope, despair, and possibility. At the time of this research study, I was a doctoral student, doubting if I would ever finish my degree (it took me seven years to finish) and questioning whether I belonged in academia (as a first-generation college student). I struggled for years to find my voice, to feel safe to reveal the other parts of myself as an artist within academia, and to engage in research as an activist for social change. I experienced discomfort with the privilege I held as a doctoral student, while I engaged in community outreach to some of the most marginalized and stigmatized women in the city that I lived in at that time, Portland, Oregon. I yearned to merge my identities as an artist-activist-feminist-researcher in order to find meaning in the work that I did and in the research that I planned to engage in. Eventually, I found my visual voice through the synthesis of critical feminist approaches and arts-based research.

I am inspired by social work research that transforms, empowers, and has the potential for creating social change, while maintaining an unpredictability that mirrors the realities of life. I view feminist praxis as creative praxis; often providing spaces for spontaneity, vulnerability, and transformation. In my own research, these moments of uncertainty and unexpectedness served as a catalyst for honest self-reflection, critical self-awareness, and acknowledgment of the struggles, rewards, and responsibilities of engaging in critical feminist research. Through the inclusion of art, my research embodies multiple layers of understanding and multiple creative media for representing experiences, thus evoking a range of emotions. I created visual art to illustrate, contextualize, process, and honor the intense emotions. I will address my engagement *with* and understanding *of* power, voice, authority, ethics, representation, reflexivity, praxis, and art throughout the duration of my research project through the visual medium of collage.

Locating Myself Within my Research

My intersecting and fluid identities, my values, my passions, and my life experiences inform the ways in which I engage with/in critical feminist social work research informed by the arts. I am a first-generation Greek-American, with dual citizenship and a transnational identity. I lived in Greece and currently reside in the United States, continuously traveling between my two parallel worlds. My engagement with the visual arts developed in childhood. As a bicultural woman, art seemed to transcend boundaries, connecting my two worlds in a way that language could not. Art served as a source of knowledge and as a form of expression for the feelings and experiences that I could not articulate. From a very young age, engaging with art and producing my own art was a source of inspiration. My self-expression has taken shape in multiple forms and through various media, such as painting, drawing, ceramics, collage, jewelry making, sewing, and photography. As I grow, I feel most at home, most safe, most alive, and most expressive behind the lens of my camera. I use each of my cameras as a tool to make sense of my reality and to document my lived experiences, perspectives, and relationships. Years of art and photography classes, the creation of my own darkroom at home, and the opportunities to display my photography in various communities have all contributed to how I see myself as a visual artist. My personal creativity and commitment to the artistic process are also inspired by the artistic images and creativity of others. It is my love for the arts and my identity as a visual artist that fuel my passion for incorporating artistic inquiry into feminist social work research with sex workers. I believe that this fusion of feminism, art, and research provided the opportunity to develop unique knowledge and a deeper insight into the experiences of sex workers. Giving sex workers cameras to represent themselves also served to shift the power dynamics, as this photovoice project manifested in unpredictable, yet meaningful, directions.

Engaging in Research *With* Sex Workers

My interest in conducting research with sex workers followed my initial interest in the feminist debates on sex work. The complexity and politicized nature of sex work challenged me to examine my own ideas about sex work, acquired through media representations and images. As a social worker, prior to engaging in this research, my clinical experience with individuals working in the sex industry was limited to working in a drug and alcohol treatment program that served dual-diagnosed, previously incarcerated individuals (some of whom worked in the sex industry) and working with children of sex workers. I never engaged in sex work, nor did I participate in other aspects of the sex industry. I acknowledged that my reality was very different from the study participants, but after getting to know the women who participated in the project, I was surprised to see where our lives intersected.

Theoretically, I believe that women's experiences of working in the sex industry can vary according to age, social location, gender, race, and even personality or mood. I consider it important to avoid moralistic positions when discussing commercial sex work between consenting adults. I believe in a sex workers' rights-based approach which demands citizenship rights for sex workers and their right to work with dignity and safety, and without discrimination.

Prior to starting this research, I wanted to immerse myself in various communities of sex workers so that I wouldn't feel like an outsider "coming in" to do research *on* a population. I sought out various opportunities to become more involved with communities of sex workers and with the social service agencies that encountered them. I volunteered with the Portland Women's Crisis Line, at a mobile outreach van that provided health services to sex workers. I was also an active member of the Sex Worker Outreach Coalition (SWOC). Through this coalition, I helped to develop a training curriculum for other volunteers and I co-facilitated sex worker outreach volunteer trainings. I participated in various SWOC subcommittees that worked in media advertisement and response. During the course of this project, I also facilitated a collage art workshop for sex workers and a film screening and dialogue session to raise awareness about violence against sex workers. Through these experiences I built relationships within various communities of sex workers and with multiple social service providers. It was important to me to build trust and feel connected to other sex worker activists in the community, prior to recruitment for the project. My status as a doctoral student and social work researcher granted me certain privileges and power that I often felt uncomfortable with. Throughout the research process, there were many times when I tried to equalize and share power with the participants in the study. Using photovoice method with sex workers allowed for a more participatory way of knowledge making and sharing, but not without its challenges.

Implementing Photovoice Method

The process of photovoice entails giving cameras to individuals who use photography to identify, represent, and enhance their communities (Wang & Burris, 1997). The three main goals of photovoice are: (1) to enable people to record and reflect their community's strengths and concerns; (2) to promote critical dialogue and knowledge about important community issues through large- and small-group discussions of photographs; and (3) to reach policy makers and others who can be mobilized for social change (Wang, Cash, & Powers, 2000, p. 82). Implementing photovoice with sex workers provides the opportunity for women to define their needs and strengths through photography, to engage in dialogue about their life experiences and perceptions, and to use photography to influence social change. As I describe the research process below, the terms participant(s), woman/women, and artist(s) are used interchangeably to capture the depth and range of embodied experiences of each individual who took part in this study.

I collaborated with a fellow sex worker activist who served as my community partner and co-facilitator on this study. We engaged in multiple methods and strategies of recruitment over a period of four months. We created and distributed a study flyer in various neighborhoods and venues in Portland where individuals working in the sex industry might be located. These locations included inside the dressing rooms and bathrooms of different exotic dance clubs, a methadone clinic, an outreach clinic for the homeless, and various drop-in centers for the homeless. We also passed out flyers to women working in the sex industry through street outreach.

Eleven female sex workers participated in this study from diverse ethnic and racial backgrounds, as well as ability status. The women were between the ages of 18 and 52 years old, with varied educational experience and social class backgrounds. The types of sex work that the women engaged in included street work, escorting, exotic dancing/stripping, pro-dominatrix/BDSM (bondage and discipline; dominance and submission; sadism and masochism) work, erotic massage, and erotic nude modeling. The years of experience working in the sex industry ranged from seven months to 39 years. Some of the women had children and/or were in a serious relationship. Their living situations varied (from living in the streets to living in a house with roommates), and, for some, changed over time.

Each woman began her participation in the project by attending a photovoice training workshop, either in a group setting or individually. These workshops ensured that all participants understood the study goals, photovoice method, procedures, risks, and ethics prior to taking their photographs. We emphasized shared power by letting the participants know that we all held joint ownership of the research project. Some training sessions were more formal in nature while others were more casual and consisted of informal conversations and relationship building. After participating in a photovoice training session, the women went out into their communities with their cameras to photograph their lived experiences, needs, and aspirations.

Once the women returned the rolls of film to me, I developed their photographs. Each artist chose a private, quiet place where she met with me individually to view and discuss her images in detail. After meeting with each woman individually, I invited all of the artists to attend two group dialogue sessions. In the group dialogue sessions, the participants shared their images with one another, planned for the art exhibit, and expressed their thoughts about the study process.

The art exhibit opening took place in a donated community space. The guests included influential community advocates, sex workers, journalists, students, professors, social workers, social service professionals, community leaders, friends, family members, and others from the community. For two years, we featured the art exhibit in different venues in Portland, including the library of a local community college, the lobby of a performance space at a community college, the café gallery of a public university, the art gallery of a private university, a social service agency, and at an independent feminist bookstore. The exhibit was also displayed in a gallery in Toronto, Canada as part of a citywide photography festival.

Reflexivity Through Collage

To capture my inner reflective processes throughout this study, I kept detailed field notes and a journal of my thoughts, feelings, observations, experiences, and interactions with participants. I created three collages throughout the stages of this study to reflect, illustrate, and contextualize my physical, mental, and emotional experiences of the research and analysis process. The opportunity to make collages allowed for the integration of both my researcher self and my artist self. I chose the art form of collage over other artistic media because the process of creating collages closely mirrored my interactive and tactile analysis process of moving images around to understand and formulate meanings.

By creating collages, I used art to reveal the intersections of my life as a researcher with the lives of the participants. This was a way of documenting my research journey and reflecting on my research process in a manner that would honor my personal approach of making sense of my world, my self, and my experiences. I created collages to make more transparent my own ideas, perspectives, and experiences throughout the study and in my analysis process. I wanted to locate my reflections and participation in the research process and present artistic representations that would provide a visual context where one could see the multiple layers of personal exploration. I didn't want to rely on language as the single form of expression. The process of creating collages allowed me to use visual images to represent the various levels of my experiences; to move from my intuitions and feelings to my thoughts and ideas.

Creating Collages

The artistic process of collage entails collecting, piecing together, and juxtaposing images and quotes from multiple sources in order to create connections and express thoughts and emotions (Vaughan, 2005). However, creating a collage is more than just cutting, moving around, and pasting images on a surface. La Jevic and Spinggay (2008) describe the collage process as "the placement of spaces, meanings and subjectivities together in a rhizomatic sequence, and from this fluid, hesitant and non-linear arrangement, multiple meanings ensue" (p. 85). My own process of creating collages began by selecting various magazine photographs and cut-out book illustrations from my personal collection. I own a large collection of vintage *National Geographic* and fashion magazines (from the 50s, 60s, and 70s) that characterize my fascination with how women were portrayed and represented in the media in previous decades. I am interested in how these representations change and continue to take different shapes and forms over time. Since I already had a plethora of words documented in my journal entries and field notes to express my experiences and emotions, I chose to use visual images in my collages for (re)imagining, (re)presenting, and critically reflecting on my experiences.

I made my selection of images based on styles, colors, and sizes of pictures that would contrast well enough that they wouldn't blend together, but rather complement each other. When going through a multitude of cut-outs, I paid attention to the color, space, directionality, position, and style of images, as well as what thoughts and emotions they invoked in me with relation to my research experiences. I also chose to incorporate various images of animals whose meanings I knew held symbolic or cultural significance. While some images I chose intentionally, based on intuition or aesthetics, other images I chose based on my interest related to the relationships and encounters I shared with the participants.

I experimented with overlapping the images and shifting open spaces within the frame. This juxtaposition of seemingly random images based on my feelings and experiences provided the potential for eliciting new awareness of hidden relationships, patterns, and associations. Sinner, Leggo, Irwin, Gouzouasis, and Grauer (2006) refer to this process as "crossing boundaries by joining things together that don't normally go together" (p. 1254). My process of composition was fluid and entailed assembling images, adding new pieces, and rearranging them intuitively until a schema was achieved. The "intuitively known content," situated with other images, allowed for the "appearance of unexpected new associations" (Davis & Butler-Kisber, 1999, p. 4) and connections that may otherwise have remained unconscious.

Understanding the power of artwork to evoke a certain mood, I emphasized a color scheme of earthy, natural colors to represent my organic relationships with the participants and the data. In their work with collage in qualitative research, Davis and Butler-Kisber (1999) reflect on the idea of framing as a metaphor for a completed piece of artwork. It is interesting to note that I began my first two collages *on* frames as opposed to framing the collages after completion. This speaks to my feelings of "duty" to the methodological steps of the photovoice research process and the "completion" of a particular stage. Since the photovoice method incorporated multiple stages, long-term involvement, and multiple interactions with the participants, I chose to look at the research process in segments so that the photovoice method wouldn't feel so overwhelming. Throughout the study, I harbored anxiety around whether or not I would be able to gather enough data and participant follow-through for this project as an "outsider." Creating a collage *on* a framed surface provided the sense of completion of the particular methodological step. In contrast, while analyzing my data, I created the third collage piece on four pieces of found wood that served as the base surface of my collage. I did not frame these pieces of wood, as they symbolized the infinite ways in which the data analysis process continuously evolved, unconfined to borders and enclosures. Also, I painted these pieces of wood orange, to reflect my sense of confidence and my rich experience working with the various forms of data. As a color, orange often represents warmth, energy, and enthusiasm. The color that I chose to paint the pieces of wood, prior to juxtaposing and pasting the images represented my excitement in working with the participants' photographs as data. In the following sections I present three collage pieces illustrating the stages of my research process: (1) recruitment and photovoice training; (2) group dialogue sessions; and (3) analysis.

Collage I: Possibilities for an Outsider

The first collage reflected the initial stages of the research process, specifically related to the recruitment process and the photovoice training workshops (Figure 12.1). It incorporated my thoughts, feelings, and experiences

Figure 12.1 Possibilities for an outsider.

with the methodology, my role as a researcher, and my initial relationships with the participants.

The gray background of the collage stands for the unknown possibilities of implementing this research and immersing my self in the communities of activists, social service providers, sex industry workers, neighborhood associations, and others who held direct and indirect interests related to the sex industry. As a color, gray represents neutrality. I wanted to use my location as an outsider to be open to every experience and every encounter without being so quick to make judgments or assumptions. I wanted to stay "neutral" while still acknowledging and documenting my personal biases and perspectives with every interaction. The repetition of the diamond pattern in the background reflected my initial sense of security in the photovoice method due to its repeated implementation by researchers with various populations all over the world. I thought that if I just followed the steps like a diligent researcher, what could possibly go wrong?

Prior to beginning this study, I spent a lot of time researching the differing feminist views and perspectives on sex work and locating my own political and theoretical perspectives within these debates. I represented these opposing perspectives in the collage through the white bird, which symbolized the idea of sexual freedom and independence, and the black birdcage which represented the idea of sexual slavery and victimhood. While these dichotomous and opposing philosophical viewpoints were prevalent in the academic literature, it surprised me to see them manifesting within the community. As an advocate for the rights and well-being of sex workers, and as a community member for the neighborhood coalition 82nd Cares, I attended numerous town hall meetings during the months of recruitment and photovoice trainings. I felt astounded in these community meetings with the ways in which those in attendance reenacted the feminist debates. Overwhelmingly present were the voices of antiprostitution activists who talked about evil pimps who forced women into sex work and sinful "johns" who needed to be arrested for "abusing" women. I felt uncomfortable with the way in which these ideas perpetuated stereotypes of sex workers and the sex industry. I included a caricature of a man in a position that displayed a sense of power and control over others. My intent was to express my own concern and fear of reinforcing stereotypes and representations of sex workers as weak, controlled, and powerless within my research, even though I did not believe that this was the case. I was aware of the well-intended motives from members of differing feminist perspectives; however, I felt a heightened sense of consciousness of who was speaking for whom, how important it was for me to be conscious of my power as a researcher, the weight of my words and the choices I made when representing the data, and what it would mean to "give voice" to someone, if this was even possible.

This collage also speaks to my diverse experiences with participant recruitment in various exotic strip clubs, adult video stores, and other

venues of the sex industry in different parts of Portland. These contradict-
ing images against the gray background correspond to the wide range of
my feelings within a continuum of extremes: from comfort to discomfort,
from fascination to disgust, from acceptance to rejection. Some venues that
I entered to pass out study flyers felt safe, comfortable, and extremely supportive of women. Other venues felt scary, unsafe, and suspicious. Some
women with whom I spoke about the study appeared very receptive and
interested in participating, while other women seemed uninterested. I had
one negative experience outside a strip club where a group of four exotic
dancers who I approached with a study flyer yelled and cursed at me. They
angrily asked me and my community partner what we were doing there, while
injecting their speech with curse words to question our motives. For hours
after this encounter I felt guilty and anxious, and wondered about how the
women perceived us, and how I might have (mis)represented myself in order
to elicit such an angry response. Questions that came up for me included:
How could I (blindly) enter this space, shaped by socioeconomic status and
race, and (naively) think that I would just be accepted? What did this reveal
about my own privilege? How might the different color of our skin, our social
and class privilege have played a role in how we were perceived, distrusted,
and rejected? Would I have received the same response if I had been alone?

The title of this first collage, *Possibilities for an Outsider,* refers to the plethora of experiences that this project was beginning to offer and had yet to
offer, my location as an outsider (a non-sex worker), and my struggle with
how to present myself to the participants in order to form a connection. I
was drawn to the image of the naked woman holding peacock feathers to
cover her body because this image embodied my own internal conflict of
how much to reveal of myself in the photovoice training sessions and my
concern of the exposure and the possibilities of what would be revealed
through this arts-based project. It also reflected my insecurity of being an
outsider and how I would be perceived by the women working in the sex
industry. I wanted to be perceived as "cool," hip, non-judgmental, strong,
and street-smart. How would I present myself to the participants as a non-sex
worker interested in their stories, lives, experiences, and artistic expression?

Along with my internal struggles I felt excitement about the possibilities
that this method offered. This also led me to question my own fascination
with a profession that was so far removed from the current reality that I
lived. I thought back to the stories my father told me about his experience
living as an undocumented immigrant in New York City in the 60s and 70s,
and his involvement with different types of illegal work. Was I trying to
understand this idea of a perceived "underworld" where an illegal economy
had a life of its own? Would I come closer to understanding my father and
his experiences if I studied the lives of individuals engaged in illegal work?
These questions led me to creatively explore the representations of the sex
industry that I subconsciously carried from films, books, media, music, and
stories.

While coming into contact with the participants to individually conduct photovoice training sessions, I found myself connecting with each woman in different ways. My interaction with each person brought forth a unique part of myself, and oftentimes, sides of my character that lay dormant for years since entering an academic setting, such as my experience with playing music and my own identification with a subculture. It was interesting to uncover those parts of myself that could be free and not feel confined to a sense of conservative professionalism that I sometimes felt among academics. Having grown up with a mother who closed her own hair salon business after moving to the United States from Greece, choosing instead to raise a family, and a father who worked in a non-professional environment as a construction worker, I was not familiar with the professionalism of educated occupations. My understanding of work was related to manual labor, in an environment that was casual and informal, so in academia I often felt cautious and reserved. For example, sometimes I felt like the interests I was able to share with colleagues were confined to research or teaching interests related to work, as opposed to hobbies or passions outside of the academy. After conducting multiple photovoice training sessions, I began to form a way of performing: a way of presenting my self and the research study that felt authentic, sincere, fluid, and adaptive to each unique participant. Rather than feeling confined to a rigid and detached role of a researcher, I opened up with the participants about my own interests in different types of music, art, and films. I shared my love for travel, outdoor adventures, and the hippy culture and bohemian style of previous decades. I identified as a photographer and shared a bit of my past to provide a context for my approach to the photovoice project. I enjoyed seeing where our interests, hobbies, and passions intersected, as well as where our interests and lived experiences completely differed.

One instance caught me off guard and led me to further explore my personal style and needs as a person, not just as a researcher. After completing a photovoice training with one of the participants at a local coffee shop, I assumed that after we discussed the process, timeline, and so on, we would spend a few moments "connecting" as I experienced with other participants thus far. For me, "connecting" usually involved an exchange of ideas, the sharing of personal information, and an expressed sense of where each one of us came from. However, after this particular photovoice training session, the participant immediately left without engaging in any conversation beyond the scope of the study. I felt a sense of rejection and questioned whether she would contact me again or discontinue her participation in the study. Why didn't she want to get to know me? Why didn't she ask any questions? Didn't she want us to connect? How could she trust me if she didn't really get to know me? While all of these questions entered my mind, I realized that these were *my* needs of wanting to establish rapport, connection, and trust, and they weren't needs and values that I could impose on someone or expect everyone to share with me. My personality and own personal needs interacted with the researcher side of me. This tension revealed my need to be informal and friendly with the participants as a way of bridging the power inequality and sense of authority that my title and role held.

Collage II: Chaotic Liberation

The second collage I created corresponded to my experience with the individual dialogue sessions, the group dialogue session, and my relationships with the participants (Figure 12.2). I collected the images for this collage over a period of a few weeks, and continued to shift in directionality and position on the frame. I chose some images to represent specific ideas and

Figure 12.2 Chaotic liberation.

perspectives; I selected others as a way for me to process some of the intense emotions that surfaced from the stories and experiences shared with me in the individual dialogue sessions.

During each of the individual dialogue sessions I traveled through a journey of emotions, images, and stories that presented a kaleidoscopic moment of time in the past, present, and future life of the artists. While some experiences brought laughter and joy, others made me angry, sad, and fearful. I felt especially affected by stories of violence and racism. I included two particular images in this collage, the black man in the center and the porcelain female head, as a way for me to process my discomfort associated with the stories shared with me. These stories included instances of violence, abuse, racism, and oppression experienced by the participants. For example, one of the women often talked about her relationship with her boyfriend, complicated by love, loyalty, and extreme violence. This particular story brought up the intersections of race, class, gender. I thought about the stereotypes of pimps, while connecting this particular story to structural oppression, perpetuated by the prison industrial complex.

In this collage, I also included a butterfly holding the weight of a zebra. The butterfly, symbolizing transformation and change, carries the weight of a zebra to show the resilience and strength that I saw in each of the women. The zebra embodies the beauty in individuality and its distinctive stripes serve as a protective camouflage against predators.

The individual dialogue sessions felt especially sacred; the women gave me their gift of trust and creative expression through their images and stories. I felt excitement with each new roll that we developed and eagerly shared that experience of curiosity with the participants. In these moments, I connected with many of the women as artists. In the individual dialogue sessions, when I learned about various "behind the scenes" occurrences at different strip clubs, among dancers, on Craigslist, and on the streets, my location as an outsider no longer seemed to be a barrier to gaining trust and openness. This was a very different perspective from what I experienced as an activist and member of SWOC. For example, an insider constitutes someone who shares a similar characteristic, role, or experience with the participants. As a non-sex worker, my location as an outsider shifted as I entered the space between that of an outsider and insider, challenging this dualistic parameter. The dichotomous reference of insider/outsider locations became more complex and fluid in order to address the multiple layers and sites on this continuum.

In the collage, the curtain signified the performance we all engaged in throughout the study; for example, the roles of researcher and researched; of artist and observer; of partner and collaborator; and the performances of our gender, race, class, sexuality, abilities, and status. The group dialogue session was like a center stage, where I felt most challenged in my performing role as a researcher who wanted to equalize my power with the participants in the study. I felt that there was a power differential inherent in my relationship with the participants by virtue of my role as the researcher, as well as elements of difference by virtue of race, class, ethnicity, age, ability, circumstances, and position. Prior to the group dialogue session, I theorized and romanticized the equalizing of power, and believed that power shifted automatically, as a result of the methodology chosen.

I did not plan or anticipate the shifting of power that took place. I prepared myself for the group dialogue session with a research "agenda," but from the responses of the participants in attendance, I realized that in order to truly shift the power dynamics, I had to set my agenda aside, allow the participants to lead the group, and feel comfortable in my role. That day, I filled my reflexive journal with words like "chaos," "loss of control," "stress," "frustrating," and "disruptive." My efforts to create structure in the group were based on what I thought I had to do as a "responsible" researcher following photovoice method protocol. However, the participants expressed resistance in various ways. Their resistance served as a space of empowerment for the artists and a location where the participants reclaimed control of the research study and agenda. The various acts, occurrences, and discussions during the group dialogue session that led to the natural shift in power felt disorienting in that moment in time, yet liberating in retrospect.

The day after the group dialogue session, five participants called me individually to discuss their experiences in the group. They decided that a second group dialogue session should take place. While my initial journal entries identified a state of bewilderment with the turn of events in the group dialogue session, after debriefing with some of the women, the subsequent journal entries identified my feelings of liberation through the process of letting go of my power. I thought back to other moments when my power as a researcher continually fluctuated throughout the stages of research, and how it shifted into the hands of the artists when they shared their visions and voices in the individual dialogue sessions. If I hadn't had the experience of the group dialogue session, if the artists had followed my agenda, would I still be making claims of a shared sense of power among us? Did certain research methodologies always lead to the equalizing of power or was it something about those particular group dynamics that day that allowed for this to take place? Was there something more than just the theoretical tenets of a method or an approach that allowed this to transpire within research? I think that particular methods like photovoice, which incorporate communal dialogue, provide the necessary spaces for balancing the power in a collective manner. Through the acknowledgment and understanding of the negotiation of power that occurs within research processes we can interrogate, recreate, and strengthen mutual researcher–participant partnerships.

It is important to illustrate that during the group dialogue session there were moments when the power not only shifted from myself to the participants, but also shifted from woman to woman based on, but not limited to, race, class, age, size, shape, ethnicity, experience, personality, and presence.

The image of the woman holding down a female head in one hand and holding up a deer's head in the other speaks to this dynamic that ensued, based on our multiple locations and shifting status. I chose the symbol of a deer, which represents gentleness and compassion for ourselves, others, and situations in life, to highlight the importance of considering how our locations and multiple identities may serve to oppress others in moments least expected.

The act of holding the deer in a particular manner, as observed in the collage, brings up the idea of ownership of the photovoice project. Throughout the research study, some women were more vocal about their participation and sought out opportunities to represent themselves and the project at the various art exhibits and within the media. Other artists were equally invested, yet less vocal. My community partner expressed an eagerness to have her participation acknowledged, while I felt uncomfortable with drawing attention to myself. Many times I struggled with issues of ownership and wanting to emphasize that the project was "ours" while also wanting to be credited for the work I contributed. Other times I felt so much pride in the photographs created by the artists, as if it was my own artwork that was on display.

The figure of the ancient Egyptian woman also raises the question and my concern of how the participants in the study perceived me. One of the artists talked about her desire to travel to exotic places, and in particular Egypt, so that she could climb the pyramids. She thought that I was from Egypt and this made me wonder if she perceived me as being foreign or exotic. If so, did this make it easier to connect with me because there were no expectations attached to my perceived identity? These questions raised to the surface my need to be liked and accepted by the participants and the importance of feeling connected with each woman. This need stems from my belief in the importance of relationships for enhancing communication, honesty, openness, commitment, and growth. I also desired to be seen in a positive light, as trustworthy, understanding, and compassionate.

While I wondered how some of the women viewed me, others voluntarily told me directly what they thought of me. I felt fascinated, pleased, and sometimes disappointed, by the variety of comments. Aside from positive comments that reaffirmed acceptance, some women saw me as a "goody-two-shoes who wanted to help losers like us," a "chicken" who didn't seem like she would ever get a tattoo, and a "hippy, indie-rocker" that cared about social issues. Throughout the research process, I found myself desiring the label of being "cool," and admiring the sense of confidence, courage, and freedom that I saw in many of the participants. I felt that being accepted by each artist would lead to the formation of a meaningful relationship and a deeper understanding of their life experiences. I assumed that if the participants liked me and perhaps even admired me (as I admired them), then they would be more willing to share more personal aspects of their lives. I associated the level and depth of participant self-disclosure with researcher acceptance, even though I understand that this correlation didn't promise a deeper understanding of each woman's life.

Collage III: The Wait, I Carry

I completed the third collage, a series of four images, during my analysis process (Figure 12.3). I created this series of collages to reflect, clarify, and contextualize the different issues that I thought about through the analysis process. I painted the pieces of wood in an orange, earthy tone to symbolize the organic process of working with the data in a physical manner (i.e., moving around the photographs and the themes on strips of paper). The painted orange color reflected my excitement with having collected such a wealth of data and my immersion in the information gathered. I began to juxtapose various images on each wood panel, shifting and altering the positions of the cut-outs, then leaving them in different arrangements to see what connections would emerge over time. I wanted to present four pieces/parts as one cohesive piece of work, to represent my cross-case analysis process of working with the data. I intended to use these fragmented pieces as one collage representation for understanding and exploring the multiple ways to merge and represent the findings of my data analysis.

Figure 12.3 The wait, I carry.

While searching for images that captured my attention for various reasons, I found myself drawn to media portrayals of femininity, representations of sexuality, and images that reflected confidence, strength, and power. These images also reflected particular stories that stood out in the analysis, while the butterflies infused in each of the four pieces characterized the transformative aspects of the multiple self-portraits presented by the artists, as well as my own transformation throughout the study.

By linking the content of this collage piece to my journal notes and interpretations of the data, I realized the potential of collage as an analytic memo. Davis and Butler-Kisber (1999) discuss the use of collage as a contextualizing analytic strategy that emulates "memoing" in ways that opens up the data for further insight. Upon closer look at the images in the collage and linking them to the content in my journal and reflexive notes, a few things stood out with relation to the data. The images of women represented in the collage depicted various aspects of the human condition, for example, laughter, fear, power, love, playfulness, safety, and spirituality. The analytic themes that surfaced among the artist's photographs and stories also reflected these expressions.

I also felt drawn to the variety of clothing and accessories worn by the women in the collage. Reflecting on this collage brought to my attention the unique clothing, or lack of clothing, that the artists wore in their self-portraits to express certain experiences or ideas. They deliberately chose to wear specific clothing in their photographs in order to tell a particular story. Some pieces of clothing were similar to costumes, depicting the performative nature of the self-portraits. Vaughan (2005) points out that clothing reflects a border between one's self and the world, between individual preferences of self-presentation and accepted societal norms. I felt intrigued and impressed by the ways in which the women used their clothing to challenge the social boundaries of self-representation.

This collage provided a portrait of my internalized world. Most of the characters in the collage are holding something, whether in their hands, on their heads, or on their feet. These symbols of "holding" or being "weighed down" correspond to my feelings of honor and burden. I felt honored to hold the participants' photographs, stories, and experiences, and sat with the data for a long time. While this allowed me to have the opportunity to revisit the data from different angles and at different moments in time, I felt burdened and weighed down with how to (re)present the participants' artwork in a written format to an audience of academics. I didn't want to use the representational space of my dissertation to further stereotype or marginalize the artists. I felt this recurring anxiety and tension around how to represent the representations of others in a way that would honor their unique voices while highlighting their common themes in a holistic manner.

My discomfort and anxiety over issues of representation were projected on to, situated within, and clarified through the collage, thus offering a sense of emotional release and transparency. This collage provided an opportunity to present the tensions in my research process and redefine them as a chance to display the interactions between my thoughts and my artistic creations. I felt the need to explore my own inner landscapes before presenting the landscapes of others (Wattsjohnson, 2005). Through the process of creating this collage, I moved through my resistance of representing the stories of others in order to tell my own story of the research process through art. This allowed me to preserve the participants' stories connected to their images and accept the co-creation of our knowledge in the presentation of the research findings. By being transparent, I found the ability to move forward in order to relay the collective vision of the represented needs and aspirations of the artists.

Navigating Continual Tensions and Struggles

The collages I created provided a space and a platform from which to understand, explore, and interpret my emotions, thoughts, and perspectives, as well as move forward with my analysis process and how to represent the findings. However, even after the photovoice project came to an "official" end with the various art exhibits held in Portland, Oregon, I was not prepared for these new complexities that have emerged and continue to unsettle me two years after the project's end.

One aspect of this project that evokes tension within is my representing the representations of sex workers' lives through their photographs at conferences, in academic publications, in my classrooms, and at community art exhibits. While the participants agreed that visually depicting their needs and aspirations was important to them, I was the one who ultimately chose the focus of representing "needs" and "aspirations." The artists decided which photographs could and could not be included in public venues and which photographs should be blurred, and they interpreted their own photographs and assigned meaning. However, this still does not address the complexity of power in the research relationship. Ultimately, I was the one who chose how these images and voices would be (re)presented to an academic audience. Even though the artists created and interpreted their own images, I continue to choose which images to share and what parts of their quotes to include, based on the shifting audience. While I tried my best to faithfully represent the themes identified by the artists, I still hold the power of representation within this research project.

Another dilemma I struggle with is regarding the ownership of the data (i.e., the photographs, captions, quotes, and artists' biographies). While presenting this research study at a conference, an art curator and gallery owner from Toronto, Canada invited my community partner and me to feature the work of the artists in an international photography exhibit. Initially, I felt honored and thrilled at the prospect, and immediately contacted the participants in the study to ask them what they thought of this proposal.

Many of the women felt ecstatic with the chance to have their photographs featured internationally. However, since I am not in contact with all of the participants, not everyone had a say in whether they felt "okay" with their photographs being displayed at an international art gallery.

Even though all of the women signed consent forms and photo releases about the public use of their photographs, this situation still felt unsettling. The recurring question that came up for me was, at what point does the traveling art show end? Is it ethical for the art exhibit to continue to be displayed without all of the women's knowledge or participation in the process? What about the women who felt thrilled to have their photographs travel to various communities? Was not accepting this opportunity fair to them? What about the impact of these images for challenging societal stereotypes and stigma of sex workers? Wasn't the act of displaying these images in public spaces a form of activism or was it bordering on exploitation? To whom was I accountable? To the few women with whom I was still in contact, or to all of us who participated and who felt like this was *our* project? The project felt like it had taken on a life of its own, and I felt really torn with what to do about displaying the body of artwork if not everyone was part of the process. Additionally, due to my class privilege, with the financial support of my university, I could afford to travel internationally with my community partner for the art opening of the photography show in Toronto. But what about the women whose artwork was *actually* featured in the art exhibit, but who did not have the financial means to attend the opening? What did this say about my power, my privilege, and the existing inequalities that I continually strived to minimize?

I also continue to grapple with my desire to stay connected to the women in the research study, even though I have since moved to another state to accept an academic position. While I am no longer in contact with most of the participants in the study since I moved two years ago, I am still writing about the women, their lives, and my interactions with them; I feel a need to stay connected. It is almost as if having these valuable artifacts that they left behind, in the form of photographs, keeps the women at the forefront of my consciousness. I still carry their memorable images around with me in my mind, and have unlimited access to their photographs and words on my computer. While this can feel endearing and evoke a similar sense to that of looking back at old pictures of friends and family, the participants don't have the same access to my lived experiences, quotes, and images of me. Also, and more importantly, I have the privilege to still gain from this project, while they do not.

As I pose these questions, I feel guilty, unethical, and ashamed, while simultaneously intrigued by the complexity of creative forms of data representation that result from arts-based methods. At the same time, I bring these questions to the forefront of my consciousness in order to continue to reflect on how unsettling some of these unanswered questions feel to me. I cannot forget the power of this project; how this research gave me the opportunity to hear the rich stories and experiences of a marginalized group of women I might not have otherwise connected with. This research challenged my own biases, fears, and assumptions about sex work and sex workers; it also stimulated, inspired, and transformed me on so many levels. I continue to self-reflect on my process and the aftermaths of this photo-voice project, and I realize that there may not be any definitive answers, just more questions. As someone who cares deeply and sincerely about the stories of others that I tell, as well as my own, I am embracing the beauty and richness in the complexity, uncertainty, and uneasiness that this project evoked.

References

Butler-Kisber, L. (2008). Collage as inquiry. In G. Knowles & A. Cole (Eds.), *Handbook of the arts in qualitative research: Perspectives, methodologies, examples & issues* (pp. 265–276). Los Angeles: Sage.

Davis, D. & Butler-Kisber, L. (1999). Arts-based representation in qualitative research: Collage as a contextualizing analytic strategy. In *Annual Meeting of the American Educational Research Association, 19–23 April 1999* (pp. 1–29). Montreal, Quebec, Canada

La Jevic, L. & Spinggay, S. (2008). A/r/tography as an ethics of embodiment. *Qualitative Inquiry, 14* (1), 67–89.

Sinner, A., Leggo, C., Irwin, R., Gouzouasis, P., & Grauer, K. (2006). Arts-based educational research dissertations: Reviewing the practices of new scholars. *Canadian Journal of Education, 29* (4), 1223–1270.

Vaughan, K. (2005). Pieced together: Collage as an artist's method for interdisciplinary research. *International Journal of Qualitative Methods, 4* (1), 27–52.

Wang, C. & Burris, M. A. (1997). Photovoice: Concept. Methodology, and use for participatory needs assessment. *Health Education & Behavior, 24* (3), 369–387.

Wang, C., Cash, J., & Powers, L. (2000). Who knows the streets as well as the homeless? Promoting personal and community action through photovoice. *Health Promotion Practice, 1* (1), 81–89.

Wattsjohnson, Y. (2005). Articulating knowledge for transformation. In F. Bodone (Ed.), *What difference does research make and for whom?* (pp. 191–201). New York: Peter Lang Publishing.

Weber, S. & Mitchell, C. (2004). Visual artistic modes of representation for self-study. In J. Loughran, M. Hamilton, V. LaBoskey, & T. Russell (Eds.), *International handbook of self-study of teaching and teacher education practices* (pp. 979–1038). New York: Springer.

13 Building Solidarity Through Collective Consciousness in Feminist Participatory Action Research

Rupaleem Bhuyan, Flavia Genovese, Rachel Mehl, Bethany J. Osborne, Margarita Pintin-Perez and Fernanda Villanueva[1,2]

Introduction

> Solidarity does not assume that our struggles are the same struggles, or that our pain is the same pain, or that our hope is for the same future. Solidarity involves commitment, and work, as well as the recognition that even if we do not have the same feelings, or the same lives, or the same bodies, we do live on common ground. (Ahmed, 2004, p. 189)

In this chapter, we consider the role of consciousness-raising in feminist participatory action research that has emancipatory goals; where knowledge that is generated to understand oppression is used to change it (Henderson, 1995). This chapter was developed by a diverse team of researchers who have been involved with the Migrant Mothers Project (MMP), which addresses the structural violence of immigration policies in Canada through research, education, and community organizing. The MMP seeks to bring visibility to how patterns of migration are engendered and how immigration policies produce conditions that fuel violence while creating barriers for women who seek safety and support (Bhuyan, Osborne, & Cruz, 2013).

From the outset, the MMP has drawn lessons from feminist, participatory, and qualitative (or interpretive) research to bring attention to women's lives, generate methods for women's voices to be heard, and mitigate the power differences between researcher and researched (Bailey, 1992; Healy & Mulholland, 1998; Henderson, 1995; Sullivan, Bhuyan, Senturia, Shiu-Thornton, & Ciske, 2006). In their review of feminist-oriented research, Gringeri, Wahab, and Anderson-Nathe (2010) identify "attention to power and authority, ethics, reflexivity, praxis and difference" as sites of struggle, where researchers reflexively engage in the dynamic social and political contexts in which their work unfolds (p. 392). As Kaufman (2007) has reiterated, attention to *"how* we study determines *what* we know" (cited in Anderson-Nathe, Gringeri, & Wahab, 2013, p. 279).

In reflecting on the praxis of the MMP's feminist and emancipatory goals, we noted that some of the most important learning has taken place through lengthy conversations we have with each other, before and after conducting different phases of our work. Henderson (1995) identifies consciousness-raising as a method for participatory action research where researchers take part in "negotiation, reciprocity, empowerment, and dialogue within the research process" (p. 60). Through reflexively considering our individual and collective experiences as women,[3] social workers/service providers, activists, immigrants, and refugees, we strengthen our capacity to engage in anti-oppression work while building a sense of sisterhood across our differences.

To illustrate the potential for consciousness-raising as a method for feminist research, we begin with a brief discussion of consciousness-raising in the contemporary women's movement in North America. We link our consciousness-raising activities to the context of research with women who are undocumented or have a precarious immigration status in Canada[4] (Goldring & Landolt, 2013; Goldring, Bernstein, & Bernhard, 2010). We then present a series of narratives from members of our research team who reflect upon their roles on the project during the first two years of the MMP (from 2010 to 2012). Our narratives illustrate how we each employ feminist and anti-oppression principles to: (1) mitigate and distribute power and authority among research staff and community partners; (2) honor our differences while seeking to build solidarity and mutual support; and (3) to blur (or queer, in a theoretical sense) the dichotomy between researcher and research subject (Gringeri et al., 2010). We draw inspiration from the quoted text by Ahmed (2004) above, to consider how, through learning about our personal and collective struggles, we foster a sisterhood that forms the basis of our collective action. Our consciousness-raising work leads us to draw upon our collective knowledge to understand the violence of immigration policy and to advocate for policy and service delivery to better address the marginalization of people living with precarious immigration status in Canada.

Consciousness-Raising as a Feminist Practice

Consciousness-raising groups of the 1970s are well known for laying the groundwork for women's activism in the contemporary women's movement. In *Feminism is for Everybody,* bell hooks (2000) recounts how consciousness-raising groups, which often took place in women's homes, were spaces where women came together to share their personal stories of oppression and to develop a political understanding of sexism and patriarchy. In hooks' words:

> Understanding the way male domination and sexism was expressed in everyday life created awareness in women of the ways we were victimized, exploited, and in worse case scenarios, oppressed . . . communication and dialogue was a central agenda at the consciousness-raising sessions . . . only through discussion and disagreement could we begin to find a realistic standpoint on gender exploitation and oppression. (pp. 7–8)

Early consciousness-raising groups, as well as their later manifestations in women's studies programs, have been critiqued for being dominated by white women with class privilege. In our approach to feminist research, we turn to structural social work and anti-oppression theory (Barnoff & Moffatt, 2007; Mullaly, 2007) to take on the ambitious goal of confronting all forms of oppression, including our own role in perpetuating interlocking oppressions as social work professionals and university-based researchers.

Our feminist consciousness in the MMP is inseparable from our attention to injustices facing women with precarious status in Canada, many of whom have endured many forms of violence in their home countries, during periods of migration, and after arriving in Canada (Bhuyan, 2012; Bhuyan et al., 2013). In particular, we seek to understand how the production of "illegality" for people with precarious immigration status corresponds to women's exposure to a spectrum of violence (i.e., ranging from interpersonal and community violence to the structural violence of poverty and deportation). Our attention to intersecting and interlocking oppressions that produce violence against im/migrant women inevitably shapes how we engage in research and social action. We continually ask ourselves, how can we authentically reach out to women who have precarious status without increasing their vulnerability? What types of meaningful solidarity is possible in a political climate where a conservative Canadian government, who has majority control, is restricting immigrant rights, while increasing criminalization and deportation of immigrants?

The MMP research team includes people with varied social locations *vis-à-vis* each other, the institutions in which we work (both academic and community-based organizations), and the broader community (i.e., an international student who is a research assistant, a doctoral candidate, a pre-tenured faculty researcher, a community member for whom the government has issued a deportation warrant). In addition to research staff (some who are paid and some who volunteer), the MMP has an active community advisory board made up of: service providers in the area of violence against women, immigration and refugee settlement, community-based lawyers, and women with precarious immigration status. In consideration of our diverse knowledges, skills, and resources we rely on dialogue (and at times debate) to increase our consciousness of interlocking oppressions and find ways to maximize to ensure that our research informs advocacy for women and children to live free of violence.

Some guiding principles that shaped our approach include:[5]

- We are the experts in our own experiences and have many different ways of knowing and getting information about our conditions.
- We promote a co-learning and empowering process that attends to inherent social inequalities between marginalized communities and researchers.
- We control the gathering and use of information about our communities. We decide what information we need to make the changes we want and how to get it.

- We gather information towards integrating knowledge and action for the mutual benefit of all partners.
- We build on the strengths and resources within our communities.

In the remainder of this chapter, we illustrate the praxis of feminist research through a series of personal reflections from different members of the research team. Due to time constraints and competing responsibilities, many key people who contribute to MMP's consciousness-raising activities were unable to contribute to this chapter. Thus, the narratives represented here are not intended to represent the whole, but rather illustrate integral parts of our ongoing growth and development as feminist researchers.

Learning to Engage With Women Ethically and Authentically in Research Interviews

We begin with a narrative by Margarita Pintin-Perez, who was hired as a graduate research assistant in the fall of 2010, to support the early development of the project before the MMP was fully funded. In addition to highlighting the importance of our collaboration with community partners, Margarita's reflection illustrates her personal development as a graduate research assistant who took part in bimonthly meetings with researchers and community partners to develop our research protocols. As Margarita discusses, our intentional reflection and consciousness-raising as a group directly informed our research protocols, but also increased Margarita's capacity to engage authentically with women who have precarious immigration status in the context of a research interview.

By Margarita Pintin-Perez (MSW student and graduate research assistant[6])

As the first research assistant hired for the Migrant Mothers Project, I was fortunate to witness the evolution and realization of this project from an idea into a concrete research study. At the time, I was gaining direct social work experience with an agency that supported migrant women who experienced various forms of violence. This proved to be an asset and also granted me access to community partners that were providing services to our proposed research participants. During the early stages of my work, I was responsible for coordinating bi-weekly meetings with the principal investigators, community researchers and community partners to develop our research design and ethical protocols. During these meetings we discussed all project details including: the project name, recruitment criteria and outreach plans, informed consent, and questions to include in our interview guide, in both English and Spanish. I noted how imperative it was for community partners to be engaged from the beginning; the initial meetings were not only helpful to develop the research study, but also to strengthen a partnership with the community members who have valuable knowledge and experience.

After several months of preparation, I was eager to speak with and learn from women with precarious status through our interviews. While we carefully organized the interview questions into themes and included gentle probes to keep the conversation on track, I had many conversations with Rupaleem (as my supervisor) about how to remain open to women's stories so that they could unfold in a natural way. Being a part of developing the research allowed me to appreciate our intention behind each interview question and how it related to the project, which resulted in an ability to also paraphrase and find plain language to pose questions differently with women, depending on their level of understanding.

As I prepared for my first interview, however, I nearly lost sight of the interview as a process. The women we were interviewing have life experiences that are often hidden, criticized or grossly stereotyped. These are women who must share their stories as a means to demonstrate that they deserve refugee status or public benefits. I grew to understand that this was more than sharing a story; our conversation offered permission for women to share their stories on their own terms.

I began to pay more attention to what I could do to help women feel safe and comfortable with me as a researcher. This meant that I needed to be comfortable bringing more of myself into the interview. I started to think about where and why these women share their stories in Canada. Who is the audience? What are the intentions and the objectives of sharing their stories?

As a research team, we understood that our interviews with women would only tap into some of the stories they share about their lives. We assumed that women adjusted and transformed their stories depending on their audience, and what they were seeking. Being conscious of how dynamics and differences can facilitate a type of variance or disconnect among women required self-reflection. This required thinking about how our appearance, background, social, political or other indicator may be received by the participants. Could this affect the research? Could you trigger the participant? Could you be perceived as unsafe to disclose certain information? It's important to review and understand these realities, because they are part of what may impact or implicate the research process. After months of preparation, it was incredibly rewarding to sit with women as they shared their stories. It is her story, and too often undermined or hurried along.

Margarita's narrative addresses the at times contradictory demands between the administrative work of composing ethical protocols for university-based research and engaging with individual women in an interview setting. Margarita also illustrates in what ways her participation in collaborative decision-making fostered her own transformative growth. Margarita's growing capacity on the project not only helped generate more meaningful interview conversations with women, but as Margarita took on leadership roles to hire and train additional research staff, she was well positioned to help create spaces for consciousness-raising as newer members of the research team joined our work.

Struggling to Ensure Principles of Equity in Participatory Action Research

We continue with a narrative by Bethany Osborne, who took on the role of Research Coordinator soon after the MMP was fully funded. Drawing on her extensive experience in community development, arts-based research, and research management, Bethany became involved in all aspects of the research, supervising graduate research assistants, networking with our community partners, and supporting data analysis and data collection activities. In the narrative below, Bethany discusses the challenges of navigating the multiple and shifting identities of our research team and community partners, where hierarchies of professionalization, knowledge, and power regularly interfere with our anti-oppression and emancipatory goals.

By Bethany J. Osborne (PhD student and research coordinator)

As a front-line community worker engaged with diverse communities for over a decade, it has been essential to develop a reflective practice to recognize my own power and privilege in relation to the people I work with. When I entered graduate school, I did not want to be an academic researcher who did the kind of research that left communities feeling like they had been used, without gaining benefit from the process. I found critical feminist scholars who were committed to similar principles (Belenky, Clinchy, Goldberger, & Tarule, 1986; Maguire, 1987; Tolman & Brydon-Miller, 2001) but the reality of the academy meant that it was difficult to do research differently.

As a PhD student, working as the Research Coordinator on the MMP, I work closely with Rupaleem and other research staff on the planning and administration of the project. One of my responsibilities has been to coordinate the Community Advisory Board (CAB) meetings and to maintain communication with our community partners. From the beginning, we discussed the importance of valuing the knowledge generated by all of the people involved in the project. We were also aware of the difficulty of demonstrating this to both committee members and to our funders. Increasingly, funders of academic research are using terms like "stakeholders," "community partnerships," "networking," and "knowledge transfer/mobilization." However, the way that research funds are designated (to fund graduate students for data collection and analysis) serves to maintain an imbalance of power and knowledge. People working in different communities are considered important in as far as they can provide access to the data held in particular spaces or communities. When they do take roles in generating knowledge, there are few (if any) resources to acknowledge their work. It is the responsibility of feminist researchers to work strategically within that system to find ways to honour the contributions of community partners. Our strategy was to do this in the form of a CAB. The CAB consists of women who differ by age, ethnicity, sexual orientation, immigration status, employment, and knowledge of immigration policy. Considering the varied social backgrounds and experience, we designated extra time and resources to get to know our community advisory board members, and to tap into their knowledge and expertise, and share leadership on project initiatives.

When I began to work with the project, one of my responsibilities was to build the CAB, bringing together people from a number of different professional backgrounds and personal commitments. I started with a core of women who had been involved in Rupaleem's previous research advisory groups and began to invite people that I knew from my work in diverse communities. Cuts to social service funding have meant that people working in the sector have increased workloads and have to be selective about the different projects that they become involved with. Knowing this, I often used my personal connections, meeting people where they were at: a local community college where we both worked, or for coffee in the neighbourhood that is convenient to them. Once people were recruited, we needed them to know that their presence and their knowledge were important. We struggled with how to do this and spent some time in our meetings discussing how people wanted to contribute. The formation of the principles guiding our research is one illustration of our collective work to articulate the common values we bring to our research, to help orient new people who join us midstream, and to identify concrete ways people on the CAB could take leadership roles related to data analysis, facilitating a solidarity group, or producing digital stories with women based on their experience with violence and immigration.

Another important group of people on the CAB were women with precarious immigration status. Early on, we noted that two women who identified themselves as "community members"[7] remained silent during the meeting, but spoke openly with our staff on a one-on-one basis. Upon reflection, we recognized that through our facilitation of the CAB meeting, we ignored a subtle dichotomy that emerged in our conversations about "us," as service providers or academics, and "them," as women with precarious status; a language that "othered" the community members we had intentionally recruited. In order to address this challenge, we worked one-on-one with "community members" prior to each CAB meeting to solicit their ideas and identify strategies for them to be more involved in the project. We took active steps to fulfill the vision of one of our community members, by creating a Solidarity Group (see Fernanda's narrative below), where a community member served as a co-leader and co-facilitator. We also co-hosted a workshop led by the Survivor Voices Inclusion Project (http://www.oaith. ca/for-survivors/the-oaith-survivor-voices-inclusion-project.html), where women from our project spoke openly about the oppression they faced when seeking services at women's shelters. Over time, we noticed a steady increase in community members' active participation, to the point that one of our "community members" who took the lead in producing digital stories with women who have precarious status to raise public awareness, stated to other community advisory board members that the MMP's strength comes from the combined efforts of three groups: academics, service providers, and immigrant women. This moment was incredibly powerful for me and others on the project, because it demonstrated that it is possible to do research differently in the academy. Though we had faced many challenges to building solidarity with women, at the start of our work, there are moments when our collaborative approach is seen as the source of our strength.

Bethany's narrative discusses our creative approach to sharing power and knowledge among the different stakeholders in the project, in both word and action. It is not easy to do this with integrity but it is essential if we are going to repurpose our research, to not just answer research questions but to actually participate in positive change in marginalized communities. In order to do this, we needed to be committed to building community.

From Community Organizing to Community Building in the Academy

In the following narrative, Rachel shares her approach to community building through her role as coordinator of the MMP's community out-reach and research interviews with migrant women. Rachel was hired at the same time as Janet Juanico Flor Cruz, who had prior experience as an ethnographic researcher in Mexico City and was working in Canada on a temporary basis. Rachel and Janet worked closely over nine months, to connect with women in different community-based organizations and conduct research interviews. Rachel and Janet were also responsible for transcribing the Spanish-language interviews and translating them into English. Rachel's prior experience as a community organizer with undocumented Spanish-speaking immigrants in the United States was evident in her capacity to recruit women for our interviews, but also in her commitment to our solidarity work. Rachel raises important questions about the limits of our solidarity work, given the constraints we faced as a university-led project that is funded for research activities as opposed to community-building.

By Rachel Mehl (MEd student and graduate research assistant)

I started working with the project, as the Graduate Research Assistant who was hired to coordinate community outreach and to recruit women to take part in the research. I brought my personal experience organizing in solidarity with undocumented migrant communities in the US and my passion for migrant justice on a global scale to this research project. As feminists seeking to practice an anti-oppression framework, we straddled multiple spheres of actors and actions that often overlap, but can also contradict one another. Individuals involved with the MMP included women who were leftist activists, community organizers, settlement and anti-violence against women workers, and academics. We did not always agree on how we should approach the barriers that we encountered, but we were committed to dialoguing about how to diminish barriers and to reflecting on the process.

Women who have experienced domestic violence, who are living in a shelter, and/or are in the process of a refugee claim have already been obliged to interact with many institutions, to repeatedly tell their stories, and to "prove" their worth. They may be reticent to interact with yet another institution to retell their stories. In almost every case, it was relationship and trust that brought participants to us, and it was the frontline workers that we had developed relationships with who mediated that trust. Initially frontline workers expressed deep concern about their clients' safety and risk of participation. For example, one women's shelter worker distrusted a recent community organizing campaign that publicly denounced cases where immigration authorities deported women who were residing in family violence shelters. This shelter worker was wary of the MMP, due to Rupaleem's affiliation with this grassroots campaign and was concerned that the MMP would expose her clients to further public scrutiny. During this meeting, Rupaleem and the worker also discussed their different perspectives on community organizing tactics for immigrant rights and the potential for women with precarious status to be caught in the crossfire (so to speak). This conversation built a sense of trust that we were working towards the same goal to eradicate sexism and interlocking oppressions; after our meeting, this shelter worker introduced the project to women in her shelter. In fact, we learned that all of our recruitment relied on our developing trust with service providers and demonstrating our long-term commitment to women's welfare.

Our recruitment challenges mirrored the contradictions of engaging in federally funded university research while attempting to make the knowledge produced and the funds themselves useful to organizations and individuals whom the state criminalizes. The Canadian government's violence toward Latin American women migrants (refugee claim denials, detentions and deportations) and the denial of rights to women with precarious status (to healthcare, freedom of movement, and safety from abuse) presented us with an urgency to use our research to support women's claims to basic rights. Despite the risks and barriers, women found their way—physically and emotionally—to the interviews. I saw women sense out the safety of places and spaces, within hostile terrains, and engage in reflective action to find ways to protect themselves, and their children in each new space.

In this context, we struggled with how to use our project and knowledge production for mutual benefit, paying careful attention to power disparities that existed between ourselves and the women who were our research participants. We struggled with what solidarity could look like in academic research where funding cycles are short term. Community organizing teaches us that this work needs to be accompanied by a long-term commitment, in order to bear fruit. At the early stages of the MMP, it was unclear how we would continue to honor the relationships that we were building through this project; the uncertainty in our own long-term commitment was a constant struggle for MMP staff, as we sought ways for our work to not become just another academic project that fails to follow through with our promises and commitment.

In Rachel's narrative, she discussed two themes that are pertinent to participatory action research: the potential risks for service providers and research participants in connecting to an academic research project; and the apprehension we encountered in service providers as well as potential interview participants, that our research would mutually benefit all stakeholders. A consistent tension in the MMP, that Rachel mentions, has involved finding ways to balance the time needed to complete tasks related to our research interviews, while also carving out time for our community-building and solidarity work. Although Rachel was deeply committed to the MMP's solidarity work and helped to develop the solidarity group that took place the winter and spring of 2012, her job responsibilities required her to spend most of her time conducting, transcribing, and translating interviews. Rachel's question of "How can we do research differently given the many restraints that we have?" thus, in part, stems from the struggle we faced as a research project where our "research" activities would often compete with our community-building and community-organizing goals.

Holding a Space for Women With Precarious Migratory Status

In our next narrative, Fernanda Villanueva reflects on her journey as co-facilitator of *Nuestra Fortaleza* (Our Strength), which was a 12-week solidarity group that we co-hosted with one of our community partner organizations. The Solidarity Group was initiated by M., a community member who has precarious immigration status and has been serving on the community advisory board for the MMP since it began. It was M.'s vision to create a safe space for women with precarious immigration status to share tips, resources, and mutual support. Through many weeks of consultation with our community partners, the MMP partnered with the Toronto Rape Crisis Centre/Multicultural Women against Rape (TRCC), to co-host a solidarity group for Spanish-speaking, adult women, with precarious status. The group was open to women irrespective of their participation in the research, and a total of ten women dropped in during the 12-week group. The group was co-facilitated by a team that included Fernanda (an MSW practicum student, supervised by Rupaleem), a staff from TRCC, a student intern at TRCC, and M. (a community member from the MMP community advisory board).

Because the MMP funds did not cover time for research assistants to coordinate community meetings for mutual aid and support, Rupaleem (as a social work faculty member) created a social work practicum for Fernanda, through the faculty of social work's practicum education office. Fernanda was in her first year of the MSW program at the time and had several years of prior experience working in a community health clinic and helping refugee claimants complete their applications in Canada. As a practicum student, Fernanda's learning goals involved group work facilitation, coalition building, communication skills, and professional writing skills that took the form of weekly reflexive essays, some of which are posted on the project website (www.migrantmothersproject.com). Through Fernanda's reflexive essay below, she illustrates the importance of honoring the differences among a team of facilitators, as a prerequisite for engaging women with precarious status in solidarity work. She also discusses how she navigated the common ground she shared with her co-facilitators and participants of the solidarity group, as a young refugee in Canada.

By Fernanda Villanueva (MSW practicum student)

When I first met the co-facilitators for the solidarity group, the power differences were very clear and all four co-facilitators took on their expected roles. The service provider with a lot of experience took the lead, while the other student intern and I took more support roles. M., who had initiated the project, maintained a quiet and reserved demeanor. I realized that before we could create solidarity with the women who we hoped would join the group, we needed to develop a sense of solidarity among the facilitators. Working from a feminist and anti-oppressive lens required that I acknowledge while all four of us were refugees from Latin America, our different social locations, histories of oppression and privileges intersect to highlight both our similarities and differences as co-facilitators and as women taking part in the group.

Developing a better sense of who I was in location to the other women allowed me to navigate and build authentic relationships with each woman in the group. I began to change the way that I interacted with my co-facilitators, validating the different strengths that each woman had and demonstrating my own strengths. Slowly, others began to do the same and as that happened, the power dynamics between us became more balanced; our interactions moved more in the direction of respect, and an acknowledgment of equity. It was this unity that gave us the foundation to begin working with women with precarious status in a way that could also uphold the vision of solidarity we were working towards. Building solidarity with women who have histories of violence and oppression by their part-ners and social structures required gently building relationships based on trust. It required that we listen to their stories of struggle, acknowledge their stories of resistance and of perseverance.

Engaging in self-reflection and being aware of my social location in respect to the women was uncomfortable and painful at times, but it was essential. I had come to Canada as a refugee from Chile when I was a child and as women talked about their experiences, I could often identify with their struggles. At the same time, I had to acknowledge the many privileges that I now have as a Canadian citizen and a graduate student in social work are privileges that women in the solidarity group, and their children, may never have access to. I realized that the process of self-reflection was not about denying my challenges or minimizing my own achievements, but it was about paying attention to what they were and how each one could potentially impact the relationships that were being formed.

Working from a feminist and anti-oppressive stance is not simply memorizing a theory discussed in school, or memorizing a sentence in your organization's mandate, it involves immersing yourself, your beliefs and your actions in the principles of working from this approach. It is being able to acknowledge the

*many intersections of oppression that exist for the individuals you work with
and ensuring that you continuously draw on the individual's personal strengths
and their expertise to shape and guide their lives. More importantly, it involves
engaging in critical self-reflection to understand who you are, what you unknowingly bring with you in the spaces you enter, and how this may impact the interactions you have. It was with these principles that the solidarity group become
a unique experience for those involved. If we had used another approach, the
solidarity group would not have been such a powerful exchange. We were able to
work together, creating a space where our collective strength supported each of us.*

Fernanda's narrative discusses the importance of acknowledging one's power
and privilege when working with a group to foster solidarity against oppression; this process intentionally blurs the conventional lines of researcher and
researched to identify commonalities among a group of women, but also brings
points of difference more closely into view. Each of the women who took part
in the MMP solidarity group had histories of violence that brought them to
seek refuge in Canada. Through engaging in critical consciousness-raising with
her fellow group facilitators, Fernanda demonstrated the necessary journey of
acknowledging her shared history with women in the group, while noting the
differences produced by Canadian immigration policy, which has offered her
and her family refugee status, while denying basic human rights to others. The
blurred lines between researcher and researched, thus, present opportunities
for shared understanding; researchers, however, continue to have the responsibility to gauge how their points of privilege may impact their relationships
among a group of diverse women, to find strategies to complement each other's strengths, while striving for equity rather than equality.

Reflexivity as a Continual Process of Becoming

Flavia Genovese further explores how the fluid nature of identity can shift
one's understanding of violence and immigration. Flavia was hired as a
research assistant during her final year in the MSW program; she had completed a practicum with one of the MMP partner organizations and was
trusted by the organization to help with recruitment and research interviews.
Flavia also worked closely with Rupaleem to code and analyze our interview
transcripts. During Flavia's tenure on the project, she experienced a shift in
her own immigration status, when her student visa expired and she entered
an uncertain period while applying to become a permanent resident in
Canada. Her reflexive essay considers how our dynamic identities and life
experiences can lead to new insights that inform feminist research.

By Flavia Genovese (MSW student and graduate research assistant)

*At the start of the project, I often reflected upon how my front-line experience as
a social service provider impacted my ability to draw upon the commonalities,
as well as differences in experiences among women we interviewed on the MMP.*

After graduating from the MSW program, however, my perspective on the project shifted when my student visa in Canada expired. After living most of my adult life in Canada as a temporary resident, I experienced some difficulties associated with precarious status while applying for permanent residency—not having health insurance, being uncertain if I would be allowed to remain in Canada, and having to pay costly immigration fees. During this time, I was in need of an expensive medical surgery but did not have health coverage. This additional personal struggle gave me first-hand knowledge of feelings of immobility and unjust limitations rooted in having a precarious status. Through my work on the MMP, I learned that several of the other researcher assistants and community partners struggled with similar experiences as part of their own stories and brought this knowledge to bear in my work analyzing our interviews with women.

Our interview approach allowed women to talk to us about the important aspects of their lives, as women who have faced violence, but who also strive to support their children and build lives in Canada. We wanted to avoid the lure to reconstruct and re-author women's narratives, so strove to understand the cultural nuances which informed their stories and whenever possible allow their words to speak for themselves. In the data analysis process, I started to pay close attention to the way women spoke about their emotions, feelings and overall health. We began to notice a common language used to speak about the impact that women's immigration journey had had on their mental health. Many of the women clearly spoke of experiencing emotionally and physically painful circumstances. But we also learned from women about their resourcefulness, strength and perseverance as they fought to support themselves and their children.

Acknowledging commonality among research staff and our community partners was one of the many strengths inherent in the MMP. It allowed women's narratives to be understood from a position of community rather than one of isolation and difference. These were important lessons for me to learn as I embark on my career as a social worker, to be willing to engage in ongoing self-reflection, willing to find spaces and places to connect and understand the different experiences of women with whom I work.

Flavia's narrative highlights one of the core values in the MMP: to ensure that our research approached women as experts of their own experiences and as people who are agents in their lives, despite encountering numerous forms of violence and oppression. Flavia's narrative also illustrates how changes in her own immigration status deepened her sensitivity to understanding how precarious status and migration contribute to women's poor health. As a research team, we had several conversations about wanting to document the effects of precarious status on women's lives, as a way to demonstrate the structural violence of immigration policy. We also were cautious about invoking a biomedical gaze, one that we are immersed in as social workers in North America. Our approach to interpreting women's narratives (through organizing interview transcripts by "code" and generating analytic "themes") thus involved playing close attention to the range of ways women talked about their health and well-being, while refraining from reducing their talk to western categories for mental illness (i.e., depression, anxiety, suicidal ideation). The result was research data and analysis that focus not just on the impact of violence on women's lives, but the ways in which they navigate difficult circumstances, to survive and thrive, building lives for themselves and their children.

Creating Space for Feminist Consciousness-Raising in Participatory Action Research

We end with a narrative by Rupaleem Bhuyan, who is the principal investigator of the MMP and a full-time social work faculty member at the University of Toronto. Rupaleem discusses the challenge of creating spaces for feminist consciousness-raising at a research intensive university. Her narrative emphasizes the politics of knowledge production where knowledge produced by university-based researchers is often assumed to be more objective and legitimate than community-generated knowledge.

By Rupaleem Bhuyan (principal investigator and full-time social work faculty member)

In the spring of 2011, I became the principal investigator for the Migrant Mothers Project, when three research proposals were funded through the Canadian government and a University of Toronto institutional award for "New Researchers." My affiliation with the University of Toronto is perhaps one of the more pivotal factors in my consciousness-raising as a feminist researcher who collaborates closely with students and community partners on the MMP. As a woman of colour of South Asian descent, with a background in feminist and immigrant rights organizing, I am committed to generating knowledge to inform collective action. I have sought to employ participatory action research methods as a means to democratize the production of knowledge, to de-center whiteness[8] within social work education, and to infuse my paid work with community engagement and activism. As a pre-tenure professor at a research-intensive university, I have the resources (and frankly, the job pressure) to apply for research funding. I also feel institutional pressure to be a "productive" scholar in the eyes of the academy.

One of the ongoing challenges on the MMP involved finding resources to support community-generated knowledge, while fulfilling our obligations as an academic research project. Gratefully, one of our funders required that 10% of our budget be spent on "community researchers." While this was a modest proportion of our overall budget, we committed to paying small honorariums ($50/meeting) to each community partner who has precarious status. The remainder of our funds, however, were allocated to pay for graduate student researchers, research travel expenses, and research-related supplies. As our community building grew to include a 12-week solidarity group, community events, and a digital story-telling project, we had to scramble to find resources to ensure that community-generated *knowledge could take form and be disseminated on terms established by our community partners. This required additional fundraising, establishing cooperation agreements with partnering community organizations, recruiting social work students through the practicum program, and volunteering countless hours above and beyond what our "jobs" required.*

The community building which we fostered through and by our collective consciousness of interlocking oppressions increased our potential as university-based researchers to mobilize the resources and status of an institution of higher education, for the benefit of those who face ongoing marginalization and exclusion. While this work is undoubtedly rewarding, both personally and collectively, it too often remains underacknowledged and less visible in institutions of higher education; the fruits of this work do not translate well to an academic talk or publication. Nevertheless, the transformative power of feminist consciousness-raising is embodied in the women who have taken part in the MMP, each of whom continue to engage in activism and social change as feminists, social workers, community-based researchers, and educators.

Conclusion

The narratives presented in this chapter illustrate in what ways members of a research team engage in collective consciousness-raising to maneuvrer around interlocking oppressions, inside and out of the university, towards developing knowledge for social action. This chapter also illustrates the key role that graduate students play in carrying out feminist participatory action research that is university-based. Graduate research assistants are often rendered invisible or neutral in analyses of power in the production of research knowledge. References to graduate research students also presume they fall on the "researcher" side of a researcher-researched dichotomy. Even when researchers—typically referring to the principal investigator and co-investigator—employ feminist and anti-oppression research methodologies, little attention has been paid to spaces within a research project that enable the development of feminist consciousness, including attention to the common ground we inhabit in our journey towards a more socially just world.

Through our narratives we highlight the blurred lines between the life experiences of women who took part in the MMP as research assistants and the lives of immigrant women we sought to understand through our research and community-building activities. We learned that our critical reflexivity and dialogue deepen the praxis of our feminist, participatory action research through: (1) considering the complex positionality and knowledge of each person who is involved in the MMP; (2) sharing leadership roles among student researchers and community partners to produce knowledge for social action; and (3) providing space for women with precarious status to generate their own knowledge to raise public awareness of their experience of marginalization and to call for social action.

We recognize that many of the lessons we share in this chapter may be specific to our project and the social and political context in which our work unfolds. We hope that through illustrating the transformative potential of engaging in feminist consciousness-raising as researchers, students, faculty, and practitioners in social work and allied fields, we inspire others to create spaces for collective consciousness-raising to deepen their knowledge of themselves, the inequalities they work against, and how a sense of community among feminist researchers can be enriching and empowering.

Notes

1 Authors' names appear in alphabetical order.
2 This research was supported by the Canadian Social Science and Humanities Research Council, CERIS – The Ontario Metropolis Centre, and the University of Toronto Connaught New Researcher Award.
3 The MMP employs a fluid definition of woman that is welcoming to people with a range of gender identities and expression.
4 We use "precarious immigration status" to refer to the range of categories in Canadian immigration policy which include temporary or dependent legal status in Canada in addition to people who are undocumented. People with precarious immigration status are not equally vulnerable, but their precariousness results from lacking one or more of the following: basic social and political rights; legal work authorization; and/or "deportability" (the right of the Canadian government to remove an individual from Canada).
5 These principles for participatory action research are adapted from Incite-National.org. Retrieved from: http://www.incite-national.org/sites/default/files/incite_files/resource_docs/5614_toolkitrev-par.pdf.
6 Job title(s) during the first two years of the project.
7 Women who take part in our CAB, who do not represent a specific organization, commonly refer to themselves as "community members."
8 I refer to whiteness, not as a social identity, but as a dominant yet highly invisible sociocultural perspective.

References

Ahmed, S. (2004). *The cultural politics of emotion.* New York: Routledge.

Anderson-Nathe, B., Gringeri, C., & Wahab, S. (2013). Nurturing "critical hope" in teaching feminist social work research. *Journal of Social Work Education, 49,* 277–291.

Bailey, D. (1992). Using participatory research in community consortia development and evaluation: Lessons from the beginning of a story. *The American Sociologist, 23* (4), 71–82.

Barnoff, L. & Moffatt, K. (2007). Contradictory tensions in anti-oppression practice in feminist social services. *Affilia, 22* (1), 56–70.

Belenky, M. F., Clinchy, B. M., Goldberger, N. R., & Tarule, J. M. (1986). *Women's ways of knowing.* New York: Basic Books.

Bhuyan, R. (2012). Negotiating citizenship on the frontlines: How the devolution of Canadian immigration policy shapes service delivery to women fleeing abuse. *Law & Policy, 3* (2), 211–236.

Bhuyan, R., Osborne, B., & Cruz, J. F. J. (2013). Unprotected and unrecognized: The ontological insecurity of migrants who are denied protection from domestic violence in their home countries as refugee claimants in Canada. *CERIS Working Paper No. 96*. Toronto: CERIS: The Ontario Metropolis Centre.

Goldring, L., & Landolt, P. (Eds.). (2013). *Producing and negotiating non-citizenship: Precarious legal status in Canada*. Toronto: University of Toronto Press.

Goldring, L., Bernstein, C., & Bernhard, J. (2010). Institutionalizing precarious migratory status in Canada. *Citizenship Studies, 13* (3), 239–265.

Gringeri, C. E., Wahab, S., & Anderson-Nathe, B. (2010). What makes it feminist? Mapping the landscape of feminist social work research. *Affilia, 25* (4), 340–405.

Healy, K. & Mulholland, J. (1998). Discourse analysis and activist social work: investigating practice processes. *Journal of Sociology and Social Welfare, 25* (3), 3–27.

Henderson, D. J. (1995). Consciousness-raising in participatory research: Method and methodology for emancipatory nursing inquiry. *Advances in Nursing Science, 17* (3), 58–69.

hooks, b. (2000). *Feminism is for everybody: Passionate politics*. Boston: South End Press.

Kaufman, D. R. (2007). From course to discourse: Mainstreaming feminist methodology. In S. N. Hesse-Biber (Ed.), *Handbook of feminist research: Theory and praxis* (pp. 681–688). Thousand Oaks, CA: SAGE.

Maguire, P. (1987). *Doing participatory research: A feminist approach*. Amherst, MA: University of Massachusetts at Amherst, Center for International Education.

Mullaly, B. (2007). *The new structural social work: Ideology, theory, practice* (3rd ed.). Oxford: Oxford University Press.

Sullivan, M., Bhuyan, R., Senturia, K., Shiu-Thornton, S., & Ciske, S. (2006). Participatory action research in practice: A case study in addressing domestic violence in nine cultural communities. *Journal of Interpersonal Violence, 20* (8), 977–995.

Tolman, D. L. & Brydon-Miller, M. (Eds.). (2001). *From subjects to subjectivities: A handbook of interpretive and participatory methods*. New York: New York University Press.

14 Positionality and Privilege in Qualitative Research

Feminist Critical Praxis

Karen Morgaine

Positionality and Privilege in Qualitative Research: Feminist Critical Praxis

As a qualitative researcher with a background in psychology and social work and who teaches social welfare and social justice in a sociology department, I am comfortable straddling disciplinary borders. I envision contributing to various fields through research that is firmly grounded in an analysis of power and the ways that structural oppressions are perpetuated. My research is feminist, critical, and queer. This research requires that I regularly confront my positionalities and privilege. I question how I can effectively navigate insider/outsider tensions without feeling that I am either ignoring crucial aspects of my own privilege or trapping myself with the expectation that I only do research where I "belong." From a theoretical perspective, I can easily dismiss the notion that my own or other's identities are fixed and that I can ever be a complete insider in anyone's life beyond my own, yet when the actual *doing* of research is on the table, I still balk at doing research with people and communities where I am clearly an outsider. Theoretically, I am most comfortable straddling intersections—queer theory, social constructivism, postcolonial and critical feminisms, and critical theory—and in these sometimes dissonant and contradictory places I have found a theoretical home. If I find comfort in theoretical tension and do not see identities as fixed, why do I often seek a simplistic resolution to the insider/outsider dilemma?

Feminist social work research prioritizes social change and social justice through centering power imbalances, privilege, and oppression (Wahab, Anderson-Nathe, & Gringeri, 2012). Critical feminist research has also been linked to anti-oppressive social work practice through critical reflexivity and attention to positionality (Daley, 2010). Wahab et al. (2012) entreat feminist social work researchers "to challenge binary categories all together and refocus gender related projects around multifaceted femininities and masculinities, foregrounding work around the intersectionalities of identities" (p. 470). Additionally, Olesen (2011) suggests that one of the ongoing challenges of feminist qualitative research is engaging intersectionality and the challenges to intersectionality, which call for an expanded vision that

examines the interactions of social identities and the "complexity of categories" (p. 134).

What follows is a deconstruction of my past and present research in an
attempt to illuminate the ways I *did* reflexivity, navigated binary tensions,
and sought comfort in the tension of praxis—where my theoretical comfort
rubs up against the *act* of research.

Reflexivity and Being an "Insider"

After ten years doing domestic violence (DV) work "on the ground," I
developed a qualitative research project aimed at discerning how the international framing of "women's rights as human rights" and DV as a human
rights issue may have influenced the DV movement in the United States.
This dissertation project came out of years of frustration with the DV movement which seemed unresponsive to the critique of women of color (Incite,
2006) and which appeared stagnant in terms of framing the issue. The project itself incorporated 29 interviews from women and men involved in the
national and regional DV and human rights fields in the United States.
My research questions focused on whether a human rights framework was
being used to define and address DV in the United States, and the benefits
and challenges of using a human rights framework (Morgaine, 2009, 2011).
I included autoethnographic/reflexive sections throughout the writing as
a way to write myself explicitly into the research process focusing specifically on my positionality and privilege. Once this project was completed,
I questioned whether this inclusion was really a way to expose and start to
dismantle white privilege or just a confessional exercise that serves little
purpose but perhaps to assuage my own feelings of anxiety.

Positioning Myself as a Researcher

I approached my dissertation project[1]

> identifying as a feminist with an affinity for postmodern feminism that embraces
> social criticism in the context of multiple oppressions (such as race/ethnicity,
> class, gender), promotes the ideal of individual agency and empowerment, and
> recognizes the importance of a social critique that is contextualized culturally,
> historically, and locally (Fraser, 1997; Fraser & Nicholson, 1988).

I then acknowledged *that my identification as an educated Caucasian[2] woman
of Western European descent contributes to my own perspective and position in
approaching this research project* (Morgaine, 2007).

Almost immediately after writing that initial statement, I began to question the role this brief section would play. While feminist and qualitative
researchers are often encouraged to practice reflexivity throughout the
research process, I wondered how I could position myself in the research
so that the reader could have a semblance of understanding of what I was

going to bring to the table, without moving too far in the direction of confessional tale or distracting nuisance, and yet giving more than a throwaway
statement about my gender/race/ethnicity/class (and so on). One solution in this project was to expose my "anxious white privilege." I wanted to
highlight my privileged position, not any possible "insiderness" that I could
claim in the research (as a woman and/or as someone who had done DV
work for years).

> *While I believe this "declaration of whiteness" (Ahmed, 2004, p. 1) is impor-*
> *tant to clarify how my own privilege influences my experiences, my observations,*
> *and how I structure the research, this declaration is also problematic. Ahmed*
> *has pointed out that the act of making whiteness visible may actually replicate*
> *the white privilege which critical whiteness studies are seeking to dismantle by*
> *recentering whiteness and by suggesting that if a white person can actually name*
> *and see their whiteness, they are essentially not claiming that which cannot be*
> *seen (whiteness), and therefore the declaration is non-performative . . . For those*
> *working within critical whiteness studies and/or examining white privilege the*
> *issues of recentering and essentializing whiteness are just two of the recurrent*
> *concerns addressed by some (see Dyer, 1997; Fine, Weis, Powell, & Wong, 1997;*
> *Frankenberg, 1993, 1997) and while beyond the scope of this study, my own*
> *"anxious whiteness" (Ahmed, p. 3) remains part of my location and my research.*
> *This anxious whiteness describes the anxiety that I and others who engage in*
> *addressing white privilege admit to—the fear of what may happen if the analysis*
> *of whiteness and white privilege becomes again that which is centered and privi-*
> *leged (Ahmed). By marking myself as white I do not want to position myself as*
> *"the good anti-racist" who, by naming herself as such has done what is necessary*
> *and can move on, yet at the same time, if I avoid the acknowledgement, I believe*
> *I become that much more an accomplice to white supremacy.*

One thing this section may have done is to complicate the issue of positioning myself in the research. Rather than merely identifying myself, it could
suggest that ongoing reflection of the *meaning* behind the identification
opens up a more complex dialogue—in this case, how can deconstructing
whiteness contribute to a more nuanced understanding of the research and
the research process? Yet being willing to open up a dialogue is not without
risks, such as the potential for this ongoing reflection to fall prey to a never-
ending cycle that, rather than providing depth, becomes a barrier to the
research process.

Navigating a Course for Privilege and Reflexivity

For many years, qualitative researchers have called for attention to
reflexivity (Denzin & Lincoln, 2011), for feminist reflexivity in research
(Ramazanoglu & Holland, 2002), and for critical qualitative researchers
to accurately position themselves in relation to their research and their

research participants/co-researchers (Foley, 2002). Particularly in regard to critical feminist research, "the invocation of feminist reflexivity is central to feminist methodological concerns with power" (Ali, 2006, p. 475). At the site of this invocation is where problems arise—a complicated terrain that has been critiqued and challenged for some time. Ali suggests that there is an all too common tendency to simplify the complexities of this position by falling into the trap of what Marcus identifies as "the practice of positioning [which] can easily get stuck in a sterile form of identity politics, reducing it to a formulaic incantation at the beginning of ethnographic papers in which one boldly 'comes clean' and confesses one's positioned identity" (as cited in Ali, 2006, p. 475). bell hooks, while calling for an examination of whiteness, also critiques this tendency: "many scholars, critics, and writers preface their work by stating that they are 'white' as though mere acknowledgement of this fact were sufficient, as though it conveyed all we need to know of standpoint, motivation, [and] direction" (hooks, 1989, para. 11).

While there have been numerous calls to examine and deconstruct whiteness—notably Morrison (1992) and hooks (1990)—there have also been cautions and an ongoing awareness by some of the very researchers that took up this task that to do so may recenter rather than deconstruct whiteness (Dyer, 1997; Fine et al., 1997; Frankenberg, 1993, 1997). At the same time, it has been suggested that to recognize what has been previously marked as "natural," "transparent," and "invisible" needs to occur first to allow for a "disruption of systems of domination" (Fox, 2002, p. 201). Another significant caveat recognized by Keating (1995) is that to examine whiteness and other racial categories may serve to continue to essentialize race rather than destabilize it. Finding a way to navigate this, in what she suggested was an "admittedly temporary" path, Keating proposes a "twofold approach where we explore the artificial, constantly changing nature of 'black,' 'white,' and other racialized identities without ignoring their concrete material effects" (Keating, 1995, p. 915).

Complicating the arena of reflexivity and whiteness is the intersecting nature of both oppression and privilege (Hurtado & Stewart, 1997, p. 300) and the question of "How, for example, do we separate 'whiteness' from masculinity and other forms of privilege? Is it 'whiteness,' masculinity, 'white' masculinity, or some other combination (Keating, 1995, p. 909)? Is it possible to untangle these intersections and look at one form of privilege in a vacuum, or, alternatively, is it possible that researchers who propose anti-oppressive critical research may get bogged down in the desire to name, locate, and deconstruct all forms of privilege? In contrast to what Fellows and Razack (1998) name the "race to innocence" in which women believe the urgency of their own gender subordination relieves them of the responsibility for subordinating other women, is there an accompanying "race to duty" in which researchers attempt to locate all their positions of privilege as they move forward with any one research project? Rather than "competing marginalities" (Fellows & Razack, 1998, p. 1) this race to duty could illustrate "competing privileges."

Attempting to enact this race to duty, qualitative researchers can incorporate a modicum of reflexivity so that they have fulfilled the expectation of the "dutiful" researcher or they can attempt to expose themselves more fully. Positioned towards one end of the continuum of the reflexivity of duty is autoethnography. Autoethnography itself can be undertaken in multi-faceted ways, including: (1) analytical—an attempt to use the researcher's insider perspective to further the social analysis being presented *vis-à-vis* the research; (2) as a key to social change; (3) as a strategy to connect the researcher's personal world to the social world which is under examination (Denzin, 2006); and (4) as a "confessional" tale (Foley, 2002). Some personal examinations of whiteness and white privilege can find a home in this form of writing and representation, where the focus is on the writer and, in these cases, on a deconstruction of white privilege (Frankenberg, 1993; Frye, 1992; Pratt, 1984).

One tool I used in this project was to go beyond the minimal reflexive naming and expose the complexity of "anxious white privilege," yet that was still rather limited. Once I opened up the dialogue, I decided it would be beneficial to thread reflexivity throughout the entire piece and so the next step was to examine how white privilege played out in the data collection process.

Positioning Myself in the Interview Relationship

My motivation for doing this study was significantly influenced by the writings of women of color in regard to the DV movement and was situated within the intersection of gender and race/ethnicity. I did not approach the study with a plan to discuss white privilege, though that rose to the surface during my interviews. I did not consciously create a plan regarding how I would present my own privileged positions during interviews, although I did presume that I would discuss how I was influenced by the critique of women of color and groups such as Incite. In reviewing transcripts, I specifically mentioned this influence in 23 out of 29 interviews. In trying to discern why I did not mention this in every interview, I noticed that in interviews with some participants who were less familiar with the DV movement, the conversations were more focused on the human rights arena in the United States. These conversations often highlighted issues of US exceptionalism rather than specific tensions in the DV movement.

In reviewing the transcripts, I was interested in examining my white privilege by identifying who I disclosed my whiteness/privilege with. Seven interviews took place in person so these participants may have determined that I am white, although this presumption is not without problems. I mentioned my whiteness to an in-person interviewee who identified as white and Jewish and three interviewees on the phone, all of whom identified as

African American. I also mentioned my white privilege when a participant who identified as an Indigenous woman and I were discussing power and oppression. All in all, I discussed the issue of privilege in the DV movement with seven participants—six of whom identified as women of color. Curiously, I did not disclose my whiteness or white privilege to any of the participants who identified exclusively as white, although two women with whom I did discuss privilege (and who I met with in person) identified as Anglo and Jewish/Jewish American and appeared to prioritize their ethnicity over their racial category. While they could both have been read as "white," they focused on their Jewish identity over their racial identity.

In looking back over the transcripts, I noticed that in the few instances where I mentioned my whiteness or white privilege, I noted feeling more comfortable looking at privilege in the DV movement, due to my own privilege, while also noting that I have been influenced significantly by women of color regarding racism in the DV movement. I also noticed that on a couple of occasions I mentioned that when I did DV work on the ground it was in a "very white community." This claim was to clarify to participants that while I was influenced by the writings of women of color, my personal DV work was almost exclusively with white women.

When I review the "hows"—how I disclosed or did not disclose my whiteness; how I examined or performed privilege; and how I "did" my whiteness and privilege in the interviews I wonder why I made the choices I did. Were they useful, "neutral," detrimental, or possibly all of the above? I could say it was because it wasn't until I was close to halfway done with my interviews that I really started to see that privilege was going to have a place in the research findings but that may only explain some of the choices I made in disclosing my whiteness.

Positioning myself in the interviews as a white ally poses both pitfalls and possible benefits. The presumption that people of color would see me as an ally simply because I identified my whiteness is problematic. Marking that which has been described by some as unmarked (Frankenberg, 1993) does not automatically give me the position of "trustworthy ally" or as somehow a "better-than-average" white woman, yet the counter-position of not identifying my race places me right back into the colorblind camp of denial. What was the intent behind the declaration? Was I intending to gain trust, an important element in any research interview, and be seen as somehow "special," or did I own my position of privilege with the hope that this "reflexive race cognizance" (O'Brien, 2001, p. 51) was part of my ongoing social justice work? Or both?

The issue of why I did not disclose my whiteness to the participants who identified solely as white or European American brings up an additional presumption—the presumption of alienation. In her work with white antiracist activists, O'Brien (2001) notes that many of the participants that she interviewed identified that while they worked within antiracist organizations and saw antiracism as a significant part of their day-to-day lives, they also worked hard not to alienate other whites around them. For some this was a way to cultivate "authentic relationships" (p. 80) in which they could continue to address issues of racism. Others such as Essed (1991) have noted that whites often fear that taking a stand against racism will "cause trouble" (p. 277). Perhaps this is the crux of the issue in this research relationship—was I afraid that to bring up privilege would "cause trouble" and the interview would falter? Or was I operating once again out of my white privilege—seeing myself and my white interviewees as the norm and therefore invisible?

Autoethnography and White Privilege: Placing Myself in the Analysis

In my attempts to step away from declaring my positionality at the front end of the research and never returning to the implications of this, I wrote myself into the project—here and there where it appeared relevant. I worked to strike a balance among participant reflections, my analysis, and my reflections on how my experiences shaped my analysis. What follows is a section from the final analysis/discussion chapter of my dissertation, entitled "White Privilege and Racism Revisited:"

> *Perhaps white privilege allows whites, myself included, to stay safely in the comfort zone of "yes, but" rather than moving outside to look at other options. If the criminal justice system affords whites a sense of security that it does not for communities of color then perhaps it is easier to believe that the justice system will deliver justice. Perhaps it is easier to see this as our best effort because whites have less to fear from the police officer, the child welfare worker, the judge, and/or the prison guard. As a white woman it is less likely that I will be assaulted by the police officer who responds to a domestic violence call (Incite, 2006) which can give me the privilege of being critical of the criminal justice system and of the trajectory of the mainstream DV movement with the comfort that I will likely experience less backlash. As a white woman I am seen as less of a threat and I am perceived as a voice of authority. Additionally, while I am critical, privilege "allows" me to feel less urgency about the problems inherent in the State entanglements with the mainstream DV movement. For women of color whose day to day existence is impacted by the criminal justice system the urgency for the system to change is much more palpable.*

> *I can best speak from my own position of privilege yet, given the insidiousness of white privilege, I can presume that the white women I spoke with and other white women in the mainstream DV movement may have similar experiences. Focusing on the criminal and civil justice systems I would say I have had a relatively disengaged or neutral experience with these systems throughout my life—a result, in part, of my position of privilege—particularly white privilege. I grew up in both suburban and rural areas that were almost entirely white—I do not recall having any impressions of the police or even seeing the police until perhaps I was of high school age. Any interaction I had was relatively benign—certainly I never considered that I was at risk of being assaulted, harassed or "profiled" in*

any way. Since moving to various urban areas throughout the US this has not changed, although I can recall a police presence a bit more, but again not as a threat to my person . . . .

In terms of the civil justice system my interactions have been solely professional in the context of my work with clients of Child Protective Services. There were occasions when I was called into juvenile court to testify and, while not particularly pleasant, the integrity of my family or community was not at stake. I do recall one of the few times I had to testify during which time I was supporting the work that my client had done in therapy and domestic violence group. The judge, an older white male, interrogated me about the domestic violence program and appeared to take a rather demeaning tone towards both myself and the program. I can recall how angry and uncomfortable I felt even 7–10 years later and remember seeing this experience as based in a sexist response to the material I was describing. While I still believe this is true, I can acknowledge that what I saw and experienced was through the eyes of a white woman and so the only oppression I had experienced and continue to experience, for the most part, comes from that place. While not wanting to fall into the trap of ranking oppression (Collins, 2008), I want to note that I was responding fully to my experience and yet need to be aware it was simply one piece in a much larger puzzle. Perhaps there may have been other issues at play too—my status as a mental health professional could be seen as "lesser" compared to a Circuit Court judge so it is possible that his treatment of me was based on more than my gender, yet for me my gender has always had more "salience" (Collins, 2008, p. 334) than any other social or identity group. Similarly, a co-worker in the same program who was a Latina woman had recounted that another older, white judge had referred to her when she was on the stand as "little lady." I recall that the small group of us—three women, two white, one Latina—all discussed this in light of the sexism that we saw as palpable in that interchange yet we did not talk about how it could have also been a racist remark.

Given that there has been substantial evidence that children of color, particularly African American children, are overrepresented in the child welfare system and the additional complexities regarding the intersection of class and gender related to child welfare (Hill, 2004; Roberts, 2002) it is apparent to me that, like my response to the criminal justice system, my response to the civil justice system and to the child welfare system is, again, based in part on white privilege. Where I saw sexism in the system—particularly when women were continually being rev-ictimized and held accountable for their partner's violence, sometimes to an even larger degree than he was—there were other systems of oppression to address such as class, race/ethnicity, sexuality, and gender identification.

Instead of simply "calling out" the white women in my study, what I attempted to do in the above excerpt was to contextualize my analysis of white privilege in the DV movement through both the participants' thoughts and my own experience. If I had "left myself out" it would seem disingenuous or perhaps too easy—to locate privilege outside myself rather than identifying the interplay of my own privilege and the privilege of others. Methodologically this was another way to integrate reflexivity, which went beyond the initial identification of self. While my conversations with my participants about white privilege during the data collection process was a more "active" process of reflexivity, the analysis of how my own privilege played out in the study and in my own participation in the DV movement was one way of maintaining engagement with the issue of privilege through the entire project rather than at the onset with a blanket statement. As I was writing myself in, I was reminded how I brought my own history into the DV work that I did for years—a history of little or no threat from the criminal justice systems that have been harnessed by the DV movement to protect women yet which do not adequately protect women of color.

In this study, I consciously positioned myself at the beginning and the end in terms of reflexively identifying my privilege both as researcher and as a part of the DV movement. I was less conscious about the active claiming of privilege during data collection. This claiming process was not consistent through all of my interviews and was mitigated by a complex interplay of my own fears, assumptions, time constraints, and pressures—all of which are commonplace in the research process, particularly as novice researchers striking out on our own. Interestingly enough, my subsequent research has continued to test and challenge me, particularly in relation to privilege.

Immobilized by "Duty"

A Dutiful Insider

Fast forward to Southern California where, one year post dissertation defense, I am teaching social welfare and social justice in a sociology department at a state university. While I had a couple of articles in the works, which meant limited external pressure to immediately begin a new research project, I had my own internal pressure to move on to something exciting, deeply relevant, and completely in line with my own ethical perspective related to being the "researcher." Unbeknownst to me, I had begun my own "race to duty" which I continue to struggle with six years later.

I was ready to move away from the DV field after ten years of work on the ground and close to five years of DV research. I was burnt out with what felt like repetitive (but pertinent) critiques and my own sense that the movement had become stagnant and co-opted by the criminal justice system. I needed something new and inspiring, yet what I had "known" for 15 years was DV. Confronted with all the fears of "not knowing," I decided to pick up where I left off with my dissertation—white privilege. I knew that, right? I was white. I could be an "insider." So what about my whiteness? I knew that what I was passionate about was social movements, framing, and how power co-opts movements. What discouraged me about the DV movement became an impetus to uncover ways that white privilege could be dismantled in the context of a movement. I found a local organization created to address white privilege—what drew me to the organization was the subgroup devoted to white antiracist activism. I thought this would be a perfect fit for me so I began to attend monthly meetings. I decided right away that if I were going to formulate some sort of research that would center this organization and/or members, I would need to be part of the organization myself. I boxed myself into thinking the only research I could ethically engage in was research in which I was truly an insider, which begs the question—when are we "truly" insiders, except perhaps in our own lives?

I dutifully attended meetings for about 18 months. While I respected the mission and many of the members, I felt frustrated and impatient early on. I felt critical of some of the members and the process, which often seemed like a once-a-month "feel good" experience where white people examine privilege and then go home. I was anxious to gain trust and become more involved with the activist subgroup, so I buried my frustration and forced myself to attend month after month. I eventually became more central to the activist group and, as a member of a small core of people, began to attend weekly planning meetings. While I clearly was experiencing some dissonance, I was also feeling enthusiasm for the potential of the group and the potential for research about the work being done. The meetings were focused and goal-oriented in terms of base building and engaging the white antiracist community to become more of a presence in local and national activism.

Unfortunately, after six to eight months the core group of the three began to be pulled in a variety of directions. While, for some, personal and professional commitments called, I wonder if we would have made more headway if we had stayed energized and found a way to continue with the workgroup? I know for myself that I was feeling discouraged and that I did not think I could sustain my own momentum alone and so I left the group.

Insider Avoidance

Around this time, a situation arose that led to another small research project. When I proposed a name change from "social welfare" to "social welfare and social justice" for the concentration that I coordinate, I naively presumed it would be viewed as a positive and timely change. The impetus for this stemmed from my desire to have the name reflect a broader macro perspective. For me, social welfare tends to evoke concepts of direct service provision, primarily to individuals and families—temporary measures to provide aid and support. While I have over ten years' experience in direct micro and mezzo practice, my teaching focuses on macro/structural issues and I was hoping the name change would be more inclusive and more dynamic. The proposal received a mixed response—from support, to lack of interest, to questions about whether it would have a negative impact on students. The questioners asked for data about the impact—what would social workers and agencies in the area think about the change? So I set out to see for myself. Once again, I protected myself from ethical conundrums—I had practiced in social services for many years and had a

PhD in social work and social research so I felt the "good enough" insider and admittedly did not even consider the issue relevant in this study. This is not to say it was a non-issue, yet by asking social workers and other social service professionals to examine the relevance of social justice in their work, something I have been doing since I began teaching, I felt my bases were covered as an insider in the field and so I did not struggle with questions about whether it was "appropriate" for me to proceed with the study.

At this point I had three projects either completed or in the works—two were grounded in social change work and my "insiderness" in relation to the field and one was a small media analysis project I had conveniently partitioned off from ethical concerns. Perhaps important to note, I felt much more inspired by my DV research than the other three projects and was itching for something to really sink my teeth into and to prove to myself that I could find a viable project. The identity I had capitalized on was my professional identity in the DV field and in social change work. To a lesser degree, I relied on my cis-gender female identity given the weight and importance that gender plays in DV work. My whiteness was an important consideration and I attempted to be cognizant of this through attention to white privilege in the DV movement.

Multiple Identities, Multiple Attempts

With the crystallizing of my own queer identity came the next foray into research as I began to prioritize queerness and the lesbian, gay, bisexual, transgender, queer, questioning, intersex (LGBTQQI) communit(ies). There was a series of false starts as projects lay fallow. These projects included an ethnographic examination of privilege in gay pride celebrations; the influence of US evangelicals in Uganda and other African nations on recent anti-gay fervor/legislation; a narrative/oral history of local pre-Stonewall LGBT social movement events; and an ethnography about faux queens. While I don't believe I am an insider solely because of my queer identity, it felt like a starting place and tapped into my interests. I had plans to highlight power and privilege in all the projects so I would not only be bringing my queerness to the table, I would be bringing my white privilege, my cis-gender privilege, my gender oppression, and so on. Easier said than done, of course. The core struggle at play in all of these ghosts-of-proposed-projects-past is the insider/ outsider dichotomy that plagues me and the challenge to find ways to move beyond the "bipolar construction of insider/outsider," which "sets up a false separation that neglects the interactive processes through which 'insiderness' and 'outsiderness' are constructed" (Naples, 2003, p. 373).

Beyond the False Separation

I am left pondering how I will begin to develop my next project with a commitment to work through this "false separation" and create a critical feminist research project that feels authentic and relevant so I can sustain it through to completion. While there has been a plethora of theorizing about the position of researchers and the relevance of the insider and outsider dichotomy (Atkinson & Hammersley, 1994; Merton, 1972; Naples, 2003), the dialogue often polarizes positionality. Voices have entered into the conversation to question this polarity and raise the issue of the complexity and fluidity of social locations (Banks, 1998; Collins, 2008; Merton, 1972; Naples, 2003), yet there continues to be a preponderance of material examining a more simplistic insider/outsider binary. I have found myself falling into the lure of that simplistic position myself as I struggle to engage in ethical critical feminist queer research.

One schema that could aid in breaking down this false separation can be found in a continuum such as Banks' "typology of crosscultural researchers" which defines the indigenous insider, the indigenous outsider, the external insider, and the external outsider (1998, pp. 7–8). While a typology is simply a tool for reflexivity, since our positions on this continuum can shift depending on context and history, it does allow for a critical reflection regarding power and relationships to individuals and communities of interest.

To further problematize the dilemma, questions about the meaning of indigenous, community, and whose voice is privileged and "authentic" continue to be raised within various communities of researchers (Brown & Strega, 2005; Smith, 2012). For example, to prioritize indigenous knowledge then begs the question about essentializing indigenous knowledge and collectivizing that which should be viewed as unique. Claiming an "indigenous identity" can also be a colonizing tool, co-opted by the dominant (Smith, 2012). While Linda Tuhiwai Smith situates her discussion of indigenous identities within the context of colonized peoples, the concept as Banks defines indigenous insider/outsider is expanded to include a variety of communities and cultures and the attendant beliefs, attitudes, knowledge, and perspectives that are dominant within the community (Banks, 1998). For myself, the appeal of this type of schema lies primarily in the expansion of the concept of insider/outsider position to make room for fluidity and as a reminder that, whether our position(s) are inside or outside, they are multilayered and need continual examination from the start of a project through to completion.

I have continued to confront what feel like rehashed theoretical and epistemological debates through my immobilization and insider avoidance. As I find some sort of solace in the intersectional spaces and overlaps, and seek out theory that suits these proclivities, it has become quite clear that the *doing* of these theories in terms of my positionality has been my *undoing* up to now. This tension continues to play itself out as I begin my next research project on pansexuality. I continue to question the ways in which I can and cannot claim insiderness and whether that is actually useful or whether it has become a worn-out relic that needs to be refashioned. I think of Plummer's (2011) use of Ulrich Beck's "zombie categories" when he speaks of "zombie research"—reusing categories (and methodology) from the past that is worn out and "masks a different reality behind them" (p. x). I hesitate to claim that the insider/outsider conceptualizations and their attendant typologies such as Banks' typology are truly zombie categories. I strongly believe we need to continually evaluate the multiple ways that our positionality influences our research. Highlighting power and privilege may serve as a platform for critical reflexivity while acknowledging Naples' (2003) interactive process and the fluidity by which our positions are constituted.

Notes

1 As I read this close to seven years after writing, I find myself flinch at the use of the term. "Caucasian"—a term I have come to wholeheartedly reject given its racist origins.
2 Italicized material comes from my dissertation (Morgaine, 2007).

References

Ahmed, S. (2004). Declarations of whiteness: The non-performativity of anti-racism. *Borderlands, 3* (2), 1–19.
Ali, S. (2006). Racializing research: Managing power and politics? *Ethnic and Racial Studies, 29* (3), 471–486.
Atkinson, P. & Hammersley, M. (1994). Ethnography and participant observation. In N.K. Denzin & Y.S. Lincoln (Eds.), *The handbook of qualitative research* (pp. 248–261). Thousand Oaks, CA: Sage.
Banks, J. A. (1998). The lives and values of researchers: Implications for educating citizens in a multicultural society. *Educational Researcher, 27* (7), 4–17.
Brown, L. & Strega, S. (2005). *Research as resistance: Critical, indigenous, and anti-oppressive approaches.* Toronto: Canadian Scholars' Press.
Collins, P. H. (2008). *Black feminist thought: Knowledge, consciousness, and the politics of empowerment.* New York: Routledge.
Daley, A. (2010). Reflections on reflexivity and critical reflection as critical research practices. *Affilia, 25* (1), 68–82.
Denzin, N. (2006). Analytical autoethnography, or déjà vu all over again. *Journal of Contemporary Ethnography, 35* (4), 419–428.
Denzin, N. & Lincoln, Y. S. (2011). *The handbook of qualitative research* (4th ed.). Thousand Oaks, CA: Sage.
Dyer, R. (1997). *White.* New York: Routledge.
Essed, P. (1991). *Understanding everyday racism: An interdisciplinary theory.* Newbury Park, CA: Sage.
Fellows, M. L. & Razack, S. (1998). The race to innocence: Confronting hierarchical relations among women. *The Journal of Gender, Race & Justice, 1,* 335–352.
Fine, M., Weis, L., Powell, L. C., & Wong, L. M. (1997). *Off white: Readings on race, power, and society.* New York: Routledge.
Foley, D. F. (2002). Critical ethnography: The reflexive turn. *International Journal of Qualitative Studies in Education, 15* (5), 469–490.
Fox, C. (2002). The race to the truth: Disarticulating critical thinking from whiteliness. *Pedagogy: Critical Approaches to Teaching Literature, Language, Composition, and Culture, 2* (2), 197–212.
Frankenberg, R. (1993). *White women, race matters: The social construction of whiteness.* Minneapolis: University of Minnesota Press.
Frankenberg, R. (1997). Introduction: Local whiteness, localizing whiteness. In R. Frankenberg (Ed.), *Displacing whiteness: Essays in social and cultural criticism* (pp. 1–33). Durham, NC: Duke University Press.

Fraser, N. (1997). *Justice interruptus: Critical reflections on the "postsocialist" condition.* New York: Routledge.

Fraser, N. & Nicolson, L. (1988). Social criticism without philosophy: An encounter between feminism and postmodernism. *Theory, Culture & Society, 5,* 373–394.

Frye, M. (1992). *Willful virgin: Essays in feminism: 1976–1992.* Freedom, CA: Crossing.

Hill, R. (2004). Institutional racism in child welfare. *Race & Society, 7*(1), 17–33.

hooks, b. (1989). Critical interrogation: Talking race, resisting racism (Reprinted, with minor revisions, from *Art Forum,* May 1989, 18–20.) Retrieved on February 28, 2013 from http://culturalstudies.ucsc.edu/PUBS/Inscriptions/vol_5/bellhooks.html

hooks, b. (1990). *Yearning: Race, gender, and cultural politics.* Boston: South End Press.

Hurtado, A. & Stewart, A. J. (1997). Through the looking glass: Implications of studying whiteness for feminist methods. In M. Fine, L. Weis, L. C. Powell, and L. M. Wong (Eds.), *Off white: Readings on race, power, and society* (pp. 297–311). New York: Routledge.

Incite! Women of Color against Violence. (2006). *Color of violence: The INCITE! anthology.* Cambridge, MA: South End Press.

Keating, A. (1995). Interrogating "whiteness," (de)constructing "race." *College English, 57* (8), 901–918.

Merton, R. K. (1972). Insiders and outsiders: A chapter in the sociology of knowledge. *American Journal of Sociology, 78* (1), 9–47.

Morgaine, K. (2007). *Creative interpretation and fluidity in a rights framework: The intersection of domestic violence and human rights in the United States.* (Doctoral dissertation). Retrieved from ProQuest. (3343775).

Morgaine, K. (2009). 'You can't bite the hand that feeds you': The state, domestic violence and human rights. *Affilia, 24* (1), 31–43.

Morgaine, K. (2011). 'How would that help our work?' Domestic violence and human rights on the ground. *Violence Against Women, 17* (1), 6–27.

Morrison, T. (1992). *Playing in the dark.* New York: Vintage.

Naples, N. (2003). *Feminism and method.* New York: Routledge.

O'Brien, E. (2001). *Whites confront racism: Antiracists and their paths to action.* New York: Rowman & Littlefield.

Olesen, V. L. (2011). Feminist qualitative research in the millennium's first decade: Developments, challenges, prospects. In N. K. Denzin & Y. S. Lincoln (Eds.), *Handbook of qualitative research* (4th ed.) (pp. 129–146). Thousand Oaks, CA: Sage.

Plummer, K. (2011). Critical humanism and queer theory: Living with the tensions. In N. Denzin & Y. S. Lincoln (Eds.), *The handbook of qualitative research* (4th ed.) (pp. 195–212). Thousand Oaks, CA: Sage.

Pratt, M. B. (1984). Identity: skin blood heart. In E. Bulkin, M. B. Pratt, & B. Smith (Eds.), *Yours in struggle: three feminist perspectives on anti-semitism and racism.* New York: Long Haul Press.

Ramazanoglu, C. & Holland, J. (2002). *Feminist methodologies: Challenges and choices.* New York: Routledge.

Roberts, D. (2002). *Shattered bonds: The color of child welfare.* New York: Basic Civitas Books.

Smith, L. T. (2012). *Decolonizing methodologies: Research and indigenous peoples.* New York: Zed Books.

Wahab, S., Anderson-Nathe, B., & Gringeri, C. (2012). Joining the conversation: Social work contributions to feminist research. In S. Hesse-Biber (Ed.), *Handbook of feminist research* (pp. 455–474). Thousand Oaks, CA: Sage.

15 Critical Feminist Social Work and the Queer Query

Jen Self

Critical Feminist Social Work and the Queer Query

Social and economic justice through practice is at the core of the social work tradition. While attending to the needs of historically marginalized communities is fundamental to our discipline's practice, research, and pedagogy, revealing and resisting logics of dominance are equally important. Complementing social work, critical queer and feminist scholarship illuminates and unsettles these logics that operate at every level of culture. As a critical queer feminist social work scholar/activist and practitioner, I build upon assertions (Anderson-Nathe, Gringeri, & Wahab, 2013; Wahab, Anderson-Nathe, & Gringeri, 2012) that social work's efforts to unveil and disrupt systems of power should extend into and through our intervention strategies. To that end, critical queer feminist research/praxis is a vital and productive tool to reveal, analyze, and interrupt dominant oppressive and normalizing systems (capitalism, racism, sexism, heterosexism, etc.) entrenched within social work research and practice. Using one example of critical queer feminist social work research, this chapter demonstrates the utility of such approaches and argues for more critically reflexive social work research and praxis, which calls into question normalizing practices and intervention strategies inherent to social work scholarship.

In this chapter, I develop this central argument and discuss its application in five sections. First, I outline a critique of social work as a normalizing practice, extending the work of feminist social work scholars (Fook, 2002; Gringeri, Wahab, & Anderson-Nathe, 2010; Orme, 2003). Second, I provide a broad overview of the study *Queering Queer Space* to set the context for the rest of the chapter. Third, I expand upon the critical queer feminist underpinnings of my study and its utility to social work at large. In the fourth section, I enumerate four concrete recommendations drawn from my scholarly process: (1) make transparent your guiding assumptions; (2) engage in critical reflexivity throughout the research project; (3) ask questions that interrogate norms; and (4) be methodologically creative. Concluding this chapter are insights, opportunities, and a call to the field for more critically reflexive social work research and praxis.

Social Work Research as a Normalizing Practice

US-based social work research and practice emphasize the conflicts, challenges, and needs of historically marginalized peoples. Yet social work primarily embraces positivism, an epistemology rooted in the scientific method of the European Enlightenment and entrenched within academia. Positivist research is understood as objective, without a politic, and assumes a privileged status within academia, thereby authenticated and normed as *research*. Consequently, positivist social work researchers and practitioners infrequently make transparent their epistemological assumptions, which legitimizes the hidden normative assumptions embedded within their research projects. Disciplinary disconnects between theory, social work scholarship, and practice (Fook, 2002; Orme, 2003; Wahab et al., 2012), combined with professionally and institutionally supported positivist research approaches, further strain tenuous links between critical theorization, knowledge production, and socially transformative praxis. In this context, social work research exerts considerable regulatory power through knowledge production and intervention strategies, which seems antithetical to our charge of social and economic justice (Wahab et al., 2012).

Similar to countless social work scholars/practitioners, social work's core value of social justice drew me to this field. Like so many of my colleagues, I experience frustration with our discipline's atheoretical leanings, disconnects between social work research, practice, and critical social theories, and our complicity with normalizing intervention strategies. Returning to graduate school after having worked for a decade as a queer activist, therapist, intimate partner violence advocate, and anti-oppression educator, this frustration felt particularly pronounced. While working toward a doctorate, I directed my university's gender and sexuality resource center, situating myself as a practitioner, burgeoning scholar, and educator. As founding director of the Q Center at the University of Washington, I had the rare opportunity to set and implement, with the collaboration of queerly minded students, faculty, and staff, a critically theorized and reflexive (given constraints of the institution) space. I was intellectually and theoretically challenged by the work of my doctoral colleagues, our first-year coursework focused almost entirely upon critical theory, and daily I connected with queer and trans* students who understood their multiply intersecting identifications as fluid amid pervasive dominant constraints of essentialized, binary categories. In this confluence, I found collegial support, institutional approval (enough), and motivation to engage a critical queer feminist interpretive study.

The Study: Queering Queer Space

Lesbian, gay, bisexual, transgender (LGBT) centers are culture jammers, defying dominant logics simply through their anti-heterosexist work. Yet, these arenas are not immune to or excused from replicating normalized interlocking systems of oppression. In this scenario, I engaged in a critical queer[1] feminist methodological study grounded in critical reflexivity. I interrogated the power and influence of LGBT centers' directors and other primary leaders by exploring how dominance in the form of "homonormative whiteness" was interrupted, resisted, and/or (re)produced discursively and spatially. Further, I analyzed the tensions that arose as center practitioners operationalized social transformation policy and praxis models while maintaining their core purpose of safety and respite from heterosexism and cis-sexism. To explore these issues, I undertook a modified extended case study of six campus centers. The data included in-depth interviews with directors and center leaders, researcher observations, photographs, hand-drawn mental maps created by center leaders, and my reflexive observations and interpretations. With critical queer feminism as my methodological foundation, the study was interpretive with specific analytic strategies that included critical discourse analysis (CDA) and spatial analysis of the interview transcripts, mental maps drawn by the participants, and the physical spaces of the centers.

Critical Queer Feminism

Critical queer feminism blends queer theory and feminisms to deconstruct racialized gender binaries and interrupt layered systems of oppression in both discourse and material realities (such as the US beauty standard or heterosexism). While some queer and feminist scholars have articulated clear distinctions between the theoretical fields, I developed my feminism and queerness within and through one another. As a gender-transgressing child of the 1970s, primarily parented by a newly feminist mother, I faced the cultural and interpersonal policing associated with discursive categories of gender, sex, and sexual orientation, as well as the material consequences of being female-bodied and gender-transgressing. Now, I claim both queer and feminist as personal, political, and professional descriptors and deploy them as politics of liberation/transformation, positioning myself in relationship to interrelated systems of power in my scholarship and praxis, and throughout my life. This discernment of one's relationship to systems of power and privilege is crucial to a critical queer feminist epistemology.

In essence, critical queer feminist scholarship reveals and disrupts heteropatriarchal power, which is inherently tied to the normalizing of whiteness (Ferguson, 2004; Frankenberg, 1993; Kobayashi & Peake, 2000; Muñoz, 1999; Smith, 2009; Ward, 2008). I attribute much of this learning to women of color feminisms, which have provided the bedrock foundation for my understanding of interlocking systems of oppression, multiple situated truths, the partial nature of research, and our (academics') frequent complicity with marginalizing, minoritizing, and oppressive institutions and processes. Patricia Hill Collins' (1990) groundbreaking *Black Feminist Thought: Knowledge, Consciousness and Pedagogy* describes how systems of oppression are constituted, articulates how negative stereotypes of Black women are produced and replicated, and presents an epistemology of liberation through critical consciousness and Black feminist intellectualism. Second, Cathy Cohen (1997/2005) articulated a radical vision of queer feminism, calling for a new queer consciousness with an intersectional analysis of regulation and policing through interconnected systems of oppression. Finally, Andrea Smith (2009), in a piece written specifically for women of color organizing, delineates heteropatriarchy and the three pillars of white supremacy: (1) slavery/capitalism; (2) genocide/colonization; and (3) orientalism/war, illustrating the multiple ways in which racism and white supremacy are enacted. These theorists inform how I understand myself as a benefactor of White supremacy and colonialism, illustrate clear and radical logics to deconstruct systematized oppression, and articulate how normalizing discourses control and harm all marginalized peoples. Consequently, critical queer feminism is my epistemological approach to scholarship, pedagogy, and practice.

Methodological Choices and Challenges

Informed by these theoretical foundations, I learned a number of central methodological lessons from the methodological choices and challenges I encountered during my investigation of LGBT campus centers. I present these here in the form of recommendations for other social work researchers hoping to engage critical queer feminisms in their work.

Make Transparent Your Guiding Assumptions

Critical queer feminist research situates the researcher within the project, requiring critical reflexivity and transparency in terms of the researcher's assumptions and orientation to the project. For me, a central assumption is that people's knowledge of reality is socially produced. Some feminisms and poststructuralism assert that universal "Truth" does not exist; rather "truth" is produced through discourse and the melding of power/knowledge (Foucault, 1977). Certain "truths" are legitimized via power/knowledge while others are delegitimized. Subsequently, though an essential "truth" cannot exist, material realities from discursively produced structures (such as interlocking systems of oppression) exist and persist. In other words, though racism is fundamentally produced through discourse, it is expressed tangibly and structurally, with real material consequences. In this way, discourse produces the object it purports to address (Foucault, 1977; Hall, 1997). For instance, the gender binary, as described by Butler (2004), is not merely discursive; the discourse itself produces gendered bodies that either conform to or refute it. Given that gender and sexuality are inextricably enmeshed with the construction of race, both are always racialized (Barnard, 2003; Collins, 2000; Crenshaw, 1991; Foucault, 1980; Fox,

2007; Kumashiro, 2001; Somerville, 1997). For example, the dominant US beauty standards for women, which privilege blond women with long hair (as recently repeated by my six-year-old daughter), indicate that women are beautiful if they are "feminine" and white.

Following poststructualist thought, I hold that nothing is free from the workings of power and discourse. Consequently, all knowledge is interpretive and conditional, and operates in relation to regulatory norms (Ronquillo, 2008). Attending to the multiple levels of power is of utmost importance to the reflexivity, clarity, and integrity of one's study. This attention renders the position of researcher as neither value-neutral nor objective. Critical queer feminist interpretive research is a subjective process with clearly stated political intentions, primarily to expose and interrogate dominant power. Finally, in this type of research, researchers must reveal their biases; it was crucial in my study to reveal my status as a director of an LGBT campus center, as that certainly influenced every part of the project.

Engage in Critical Reflexivity Throughout the Research Project

Critical reflexivity throughout research, pedagogy, and practice is essentially to understand the ways in which social work researchers and practitioners (re)produce the very sources of injustice we seek to disrupt (Marinucci, 2010; Nieto, 2010; Orme, 2003). This is a key utilitarian feature of queer feminist research: to render evident the intractable heteropatriarchal norms pervasive in positivist social work theorizing, research, and practice. Framing our research through critical reflexivity extends to all aspects of one's study, from defining parameters, to delineating the research questions, to methodological choices, through analysis, and to reporting conclusions and implications. In this section, I provide concrete examples of critical reflexivity from the study.

Positionality

When the University of Washington hired me as the director, fewer than 150 LGBT centers existed on college campuses across the United States. Campus centers were born of resistance to heterosexism and developed in response to calls for greater institutional responsiveness to violence and discrimination against those who transgress heterogender normativity (National Consortium of Higher Education LGBT Resource Professionals, 2013). Unsurprisingly, as direct outcomes of the US gay pride movement, campus centers developed primarily through an essentialized identity-based framework that conceptualized "gayness" as unified and fixed, constituting a broad-enough experience to define a community regardless of race, class, gender, or other subjectivities (Barnard, 2003; Cohen, 1997/2005). From the vantage point of critical queer feminism, I saw campus-based LGBT centers in need of coherent theorization leading to practice that is more responsive to multiply positioned/marginalized constituents. Centers relied too heavily upon outmoded essentialized identity politics and research that reproduced normalizing power regimes (racism, cis-sexism, and classism). These observations and critiques fueled my development of the Q Center and the framing of my research. In theorizing the Q Center, I turned to the thinking of feminists of color (Cohen, 1997/2005; Hill Collins, 1990, 2000; hooks, 1990; Lorde, 1984; Razack, 1999/2001/2006), queer theorists (Butler, 2004; Duggan, 2003; Ferguson, 2004), and critical social workers, psychologists, and educators (Bonilla-Silva, 2010; DiAngelo, 2004; Kumashiro, 2001; Nieto & Boyer, 2006). However, my identities impelled both a passion for queer academic and service work as well as privileged my ability to pursue these interests.

Though marked "other" by cultural signifiers such as queer, gender-queer and non-apparently disabled, I also hold a number of privileged positionalities. I am a US-born, white, non-indigenous adult who was raised in an upper-middle-class family and had ample access to higher education. I repeatedly positioned myself throughout the study process, whether in relationship to my dissertation committee, the study participants, colleagues, or the students with whom I worked at the center I directed. While my identity markers did not fluctuate throughout the research process, my relationship to dominant power changed from situation to situation. For example, when relating to my university administrators and dissertation committee, I experienced less influential power than when I interviewed study participants. Though I was a colleague of the participants, I was also a researcher with the power to analyze and make determinations about their contributions. My committee, however, had a similar power to analyze and make determinations about my contributions.

Consequently, I caution against understanding positionalities as fixed to time and space; rather, they are fluid and mobile. It is tempting to essentialize the "self" and exclude analysis of how one's positions are (re)constituted throughout the various parts of a study (Swarr & Nagar, 2010). As a researcher, I am never external to the power systems I seek to reveal and disrupt; thus, I easily recognize myself as squarely within the larger discourses of positivism, postmodernism, liberation and racial, sexual, gender, and class binaries. During my study, in this chapter, and in my work in general, I strive to challenge these logics while still attending to my positions within them.

Ethics

Throughout the study, I faced ethical questions at nearly every stage. Often, I faced difficult and challenging questions given my multiple positionalities and competing interests. As a somewhat marginalized, queer feminist scholar within a Research I institution, conducting research on queer spaces with privately raised funding, I had limited time, financial resources, and institutional support for my work. However, I did have strong support from my committee chair, Susan Kemp, a highly respected feminist social work scholar and ally. Further, I had created tight networks of scholarly and emotional support with my friends and colleagues, who were primarily marginalized scholars. To complicate matters, my daughter was two years old and becoming more active and engaged, my partner had been working as an oncology nurse for 14 years and was experiencing compassion fatigue, and I was in the midst of a severe metabolic disruption that caused extreme exhaustion, lethargy, and problems with concentration.

In the midst of these circumstances, I made choices, many in alignment with my critical queer feminist epistemology and some more aligned with a pragmatic need to finish my dissertation quickly. For instance, I considered whether to maintain the confidentiality of the study sites. All were public universities, public spaces, and public employees answering questions and engaging in activities to be expected of someone in their position. Nevertheless, I ultimately erred on the side of maintaining confidentiality. I did so for a number of reasons but primarily because that choice allowed for an exempt Institutional Review Board application, meaning that it took one day for approval versus weeks to months. This choice, made in an effort to speed my process along, had consequences for my study. This meant that I could only present data in the aggregate, rather than specify to a particular geographic location and/or person. It meant that I was less able to take into account the positionalities of the leaders of the centers, something I think is incredibly important in terms of the philosophical and practical choices they made. Further, this choice made it virtually impossible to speak to the internal politics and struggles of each center without the centers being identifiable to other professionals in the field.

I share this information to illustrate that a great many factors influence our research choices. I would love to say that my politics and commitment to a critical queer feminist methodology were unwavering, yet that simply is not the case. At all times, I weighed the costs and benefits of my health, the emotional, financial, and physical stress of graduate school, my family's wellbeing, institutional limitations, funding limitations, my internalized oppression, the importance of my political and heart commitments, and my connection to and support of colleagues and friends. Having declared this, I can say unequivocally that at every juncture I did the best I could do in the moment to make decisions in alignment with a critical queer feminist methodological frame.

Ask Questions That Interrogate Norms

In my experience, identifying the research question and aims is more than half the hike. I was committed to developing a study that did not focus on identities, the needs of marginalized communities, or how to serve better populations that did not align with the privileged norms. These types of studies are important but rarely address social work's adherence to normalizing interventions. I was intent upon asking questions that deconstructed systems of power rather than focusing on how marginalized communities respond to oppression. Additionally, I wanted to contribute to a different body of knowledge which could provide deep, nuanced insight into the (re)production of homonormativity (Andrade, 2009). To that end, my primary inquiries were:

1   How was resistance to/(re)production of homonormative whiteness embodied and engendered in the space of LGBT campus centers?
2   How did LGBT campus centers resist/(re)produce homonormative whiteness discursively and programmatically?
3   What were the tensions and new questions for praxis (if any) that arose as campus centers acted as sites of resistance, anti-oppression, and social transformation?

In coming to these questions, I first interrogated myself. What were my spheres of influence? What were my commitments, to whom, and to what? What were the limitations over which I had no control; e.g., structure and format of a dissertation, what counts as rigorous scholarship in the academy? What were my personal limitations (length of time I wanted to spend, family concerns, timing my graduation to coincide with ideal work transitions)? Each consideration played a factor, not only in the question formulation, but also throughout the entire research process. Many of my answers were not clear-cut or simple due to what felt like competing interests. For instance, I was committed to the efforts of LGBT campus resource centers. Yet, I was about to embark on what I feared might be viewed as a vicious attack on their practices due to the focus of the study and my chosen analytic strategy of CDA. Call it internalized dominance, heterosexism, cis-sexism, or just wanting my colleagues to like me, I worried nonetheless. I wondered: Could I be the loyal critic? Would I feel protective of my colleagues? Would I be overly critical of my colleagues? Would I be seduced by the impossible notion that my own practices were free of homonormative whiteness?

The answer to all of these questions was yes. At one point or another, I experienced each of these concerns. As a practitioner and activist who knew from experience that LGBT spaces reinforced dominant cultural norms, I remained anchored in my concerns as to how such spaces, including mine, were complicit with the (re)production of homonormativity. My commitments—to colleagues, constituents, and other activists—held me accountable to my multiple roles as a scholar, practitioner, educator, and activist invested in deconstructing and disrupting dominant norms with the intent of retheorizing a critical praxis for queer[2] spaces. With these concerns in mind, I investigated the dialogic and spatial praxis of LGBT centers and leadership.

Be Methodologically Creative

While every piece of one's methodological approach is important, I cover two specific parts of the methodology: data collection methods and analytic strategy. These steps caused me the most concern throughout the study process. I had misgivings about the number of sites I visited. Was six sites enough for an interpretive study? I questioned whether I should conduct interviews. If yes, how would I manage them? How would my management affect the answers provided by the participants? I worried about the privileging of some forms of discourse (interview transcripts, mental maps, photographs) over others (websites, brochures). I wondered if my choice of CDA would do more violence to the interview narratives than illuminate power structures. Would my interpretations and critiques of the interviews and maps simply be decontextualized misinterpretations? With every misgiving, I engaged in conversation with my committee chair and colleagues, talking through my apprehensions and devising strategies for mitigating the concerns. For instance, I checked my interpretations against those of my committee chair. I consulted with a geographer to consider how to analyze the mental maps. While some of these strategies seemed to have a modernist bent and to be at odds with my epistemological assumptions, I used them as tools to keep my bearings. Additionally, the ongoing conversations I had with my chair and colleague circle were critical to my own reflexive process as well as presenting me with opportunities to speak back to institutional power and shape the dissertation structure, in particular by developing innovative methods.

Innovative Methods Capture Untapped Data (Mental Mapping)

bell hooks' (1990) work framing homeplaces and margins as sites of refuge and resistance, coupled with Nancy Fraser's (1990) description of counterpublics as subversive public spheres created by marginalized groups, led me to study physical and metaphorical space. Space directly intertwined with my core research questions, given both critical and queer epistemological understandings of space as socially produced through processes of negotiation and contestation regarding power/knowledge (Knopp, 2007; Oswin, 2008; Valentine, 2002). Critical geographers theorize space as fluid, multiple, and always being made and unmade (Knopp, 2007). Space, materially, affectively, and discursively, develops within and through the (re)production or resistance of dominant power systems, such as white homonormativity. Further, space refuses stagnation, changing moment to moment via relationship to social and discursive processes. LGBT centers are everchanging spaces because their structures are in constant dialogue with their universities, constituents, and staff. I wanted to capture the spatial dynamics of the centers through a number of different methods, one of which was mental mapping.

Mental mapping is used frequently in psychology and geography to study cognitive orientation and spatial behavior (Downs & Stea, 1977; Gould & White, 1974; Lynch, 1950; Sommer & Aitkens, 1982) and by therapists to help people represent how they internalize the external world into their emotional schema (Diem-Wille, 2001). As part of a semi-structured interview, I asked participants to draw their maps literally, figuratively, metaphorically, or in any way in which "their brain worked" to think about these spatial relationships. I provided all participants with the same materials to create their maps and prompted the participants with the following suggestions:

Map and space: Draw a map of the center:

1 On your map, please draw another map of how you and your center interact with various communities of people. You can talk about this either while you are drawing or explain to me after you have completed your drawing. Tell me about who these people are.

2 On the map write or draw or indicate the kinds of pressures/ challenges (institutionally, socially, culturally) they are dealing with daily. On this same map draw how you and your center interact with these various pressures/challenges. You can talk about this either while you are drawing or explain to me after you have completed your drawing.

3 Please talk about the center space, its functions, different aspects, rooms, decorations, etc.

   Talk about how you decided what went on the walls, colors, furniture

   Books in the library

   Your physicality in the space

4 Tell me about the center as a space. What is the center space?

   Tell me about the importance of this space.

   Why? For whom?

   What does the space provide? Both in tangible services but also in intangible qualities.

Mental mapping gave me an innovative glimpse into the participants' understandings and accounts of the center space and their relationships to constituents, communities, intervention practices, and systems of power (Self, 2010). Additionally, the participants conveyed different information graphically and spatially than they did verbally. The mental map shown in Figure 15.1 was drawn by a center director who spoke about their center[3] as a refuge, a place of safety in a politically conservative climate.

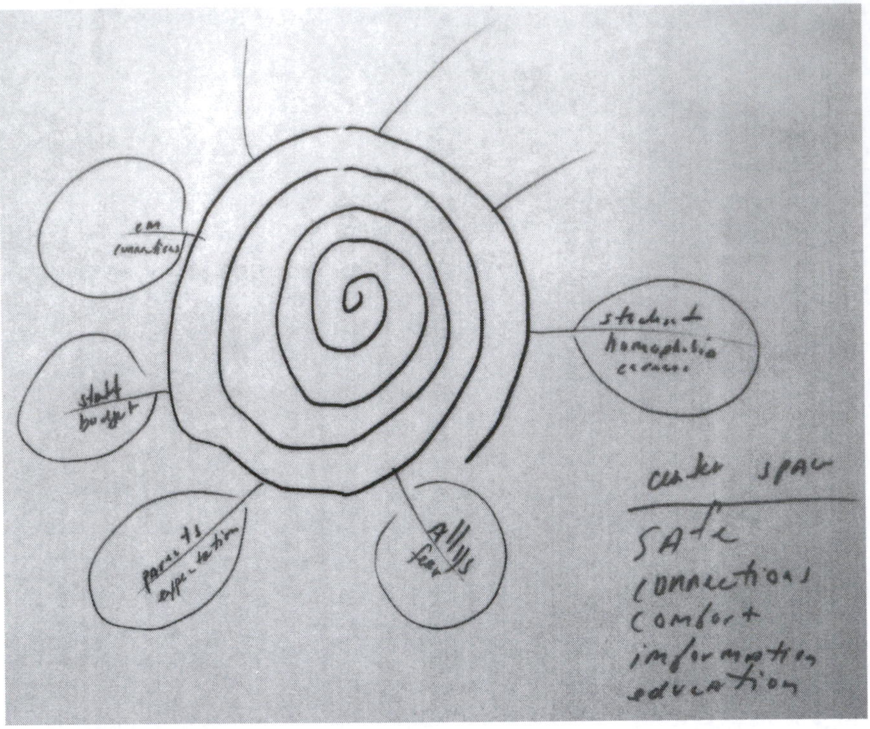

Figure 15.1

While the map could be interpreted as spiraling inward, with a focus on safety, comfort, and refuge from the outside world, it also clearly depicts a spiral with ray-like lines extending from its exterior. A common shape in nature, often associated with the sun, solstice events, evolution, and migration, ancient Chinese art, and petroglyphs, spirals hold what many believe is universal symbolic meaning. The director's symbolic representation seemed to transmit these meanings of evolution, sun/center of the universe, and light, meanings encouraged by the rays extending out from the active spiral. This particular map conveyed an active, evolving space of central importance to its constituents. This dynamic representation is a provocative example of how this method allowed me to access different information.

Critical Discourse Analysis

CDA is a purposeful and decisive strategy to reveal and disrupt systemic power. Rooted in progressive social change and emancipatory knowledge, CDA blends analysis and operation (Fairclough, 2001). That is, a finite goal of CDA is to move from critique to action to demystify, reveal, raise consciousness, and emancipate. CDA requires the analyst to take a position on social problems, social/cultural power relations, and discursive structures that do ideological work (Wodak & Fairclough, 1997). Feminist and other critical discourse analysts have asserted that CDA is inherently reflexive, given that it is a critical methodology with assumptions about the productive powers of language and that any CDA must "implicitly constitute itself as constructed from the effects of language, or risk incoherence" (Rose, 2007, p. 148). A fundamental assumption of my study was that all queer people living in the United States inherently have relationships to the discursive power structures of homonormative whiteness. Further, I recognized throughout my research the inescapable fact of discourse and that I would surely "present [my] discourse through the structure that [I was] critiquing" (Spivak, 1989, p. 214). Hence, reflexivity played a heavy role in my CDA process (see example below).

An important aspect of the way in which I approached CDA was through deconstruction. One central assumption of poststructuralism is a hierarchical linguistic structuring of common binaries—such as male/female or straight/gay—which privileges one term as the original or center of the system and the other known only in relation to the first (Derrida, 1976). Deconstruction thus examines text closely for these signs of privileging, places of paradox, and/or contradictions. Reading for the places of privileging, deconstruction interrogates what is often accepted as "normal" or "natural" and reveals that these normalizing processes privilege and subordinate simultaneously. Further, Derrida asserted that all text was contestable and, while clearly powerful, also unstable and vulnerable. Within that instability, I brought the narratives, the discursive structures of the mental maps, and the spatiality of the centers into question or crisis (Butler, 2004).

To offer an example of the analytic process using both the mental maps and participant narrative, I provide two maps drawn by the Director and Assistant Director at an East Coast university (Figure 15.2) (Self, 2010).

Interviewed independently, the Director and the Assistant Director both drew seemingly isolated, difficult to reach, dangerous to access, and disconnected representations of their center space. The Director explained that their drawing depicted the center as surrounded by a moat (complete with a couple of sharks) with access to the space by way of a single bridge. When asked to describe the sharks, they made the following comments:

> Oh, just the difficulties for someone to get assistance to cross over, you know, the fears that people have. And I think that's one of the misperceptions that still, just something that's out there because people see that there's more resources available. There's the internet. There's images in pop culture of people who are out that means so that it's easy for someone to come out and seek support, get help if they need help coming to terms with their gender identity or sexual orientation. But I think it can still be a pretty scary place for people and, you know, it's still dangerous water. There's still sharks in that water and in getting over the little bridge here. You know, you could leave the bridge down, although it's a non-accessible bridge.

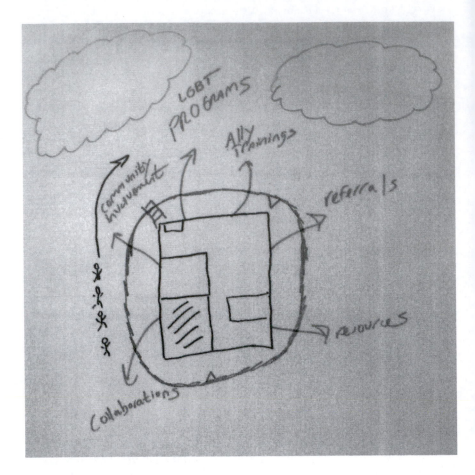

Figure 15.2

These statements spoke to the difficulties faced by queer people given hetero-sexism and cis-sexism. However, they drew the sharks as part of the moat sur-rounding the center. Historically, moats have served as a preliminary line of defense. Arguably, therefore, the moat and sharks drawn by the Directors are representations of center space containing "dangerous water" with little provi-sion, just a small bridge, to access the seemingly sealed center (no open door). The sharks might be protectors of the center, mechanisms to keep danger out of the space. However, in conjunction with the Director's words, the sharks may represent dangerous waters that engulf rather than protect the center. In this light, the center seems to embody the fears, doubts, and danger of internal-ized heteronormative regulations without productively spatializing resistance to the same (e.g., no accessible bridge to cross, it is a small bridge).

Graphically different from the Director's rendition, the Assistant Director's center mapbrought forth many of the same themes of danger, isolation, and disconnection. Figure 15.3, the photograph of the Assistant Director's mental

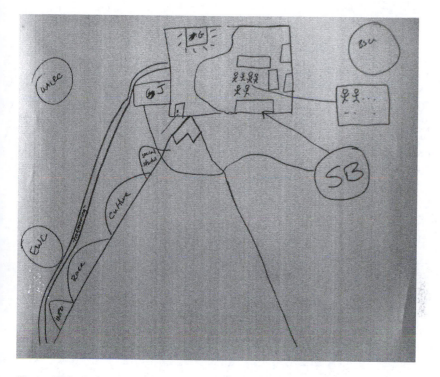

Figure 15.3

map, portrays a center teetering on the edge of a steeply pitched mountain-top. Hills or bumps filled with words such as "info, race, culture" and "social status" are visible on the left-hand side of the mountain. They explained that "it seems like for a lot of students just getting here is an effort, finding us, location, feeling comfortable, the location on the part of campus" and that "race and culture are huge hurdles and then I think also just in terms of people's social comforts, status," people had difficulties feeling connected with others in the space. I interpret these bumps as hills, rocks, or difficult parts of the climb up the mountain. They explained these difficulties by describing the work of a white student staff member and the organizational whiteness of the center:

> But she's right now involved in trying to organize some programming with the student of color groups and trying to kind of look at intersections there. And so I guess with my identity as a white person and also my background in kind of race issues and how to facilitate dialogs and things like that, I'm kind of trying to gently kind of coach them along in kind of different approaches, and that it's okay to actually acknowl-edge to these groups that yes, our organization is seen as very white and dominant. We see that there's a reason why people of color aren't often at our events and we want to do something about that with you, not for you, or asking you to do it all.

This text had layered complexity, given the Assistant Director's position as the secondary center leader, their efforts to increase the critical consciousness of white staff, and the acknowledgment of center regulatory norms. The Assistant Director arguably "see-sawed" between accountability and externalization regarding center safety, accessibility, and connection spatial processes. The statement "our organization is *seen* as very white and dominant" externalizes responsibility for whiteness and dominance by contextualizing it through the view of "the other." The Assistant Director acknowledged the view of the center as both white and dominant but not that staff actively (re)produced center space through those norms. One could interpret their commentary as "that's how we are viewed but not how we are." However, the Assistant Director's mental map and further comment that "we see that there's a reason why people of color aren't often at our events" reveals some acknowledgment of spatialized white homonormativity at play.

Conclusion

The study discussed in this chapter brought together bodies of knowledge (critical queer feminist theory and social work practice) that scholars infrequently commingle. This chapter illustrates the utility of a critical queer feminist approach to social work research, the challenges and choices faced when taking up such an approach, and argues for more critically reflexive research/praxis, which calls our normalizing practices into question. My findings were unsurprising; indeed, homonormative whiteness was reproduced virally throughout the LGBT centers I investigated. When I talked with each participant, I felt moved by their lives, thoughts, experiences, and strategies regarding what they faced. When confronted with the material realities of the challenges facing the directors and constituents in each region as analyzed through my urban, critical queer feminist lens, I balked. The difficulty and complexity of engaging critical theory and practice were profound. Enhancing the difficulty of these conversations in social work is our discipline's lack of conscious and overt acknowledgment of dominant theoretical frameworks within both scholarship and practice.

Due to the promulgation of modernist dominant research/practice discourses, the deep theoretical underpinnings in our discipline pass for "Truth," "normal," and "how the world works." While critical scholars aim to disrupt and unseat these "truths," US social work scholars and practitioners frequently begin with them as unconscious underlying assumptions and tend to be trained in exclusively modernist, positivist traditions rooted in epistemological unconsciousness (Steinmetz, 2005). Consequently, practitioners educated in the positivist vein infrequently question undergirding epistemologies. To that end, Karen Staller (2012) encourages scholars to understand the framework of the scholars they read, note differences between scholars, and make conscious decisions as to how to put concepts together and apply them.

If feminist social work scholars/practitioners are committed to social work as social justice, then we must become traitors to any of our positions of privilege in order to open spaces within movements to locate our legibility differently, across issues, across differences, to radically politicize and transform dominant mechanisms of oppression (Butler, 2004). For instance, through critical reflexivity and intentional writing, I attempted to attend to and make transparent the multiple levels of dominant power at play throughout the research process, whether I was privileged or marginalized by those systems.

We must connect critical theory more directly with scholarship and practice. We must engage critical reflexivity not just as individuals within our own work, but as a discipline critically evaluating the normalizing impacts of our intervention strategies with the intention of rigorously unsettling our practices and exposing hidden assumptions and embedded power (Fook, 2004; Pollner, 1991). Certainly, I do not suggest that we can disavow our privileged or marginalized subjectivities; rather we can acknowledge the power structures that produce them and work to reshape radically our discursive choices. In addition, queer feminism is a vital tool in our repertoire to conquer these challenges: linking overt and transformative theory to research/praxis, demanding critically reflexive praxis as individuals and as a discipline, and exposing dominant logics and normalizing regimes within our research and intervention strategies.

Notes

1 I use queer to identify a critical epistemology of placing the familiar and the assumed into doubt. I use LGBT to refer to the sites of the study and queer to refer to people who might be served by the centers, those who resist and/or transgress heteronormativity or question gender and sexual binaries.

2 I switch to the use of queer here to describe campus resource centers, denoting a queering of the spaces placed under analysis and a shift toward praxis frameworks that hold social transformation as a values base. Further, this switch marks a shift in the current dominant language. I am not arguing for centers to be named "The Queer Center," rather I am using queer as a signifier of the fluidity and mobility of sexuality and gender and the interconnected nature of oppressions and identifications.

3 "They" and "their" are used as gender-neutral pronouns in this chapter, to avoid using "his or her," as well as to avoid disclosing clues to the identity of a participant.

References

Anderson-Nathe, B., Gringeri, C., & Wahab, S. (2013). Nurturing "critical hope" in teaching feminist social work research. *Journal of Social Work Education, 49* (2), 277–291.

Andrade, A. D. (2009). Interpretive research aiming at theory building: Adopting and adapting the case study design. *The Qualitative Report, 14* (1), 42–60.

Barnard, I. (2003). *Queer race: Cultural interventions in the racial politics of queer theory.* New York: Peter Lang.

Bonilla-Silva, E. (2010). *Racism without racists: Color-blind racism and the persistence of racial inequality in the United States.* Lanham, MD: Rowman & Littlefield.

Butler, J. (2004). *Undoing gender.* New York: Routledge.

Cohen, C. J. (1997/2005). Punks, bulldaggers, and welfare queens: The radical potential of queer politics? *Gay and Lesbian Quarterly, 3,* 437–465. [Reprinted in P. E. Johnson & M. G. Henderson (Eds.), *Black queer studies: A critical anthology* (pp. 21–51). Durham: Duke, 2005.]

Crenshaw, K. W. (1991). Mapping the margins: Intersectionality, identity politics, and violence against women of color. *Stanford Law Review, 43* (6), 1241–1299.

Derrida, J. (1976). *Of grammatology.* (G. C. Spivak, Trans.). Baltimore: John Hopkins University Press. (Original work published 1967.)

DiAngelo, R. (2004). Whiteness in racial dialogue: A discourse analysis. (Doctoral dissertation, University of Washington, 2004.) UMI 3131146.

Diem-Wille, G. (2001). A therapeutic perspective: The use of drawings in child psychoanalysis and social science. In T. van Leeuwen & C. Jewitt (Eds.), *Handbook of visual analysis* (pp. 119–133). London: Sage.

Downs, R., & Stea, D. (1977). *Maps in minds.* New York: Harper and Row.

Duggan, L. (2003). *The twilight of equality: Neoliberalism, cultural politics, and the attack on democracy.* New York: Beacon Press.

Fairclough, N. (2001). The discourse of new labour: Critical discourse analysis. In M. Wetherell, S. Taylor, & S. Yates (Eds.), *Discourse as data: A guide for analysis* (pp. 229–266). London: Sage.

Ferguson, R. A. (2004). *Aberrations in black: Toward a queer of color critique.* Minneapolis: University of Minnesota Press.

Fook, J. (2002). Theorizing from practice towards an inclusive approach for social work research. *Qualitative Social Work, 1* (1), 79–95.

Fook, J. (2004). Critical reflection and transformative possibilities. In L. Davies & P. Leonard (Eds.), *Social work in a corporate era: Practices of power and resistance* (pp. 28–42). Burlington: Ashgate.

Foucault, M. (1977). *Discipline and punish: The birth of the prison* (Sheridan trans.). New York: Pantheon Books.

Foucault, M. (1980). *The history of sexuality Volume I: An introduction.* (Hurley trans.). New York: Vintage.

Fox, C. (2007). Texts of our institutional lives: From transaction to transformation: (En)countering white heteronormativity in safe spaces. *College English, 69* (5), 496–511.

Frankenberg, R. (1993). *White women, race matters: The social construction of whiteness.* Minneapolis: University of Minnesota Press.

Fraser, N. (1990). Rethinking the public sphere: A contribution to the critique of actually existing democracy. *Social Text, 25/26,* 56–80.

Gould, P. & White, R. (1974). *Mental maps.* Middlesex: Penguin Books.

Gringeri, C. E., Wahab, S., & Anderson-Nathe, B. (2010). What makes it feminist? Mapping the landscape of feminist social work research. *Affilia, 25* (4), 390–405.

Hall, S. (1997). *Foucault: Power, knowledge, and discourse.* In M. Wetherell, S. Taylor, & S.J. Yates (Eds.), *Discourse theory and practice: A reader* (pp. 72–81). London: Sage.

Hill Collins, P. (1990). *Black feminist thought: Knowledge, consciousness and pedagogy.* Boston: Unwin Hyman.

Hill Collins, P. (2000). *Black feminist thought: Knowledge, consciousness, and the politics of empowerment* (2nd ed.). New York: Routledge.

hooks, b. (1990). *Yearning: Race, gender, and cultural politics.* Boston: South End Press.

Knopp, L. (2007). On the relationship between queer and feminist geographies. *The Professional Geographer, 59* (1), 47–55.

Kobayashi, A., & Peake, L. (2000). Racism out of place: Thoughts on whiteness and an antiracist geography in the new millennium. *Annals of the Association of American Geographers, 90* (2), 392–403.

Kumashiro, K. (Ed.). (2001). *Troubling intersections of race and sexuality: Queer students of color and anti-oppressive education.* Boston: Rowman & Littlefield.

Lorde, A. (1984). *Sister outsider.* Berkeley, CA: The Crossing Press.

Lynch, K. (1950). *The image of the city.* Cambridge: The Technology Press.

Marinucci, M. (2010). *Feminism is queer.* New York: Zed Books.

Muñoz, J. E. (1999). *Disidentifications: Queers of color and the performance of politics.* Minneapolis: University of Minnesota Press.

National Consortium of Higher Education LGBT Resource Professionals. (2013). www.lgbtcampus.org.

Nieto, L. (2010). *Beyond inclusion, beyond empowerment: A developmental strategy to liberate everyone.* Olympia, WA: Cuetzpalin.

Nieto, L. & Boyer, M. (2006). Understanding oppression: Strategies in addressing power and privilege. *ColorsNW,* March, 30–33.

Orme, J. (2003). It's feminist because I say so!' Feminism, social work and critical practice in the UK. *Qualitative Social Work, 2* (2), 131–153.

Oswin, N. (2008). Critical geographies and the uses of sexuality: Deconstructing queer space. *Progress in Human Geography, 32* (1), 89–103.

Pollner, M. (1991). Left of ethnomethodology: The rise and decline of radical reflexivity. *American Sociological Review, 56,* 370–380.

Razack, S. H. (1999/2001/2006). *Looking white people in the eye: Gender, race, and culture in courtrooms and classrooms.* Toronto: University of Toronto Press.

Ronquillo, T. M. (2008). Normalizing knowledge and practices: Interrogating the representation of the ethnic other in human behavior and the social environment (HBSE) textbooks. (Doctoral dissertation, University of Washington, 2008.) OCLC 326877690.

Rose, G. (2007). *Visual methodologies: An introduction to the interpretation of visual materials.* London: Sage.

Self, J. M. (2010). Queering queer space. (Doctoral dissertation, University of Washington, 2010.) UMI 3431722.

Smith, A. (2009). Heteropatriarchy and the three pillars of white supremacy. Rethinking women of color organizing. In INCITE (Ed.), *Color of Violence: The Anthology* (pp. 66–73), Cambridge: MA. South End Press.

Somerville, S. (1997). Scientific racism and the invention of the homosexual body. In R. N. Lancaster & M. Di Leonardo (Eds.), *The gender/sexuality reader* (pp. 37–52). New York: Routledge.

Sommer, R. & Aitkens, S. (1982). Mental mapping of two supermarkets. *The Journal of Consumer Research, 9* (2), 211–215.

Spivak, G. C. (1989). A response to the difference within: Feminism and critical theory. In E. Meese & A. Parker (Eds.), *The difference within: feminism and critical theory* (pp. 207–220). Amsterdam: John Benjamin.

Staller, K. M. (2012). Epistemological boot camp: The politics of science and what every qualitative researcher needs to know to survive in the academy. *Qualitative Social Work, 12,* 395–413.

Steinmetz, G. (2005). The epistemological unconscious of US sociology and the transition to post-Fordism: The case of historical sociology. In J. Adams, E. Clemens, & A. Orloff (Eds.), *Remaking modernity: politics, history, and sociology* (pp. 109–157). Durham, NC: Duke University Press.

Swarr, A. & Nagar, R. (Eds.). (2010). *Critical transnational feminist praxis*. Albany: State University of New York Press.

Valentine, G. (2002). Queer bodies and the production of space. In D. Richardson & S. Seidman (Eds.), *Handbook of lesbian and gay studies* (pp. 145–160). London: Sage.

Wahab, S., Anderson-Nathe, B., & Gringeri, C. (2012). Joining the conversation: social work contributions to feminist research. In S. Hesse-Biber (Ed.), *Handbook of feminist research* (pp. 455–474). Los Angeles: SAGE.

Ward, J. (2008). *Respectably queer: Diversity culture in LGBT activist organizations*. Nashville: Vanderbilt University Press.

Wodak, R., & Fairclough, N. (1997). Critical discourse analysis. In T. van Dijk (Ed.), *Discourse as social interaction* (pp. 258–284). London: Sage.

16 Considering Emotion and Emotional Labor in Feminist Social Work Research

Gita Mehrotra

A queer Asian American woman whose work critiques the ways we remember and re-create the civil rights movement revealed to me that the process of doing her research had been a deeply emotional experience. She also mentioned that she had often cried when giving academic presentation on this work. After hearing about this, some of the questions I was left with were: What are the emotional stakes and affective impacts of doing this kind of research as a woman of color within academia, particularly in spaces that assert a commitment to issues of social justice? How do we manage this in the research process within institutions and discourses that continue to privilege a white/western, disembodied, and masculinist way of knowing and are dismissive of (or oblivious to) the emotional impacts of doing this kind of scholarship?[1]

At a recent conference session on qualitative research, a panelist shared with the audience about a doctoral student who had been experiencing trauma symptoms, possibly even PTSD [posttraumatic stress disorder], *as a result of her fieldwork. From there, the conversation moved on. There was no acknowledgment that this experience of trauma was part of the research work, or that this emotional response may have had impact on the research process. It was simply seen as an inevitability of doing qualitative research on a difficult issue.*

I feel emotionally exhausted . . . still holding so much from the interviews . . . Marriage, nuclear family . . . it's hard . . . I don't have time to be emotionally affected by this process! I didn't account for the fact that this process was going to make me feel triggered (from research journal, 2011).

I think that part of why this chapter is so hard for me to write is because it is such emotional content. I am engaging with this material from such a specific location as a queer South Asian woman (from research journal, 2012).

My own research experience, combined with hearing numerous accounts from colleagues. such as the examples shared above, have led me to think about the role and significance of emotion in feminist social work research, and more specifically about the emotional labor exerted as part of the work of conducting research.[2] For example, in my dissertation research focused on South Asian women's narratives of race, gender, sexuality, and migration, emotion was a significant part of my research experience throughout different stages of the study, and, in my view, it affected various aspects of the project from formulating my research questions to dissemination of findings. Drawing on Gould's

(2009) connection between emotion and political life, I am interested in raising questions about affect and emotions as part of the research experience

> not in the sense that they overtake reason and interfere with deliberative processes as they are sometimes disparagingly construed to do, but in the sense that there is an affective dimension to the processes and practices that make up "the political" broadly defined. (p. 4).

If we understand feminist social work research as a political project, then attention to the affective dimensions of the work is consistent with our purpose and goals.

The primary aim of this chapter is to pose questions to other feminist social work researchers about emotionality and emotional labor in our research and scholarship. Instead of offering answers or a mandated direction we should take in regard to these issues, I am interested in asking questions about what it might mean for feminist social work scholars to: (1) better understand and acknowledge the emotional component of knowledge production; and (2) view emotional labor as an integral, salient, and legible part of the research work we do. It is my hope that the ideas here will provide an opening for further discussion and dialogue about these issues as we continue to grow emancipatory feminist social work scholarship and research practices.

In the exploratory essay that follows, I start with a brief discussion of how emotion (as experienced by the researcher) is being taken up in social research. Building on this work, I invite feminist social work scholars to question the role of emotion in our work and what it might mean to understand emotional labor as part of our research processes. Using my own research as an example, I will share the experience of managing intersectional social identities and power dynamics in the research process as a form of emotional labor. I will end this call to the field by raising challenges and questions for further discussion in regard to emotionality and affective labor in feminist social work scholarship.

Considering Emotions in Qualitative Research

> As we have already seen, Western epistemology has tended to view emotion with suspicion and even hostility. (Jaggar, 1989, p. 154)

> *Emotions are culturally and discursively produced, physically felt, and cognitively mediated. They are embodied and messy. Emotions cannot easily be measured, quantified, known; and yet they must be controlled, eliminated, compartmentalized, managed to produce academic knowledge. What if that were not the case and we could create space for emotion in our work?*

Emotions are indisputably a part of individual and social life[3]; however, in the Western, masculinist, positivist tradition of knowledge production, they have been suspect. In this view, emotion must be removed from the process of research so as not to taint the "objectivity" of the researcher. Jaggar (1989), in her discussion of emotion and feminist epistemology, argues that, rather than repressing emotion, it is necessary to see reason and emotion as mutually constitutive parts of feminist epistemology. Other feminist researchers have similarly posited the importance of emotion, though most have asserted it as a part of feminist methodology or ideology as opposed to proposing a method by which to incorporate this component in practical ways in research (see, for example, Campbell & Wasco, 2000; Jaggar, 1989; Kleinman & Copp, 1993). Although a tenet of Western feminism has been a desire to dismantle the emotion/rationality hierarchy, discussion of emotionality is still relatively sparse within the realm of feminist scholarship. Even within feminisms that have enthusiastically engaged in discussions about subjectivity, reflexivity, and different ways of knowing, there is still a reticence to explicitly naming the reality and role of emotion in the research process. Consistent with Jaggar's argument (1989), I suggest that this reluctance to attend to emotion is connected to the continued devaluing of qualities associated with the "feminine" (such as emotion) as well as the ongoing pervasiveness of positivism and objectivity as dominant epistemological forces shaping academic research. As Widdowfield (2000) importantly points out:

> Emotions have an important bearing on both how and what we know . . . Yet despite increasing recognition in recent years of the subjective nature of much research and a predilection on the part of many researchers towards adopting a reflexive approach to their work, the influence of emotions on the research process has been largely omitted from accounts of that process. (p. 199)

In social science research, there are a few scholars who look at the emotional and personal aspects of conducting qualitative research, particularly naming the emotional difficulty of studying sensitive or difficult topics, such as death and dying, illness, or violence (e.g., Campbell, 2002; Dickson-Swift, James, Kippen, & Liamputtong, 2009; Lalor, Begley, & Devane, 2006; Rager, 2005; Woodthorpe, 2009). This small body of work focuses on the emotional nature of the content and psychological impacts of research topics on the researcher (such as secondary trauma), most often during the fieldwork or data collection phase of the research.

While this literature is significant in elucidating the ways that researchers are affected by research, and the psychological challenges of holding difficult information from participants, I am interested in delving deeper into the importance and role of emotion in social research. For example, what are some of the ways that emotion influences research processes, not only the researcher's psychological state? How does this play out across different stages of a research project beyond the fieldwork or data collection phase? An additional challenge to engaging with the role of emotions in research is the ways in which feelings and emotion are most often relegated to the private domain, as opposed to academic knowledge, which is seen as a public enterprise.

Emotion Work as Private

> *I am continually struck by how much emotion is a part of the private conversations we have about our research experience—our sadness or anger about participants' experiences of injustice, our frustrations with institutional constraints, our personal and political conflicts about representation, our relationships to the issues and communities we study, and the impacts of holding people's traumatic experiences . . . the list goes on. And yet, when these aspects of the work are talked about, it is in the private domains of an individual's office, a passing hallway conversation, or—as is most frequently advised by research "experts"—in the pages of our research journal or fieldnotes.*

This reflection about the somewhat hidden and compartmentalized nature of emotion work in research parallels the ways that we have historically privatized emotion in different spheres of social life. Clark and Lange (1979), as cited in Parkin (1993), write that there are two spheres of life—"Sphere A," that is the arena of productive, political, public activity and reason, and "Sphere B," that is non-productive, non-political, private, and emotional. Within our research practices, we have replicated this divide, even in most feminist projects that are explicitly political, and/or in critical feminist spaces that call for the disruption of binaries and the embracing of the fluidity and complexities of categories and experiences.

A key example of this public/private dichotomy is in the emphasis placed on journaling as a way to process emotions while conducting research. Widdowfield (2000) points out that the way that most researchers are advised to deal with their emotions is by keeping a research journal, which is an inherently private and personal activity (e.g., Rager, 2005; Valentine, 2007). I am not suggesting that such a practice doesn't have utility, but rather want to draw attention to the ways that this strategy exemplifies the separation of emotion from the public production of knowledge. This practice is also based on an assumption that feelings can be "bracketed" in the pages of a notebook and kept outside of the "real" work of academic research. *What other structures could we imagine to hold this piece of research labor? What would it mean to more publicly recognize emotionality as part of research?*

Emotional Labor as a Dimension of Emotion in Research Work

> . . . full emotional labor involves working with feelings rather than denying them. (James, 1993, p. 95)

> *What would it mean to acknowledge that managing emotion is a part of the work of research? What if we considered emotional labor in the same way that data collection, analysis, writing, and reflexivity have become assumed components of the work of conducting qualitative feminist research? What support, processes, and conversations could this make room for?*

Once we open up the possibility of considering emotion as part of research work, I want to go one step further to look at what it might mean to consider emotion as a component of research labor. The term "emotional labor" was coined by Hochschild (1983), who specifically wrote about how, within certain domains of gendered labor, including the service industry, nursing, and other care work, workers regulate their emotional lives in order to publicly express certain feelings and evoke certain emotions in those they are serving. In this formulation, workers need to communicate the "right" or appropriate feeling for the job and try to induce the "right" feeling in others. In such settings, then, a high level of control of emotions is required by the laborer. Hochschild (1983) argues that emotional labor is both gendered and commodified through this public care work. While there are elements of this definition that are relevant for the context of research and questions I am posing here—in particular the mandate to emotionally regulate to display the "right" emotion for the (research or academic) setting (which could include displaying no emotion)—I propose a broader conceptualization of emotional labor. In my definition, emotional labor can be understood as the *affective impacts and processes that are a part of our research work* that may include efforts such as emotional regulation/management (in a variety of research-related circumstances), holding and processing participants' experiences (including trauma, injustice, etc.), and the affective components of navigating various forms of power and positionality in the research.

As James (1993) articulates, "The phrase 'emotional labour' is intended to highlight similarities as well as differences between emotional and physical labour with both being hard, skilled, work requiring experience, affected by immediate conditions, external controls and subject to divisions of labour" (p. 95). I would also add that the term "emotional labor" can differentiate this kind of effort from the "intellectual labor" that is assumed to be central to academic research. As discussed above, there is a burgeoning interest in understanding the role and impact of emotion in social research; however, as a subtheme within this broader discussion, I am interested in what it could look like to think about the emotional component of research as a form of work, particularly given how prevalent emotion seems to be as a component of conducting feminist social work research, the epistemological potential for taking emotion seriously in our knowledge production, and the feminist history of valuing emotional work as labor.

Emotional Labor From the Faultlines: Navigating Social Positionality as a Form of Emotional Labor at Various Stages of the Research Process

> In reality, in more than 20 years in the US, I have routinely fallen through the cracks of gender, class, and race, of culture, nationality, and sexuality, all predicated largely on binary oppositions that continue to feel unsatisfactory and almost infantile long after I have come

to understand them intellectually. My responses to being positioned and re-positioned, of turning my yearning one way and then another, tripping all over myself, experimenting demurely or equally without restraint, risking money, shelter, status, affection, pushing the envelope on all sides, and finally grappling with the immense fund of self-knowledge that now dogs me down every alleyway of action and reaction—all have transformed me into a thinker and writer situated on the intersection of various destabilizing fault lines. (Kamani, 2000, p. 96)

Within the social sciences, most significantly in anthropology, there is a growing discourse about the role of the "native," "indigenous," or "insider" researcher—most often minoritized scholars doing work in racial/ethnic groups they are a part of.[4] In social work scholarship, writers such as Kanuha (2000) and Al-Makhamreh and Lewando-Hundt (2008) have written about "insider" positionality in relation to research, though exploration of these issues has been very limited within the discipline.

Perspectives on "insider" research have largely focused on the concept of the "native" researcher in which the researcher shares a key characteristic, demographic, or community experience with participants, such as scholars of color who are doing research work within their own racial/ethnic communities (see Baca-Zinn, 1979; Ohnuki-Tierney, 1984 for early writing on this premise). The assumptions underlying much of these viewpoints is that it is practically and/or epistemologically advantageous to be an "insider." As Labaree (2002) lays out, across the literature, the primary advantages to being an "insider" researcher are most often cited as the value of shared experience, the value of greater access to and potential trust with the community, and potential for greater depth of cultural understanding wherein the "insider" researcher may see certain texture or nuance in the research process that would be missed by a researcher from outside the community. Some writers also assert that if members of marginalized groups are themselves conducting research, there is potential for more liberatory representation of historically oppressed groups (e.g., Jacobs-Huey, 2002). Anyidoho (2008), for instance, posits that insider scholarship is often borne out of a general "disaffection with positivism" (p. 29) and a desire for more just representation.

Despite these aforementioned perceived benefits to an "insider" perspective, a number of writers have also challenged the dichotomous understanding of the researcher as an "insider" or "outsider" to a community and have instead argued for an understanding of fluid, intersectional, and multiple positionalities that may be negotiated and at play in different ways throughout the research process (e.g., Beoku-Betts, 1994; Kusow, 2003; Lomba de Andrade, 2000; Naples, 1996; Narayan, 1993). Narayan (1993) writes:

at this historical moment we might more profitably view each anthropologist in terms of shifting identifications amid a field of interpenetrating communities and power relations. The loci alone which we are aligned with or set apart from those whom we study are multiple and in flux. Factors such as education, gender, sexual orientation, class, race or sheer duration of contacts may at different times outweigh the cultural identity we associate with insider or outsider status. (p. 672)

Consistent with Narayan's call to complicate the "insider/outsider" binary in locating a researcher's social positionality, other authors, such as Labaree (2002) and Nelson (1996), propose continuum models in which researchers may locate themselves differently at different times and contexts within the research process. For example, Nelson (1996) suggests the idea that native anthropologists are rarely viewed as insiders by default but rather they experience "gradations of endogamy" (p. 184) in relation to research participants.

Across this scholarship, minoritized scholars have written consistently about the unique challenges and dilemmas facing "insider" researchers, some of which include: negotiating multiple roles and relationships within the community (including the role of researcher), greater sense of accountability to research participants, and a unique process of "leaving the field" (e.g., Chavez, 2008; Hill, 2006; Labaree, 2002; Sherif, 2001; Zavella, 1993). While these challenges have been most written about in relationship to fieldwork, authors have also noted the difficulty of locating themselves in written texts (Hill, 2006), or being seen as self-centered if they explore their own experience of the research process in written work (Behar, 1996; Jacobs-Huey, 2002; Smith, 1999). In addition, some scholars have noted that participants may be less likely to share information about some topics to someone perceived as being within the community and that "insider" researchers may be held to particular social expectations that outsiders would not (Beoku-Betts, 1994; Kusow, 2003; Sherif, 2001).

Throughout this work on researcher positionality, even in the discussions that focus on the dilemmas of negotiating "insider" positionality in the academic research process, no accounts have overtly named the emotional labor of managing these unique challenges. In the section that follows, I discuss some aspects of my dissertation research with South Asian women to highlight the emotional labor that was employed in navigating my social positionality in my research, particularly when I had an assumed "insider" role within the community.

Traversing the Intersections

The focus of my study was to critically explore how South Asian women understand and talk about their social identities and life experiences. I utilized a local performance project Yoni Ki Baat (YKB) ("Talk of the Vagina") as a unique community-based site in which South Asian women individually and collectively narrate their experiences.

As a US-raised, South Asian woman who was familiar with YKB and connected to organizations involved with the project, I entered my research with a sense of being an "insider" to this community of women. Though I felt cognizant of similarities and differences in life experience and social identities that I had with a number of the women involved, I had also received positive feedback from community members about conducting my research with YKB participants. I was also seen as someone who was familiar with the YKB project and supporting organizations as I had performed in the first YKB when it started in the local area, and had been involved with the project as a volunteer in subsequent years. In addition, I perceived that within this largely middle- and upper-middle-class, highly educated community, my status as a doctoral student was valued and getting a PhD was seen as an important endeavor, hence giving me credibility with participants. While some of these things were true, I also experienced oppressive dynamics of power and privilege in the research process that made clear that the "insider–outsider" conceptualization was a false dichotomy—that in fact I was negotiating many different dynamics of power throughout the research process which required a great deal of emotional labor.

For my study, I conducted in-depth interviews with participants regarding issues of gender, sexuality, race/ethnicity, diaspora, and significant life experiences (such as turning points, migration history, etc.). It was in these interactions that the continual shifting of similarities, differences, and power became apparent. Generational differences, class differences, and differences in sexual orientation were only a few of the significant dynamics that I was navigating in these encounters. Simultaneously, there were also meaningful shared experiences I had with participants, such as family immigration stories and experiences of gender oppression. Thus, at times I over-identified with women's narratives—to the point of having strong emotional reactions (about my own experiences) following interviews. There were also instances of "microaggressions" based on sexual orientation, class, generation, and cultural authenticity that I experienced in interactions with participants. For instance, many women asked why I wasn't married, or talked to me about their class privilege in unreflective ways (assuming what my class experience had been growing up). As I wrote in my research journal during the data collection phase (July 2011):

> Sometimes I feel exhausted by the privilege in these women's lives and narratives. Their class privilege, their heteronormativity, their apparent simplicity in understanding who they are. It was weirdly kind of a relief when (P18) said today that what was most challenging about being a South Asian woman living in the US was dealing with oppressions like racism and sexism. Obviously it's not that I want people to have these negative experiences . . . but maybe it makes me feel less crazy. (P25) and I had a good 'offline' conversation today about the privilege in the South Asian community here, too (mostly around class). She suggested I should research some writing about "studying up" . . . but it's weird to think about how to define "up." It's more like a non-linear sense of sameness and difference and oppression and privilege in lots of ways happening all the time in this process.

By far the biggest component of emotional labor that I undertook in relationship to navigating my social positionality with participants was in regard to my sexual orientation (and marital status). While this was somewhat present during the data collection phase of the project, it became even more salient in the analysis, writing, and dissemination phases of the work.

The Point of View of the Inappropriate/d

> I have attended many conferences at which anthropologists make a virtue of the need to avoid projecting colonial relations of power into the fieldwork situation . . . not many anthropologists, on the other hand like to talk about the opposite process of being inferiorized by your informants. (Hage, 2010, p. 133)

Interviewer: What did you learn growing up about what it meant to be South Asian-American woman?

Interviewee: That I was going to get married, whether it was arranged or not. Probably in my early to mid-20s. I was going to—I wasn't necessarily going to be like a homemaker, but I'd be like respected if I was. I was going to have kids. My own kids, like from my body or whatever. I was going to wear saris.

This response above reflects the central cultural script about South Asian (and South Asian American) womanhood that was continually talked about in various ways by participants in my study: To be a good, middle-class, South Asian woman is to be married. Overwhelming throughout the interviews, what was repeatedly articulated by South Asian women, across generations and other divergent experiences and identities, was that heterosexual marriage is central to producing (hegemonic) South Asian womanhood. Further, women consistently narrated that their families and communities were the primary communicators and enforcers of this cultural script; thus social relationships within family/community were the sites of struggle if/when scripted expectations were not met.

Kofoed (2008) importantly observes that "the point of view of the inappropriate/d confirms the existence and content of the hegemonic narrative, at the same time as it challenges the demands to conform" (p. 421). In many ways, in terms of the cultural script of South Asian womanhood, as a South Asian queer female, unmarried subject, I am "the inappropriate/d," and my perspective does confirm the cultural script, or the hegemonic narrative, of South Asian womanhood in a particular way. In the process of conducting the research, being immersed in the cultural discourses around gender and marriage within South Asian families and communities was a significant aspect of emotional labor in my research process. The work was intellectually challenging, but, in addition, this work was emotionally taxing for me as a South Asian queer woman who has lived and negotiated these hegemonic constructions and their material consequences for all of my adult life, including during the time of working on this project. While immersed in this study, I faced a number of personal circumstances in relationship to my family and community that were directly related to my positionality as a queer (and unmarried) woman in those spaces. This interface, between the personal and the intellectual work, added a dimension of emotionality to navigate which ultimately impacted my writing, particularly in terms of pace and timeline. It was no coincidence that the dissertation chapter on this material took me the longest to write! The emotional toll of the content significantly influenced my writing process as well as considerations about how to disseminate this piece of my findings in diverse academic and community settings. The experience of emotionality and emotional labor in this project illuminated for me the value of engaging with these concerns in feminist social work research more broadly.

Where Could We Go From Here?

As feminist social work scholars, as is true with any of our methodological and epistemological choices, how we engage with emotion in any given project should be specific to the goals and nature of that particular study. I view the emotional labor that is part of research as multidimensional, specific, and personal to each project, context, and researcher. There are some studies that may elicit greater emotion than others, or require more emotional labor, based on any number of factors, such as the issues being studied, methodology, or the social positionality of the researcher. In general, however, I am asserting the need to acknowledge and evaluate the potential of emotionality as part of our research work and proposing that we think seriously about how to engage with it as part of the labor involved with our feminist research efforts. Borrowing from Smith and Kleinman (2010), I am interested in what it would look like if we were to create space for "the affective-political-analytical" dimensions of research labor (p. 172). It is also my stance that such an approach is consistent with the potential of feminist epistemology (e.g., Jaggar, 1989) and feminist research traditions that have sustained ongoing engagement with questions of the role of the researcher, subjectivity in research, the politics of representation, and researcher reflexivity.

Possibilities for Considering Emotional Labor as Part of the Work of Feminist Research

Over time, I have repeatedly seen the emotional labor of research coming up in conversation amongst feminist and other critical scholars in relation to carrying out various aspects of qualitative work. As the vignettes at the beginning of this chapter illustrate, emotional labor is part of our research experience, yet it is not visible in discourse about academic knowledge production, even in feminist spaces that may be more open to disruptions of positivism, use of creative methods, and/or alternative forms of writing and representation.

Recognizing the emotional domain of our work and viewing it as an important part of the "affective-political-analytical" trifecta of feminist research could create stronger infrastructure and support for this component of research. For example, what if we discussed emotion in social work courses on qualitative and/or feminist research methods? What if in planning timelines for research projects we took into consideration the ways that emotional labor might be a piece of the work at various stages of the research process? What could it look like to talk about emotionality amongst feminist researchers in order to deepen understandings of core concerns of feminist methodology such as reflexivity, representation, and power?

Campbell and Wasco (2000) write that emotionally engaged research has the potential to yield important theoretical insights, particularly in the domain of feminist social research. Similarly, Behar (1996) posits that by using emotions intelligently we can be better researchers and, ultimately, our research can be more truthful. Building on such positions, attention to emotion and emotional labor could add nuance and texture to accounts of reflexivity, the role of the researcher, and rigor. For instance, discussion about how researchers emotionally manage the challenges of negotiating power and social positionalities in the field could augment existing representations of reflexivity that most often rely on researchers simply listing their salient identities. Accounting for emotion could also contribute to stronger rigor in feminist scholarship by making visible the affective influences on the work—from data collection through writing. Lastly, consideration of emotional labor could also expand discourses around the dilemmas and negotiations of researcher positionality, including unique issues facing "native" researchers.

Ongoing Questions and Tensions

How and at what stages of the process should emotionality be attended to? What is achieved by engaging with the affective pieces of the work? Who benefits? Is it helping to further goals of social and gender justice? Who is the audience for these discussions? Can it contribute to rigor and more nuanced accounting for researcher reflexivity? Or is it simply self-indulgent navel-gazing on the part of the researcher?

While I am advocating for a broader and more intentional accounting for emotionality as part of the research labor employed in feminist research, it is also critical to exercise caution and judgment in thinking about how to engage with affective aspects of our research processes. There are a myriad of potential challenges to incorporating more content, analysis, and discussion of emotion in feminist academic research. Attention to the "affective properties of research labour" (Fraser & Puwar, 2008), if not done thought-fully, could inadvertently privilege the researcher's experience over the experiences of research participants or appear to be "navel-gazing" on the part of the researcher. It could also detract from research findings/analyses or perspectives of participants. In the worst-case scenario, explicit attention to emotion from the researcher's perspective could contribute to problem-atic representations of those being studied or stereotypes of research par-ticipants, particularly in instances in which the researcher is not a member of the group being studied (Widdowfield, 2000). As is true with any of our feminist inquiry, engagement with emotional aspects of our work must also be serving our larger commitments to gender and social justice.

Behar (1996) also highlights some of the difficulties in writing about emotion in our work. For example, what is meant by emotions? How do you write well about emotion to go beyond the "confessional tale" approach taken by many researchers? She importantly notes the challenge of writing emotion into our research as she states, "writing vulnerably takes as much skill, nuance, and willingness to follow through on all the ramifications of a complicated idea as does writing invulnerably and distantly" (p. 13). Hage (2010) also cautions against trying to reduce the complex affective dimensions of research into discrete and analyzable data. These perspec-tives raise the questions: Do we even have language to make meaning of affective labor in the research process? Would it require new and different forms of writing?

Institutional Constraints and Challenges

Taking emotions seriously into account requires an ongoing commitment to articulating alternative narratives about the nature of academic knowl-edge production (Harris & Huntington, 2001, p. 130).

I also understand that to take emotion into account in research would require substantive work in intervening into masculinist, positivist, and neo-lib-eral forces that drive most aspects of academic knowledge production in social work. Within most dominant paradigms, it is epistemologically impossible to do the kind of work I am proposing. In addition, for many of us, the institutional and practical constraints and the personal and professional vulnerability that it could take to do this may make it unmanageable to grapple with the emotional dimensions of research work. For example, emotional labor and emotion in our research can be unpredictable and cannot always be planned for ahead of time or "bracketed off" as we move through our research. Accounting for emotion or finding ways to meaningfully engage with it can take time and/or resources in the research process. This could come into conflict with other institutional or professional timelines and constraints.

An additional challenge can be in the realm of academic publication. As a critical component of institutionally based academic success, publication requires particular forms of writing and feminist scholars can be made even more vulnerable when we take risks to account for emotion in writing in most traditional academic venues. The "gatekeepers to academic success" (Staller, 2013), such as peer reviewers, may be steeped in positivist epistemology and have differing understanding of feminist methodologies which could render discussion of emotion incomprehensible or completely outside the bounds of what is acceptable to publish. It can also be personally risky or uncomfortable to expose personal emotion or disclose aspects of emotional labor in public venues. Even in the writing of this piece, I was unwilling to share the most intimate details of the emotional aspects of my research experience because of such considerations! Intentionally attending to the affective along with the political and analytical dimensions of our work requires risk-taking which may or may not be possible depending on our personal and professional circumstances. Clearly, there are many factors to contemplate in considering how, when, and why we take on this work and what the stakes might be.

Continuing the Conversation

> Emotion has only gotten a foot inside the academy—how much space to we want to give it? (Behar, 1996, p. 16)

In this chapter, I have barely scratched the surface in beginning to asking questions about emotion and emotional labor as part of feminist research. It is my hope that this preliminary discussion will contribute to and catalyze more ongoing attention to these issues and their implications for feminist social work research in the future. Because of the paucity of writing in this domain, there are many directions to go in terms of future exploration of the ideas presented here. In particular, I encourage feminist scholars to more intentionally pay attention to emotionality in feminist knowledge production and begin to think in creative and critical ways about the way emotion and emotional labor play out and are negotiated in our diverse research projects. What strategies do we currently use to manage and account for emotion in different stages of our research processes? Also, attention to the differences in emotional labor experienced in feminist projects that utilize diverse methodologies and focus on different types of topics and communities could provide useful insights and inform future approaches to thinking about the range of what emotionality looks like in social research. For instance, what might be some of the unique issues around emotional labor that may emerge in conducting quantitative projects? By engaging in these conversations in more formalized ways, we have the potential to learn from strategies that feminist scholars are already employing. Sharing concrete examples with one another about how we see emotion as part of different phases of the work could open up deeper conversations about how we approach our research, how we teach it, and the implications for publishing such aspects of feminist studies.

Attention to emotion and emotional labor also has the potential to deepen and add texture to how we think about reflexivity and rigor in feminist social work research. Again, accounting for the affective aspects of our research endeavor at all stages of the work may provide new avenues of understanding issues of power, reflexivity, and positionality—all currently issues of deep concern to feminist researchers. For example, how does our social positionality and relationship(s) to the issues and communities we are doing research with intersect with (or even co-constitute) the emotional labor we do in the research process? How is negotiating power/positionality a form of emotional labor? How is this connected to reflexivity? It is my hope that feminist social workers will continue to engage with these questions through future research and writing.

Lastly, as discussed above, the institutional constraints of the masculinist, neo-liberal university, the tenure and promotion process, norms of academic publication, and dominant, positivist epistemologies that drive social work knowledge production all present serious challenges to being able to think, write, and talk about emotion and emotional labor in many institutional contexts. It is my hope that, as we do our work to push the boundaries of social work scholarship from a feminist perspective, we keep thinking creatively about how to make space for emotion and emotional labor as important to feminist research processes and scholarship. This work will not be easy or one-dimensional. It may take trying out new forms of writing to avoid "navel-gazing" or the tone of "confessional tales" from researchers (Behar, 1996), risk-taking from those who have institutionally more secure positions, and collective strategizing to create publication and presentation venues that can hold emotion as part of feminist epistemologies and projects. Through continuing this conversation we have the potential to develop deeper and more complex ways to understand emotion and emotional labor in feminist social work scholarship in order to continue to work toward our collective visions of social and gender justice.

Notes

1 This chapter aims to make small disruptions in traditional academic approaches to writing, thus I have played with form in this text, including the sharing of quotes from others, anecdotes or thoughts of my own, and clips from my research journal. This is done in the spirit of promoting creativity, questions, and dialogue about the ideas presented. In this chapter, when quotes are italicized and not referenced explicitly, they represent my own thoughts, stories, and/or questions.

2 This discussion focuses on qualitative work. Given the assumptions undergirding the questions raised, the discussion applies most to projects grounded in interpretive, feminist, and critical method/ologies.

3 The concept of "emotion" has been defined and studied extensively in a range of disciplines ranging from psychology to philosophy. An explication of these definitions is beyond the scope of this discussion and instead I invite the reader to interpret the concept of emotion broadly (e.g., Denzin, 2007; Ellis, 1991).

4 A comprehensive view of this literature is beyond the scope of this chapter. However, I have cited some relevant scholarship in this domain to contextualize my discussion and point to some of the scholarship that has informed my thinking here.

References

Al-Makhamreh, S. & Lewandow-Hundt, G. (2008). Researching "at home" as an insider outsider: Gender and culture in an ethnographic study of social work practice in an Arab society. *Qualitative Social Work, 7* (1), 9–23.

Anyidoho, N. A. (2008). Identity and knowledge production in the fourth generation. *Africa Development, 33* (1), 25–39.

Baca-Zinn, M. (1979). Field research in minority communities: Ethical, methodological and political observations by an insider. *Social Problems, 27,* 209–219.

Behar, R. (1996). *The vulnerable observer: Anthropology that breaks your heart.* Boston: Beacon Press.

Beoku-Betts, J. (1994). When black is not enough: Doing field research among Gullah women, *NWSA Journal, 6* (3), 413–433.

Campbell, R. (2002). *Emotionally involved: The impact of researching rape.* New York: Routledge.

Campbell, R. & Wasco, S. M. (2000). Feminist approaches to social science: Epistemological and methodological tenets. *American Journal of Community Psychology, 28* (6), 773–791.

Chavez, C. (2008). Conceptualizing from the inside: Advantages, complications, and demands on insider positionality. *The Qualitative Report, 13* (3), 474–494.

Clark, L. M. & Lange, L. (1979). *The sexism of social and political theory: Women and reproduction from Plato to Nietzsche.* Toronto: University of Toronto Press.

Denzin, N. K. (2007). *On understanding emotion.* New Brunswick, NJ: Transaction Publishers.

Dickson-Swift, V., James, E. L., Kippen, S., & Liamputtong, P. (2009). Researching sensitive topics: qualitative research as emotion work. *Qualitative Research, 9* (1), 61–79.

Ellis, C. (1991). Sociological introspection and emotional experience. *Symbolic Interaction, 14* (1), 23–50.

Fraser, M. & Puwar, N. (2008). Introduction: Intimacy in research. *History of the Human Sciences, 21* (4), 1–16.

Gould, D. B. (2009). *Moving politics: Emotion and ACT UP's fight against AIDS.* Chicago: University of Chicago Press.

Hage, G. (2010). Hating Israel in the field: On ethnography and political emotions. In J. Davies & D. Spencer (Eds.), *Emotions in the field: The psychology and anthropology of fieldwork experience* (pp. 129–170). Stanford, CA: Stanford University Press.

Harris, J. & Huntington, A. (2001). Emotions as analytic tools: Qualitative research, feelings, and psychotherapeutic insight. In K.R. Gilbert (Ed.), *The emotional nature of qualitative research* (pp. 129–146). Boca Raton, FL: CRC Press.

Hill, M. L. (2006). Representin(g): Negotiating multiple roles and identities in the field and behind the desk. *Qualitative Inquiry, 12* (5), 926–949.

Hochschild, A. R. (1983). *The managed heart: Commercialization of human feeling.* Berkeley, CA: University of California Press.

Jacobs-Huey, L. (2002). The natives are gazing and talking back: Reviewing the problematics of positionality, voice, and accountability among "native" anthropologists. *American Anthropologist, 104* (3), 791–804.

Jaggar, A. M. (1989). Love and knowledge: Emotion in feminist epistemology. In A. M. Jaggar & S. Bordo (Eds.), *Gender/body/knowledge* (pp. 145–171). New Brunswick, NJ: Rutgers University Press.

James, N. (1993). Divisions of emotional labour: Disclosure and cancer. In S. Fineman (Ed.), *Emotion in Organizations* (pp. 94–117). London: Sage.

Kamani, G. (2000). Code switching. In M. N.A. Danquah (Ed.), *Becoming American: personal essays by first generation immigrant women* (pp. 95–103). New York: Hyperion.

Kanuha, V. K. (2000). "Being" native vs. "going native:" The challenge of doing research as an insider. *Social Work, 45* (5), 439–447.

Kleinman, S. & Copp, M. A. (1993). *Emotions and fieldwork.* Newbury Park, CA: Sage.

Kofoed, J. (2008). Appropriate pupilness. *Childhood, 15* (3), 415–430.

Kusow, A. M. (2003). Beyond indigenous authenticity: Reflections on the insider/outsider debate in immigration research. *Symbolic Interaction, 26* (4), 591–599.

Labaree, R. V. (2002). The risk of "going observationalist": negotiating the hidden dilemmas of being an insider participant observer. *Qualitative Research, 2* (1), 97–122.

Lalor, J. G., Begley, C. M., & Devane, D. (2006). Exploring painful experiences: Impact of emotional narratives on members of a qualitative research team. *Journal of Advanced Nursing, 56* (6), 607–616.

Lomba de Andrade, L. (2000). Negotiating from the inside: Constructing racial and ethnic identity in qualitative research. *Journal of Contemporary Ethnography, 29* (3), 268–290.

Naples, N. A. (1996). A feminist revisiting of the insider/outsider debate: The "outsider phenomenon" in rural Iowa. *Qualitative Sociology, 19* (1), 83–106.

Narayan, K. (1993). How native is a "native" anthropologist? *American Anthropologist, 95* (3), 671–686.

Nelson, L. W. (1996). Hands in the chit'lins: Notes on native anthropological research among African American women. In G. Etter-Lewis & M. Foster (Eds.), *Unrelated kin: Race and gender and women's personal narratives* (pp. 183–200). New York: Routledge.

Ohnuki-Tierney, E. (1984). "Native" anthropologists. *American Ethnologist, 11* (3), 584–586.

Parkin, W. (1993). The public and the private: Gender, sexuality, and emotion. In S. Fineman (Ed.), *Emotion in organizations* (pp. 167–189). London: Sage.

Rager, K. B. (2005). Self-care and the qualitative researcher: When collecting data can break your heart. *Educational Researcher, 34* (4), 23–27.

Sherif, B. (2001). The ambiguity of boundaries in the fieldwork experience: Establishing rapport and negotiating insider/outsider status. *Qualitative Inquiry, 7* (4), 436–447.

Smith, L. T. (1999). *Decolonizing methodologies: Research and indigenous peoples.* London: Zed Books.

Smith, L. & Kleinman, A. (2010). Emotional engagements: Acknowledgment, advocacy, and direct action. In J. Davies and D. Spencer (Eds.), *Emotions in the field: The psychology and anthropology of fieldwork experience* (pp. 171–187). Stanford, CA: Stanford University Press.

Staller, K. (2013). Epistemological boot camp: The politics of science and what every qualitative researcher needs to know to survive in the academy. *Qualitative Social Work, 12* (4), 395–413.

Valentine, C. (2007). Methodological reflections: Attending and tending to the role of the researcher in the construction of bereavement narratives. *Qualitative Social Work, 6* (2), 159–176.

Widdowfield, R. (2000). The place of emotions in academic research. *Area, 32* (2), 198–208.

Woodthorpe, K. (2009). Reflecting on death: The emotionality of the research encounter. *Mortality, 14* (1), 70–86.

Zavella, P. (1993). Feminist insider dilemmas: Constructing ethnic identity with "Chicana" informants. *Frontiers: A Journal of Women Studies, 13* (3), 53–76.

17 Conclusion

*Stéphanie Wahab, Ben Anderson-Nathe and
Christina Gringeri*

In a qualitative research session on feminist social work research, one student sat quietly, listening pensively, as I extolled the virtues and contributions of feminist perspectives and critiques in research. I shared with them my bias, that feminist perspectives had a lot to offer social work research, because the values, ethics and standpoints of both had so much in common: focus on power, oppression and privilege; reflexivity; praxis; commitment to social justice; self-determination; and a deep appreciation for lived experiences and their contribution to knowledge development. This student raised his hand, and said, "I agree with all that, Christina. But what I wonder is, if social work researchers actually did everything social work says it does and is about, would we even need feminisms in social work research?"

Maybe we need feminisms to keep social work research accountable to its ideals and visions, to help slowly move the rudder driving research back on course. Perhaps that is one of the purposes of this volume: to help re-center professional values and ethics in social work research, and to recognize the important contributions of feminisms in that process.

(Christina Gringeri)

While many have written about what constitutes feminist research, few besides the contributors in this book have written about what constitutes feminist social work research. In addition to shedding light on how feminist social work researchers engage theory, treat binaries, and engage praxis as well as other methods issues, this book takes up issues of difference as they relate to the intersections of race, class, gender, nationality, sexual orientation, and ability on gendered bodies. Difference remains a challenging topic for feminist scholars, including social work scholars, as our politics of difference expose our relationships to categories, grand narratives, and materialist claims often in conflict with more postmodern and poststructuralist realities that regard categories like gender as socially constructed. On the one hand, categories (like woman) help social workers fulfill our mission to critique and resist oppression; such categories can support us to organize and advocate with marginalized populations (Gringeri, Anderson-Nathe, & Wahab, 2010) as well as challenge the perpetuation of privilege among "dominant" groups (Harro, 2000). On the other hand, categories can function as stagnant and fixed (rather than fluid) labels and consequently promulgate oppression in their superficiality (Sands & Nuccio, 1992). While some have contested the use of "waves" to depict differences across feminisms (Laughlin, Gallager, Cobble, Boris, Nadasen, Gilmore, & Zarnow, 2010), we lean on the wave metaphor simply to assert that whether the category "woman/en" needs to be at the center of feminist research in order for the research to be considered feminist is a question that divides many second- and third/fourth-wave feminists.

While many of the feminist contributions in this book address research on or about women, not all of them do. Researchers like Ann Curry-Stevens demonstrate that feminist research can also center racism, disparities, and whiteness without specifically focusing on the category woman. Her claims to feminisms in the research rest within feminist commitments to social justice and anti-racist work that seeks to equalize disparities and interrupt oppression. Similarly, Wendy Hulko demonstrates how the application of intersectionality can inform knowledge creation so it is ontologically coherent and produces epistemologically sound results in research with equity-seeking groups. While women are not the focus of the research, Hulko interrogates the process of knowing and doing (a feminist practice) by engaging research informed by intersectionality and by highlighting how theory informed her choice of methods consistent with an anti-oppressive feminist approach. Also attending to the knowing and doing of research through an intersectional lens is Carole Zufferey's research on social work engagement with homelessness in Australia. Again, claims to feminisms are not dependent on the centering of women in research. Rather, she stakes her feminist claims on an epistemology that attends to issues of power, difference, oppression, and privilege in the research process.

Other contributors who did not center women in their research, yet situate their work within feminisms, include Bob Pease's research with men, focused on masculinities, resulting in a profeminist epistemology for researching men's lives. Ending sexist oppression and dismantling patriarchy grounds Pease's research on men and multiple masculinities. Joseph DeFilippis centers feminist praxis as he discusses his transition from activism to academia. Finally, Karen Morgaine stakes her feminist claims across multiple critical theories and practices, including troubling the insider/outsider binary, engaging in praxis and reflexivity in research, as well as engaging in research that has explicit anti-racist, social justice aims.

As Joan Orme was deeply influential in our thinking, we once again echo her argument that claiming research as feminist "because I say so" is not enough, and we add to her call to duty by arguing that social work research can be feminist without necessarily centering women's experiences. Claims to feminisms in social work research can also be made by engaging feminist principles, theories, praxis, and intersectional lenses that help guide both gendered and material analyses of people's lives and phenomena.

These feminist principles, when implemented in research, center the project in core social work values of self-determination, value, and dignity of the individual and community, and an emphasis on social justice. Taken seriously, and implemented in our research, our professional values should compel us to revision post-positivist paradigms to decenter the researcher's agenda, and move toward developing paradigms which value the "person in environment" and liberation in and through the process of knowledge-building. DeFillippis' chapter addresses this point by encouraging activist-scholars who:

> can enable the production of new forms of emancipatory scholarship and pedagogy. We can continue our work in social movement spaces as we simultaneously work in academia. . . . By participating in grass-roots movements, activist-scholars build knowledge, collaborations and accountabilities that nourish and inform our research agenda.

Recentering feminisms in social work research is congruent with center-ing our professional values in research, rather than having post-positivism as a dominant research paradigm that diminishes or ignores those values. Capous-Desyllas merges critical feminisms with an arts-based approach for the purpose of "deconstructing dualistic relationships that can be per-petuated in research, such as researcher/participant, layperson/expert, artist/audience, and art/science." She also engages feminist research to "unsettle stereotypes, challenge dominant ideologies and hegemonic ways of representing knowledge, build bridges across differences, promote understanding, foster empathetic connections, and raise critical conscious-ness." Capous-Desyllas and others make clear claims to feminist research approaches, and use those approaches to center their work within social work values.

Research paradigms that incorporate reflexivity, ethics, praxis, an exami-nation of power dynamics, and insider/outsider binaries, and question who is involved in knowledge production and whose knowledge counts, disrupt hegemonic methodological assumptions present in post-positivist research. Hudson refers to disruptive research as being in the "borderlands" between "disciplinary boundaries and thresholds of acceptability/acceptance" pre-cisely because it represents a departure from the post-positivist paradigm that dominates research in social work and the social sciences in general. Through most doctoral programs, social work academics are socialized in the post-positivist paradigm, emphasizing objectivity, distance, and discon-nection, and lack of reflexivity and praxis. To implement feminisms in research is to struggle upstream against a dominant paradigm that is in conflict with our professional values. Morgaine's work aptly illustrates the struggle to deal with developing a research agenda that fits both academic expectations and feminist social work values and ethics. These struggles, located in the deep connection feminist researchers tend to have with their work and those who participate in the process with them, intensify the emotional labor experienced in the process, and thus, as Mehrotra argues, we need "to view emotional labor as an integral, salient, and legible part of the research work we do." To do so, however, is yet another departure (or degree of freedom?) from post-positivism, and another step toward grounding our research in our professional values.

In working on this project and reviewing the creative and insightful research that our feminist colleagues are producing, we have arrived at the idea that we need a signature epistemology for our profession—one that speaks to social work's values of inclusivity, equality, enhanced well-being, and commitment to social justice and structural change. We need to pull the covers back on *epistemological unconsciousness* (Staller, 2012; Steinmetz, 2005) in schools of social work to trouble the unquestioned preference for objectivist episetmologies. We need to base our work in an epistemological stance that moves social work students, researchers, educators, and practitioners away from the need for certainty and towards a deep understanding of context, power, and our own subjectivities as we impact practice and research. This body of research argues for just that: an epistemology for social work research that centers our professional values in the process of knowledge production rather than "indirectly produce consequences that contradict the profession's mission of social justice" (Reisch, 2013, p. 722).

Feminisms can help social work develop this epistemology that incorporates professional values and ethics and multiple ways of knowing into research processes so that knowledge production is congruent with and serves our professional values, and the processes and products of research support individual and community well-being and social justice. As Reisch (2013) argues, social work's enthusiastic embrace of evidence-based practice and intervention research "has altered the substance and direction of social work scholarship. It now emphasizes assessment of the effectiveness of established interventions designed to address symptoms of systemic problems, rather than their structural roots" (Reisch & Jani, 2012 in Reisch, 2013, p. 719). Reisch (2013) also argues (and we agree) that the turn towards competency-based social work education "inhibits the development of innovative curriculum content" (p. 720).

While we argue for an inclusive epistemology in social work research, we also think it is useful and important to consider tensions, ruptures, and dilemmas. Some authors, like Capous-Desyllas and Bhuyan's team, invite readers to consider the tensions and incongruities of the relationships involved in feminist social work research. For Capous-Desyllas, this coalesced in her self-examination around the realization that, although she remained emotionally connected to the participants in her research study, those same participants may not have shared a similar sustained closeness with her. This raises important questions about reciprocity in the research relationship, which echoes through the consciousness-raising work of Bhuyan and her team. Both chapters encourage readers to consider deeply the meaning (including issues of power, reciprocity, ownership, and so much more) of their research relationships, both within the research team and between researchers and participants.

Gita Mehrotra, K. D. Hudson, and Martha Kuwee Kumsa point to similarly intense experiences navigating the role of the self in the entire endeavor of both feminisms and research. Through their deeply insightful and personal narratives, they ask fellow feminist social work researchers to examine the in-between spaces where researcher and researched blur. What does it mean, for the researcher and the research process, when self and other cannot—and must not—be cleanly separated? How do researchers account for and communicate their claims to feminisms when those come from deeply and profoundly personal—not to mention often contested—experiences, as illustrated by Kumsa's narrative?

What unites these chapters is, among other things, a commitment to honest, relational involvement in the research process. This is a commitment that demands ongoing attention to the process of the research, not merely its procedures or its outcomes. In a social work climate increasingly concerned with technical and instrumental knowledge (Reisch, 2013) in the form of evidence-based practices and competency-based education, feminist social work research offers an opportunity to refocus on the process of knowledge production. It introduces to social work research a theory of being, not only of doing, grounded in principles that are central to the social work tradition but that often get lost along the way.

> A vision for the future of social work might also include a reassertion of its historic commitment to its fundamental social justice purposes and recognition that it is a value-based profession, not merely an agglomeration of sophisticated research and practice techniques. Its deep intellectual and cultural roots can play a major role in shaping US society in the future . . . We do not need to abandon the pursuit of methodological expertise in order to retain a focus on the big picture, but without recognizing the relationship between knowledge and values, between methods and goals, we are merely adapting to existing trends and abdicating our responsibility for shaping the future. (Reisch, 2013, p. 728)

Of course, engaging this signature epistemology in our work requires more of a researcher than those demands associated with employing more positivist orientations to the research project. Reflective of a critical epistemology, situating oneself in engaged and reflexive conversation with one's work—from inception to dissemination and beyond—is taxing. It demands that researchers commit to a uniquely affective and emotional form of labor. In this commitment, we cannot distance ourselves from our work, from the origins of our questions, the competing demands of this work on other facets of our lives and selves, or the impact of our work on those who choose to participate with us in it. Rather, as much as we center our professional values in the process of knowledge production, we also give critical attention to our personal and interpersonal values, experiences, and relationships.

It is perhaps an understatement to say that this commitment is emotionally taxing. As editors, much of our work shaping this text involved supporting and encouraging contributors to go ahead and "go there," to those places where they pulled back the veil from their research and from themselves as researchers. In countless email exchanges, phone calls, and face-to-face conversations, we worked with authors to write themselves into their work, with all the fear and trepidation involved, to honestly articulate the affective labor they expended during their research projects. As editors, we routinely remarked that the process of creating this collection was as significant to us as we hoped the product would be. We hoped that the chapters contained here would invite others into a similarly reflexive, emotional, affective, and ultimately generative conversation with their own research. We hope that the authors' experiences step off these pages as models of feminist social work research. To those who wonder, "Is it worth it?"—we believe it is.

References

Gringeri, C., Wahab, S., & Anderson-Nathe, B. (2010). What makes it feminist? Mapping the landscape of social work feminist research. *Affilia, 25* (4), 390–405.

Harro, B. (2000). The cycle of socialization. In M. Adams, W. J. Blumenfeld, C. Castañeda, H. W. Hackman, M. L. Peters, & X. Zúñiga (Eds.), *Readings for diversity and social justice* (pp. 45–58). New York: Routledge.

Laughlin, K.A., Gallager, J., Cobble, D.S., Boris, E., Nadasen, P., Gilmore, S., & Zarnow, L. (2010). Is it time to jump ship? Historians rethink the waves metaphor. *Feminist Formations, 22* (1), 76–135.

Reisch, M. (2013). Social work education and the neo-liberal challenge: The US response to increasing global inequality. *Social Work Education: The International Journal, 32* (6), 715–733.

Reisch, M. & Jani, J. S. (2012). The new politics of social work practice: Understanding context to promote change. *British Journal of Social Work, 42* (6), 1132–1150.

Sands, G. R. & Nuccio, K. (1992). Postmodern feminist theory and social work. *Social Work, 37* (6), 489–494.

Staller, K. (2012). Epistemological boot camp: The politics of science and what every qualitative researcher needs to know to survive in the academy. *Qualitative Social Work, 12* (4), 395–413.

Steinmetz, G. (2005). The epistemological unconsciousness of US sociology and the transition to post-Fordism: The case of historical sociology. In: J. Adams, E. S. Clemens, & A. S. Orloff (Eds.), *Remaking modernity: Politics, history, and sociology* (pp. 109–157). Durham, NC: Duke University Press.

Index

immigrant 58; men's violence against 52, 93; myth of poor working-class 120; oppression/subordination of 60, 98, 160, 215; poverty 131–2; as problematic 121; psychiatric regulation of 24, 25; regulation of 121; representation in media 194–5; resistance of 163; subversive agency of 163; surveillance of 121, 132; violence against immigrant 211

working-class mothers, stereotyping of 127
Wright, C. 147
writing: about emotion in work 270; inaccessible 183

Yoni Ki Baat (YKB) 265–6
Young, I. M. 72

zombie categories 237–8

![Taylor & Francis eBooks]

eBooks
from Taylor & Francis

Helping you to choose the right eBooks for your Library

Add to your library's digital collection today with Taylor & Francis eBooks. We have over 45,000 eBooks in the Humanities, Social Sciences, Behavioural Sciences, Built Environment and Law, from leading imprints, including Routledge, Focal Press and Psychology Press.

Choose from a range of subject packages or create your own!

Benefits for you
- Free MARC records
- COUNTER-compliant usage statistics
- Flexible purchase and pricing options
- 70% approx of our eBooks are now DRM-free.

Benefits for your user
- Off-site, anytime access via Athens or referring URL
- Print or copy pages or chapters
- Full content search
- Bookmark, highlight and annotate text
- Access to thousands of pages of quality research at the click of a button.

ORDER YOUR **FREE** INSTITUTIONAL TRIAL TODAY

Free Trials Available

We offer free trials to qualifying academic, corporate and government customers.

eCollections

Choose from 20 different subject eCollections, including:

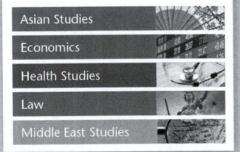

Asian Studies

Economics

Health Studies

Law

Middle East Studies

eFocus

We have 16 cutting-edge interdisciplinary collections, including:

Development Studies

The Environment

Islam

Korea

Urban Studies

For more information, pricing enquiries or to order a free trial, please contact your local sales team:

UK/Rest of World: **online.sales@tandf.co.uk**
USA/Canada/Latin America: **e-reference@taylorandfrancis.com**
East/Southeast Asia: **martin.jack@tandf.com.sg**
India: **journalsales@tandfindia.com**

www.tandfebooks.com